SOCIETY
IN
EARLY HISTORIC TAMIḺAKAM

SOCIETY IN EARLY HISTORIC TAMIḶAKAM

RADHIKA RAJAMANI

BKP

BHARATIYA KALA PRAKASHAN
DELHI (INDIA)

First Edition : 2009

Published by **C.P. Gautam**
BHARATIYA KALA PRAKASHAN
3421-A, IInd Floor, Narang Colony, Tri Nagar,
Delhi-110035. Ph. : 32967505, Telefax : 011-27393083
E-mail : 3421bkp@yahoo.co.in

ISBN : 978-81-8090-183-6

Laser Typesetting by
A-ONE GRAPHICS
Pitampura, New Delhi-110088

Printed by
BDH Printer at Salasar Imaging System, Delhi.

CONTENTS

ACKNOWLEDGEMENTS

A doctoral thesis in the history of a period somewhat shrouded in the mists of antiquity and the realms of analytical speculation of all the evidence, mostly literary, has necessarily to be the product of not a solo effort but an effort aided by all the scholarship that has gone before and all the help one can muster from contemporary sources both physical and human. In such an effort, an admirer and student of history like me had to turn to several distinguished persons for guidance and support. It is my endeavour to acknowledge my debt of gratitude to all of them including those I may have missed out unwittingly.

First and foremost my deep sense of gratitude goes to my supervisor Dr. R. Champakalakshmi. This thesis would not have been possible but for her constant interest, invaluable guidance, erudite advice and encouragement. She did not spare herself in this effort and I am thankful to her for spending many hours of her precious time in discussing every detail of the sources and particularly pointing out the methodological problems and raising conceptual questions.

I would like to sincerely thank Mr. R. Viswanathan for invaluable help in translation and general understanding of the Tamil sources used in this study and spending may hours with me for more than two years. Without his help and interest, this work would scarcely have been completed. I am really grateful to him and Mrs. Lakshmi Viswanathan for their constant words of encouragement and good wishes which has been a source of inspiration.

I owe my thanks to Mrs. I. Manian (New Delhi), Mr. Rajagopalan (New Delhi) and Ms. Sasivalli (Madras) for extending help in the translation of Tamil works in the initial stages.

I am grateful to Dr. M. G. S. Narayanan, Dr. S. F. Ratnagar, Dr. Rajan Gurukkal and Dr. R. Vanaja for suggestions on references and books.

I would like to thank the staff of the libraries mentioned below for the help extended by them :—

NEW DELHI

Central Archaeological Library.

Central Secretariat Library.

Indian Council of Historical Research.

Indira Gandhi National Centre for the Arts.
Jawaharlal Nehru University.
National Museum.
Nehru Memorial Museum and Library.
Sahitya Akademi.

MADRAS

Adyar Library.
Institute of Asian Studies.
International Institute of Tamil Studies.
Madras University Library.
State Department of Archaeology, Tamil Nadu.
U. V. Swaminatha Aiyar Library.

MYSORE

Mysore University Library.

PUNE

Deccan College.

I would like to thank Shri P. T. Deshpande for the cartographic work (2 maps) with his special technical expertise.

Among those who gave me great deal of encouragement and help I must particularly mention Dr. Kapila Vatsyayan, Ms. Krishna Dutt, Mr. R. G., Mukopadhyaya and other friends in the Indira Gandhi National Centre for the Arts, Mr. and Mrs. S. Narayanan and Mr and Mrs. N. Srinivasan.

I am grateful to Mr. S. Krishnan, Mr. Sundaresan, Dr. S. S. Murali, Mr. A. K. Jain, Mr. K. K. Bhalla, Mr. A. N. Narayanan, Mr. S. C. Garkoti, Mr. B. K. Bhattacharya and Mr. Ravi Shankar for all the assistance in getting access to books, word processing etc.

I am specially grateful to Shri A. N. Narayanan and Shri C. K. Saxena for helping me to present a neatly produced thesis.

For the help rendered in the preparation of appendices I would like to thank Ms. Jennifer and Ms. Janaki.

Last but not the least I would like to thank my family which has been my main source of strength. My aunts, brother, Mrs. Revathi and grandmothers encouraged me at every stage. My cousin R. S. Krishna helped me in proof-reading. More importantly, my parents Mr. R. Rajamani and Mrs. Prema were constantly at my side, encouraging and prodding me and providing moral and physical support at every stage of this work.

I thank Dr. Aloka Parasher Sen for all the guidance and advice given to me and introducing me to Shri C.P. Gautam. I am thankful to Shri Gautam for publishing this book.

(Radhika Rajamani)

CHAPTER - I

INTRODUCTION : HISTORIOGRAPHY AND SOURCES

Till the Sixties or early Seventies of this century, studies in the history of south Indian based on early Tamil literature have focussed mainly on the political aspects though a few dwell upon the social aspects. Scholars belonging to this period have viewed the social, economic, political, religious, cultural as mutually exclusive categories and not as a whole[1]. Therefore. society is described to be a stagnant one over centuries without any change or development. Most of this research has not effectively tried to integrate and correlate evidence from different categories of sources, literary, archaeological, epigraphical and numismatic.

Researches till the early Sixties or Seventies of this century were essentially concerned with the cultural and political history of the early Tamils[2]. The pioneering work in the reconstruction of early Tamil history was done by V. Kanakasabhai who wrote at a time when all the Tamil texts had not been properly edited and printed. Further, he made use of information from foreign accounts while discussing trade and georaphy of the ancient Tamils. He was the first to date early Tamil literature to the early centuries of the Christian era which has generally been accepted by other scholars. However, his work is essentially of a descriptive nature and confines itself to discussing the geography, foreign trade, Tamil races, tribes, princes and ruling lineages, social life, religion and philosophy between 50 A. D. and 150 A. D.

Most of the later writings also focussed on political aspects and were generally descriptive accounts. Historians like K. A. Nilakanta Sastri, K. K. Pillay, N. Subrahmanian who provide descriptions of Society in the 'Sangam' age failed to see the interrelationships between the political, social and economic aspects and hence adopted the conventional pattern of describing the economy, society, religion etc. in mutually exclusive chapters or sections. Their writings viewed society as a static one and failed to take note of transformation or change in it. Moreover, the above scholars with the exception of Nilakanta Sastri made no attempt to establish even a relative chronology of early Tamil literature. Another important lacuna in the writings of Pillay and Subrahmanian is their heavy reliance on literary works and the tendency to ignore or play down the importance of correlating literary evidence with archaeological data.

K. A. Nilakanta Sastri was the most prolific writer on the history of south India. Nilakanta Sastri alone, amongst the conventional historians, used archaeological evidence to substantiate the literary evidence. His chapter on the "Age of Sangam and After" in *A History of South India from Prehistoric Times to the Fall of Vijayanagar* provides a brief account of the political, socio-economic and cultural aspects. However, the concept of the *tiṇai* or the ecological- situations or zones, the social groups inhabiting the region and the nature of society in each *tiṇai* were not serious concerns in his work.

N. Subrahmanian in his comprehensive account on *Śaṅgam Polity,* dealing with all aspects of life, perceives a highly advanced Tamil society with a full-fledged administration, military organisation, law and justice, revenue system, agriculture and flourishing trade. He clubs all the anthologies, the Ten poems, epics and the Eighteen Minor Works together as Śaṅgam Works and uses their evidence without attempting a relative chronology of these works or to substantiate his assessment of early Tamil society wherein he perceives such institutional development[3]. By doing so Subrahmanian fails to take note of the changes in early Tamil society. Moreover, we shall attempt to show in the course of this work that the society of the early Tamils as portrayed in the early anthologies was not so advanced as to have a full fledged administrative machinery, revenue system and law and justice. It was more in the nature of tribal society being transformed into a farming society wherein a full-blown state apparatus had not developed. On the other hand, the epics and the Eighteen Minor Works seem to reflect the beginning of such institutional development.

Singaravelu made some attempts in using anthropological/ sociological concepts to study the social life of the early Tamils[4]. However, his account is essentially descriptive in nature similar to the conventional historiography. In the sections on habitat and material culture of his work Singaravelu focusses essentially on themes like food, agriculture, barter, means of transport, dress, ornament and adornment like the conventional historians. It is only in the section on religious beliefs that he tries to interpret early religion as an animistic and totemistic one. Towards the concluding section of his book Singraravelu discusses in brief the types of settlement and the family. Although the discussion touches upon kinship, it is limited to highlighting the customs of fosterage, courtship and marriage. The role of kinship is hardly discussed in relation to the production process or redistributive system. Thus, we find that conventional historiography is basically descriptive and lacks a change oriented approach. While the importance of these scholarly essays cannot be minimised, their studies did not seek to analyse the nature of the society of those times in general.

In the last 20-25 years new perspectives have emerged in the researches of scholars like K. Sivathamby, M.G.S Narayanan, Rajan Gurukkal and R. Champakalakshmi who have adopted critical methods of enquiry and analysed the nature and content of the sources and have hence looked at the interrelationship between the soci-economic, religious and political factors and viewed society as a whole. Scholars like K. Kailasapathy[5], G. L. Hart[6], J. R. Marr[7] and K. V. Zvelebil[8] are more interested in the literary aspects of the early Tamil sources which are of major concern to them.Nevertheless, they have made some attempts to focus on socio-cultural aspects.

Infact Kailasapathy was one of the foremost to designate the poetry as heroic on the basis of a comparison with Greek heroic poetry. G. L. Hart after comparing the common elements between early Tamil literature and classical Sanskrit literature points to Aryan influence on early Tamil literatures as negligible. The customs of the Dravidians, which he describes, are said to be characterised by minimal Aryan influence

Kamil Zvelebil is generally concerned with the poetic genre, chronology and the contents of the early Tamil texts. In the course of discussing these he provides some information on socio-cultural aspects. His discussion on the chronology of the texts in illuminating, useful and generally accepted by scholars. The issue of chronology will be taken up in a later section.

John Ralston Marr attempts to reconstruct the social and cultural life of the early Tamils after an intensive study of the Tamil texts, their invocatory verses and their commentaries. The work concentrates mainly on political history i.e. providing lists of kings and chieftains on the basis of two main texts the *Puṟanāṉūṟu* and the *Patiṟṟuppattu*.

K. Sivathamby's work denotes a considerable change in South Indian historiography. He is one of the few who have effectively integrated the various types of source material, used anthropological methods and applied the concept of historical materialism in understanding the *tiṇai* or eco-situation and the socieconomic milieu of ancient Tamil society[9].

Clarence Maloney emphasises on the role of the sea trade in bringing about civilisation in South India[10]. For Maloney the stimulus provided by sea trade was more important than the "diffusion over land down the peninsula" for the emergence of civilisation in south India. Although trade could have been one variable resulting in the emergence of civilisation, the stimulus provided by the contact with the Mauryan empire (attested in literary and archaeological evidence as will be seen in a later section) in the north cannot be undermined. Further Maloney asserts that the causal factors contributing to the development of civilisation in the Pāṇṭiyaṉ country (which is his specific area of study) are applicable to the Cōḻa and Cēra countries also.

However, a case study of Trade of the early Cōḻas points out differences in the nature of trade between the Cōḻa country and the Pāṇṭiyaṉ country which Maloney has focussed on.

In the researches of M. G. S. Narayanan and Rajan Gurukkal attempts are made to analyse the nature of the social and economic structure of Tamiḻakam in general and the forces of change or developments within it.

Out of the eight articles in M. G. S. Narayanan's *Re-interpretations in South Indian History*[11], three which deal with the chronology of the epic *Cilappatikāram* and the northern 'Aryan' and Mauryan influences over Tamil society are relevant to our study. In the article on "Social and Economic Structure of India" Narayanan characterises the polity to be in a state of transition from a tribal stage to a stage of state formation. He has also contended that the Sangam literature is permeated with the concept of the *varṇa* or caste, references to *yajñas,* Aryan deities and Sanskrit words[12]. As regards the percentage of Sanskrit words in *Caṅkam* literature George Hart has pointed out that this literature contains very few words of Sanskritic origin. M. G. S. Narayanan has laid a lot of emphasis on the precence of Aryan deities, *yajñas,* caste system, brahmins etc. Moreover, as we shall attempt to show later, such notions of caste, *yajñas,* brahmins, etc. were limited to the two most advanced *tiṇais, marutam* and *neytal* (the riverine and coastal belts) where arose the three main 'kingdoms' namely those of Cēra, Cōḻa and Pāṇṭiya. The rest of the region did not appear to have been brought into the oribit of the caste system and remained essentially in the tribal stage. An important lacuna/ drawback in Narayanan's writing is the general absence of the discussion pertaining to concept of the *tiṇai* (ecozones) and their development potential.

In the article on "Newlight on Kunavayir Kottam and the Date of Cilappatikaram" Narayanan dates the *Cilappatikāram* to the 8th - 9th centuries A. D. The reasons for the unacceptability of this dating will be stated in the section on chronology[13]. Another article "The Mauryan Problem in Sangam Works" attempts at a reconstruction of the relations between the Mauryan empire and extreme South India[14].

A number of articles of M. G. S. Naryanan focussing on socio-economic history of early Tamiḻakam have appeared. however, in none of these works is the concept of the *tiṇai* used to explain the ecological basis of socio-economic organisation and difference between *tiṇais*. He characterises early Tamil society as a tribal one but at the same time recognises features akin to a feudal society like land grants to bards, warriors and brahmanas[15]. The idea of feudal relationship according to Narayanan is further indicated by the nature of peasantry[16], their subjugation which he perceives mainly in the cult of war as class ideology[17] resulting in the extraction of surplus from the peasantry. This, he recognises in the activities of the '*maṛavar*', who were highly war like or militant in their attitude. No doubt the cult of war was important in this age. It is true that war brought about destruction of agricultural fields but there is no direct evidence on the subjugation of the peasantry in this period as it was in the later or early medieval period. We have no evidence of regular taxation system and an administrative machinery to effectively collect the taxes from the peasants in the period of the early anthologies. There are references to grants of land in some texts but such grants do not seem to correspond to the institutionalised land grants of the early medieval times and hence did not necessarily bring about feudal relations. Hence, the use of terms such as class ideology, subjugation of peasantry and extraction of surplus are not warranted/justified by the evidence of the texts.

Another article tries to reconstruct the social history from the work on grammar i. e. *Tolkāppiyam*[18]. In this the author seeks to show that this text presents an ethos different from that of the egalitarian society reflected in some early poems. In other words, it shows the Sanskritic influence when the concept of the *varṇa* system, types of marriage, social rights and privileges of groups are discussed.

Rajan Gurukkal uses literary, archaeological epigraphic and numismatic evidence to study the socio-economic processes[19]. In an article on 'Forms of Production and Forces of change[20]' he is essentially concerned with forces of change within the region and does not assign any significance to trade as an important variable in historical change in early Tamiḻakam.

Both Narayanan and Gurukkal's writings mark a departure from the traditional historiography. Their essays are based on a rigorous analysis of the source material (they establish a relative chronology of the early Tamil literature) and integration of literary and archaeological evidence. Gurukkal, in fact, advocates the integration of all types of source material and adopts an interpretation on the basis of anthropological methods. By using such methods they are able to show developments in socio-economic life over a period of six to eight centuries. Although their works are concerned with viewing societal changes in the period of the anthologies (or the early texts), they have not focussed attention on the religious beliefs of the early Tamil people.

The studies of R. Champakalakshmi on urbanisation based on the use of literary as well as archaeological evidence show that urbanisation and emergence of urban centres have to understood in the context of the eco-systems (*tiṇais)* and the impact of maritime trade[21]. The urbanisation of the early period is discussed as the first urbanisation of the region and as distinct from the urbanisation of the early Medieval period, which she attributes mainly to the degree of agricultural expansion and the need for marketing network.

In another article entitled "Ideology and the State in South India", she suggests that the collection of the oral bardic verses by the end of the 3rd century A. D. was the "first attempt by the Cōḻa-Pāṇṭiya ruling families to legitimate their sovereignty through emphasising lineage connections i.e. consolidating their lineage claims to territorial sovereieignty." Further, she is of the view that the invocatory verses in praise of the Purāṇic Śiva and Viṣṇu added to the collection of anthologies were an attempt to 'brahmanise' or Puranise the Tamil classics and their religion[22]. While the early portions of this essay dealing with the *Caṅkam* are directly relevant to our study, the main thrust of the article is the ideological basis of the emergence of the state in early medieval South India.

The present study seeks to illustrate the nature of society over a period of six-eight centuries and point out changes in the socio-religious sphere till the period of the epics and eighteen minor works.

The major source for a study of this nature is the corpus of *Caṅkam* literary works plus the two epics and eighteen minor works. The Graeco-Roman works (classical texts) represent a second group of texts. Archaeological data for this study comprises evidence from Megalithic sites and excavated sites mentioned in the *Caṅkam* classics. While epigraphic evidence is in the from of early Tamil Brahmi inscriptions, numismatic evidence includes punch marked and Roman coins found in the region.

The earliest stratum of Tamil literature is assigned to a literary Academy known as *Caṅkam*[23]. Tradition assigns the third Caṅkam to Madurai and the two earlier ones to other centres[24] viz. Teṉ Madurai and Kapāṭapuram. The word *Caṅkam* is not known to the collections but is mentioned only in the commentary to the *Iṛaiyaṉār Akapporuḷ* of the 7th-8th centuries A. D. In fact it is only in the commentary to the text *Iṛaiyaṉār Akapporuḷ* does one find an elaborate account of the three Tamil *Caṅkams* called the First or *Talai Caṅkam*, Middle or *Iṭai Caṅkam* and the Last or *Kaṭai Caṅkam*. While the account of the first two *Caṅkams* appear to be legendary on account of the time span (all the three *Caṅkams* are said to have lasted at long intervals for 9,990 years) and places mentioned which do not exist in the historical records, the last one appears to be historical as the works assigned to this *Caṅkam* survive in the form of the early *Caṅkam* literary records. This legend in the commentary dated tc around the 7th century A. D. has been questioned by several scholars[25]. However, one can agree with K. A. Nilakanta Sastri who states "That a college (*sangam*) of Tamil poets flourished for a time under royal patronage in Madura may well be a fact. but the earliest account of it which occurs in the introduction to the commentary on the Iraiyanar Akapporul (A. D. 750) is enveloped in legend.....Some of the names of the kings and poets such as Kadungon and Ugrapperuvaludi are found in inscriptions and other authentic records showing that some facts have got mixed up with much fiction, so that no conclusions of value can be based on it[26]". K. Sivathamby interprets this legend in the *Iṛaiyaṉār Akapporuḷ* differently. According to him the text which is dated around 750 A. D. appears after the Jaina oriented didactic literature. The word *Caṅkam* could have been borrowed from Sangha as a Drāviḍa Saṅgha of the Jains was established around 470 A. D[27]. Therefore. in Sivathamby's view due to the hostility of the Śaivites and Vaiṣnavites towards the Jains this legend is clearly an effort to 'hinduise' Tamil literature and especially make it part of the Saivite tradition. Further, it attempts to take over an obviously Jaina and Buddhist institution (saṅgha) and give it a Hindu form and content[28]. The early Tamil texts comprise the Eight Anthologies or *Eṭṭuttokai*; Ten poems or *Pattuppāṭṭu*; a treatise on grammar *Tolkāppiyam* and Eighteen Minor works or *Patiṉeṉkiḻkkaṇakku*. Kamil Zvelebil has suggested that the poems were written, edited and compiled when the poems ceased to be an orally transmitted poetry. These poems were collected into individual anthologies as they are mentioned for the first time in Nakkīrar's commentary on *Iṛaiyaṉār Akkapporuḷ* (8th century AD) and Ilampuranar's commentary on *Tolkāppiyam* and later on codified into two categories *Eṭṭuttokai* and *Pattuppāṭṭu*[29].

The basic information on the texts as discussed by Zvelebil[30] will be dealt with briefly before the issue of chronology of the texts is taken up for discussion. The *Eṭṭuttokai* comprises the following texts:

(1) *Aiṅkuṟunūṟu* (collection of 500 short poems): It is divided into five groups of 100 stanzas each, each set against the five physiographic regions (i.e *marutam* or riverine; *neytal* or littoral; *kuṟiñci* or mountains; *pālai* or arid and *mullai* or pastoral). Five poets composed this work; the poems on *marutam* are credited to Ōrampōki; on *neytal* to Ammūvaṉār; on *kuṟiñci* by Kapilar, the Elder; on *pālai* by Otalāntai and on *mullai* by Pēyaṉ.

(2) *Kuṟuntokai* (the collection of short poems) includes 400 poems (on *akam* or love theme) and one invocatory stanza. It is said to have been compiled under a certain king Pūrikkō.

(3) *Naṟṟiṇai* According to Zvelebil, the name means "(the collection of poems) on excellent *tiṇais*" or (the collection of excellent (poems) on the *tiṇais*[31]. This text has 400 songs and it was compiled under the patronage of Pāṇṭiya Māṟaṉ Vaḻuti.

(4) *Patiṟṟuppattu* (Ten Tens):— It is a collection of panegyric poems arranged in ten sections. Each ten sings the praise of a Cēra king and is accompanied by a colophon (*patikam*) providing details regarding the hero, his lineage etc.

(5) *Akanāṉūṟu* (400 poems of *Akam*): This also includes an invocatory song by Peruntevaṉār. The work was compiled by Uruttiracaṉmaṉ (a brāhmaṇa) under the patronage of Pāṇṭiyaṉ king Ukkiraperuvaḻuti. There are quite a few historical allusions (even to *Yavaṉas*) and puranic legends in this anthology.

(6) *Puṟanāṉūṟu* (400 poems of *puṟam*): The text has an invocatory verse by Perumtēvaṉār and consists of heroic songs singing praises of chiefs, kings etc. and is a valuable work.

(7) *Kalittokai* is a work composed in the *kali* metre (the other six being in *akaval* metre). It opens with an invocatory verse and has all types of songs on love themes. This work was compiled by Nallantuvaṉār.

(8) *Paripāṭal* comprises love poetry as well as devotional poetry. Only 24 poems are available in full as several verses are believed to have been lost. Out of this 24, 7 are dedicated to Tirumāl, 8 to Cevvēl (Murukan) and 9 to the river Vaikai. Each is accompanied by a colophon which gives the name of the composer who set the poem to music and the tune to which it was set. The *Pattuppāṭṭu* includes the following plays

(1) *Porunarāṟṟuppaṭai* (The guide for war bards. This poem consisting of 248 lines in *akaval metre* (with a few in *vanci* lines) sung by Muṭattamakkaṇṇiyār is about a war bard who goes to the court of Cōḻa king Karikāla. It provides a good account of the king, his valour and achievements and a general account of *Cōḻanāṭu.*

(2) *Perumpāṇāṟṟuppaṭai* (The guide for bards with a large lute): This work written by Uruttiraṅkaṇṇaṉār in praise of the ruler of Kāñci Toṇṭaimāṉ, Ilantiraiyan consisting of 500 lines provides a graphic account of the five ecological *tiṇais*.

(3) *Paṭṭinappālai:* It is attributed to Uruttiraṅkaṇṇaṉār. Comprising 301 lines, this

poem gives a vivid picture of the life of Kāveripaṭṭiṉam while singing the praise of king Karikāla.

(4) *Kuṟiñcippāṭṭu* (The song of the mountains) This poem written by Kapilar in 261 lines in *akaval* metre highlights the story of per-marital love among the people living in the hilly regions and mentions 99 flowers growing in the *kuṟiñci* region.

(5) *Malaipaṭukaṭām,* "which according to Zvelebil, means either the 'secretion oozing from the mountain' or the sound of *kaṭām* which appears in the mountains composed by Peruṅkuṉṟūr Peruṅkaucikaṉār (a *brāhmaṇa*) in 583 lines sings the exploits of chieftain Naṉṉaṉ.

(6) *Neṭunalvāṭai* (the good North wind). This was written by Nakkirar in 188 lines in the akaval metre. It is a blend of love and heroic elements, with the pains of separation being its predominant features [32].

(7) *Maturaikkāñci* is the longest lay consisting of 792 lines mainly in the *akaval* metre. The authorship of this is attributed to Māṅkuṭi Marutaṉār who gives a good description of the city of Madurai and the king Neṭuñceḻiyaṉ's achievements.

(8) *Mullaippāṭṭu*: It is attributed to Nappūtaṉār containing 103 lines and deals with a variety of themes love theme, heroic theme-(the expedition of the hero, the war camp, hero chamber).

(9) *Ciṟupāṇāṟṟuppaṭai* (A guide of the minstrel playing the small flute): The poet Nattattaṉār composed this poem in 296 lines in the metre praising the chief Nalliyakkōṭaṉ of the Ōy thribe.

(10) *Tirumurukāṟṟuppaṭai* (the guide to Lord Muruka): Written by Nakkīrar, this poem in 312 lines in *akaval* metre, gives a vivid portrayal of the various shrines of Lord Muruka.

The 18 minor works stated below are primarily didactic works[33] i.e ethical literature except a few which deal with love and war.

i. *Nālaṭiyār*
ii. *Nāṉmaṇikkaṭikai*
iii. *Kār Nāṟpatu*
iv. *Kaḷavaḻi Nāṟpatu*
v. *Iṉṉa Nāṟpatu*
vi. *Iṉiyavai Nāṟpatu*
vii. *Aintiṇai Aimpatu*
viii. *Aintiṇai Eḻupatu*
ix. *Tirukkuṟal*
x. *Tirikaṭukam*
xi. *Ācārakkōvai*

xii. *Paḻamoḻi*

xiii. *Ciṟupañcamūlam*

xiv. *Kainnilai*

xv. *Mutumoḻikkañci*

xvi. *Ēlāti*

xvii. *Tiṇaimālai Nūṟraimpater*

xviii. *Tiṇamoḻi Aimpatu*

There have been scholars of Tamil language and literature who have tried to give great antiquity to Tamil literary works by pushing it back to the pre-3rd century B.C. period[34]. Even within this school Vaiyapuri Pillai[35] recognises an internal chronology of the *Cankam* corpus and assigns some on the basis of the contents, style of the language to the early centuries of the Christian era and some like the epics to as late as even the 9th centuries A.D. This trend of assigning the epics on the basis of the contents to a late period as we shall see later in this section has been revived by historians like M.G.S. Narayanan and scholars interested in Buddhist literature like S. Hikosaka.

There has been much debate over the dating of the Tamil texts with each scholar propounding a chronological scheme[36]. However, there has also been some consensus among scholars who ascribe the anthologies to the early centuries of the Christian ear on the basis of the internal evidence (linguistic style and prosodic nature and historical clues in the Tamil texts and colophons) and external evidence i.e archaeological (numismatic) and the Graeco Roman textual evidence[37].

Even amongst the texts there is internal stratification. While some of the texts belong to a slightly earlier period (around the first two or three centuries of the Christian era) some like the epics and the 18 minor works belong to a later period (around 5th or 6th centuries)—i.e Pre-Pallavan and these are generally taken to be post *Caṅkam* works.

These texts are generally said to belong to the Pre-Pallava period as the Pallavas are not mentioned in them. However, Hardy is of the view that since the word Pallavas does not occur in the literature it could imply that they were known by a different name. He suggests that references to *Toṇṭai Manyar* and *vaṭavar* in the texts could be associated with Pallavas[38].

The term *Caṅkam,* according to Sivathamby, is applied only to the following six anthologies[39] which are considered to be the earliest works by scholars[40] dating back to the first three centuries of the Christian era.

1. *Naṟṟiṇai*
2. *Kuṟuntokai*
3. *Patiṟṟuppattu*
4. *Akanāṉūṟu*

5. *Puṛanaṉūṛu*
6. *Aiṅkuṛunūṛu*

Further, within the texts there are four different components which probably represent four chronological layers: the texts, the colophons, invocatory stanzas (which are invocations of Śiva; Viṣṇu and Murukaṉ generally dated to the 7-8th centuries A.D) and the commentaries[41]. The invocatory stanzas to the texts *Akanāṉūṛu, Aiṅkuṛuṉūṛu, Kuṛuntokai, Naṟṟinai* and *Puṛanāṉuṛu* were written by a person called Peruntēvaṉār. A Peruntēvaṉār is said to have sung the *Mahābhārata* in Tamil probably in the middle of the 8th Century A.D. Therefore, in Zvelebil's view the two Peruntēvaṉārs who sang the *Bhārata* and composed the invocatory verses could be presumed to be the same[42]. The colophons/*patikams* at the end of verses giving information on poets, rulers etc. are also attributed to a period later than the texts. Most of the commentators of the texts like Nakkīrar, Nacciṉarkkiṉiyar, Perāciriyar, Iḷampuraṇar lived in the medieval period mostly in the 13th-14th centuries A.D. with the exception of Nakkīrar. The social conditions of that period are reflected consciously or unconsciously in the writings of these commentators.

The following nine lays of the *Pattuppāṭṭu* may be dated a little later than the six anothologies:—

1. *Porunarāṟṟuppaṭai*
2. *Perumpāṇāṟṟuppaṭai*
3. *Paṭṭinappālai*
4. *Kuṛiñcipāṭṭu*
5. *Malaipaṭukaṭām*
6. *Netunalvāṭai*
7. *Maturaikkāñci*
8. *Mullaippāṭṭu*
9. *Ciṛupāṇāṟṟuppaṭai*[43]

Kamil Zvelebil furnishes an internal chronology for the poems[44]. Friedhelm Hardy also provides the tentative dates for this literature[45]. While Zvelebil dates the poems of the anthologies on the basis of the authorship of the poems (they are placed within a time span of 5 centuries i.e. 1st C.B.C.-4 C.A.D.), Hardy fixes the chronology of the texts as a whole (and not on the basis of authorship of the poems). Nevertheless the chronologies of thexts provided by Hardy and Zvelebil coincide with regard to the dating of texts such as various lays of the *Pattuppāṭṭu, Kalittokai, Paripāṭal, Cilappatikāram* and *Tolkāppiyam*.

Both Hart[46] and Sivathamby[47] date the *Paripāṭal* and *Kalittokai* to a period later that the six anthologies on the basis of stylistic and linguistic grounds.

As far as the epics are concerned most scholars date them to a late period i.e.

5th-6th centuries A.D [48]. on the basis of the language and the internal evidence presented in them i.e they depict a social setting which differs from that of the anthologies.

The *Tolkāppiyam,* the earliest extant treatise on grammar, can be said to have been written over different periods of time. While scholars like Subrahmanian[49] and Meenakshi Sundaram Pillai argue for an early date of this text[50] (a few centuries before Christ) on the basis of linguistic grounds, others like Hart[51], Zvelebil[52] and Sivathamby[53] feel that the first two portions of the text (on Orthography and Morphology) are earlier than the third section on Poetics which can be assigned to a period around 5th Century A.D. This section is more useful in a study like ours. Vaiyapuri Pillai also views the *Tolkāppiyam* as a late text [54]. Hardy places the *Porulatikāram* of *Tolkkāppiyam* in the 5th Century A.D.[55].

The eighteen minor works have no uniform chronology but have been generally dated to the 5th-6th Centuries A.D., i.e. after the anthologies but as pre-Pallavan by most scholars except Subrahmanian who treats them as part of the *Caṅkam* traditions and assigns them along with the anthologies to the few centuries immediately preceding and following the Christian era.

Thus we see that chronology of the texts is baffling and problematic. But by and large we notice some sort of a consensus among scholars.

For the purpose of this study the chronologies put forth by scholars like Hart, Hardy and Zvelebil are generally accepted. In the light of the views put forth by scholars, two broad phases (based on chronology) have been identified to discuss the changes and nature of society. Phase I- would include the six anthologies and Nine lays of the *Pattuppāṭṭu* except *Tirumurukāṟṟuppaṭai*. Out of these, four namely *Aiṅkuṟunūṟu, Akanaṉūṟu, Kuṟuntokai* and *Naṟṟiṇai* deal with the theme of love and two *Puṟanāṉūṟu* and *Patiṟṟuppattu* deal with the theme of war. The *kalittokai,* although it is assignable to a later phase, is still of greater relevance to phase I and of some relevance to phase II. For Phase II the material from the epics and the minor didactic works and *Tirumurukāṟṟuppatai* and *Paripāṭal* would be used to show the change in the social setting. Here it would be necessary to state that a certain overlap of dates is seen in the epics, *Kalittokkai* and *Paripāṭal.*

In addition to this vast corpus of early Tamil literature we have the foreign accounts viz the Graeco-Roman works such as Pliny's *Natural History,* Ptolemy's *Guide to Geography* and the *Periplus of the Erythraen Sea* (by an unknown author). These texts are contemporaneous with portions of the *Caṅkam* texts and provide corroborative information. The main advantage of these texts is their reliable chronology[56]. They are more like travelogues and geographical accounts, mundane in nature providing a wealth of information regarding the trade relations between Indian and the West, the trade routes, articles of trade and the ports and inland centres of South India. As far as our study is concerned they do not give much information on the social groups involved in this trade.

Archaeological data is indispensable in a study such as this. The period 3td century B.C.-3rd Century A.D. coincided with what is termed as the last phases of the megalithic culture[57]. A study of these megalithic burials needs to be undertaken to attempt a correlation with the ecological regions mentioned in literature. Data from habitation sites of megalithic association is limited as very few excavations have been conducted.

In this context Leshnik observes that the quantitative and relational reports is seldom detailed enough to permit the application of the kind of sophisticated analysis now almost standard in archaeological studies[58].

In many cases the chronology of the sites has not been clearly worked out with the exception of Arikamedu.

Archaeological data from excavations of early historical sites can also be made use of. Future scientific excavations[59] and under water archaeology (no being conducted at Kaveripattinam) may provide more information ot corroborate literary evidence.

The nature of archaeological data is limited because no regular excavations were conducted at many sites and no systematic excavations could be conducted at modern cities like Kanchipuram, Madurai and Uraiyur due to continuous occupation and lack of potential areas for digging[60].

As for epigraphic evidence there are some Tamil Brahmi inscriptions in the southern part of Tamilakam inscribed in natural caverns mostly in the districts of Madurai, Ramanathapuram and Tirunelveli with a few in the districts of Tiruchirapalli, Chingelput and South Arcot[61]. Though some of these inscriptions are incomplete and short, they throw light on various social and occupational groups as well as mention place names and personal names.

Numismatic evidence mainly comprises abundant Roman coins (mostly gold, silver and few copper), punch marked issues and some indigenous issues[62]. Roman coins mostly occur in hoards, sometimes as surface finds and very rarely in stratified layers of the excavated sites. The Roman numismatic evidence is problematic as one is not clear on how the coins were used. Further, as there is hardly any information on the usage of these coins by the general populace it can be assumed that only certain social groups like merchants and traders used them probably as money.

Nature of Early Tamil Literature

There have been diverse opinions regarding the nature and authorship of this poetry.It would be useful to understand their nature and authorship in the light of views put forth by scholars on (a) whether the poetry was bardic/heroic or courtly (b) the indebtedness of this literature to Sanskrit literature.

One of the earliest scholars who used the appellation 'heroic age' for the age of the early Tamil texts was Kailasapathy after an analysis of the Tamil poetry in comparison with the heroic epics of Greece[63]. In his work *'Tamil Heroic Poetry'* Kailasapathy opined that these texts were orally transmitted by bards as writting of the poems is not indicated anywhere in the poems. Moreover, he postulates a heroic character for the poems on the anaylsis of the various categories of bards and minstrels, the formulae, metre, themes, catalogues and geneologies present in the Tamil texts and in the light of the Greek evidence provided by the Homeric epics[64] and the application of theories propounded by Chadwicks, Parry, Thomson, Bowra and Lord for the study of the Homeric works. Besides, Kailasapathy was of the view that the personnel of the heroic poems (whether named or anonymous) were aristocratic. The *akam* and *puṟam* poems dealt with an aristocractic society dominated by war like chiefs. Even terms like *Talaivaṉ, Kurucil* etc. used in the poems are taken to mean words connoting high social rank by Kailasapathy. This is postulated on the evidence in the *Tolkāppiyam* which states that servants, slaves, errand men etc. are not to be sung of as heroes in poems treating the five divisions of mutual love[65].

G.L. Hart, on the other hand, is of the view that ancient Tamil literature was written by high class poets who followed the model of the oral poetry of the *Pāṇaṉs* and *Paṟaiyaṉs*-men of the lowest castes but is devoid of both high class and brahmanical bias. Hart disagrees with Kailasapathy on the oral nature of transmission of the poems as he feels that some of the poems in the *Caṅkam* anthologies are "polished productions of essentially literate men, far more sophisticated in grammar and diction than their oral models could have been". Further, he is of the view as indicated earlier that a few centuries after the Brahmi script was introduced and adapted to Tamil the class of people called *pulavaṉs* who arose from mostly higher classes looked for subject matter for their poems. For this they turned to the poetry of the bards and may have put many poems into the mouths of the low caste oral bards[66].

John Ralston Marr has used the term 'court poetry' to denote the poems of the Anthologies. he has also suggested that the Tamil poems are similar to other heroic poems on the basis of the use of the metre, the forms of address in *puṟam* poems and the recurrence of stock epithets[67]. These poems, according to him, were recited orally or chanted loudly before the king and his courtiers. It is difficult to fix the date of the actual redaction of these poems. According to Marr they were probably written before the commentary to the *Iṟaiyaṉār Akapporuḷ* was written around the 8th century A.D.[68]. Further, Marr mentions two more features which suggest their association with heroic poetry. Firstly the names of the poets are known only from the colophons. Secondly, the heroic poets are little concerned with outside events or dates[69].

In Kamil Zvelebil's view classical Tamil literature is not "the literature of the barons, neither is it the literature of a monastic order; nor the literature of a elite, of a *nagarika;* it is thus not the literature of a particular social class". The poets, male and female, were from different sections and communities of society. While the characters in heroic poetry are aristocratic those of the love poems are anonymous common people or people in general without any determination of their social status, their occupations etc. Even amongst the anonymous love poems Zvelebil states that some heroes belong to the leisure class and "with some exceptions one and the same type of male is the hero of both - the war exploits and the erotic feats"[70].

In Zvelebil's view the literature is predominantly secular with the absence of religious sentiment. Here he agrees with Kailasapathy's 'comments that' "early poetry of the Tamils is founded on secular oral bardic traditions." Besides the literature is worldly - it does not make any allusions to supernatural meddling in worldy affairs[71]. In the words of Zvelebil "this early bardic poetry transmitted orally during the pre-literary stage refined and transformed into court poetry began to crystallise around certain nuclei which become later, upon the application of a lively criticism by a body of scholars, the core of the anthologies"[72].

G. John Samuel views *Caṅkam* poetry as "the product of a class society in which division of labour has paved the way for the emergence of minstrels, bards and poets as separate classes isolated from the other working communities. The economic conditions and the nature of their vocation forced the minstrels and poets to depend upon the aristocracy under whose patronge they happened to meet the financial requirements for their existence. So they had to cultivate their art in such a manner as to please the whims and fanicies of the ruling class, the political tendencies of the age and the literary tastes of the aristocracy whose ideals and aspirations were shaped and conditioned by the social and political milieu of that age. Since Cankam poems were cultivated under such a patronised system they happened to be bardic in character and courtly in nature"[73]. Further, Samuel, like Kailasapathy and Zvelebil notes the aristocratic nature and classical character of the poems.

Initially G. John Samuel seems to disagree with the concept of Heroic age put forth by Chadwick and borrowed by Kailasapathy. He seems to find evidence in the poems depicting well established monarchies entailing the necessities for construction of water tanks, increasing production and fixation moderate taxation - 'facts' which are questionable. While stating this the author seems to be influenced by modern concepts of class, aristocracy, monarchy and a taxation system which are not justified by the evidence of the *Caṅkam* texts. Besides, he states that many of the characteristic features put forth by the Chadwicks for gnomic poetry are found in poems of *Puṟanaṉūṟu*. A salient feature of gnomic poetry which is discernible in the poems of *Puṟanaṉūṟu* is the predominance of scholar poets (*pulavar*) apart from minstrels and bards. Therefore part of the poems in *Puṟanāṉūṟu* represent a transitional stage i.e. transition from heroic content to gnomic content. So the author deduces that the 'whole anthology of *Puṟanāṉūṟu* seems to be an intermingling of heroic as well as post-heroic poems both in structure and content'. Moreover, the poems of *Puṟanāṉūṟu* are not heroic stories in long narrative interspaced with supernatural events as the poets are more concerned with particular martial activities. The length of time covered in the poem is shorter as compared to other heroic literatures[74].

Therefore, he views the *Puṟanāṉūṟu* to be a text comprising heroic as well as gnomic poems. Towards the latter half of the article the author agrees with the appellation 'heroic' to the poetry on account of certain features. The poets saw to it that they maintained close ties with the patrons i.e. kings as they were dependent on their patronage for their existential sustenance. Like the Greek bards, the poets also tried to avoid war between kings or brought about reconciliation. Their main purpose seems to have been to instil or kindle the heroic sentiments of the kings and warriors and justify their deeds by singing their glory. There are numerous references to court feasting in the *Puṛanāṉūṛu* which add to the grandeur of heroic poetry[75]. Besides the poets made use of similes, formulae, allusions to mythical accounts and provided catalogues and geneologies to enhance the glory of the hero[76]. Regarding the nature of transmission the author opines that while some poems in the *Puṛanāṉūṛu* or general nature were transmitted orally, there were other panegyrics which were sung by individual poets to celebrate the particular victory a hero won in a battle and such poems have only an occasional and temporal value. The singing of the poem may not have been necessary when the political situation changed[77].

K. Sivathamby holds that the term 'heroic' would be an apt appellation for the period upto 250 A.D. but points out that Tamil literature has certain features listed below which distinguish it from the other heroic literatures.

1. Among the Tamil literary texts there is no heroic epic of any sizeable length as the Homerian Illiad or Odyssey.
2. The corpus or *Caṅkam* literature available has been anthologised in a highly conscious literary pattern.
3. The highest unit of *akaval* metre which is the most employed bardic metre prescribed by Tolkāppiyar is only thousand lines which is not sufficent for a full bardic epic.
4. Political motivations seemed to have played a significant role in the preservation of the *Caṅkam* texts as the *Puṛam* literature is political and the *Akam* literature contains a number of political allusions.
5. There is no evidence on the practice of bardism and the transmission of the bardic art in Tamilnad[78].

He traces the origins of *Akam* poetry to the primitive songs of ancient South India and the evidences for the antiquity and the continuity of it are seen in Hala's *Saptasati* and Toda oral poetry. Some features of *akam* poetry continue in the Tamil folk songs on love theme even today[79]. As regards the compilation of the texts he holds that this compilation of the poems of the bardic phase was to consolidate the literary gains of the immediate past and thus ensure the continuity of the royal lines and perhaps this comilation was connected with increasing use of writing[80].

F. Hardy views the early Tamil texts as belonging to two periods which he describes as classical and renaissance periods. The classical period includes the anthologies and nine songs of the *Pattuppāṭṭu*. In Hardy's words, *Caṅkam* poetry is a "refined sophisticated and idealised form of literature, which by virtue of that character can be related to the elitist class of the *cāṉṟōr"*. Works of the renaissance period are said to be the *Kalittokai, Cilappatikāram* and *Paripāṭal*. This renaissance poetry, which was fresh and popular, had in it folk songs, village religion, popular customs vulgarism and this can be linked to the re-emergence of the Pāṇṭiya kingdom in Madurai (the seat of the *Caṅkam*) Most of the poems sing of the Pāṇṭiya king. Hardy after an analysis of the references of Māyōṉ in these works shows that mythical episodes of Kṛṣṇa exploits in Vrindavan figures in these poems[81].

As far as the "*Tolkāppiyam*" is concerned, Hardy differs with Zvelebil. Hardy suggests that the *Tolkāppiyam* must be interpreted as "the reflection and codification of the literary practice of early poetry"[82].

In our view, the poems of the *Puṟanāṉūṟu* and *Patiṟṟuppattu* are heroic because they deal with men and their deeds (though Gods are mentioned in the poems); they concentrate mostly on a few (mainly kings and warriors) and neglect others (even if they discuss others, they do so with reference to the happy few): death is glorified: they refer to feasts (*uṇṭāṭṭu*) given by kings which is a sign of princely generosity. Repetitions, similes and formulae are used[83]. These songs served as an important link between ruler and ruled. Bards/poets sang songs to inspire the kings/warriors in battle or they praise the glory and generosity of the kings.

Though these poems are heroic in certain respects they have certain features which distinguish them from other heroic poems. In heroic poetry, the heroes attempt feats which are beyond the reach of nearly all other men; in other words, superhuman feats like the characters in the Homeric epics. There are no superhuman feats in early Tamil texts. Bowra states that description of natural scenery is rare in heroic poetry and heroic poets describe natural scenes when they are to fulfil some special functions in the story[84]. The early Tamil poems do provide descriptions of natural scenery. Unlike the other heroic poems, the early Tamil poems do not abound in miraculous elements. Men and women do not transform into other forms - human and animal[85]. These poems of the early anthologies seem to belong to oral tradition[86]. They can be characterised as what Vansina termed 'unintentional testimony' as a testimony always has an aim of some kind but it is not aimed at recording history[87]. Also, Vansina holds that most oral texts have an internal pattern of arrangement where "content is not presented in random fashion but is set forth in accordance with certain rules and these rules enable a further classfication of oral literature to be made based on the kind of internal structure displayed"[88]. The early Tamil Poems were broadly classified as *akam* and *puṟam* and further divided into *tiṇais* and *tuṟais*. Most of the *puṟam* poems were panegyric in nature[89].

Regarding the indebtedness of early Tamil literature to classical Sanskrit literature, scholars like Nilakanta Sastri and M.G.S. Narayanan are of the view that early Tamil literature is indebted to Sanskrit and contains not only Sanskrit words but Aryan elements like *yajñas,* references to Aryan deities, familiarity with the epics in the form of allusions to episodes etc[90]. on the other hand Hart, after studying the relation between Tamil and classical Sanskrit literature is of the opinion that the early Tamil literature is fairly devoid of words of Sanskritic origin. According to him, "words of Sanskritic origin are quite few comprising less than two percent of the *Murukāṟṟuppaṭai* and one percent of the *Pattuppāṭṭu,* itself later than the earliest works". Thereby Hart shows that "Tamil literature developed at a time when Sanskrit did not have the boundless prestige it had attained when the other south Indian languages which from the beginning are full of Sanskrit words, developed literatures. It follows that Sanskrit and the northern culture for which it was the vehicle, had not penetrated into Tamilnad to a degree sufficient to supplant indigenous coustoms at the time when Tamil literature developed in the first centuries A.D."[91].

A.K. Ramanujan is essentially concerned with the poetic genre of the poems and their symbols and structures. While not denying the oral base of classical Tamil poetry, Ramanujan believes that these poems were compiled by editors who wrote them down from either their own or others' memories in the early centuries before or after the Christian era. He makes a distinction between the bards in the poems and the poets/ authors of the poems. These were not the same as he mentions that poems were not rapidly composed like oral epics but were reworked with care. It is not clear whether they were composed mentally or in writing. The poets may have used the metre, diction of the verse, traditional formulae and stock of themes from the Academies or *Caṅkams* of previous ages[92] .

Inspite of the fact that *Caṅkam* poetry follows stylised conventions which allowed the treatment of certain themes, the poems can be examined for clues to understand the social life of different groups. These poems have been used as source materrial by scholars working on different aspects of society, economy, polity and religion right from the time they have been published. Analysis on the nature of this poetry has however been done only from 1960s. Scholars interested in poetic genre of this literature like Hart, Zvelebil and A.K. Ramanujan have analysed this literature by going into details such as metre, chronology, contents etc., and Hart has gone a step further by tracing the relationshiop of this literature with classical Sanskrit literature. Ramanujan focusses mainly on providing good translations of select poems from the anthologies keeping in view their context, syntax etc. Scholars like Hart and Zvelebil working in literature or scholars working on socio-economic and cultural formations like M.G.S. Narayanan, Rajan Gurukkal and Sivathamby have adopted critical methods of enquiry in handling the sources and have tried to present an integrated view by correlating the information gleaned from the texts with archaeological data. They have viewed the poems as belonging to different chronological periods, spanning a period of six-eight centuries.

Rajan Gurukkal has highlighted the problems in using this literature as source material. In his view, as this literature consists of heroic poems there are difficulties in using this to understand society. "This literature broadly belongs to the traditions of oral compositions characterised by formulaic diction, stock phrases, highly stylised expression and administration of symbols of unconscious meaning"[93] of which we are doing a content-wise analysis in a chronological framework perpared on the basis of the most accepted dating of the texts by scholars. So in Gurukkal's view "the use of this literature as source material has to be preceded by a series of difficult exericses starting from the basic syntagmatic analysis of morphology to the complex paradigmatic psycho-analytical and semiological analyses for grasping the principles of versification and the genuine meaning of the poems"[94]. Such exercises for understading the poems have just begun.

The Eighteen Minor works constitute a new type of literature different from the earlier heroic ones[95]. Some of the Eighteen Minor works like the *Nālaṭiyār, Kuṟaḷ, Iṉṉa Nāṟpatu, Iṉiyavai Nāṟpatu, Mutumoḻikkāñci, Naṉmaṇikkaṭikai, Tirikaṭukam, Ācārakkōvai, Paḻamoḻi. Ēlati* and *Ciṟupañcamulam* are mainly ethical didactic texts, perscriptive in nature, preaching morals and laying emphasis on good conduct, vegetarianism, maintenance of peace, etc, presumably due to the influence of Jainism and Buddhism. Other texts like the *Aintiṇai Aimpatu, Aintiṇai Eḻupatu, Tiṇaimālai Nuṟraimpathu, Tiṇaimoḻi Aimpatu, Kainnilai* and *kār Nāṟpatu* include love poems in the *akattiṇai* framework like the early anthologies. The *Kaḷavaḻi* Nā*ṟpatu* is mainly a *Puṟam* text giving gory descriptions of the battlefield during a war between the Cōḻa king Cenkaṇ*āṉ* and the Cēra ruler Irumpoṟai.

This corpus of early Tamil literature though compounded by problems of exaggeration in many poems, baffling chronology and lack of clear evidence for definite internal stratification, problem of the presence of four layers of text (text, colophon, invocatory stanzas and commentaries) on account of collection and classification at different points of time, absence of good and adequate translations of texts[96] and being oral and representing to a certain extent heroic traditions, is nevertheless useful in stydying socio-economic and religious history. Even though information relating to society was not the direct concern of the poets and hence incidental, indirect, or metaphoric, this information is extremely helpful in understanding society, This information from literature has to be decoded from a stylised languages.

The above discussion on the nature of the literary sources, the problem of fixing their chronology and the historiography of early Tamiḻakam make it clear that there are inherent difficulties involved in a study of the present kind. However, an attempt is made here to examine the nature of early historical Tamil society by integrating literary data culled out from a content wise analysis of the texts within a relative chronological framework and archaeological data with concepts borrowed from social anthropology. Given the limitations in understanding the hidden and symbolic meanings which the *Caṅkam* classics abound in, and the methodological problems in using the proto-historic/megalithic and early historical archaelogical data from a limited number of excavations, the present thesis does not claim to provide major conclusions. What it hopes to do is to present new ways of interpretation of the available data to understand the nature of early Tamil society.

This introduction is followed by an analysis of the geography, ecology and settlement patters of the region wherein the *tiṇai* concept will be elaborated to set the background to the discussion on early Tamil society. The thesis will then focus on the nature of organisation and transformation of society. This will be discussed in the light of two phases—an early phase indicating a clan, kin and lineage based organisation and a later phase highlighting the changes in the social sphere, where in the impact of *varṇa* will be taken up. This will be followed by a discussion of the changes which set in, which subsequently resulted in the transformation of society. Similarly, the analysis of religion will be done in two sections, one focussing on the folk forms in the worship of deities and the other on assessing the influence of the northern Sanskritic traditions. A section will deal with the role of the women in early Tamil society.

The analysis of the nature of society is taken up in the light of two phases as the evidence of *Caṅkam* corpus itself shows a society in transition. As part of society the nature of the political organisation or the change from chiefdom towards kingdom will also be studied in the following section.

FOOTNOTES

1. Most of these authors were involved in the debates sentering around the Aryan Dravidian issue. In order to prove the superiority of the Dravidian civilisation they projected a highly advanced society (characterised by a state, revenue system, administrative machinery etc.) of the early Tamils.

2. V. Kanakasabhai, *The Tamils Eighteen Hundred Years ago,* Madras 1956 (2nd edition).

   K.N. Sivaraja Pillai, *Chronology of the early Tamils,* New Delhi, 1984 (Rp). The author compiled lists of kings in a tabular form from the early Taml literature and foreign accounts and dated the reigns of kings and literary texts between 50 BC and 200 AD. This account is very confusing.

   S. Krishnaswami Iyengar, *Beginning of South Indian History,* Madras 1918.

   P.T. Srinivasa Iyengar, *History of the Tamils,* 1918 (Rp)

   K.A. Nilakanta Sastri, *A History of South India,* Madras 1955 is a text book for students of South Indian History.

   K.A. Nilakanta Sastri, *Sangam Literature: Its cult and culture.,* Madras, 1972.

   K.K. Pillay, *A Social History of the Tamils,* Madras 1975.

   N. Subrahmanian, *Sangam Polity,* (Rp.) Madurai, 1980.

   S. Singaravelu, *Social life of the Early Tamils: Classical period,* Kuala Lampur, 1966.

3. Subrahmanian clubs all the anthologies, 10 poems, epics and the 18 Minor works as Sangam Works and assigns them to the first three centuries A.D. At the same time, he assigns all these works to what he calls pre-Pallavan period, thereby implying that they were composed between 1st century A.D. and 600 A.D. - 1980, p. 26.

4. S. Singaravelu: *Social life of the early Tamils: The classical Period,* Kuala Lampur 1966.

5. Kailasapathy : *Tamil Heroic Poetry,* Clarendon Press, Oxford, 1968.

   "Tamil Heroic Poetry" A comparative study in *Proceedings of the Second Conference, Seminar of Tamil Studies,* Vol.II Madras, 1968, pp. 152-57.

6. G.L.Hart : *The poems of Ancient Tamil: Their milieu and Sanskrit counterparts* Berkeley, 1975

   "Ancient Tamil literature its scholarly past and future" in B. Sten (ed) *Essays on South India, New Delhi* 1976, pp. 41-63" "*Relation between Tamil and classical Sanskrit literature, Wiesbaden, 1976.*

7. J.R. Marr, *The Eight Anthologies,* Madras, 1985.

8. K.V. Zvelebil : *The smile of Murukaṉ on Tamil literature of South India,* Leiden, 1973.

   Tamil literature, Leiden, 1974.

9. K. Sivathamby : "An Analysis of the Anthropological significance of the Economic Activities and conduct code ascribed to Mullai tiṇai" *Proceedings of the First International Conference Seminar on Tamil Studies* Vol. I, Kuala Lampur, 1986, pp. 320-31.

   "Early South Indian Society and Economy: The Tinai concept" *Social Scientist,* Vol. 29, 1974, pp. 20-37.

   He uses this method for studying *Drama in Ancinet Tamil Society* Madars, 1981.

10. Clarence Maloney "The Beginnings of Civilization in South India" *Journal of Asian Studies,* vol. XXIX, no. 3, pp. 603-616.

11. Trivandrum, 1977 (a).

12. *Ibid* pp. 1-23

    This tendency is visible in another essay by Narayanan "Vedic Puranic Sastraic element in Tamil Sangam Society and Culture", *Indian History Congress,* Proceedings of the thirty sixth session, Aligarh, 1975 pp. 76-91.

13. 1977 (a), pp. 66-82.

14. *Ibid* pp. 83-98.

15. "The Warrior settlements of the Sangam Age", *Indian History Congress,* Proceedings of the 43rd Session, Kurukshetra 1982, pp. 102-109.

16. "The role of peasants in the early history of Tamilakam in South India", paper presented at the Indo Soviet *Seminar on the History of Peasants struggle,* Moscow 26th-28th September, 1988.

17. "The cult of war as class ideology in the Sangam age in South India "*Indian History Congress,* Proceedings of the 49th Session, Karnatak University, Dharwad 1988 (1989) pp. 109-13.

18. "Social History from the Text Book of poetics in the Sangam age (A study of Tolkāppiyam-Section IV Porulatikaram)" *Indian History Congress,* Proceedings of the 51st session, Calcutta, December, 1990.

19. "*Studies in History* 5.2 ns (1989) pp. 159-75.

20. For this see "Political process and social formation in Early Tamilakam" paper presented at the Seminar on *The State in Precolonial South India* held at Jawaharlal Nehru University, 1989.

21. "Urban Process in Tamil Nadu", occasional papers Urban History Association of Indian, 1982.

"Urbanisation in South India:The role of ideology and polity;" *Indian History Congress,* Proceedings of the 47th Session Srinagar, 1986, Section 1.

22. "Ideology and the State in the South India", Mamidipudi Venkatarangaiah memorial lecture, 1989. Published in the *Andhra Pradesh History Congress,* Proceedings of the 13th Session, Srisailam, 1989, pp. 278-307.

23. The use of the terms '*Caṅkam* literature' and '*Caṅkam* period' have been questioned by scholars who state that these terms are misleading and should not be used. The Jesudasans in their (History of Tamil literature) 1961: p8 State that *Caṅkam* literature is a term used for the sake of convenience Zvelebil does not favour the use of the term 'Augustan literature coined by S. Krishnaswami Iyengar. He finds it appropriate to use the term 'classical' to this literature (Zvelebil 1973, pp. 49-50) Rajan Gurukkal however disagrees on the use of the term classical. He states that this team classical which was used in the context of the hellenistic Greece or Mauryan India cannot be used in the context of ancient south India as the level of culture bears no comparison with that of the former (Gurukkal 1981, p. 79)

24. The three *Caṅkams* lasted at long intervals for 9990 years all together. Mention is made of 8598 poets (including a few gods of the Saiva persuasion) as members and 197 Pāṇṭiyaṉ Rings as patrons.

25. N. Subramanian 1980, p. 6.

    K.A. Nilakanta Sastri 1955, p. 111.

    Kailasapathy 1968, pp. 2-3.

    Zvelebil 1973, pp. 46-49.

    Hart 1975. pp. 9-10.

    Marr 1985, pp. 2-7.

26. K.A. Nilakanta Sastri, 1955, p. 111.

27. For details of the Jain Sangha see A. Chakravarti *Jaina Literature in Tamil,* New Delhi 1974, pp. 14-16.

28. Sivathamby states that reference is made to the number of kings who took part in literary activities. This is made the vital part of the story. The opening lines of that part of the commentary are "The Pandyas established three *Caṅkams* known as Primeval, the Medieval and the Final *Caṅkams.* By constructing a royal base for the *Caṅkams* in which the Gods themselves take part the rule of the newly emerging Pandyas was legitimised. Further, the author adds that it is the first attempt at a Saivite history of Tamil literature", Sivathamby, *Literary History of Tamilnad* 1986:, pp. 34-36.

29. K. Zvelebil, 1974, p. 11.

30. K. Zvelebil furnishes information on the commentaries and publications of the texts 1973, pp. 50-64.

31. K. Zvelebil, 1973, p. 51.

32. K. Zvelebil, 1973, pp. 59-60.

33. For a discussion on the contents of this literature see X.S. Thaninayagam "The period of Ethical Literature in Tamil : Third century to the Seventh century A.D." in J.C. Heesterman, G.H. Schokker and V.I. Subramoniam (ed.) *Pratidānam : Indian, Iranian and Indo-European*

Studies, Franciscus Bernadus Jacobus Kuiper on his 60th Birthday, Mouton, The Hague, Paris, 1968, pp. 601-14.

34. T.P. Meenakshi Sundaram, *A History of Tamil Literature,* Annamalai, 1965.

M.S. Purnalingam Pillai, *Tamil Literature,* Tancavur, 1985 (Rev. ed.).

35. *A History of Tamil Language and Literature,* Madras 1956.

36. N. Subrahmanian, 1980, pp. 25-34.

K. Zvelebil, 1973, pp. 23-41.

37. V. Kanakasabhai, 1956 pp. 2-7.

K. Zvelebil. 1973, p. 4; 1974, p. 41.

38. Hardy, 1983, pp. 124-25.

39. Sivathamby, 1981, p. 66.

40. Scholars date them on the basis of the cumulative evidence in the form of linguistic evidence in the texts, the epigraphic evidence (the Pukaḻūr inscription referring to the geneology of the Cēras, the inscriptions at Mangulam referring to the Pandya Neṭuñceḻiyaṉ) the references to trade with *yavaṉas* in the early anthologies corroborated by numismatic finds and Graeco Roman textual records and historical data. Few of the poems may have been written after 3rd century A.D.

Zvelebil, 1973, pp. 41-43.

Hart, 1975, pp. 8-9; 1976 (a), p. 41. Hart states that the language of these anthologies is consistent and the people mentioned in them seem to have lived within about ten generations. These six were "written after the use of the old Brahmi script which was probably first adapted for Tamil during the reign of Asoka (272-232 B.C) had become standardised and after literacy had spread widely.

41. Zvelebil, 1974, p. 11.

42. Zvelebil, 1973, p. 30.

43. Zvelebil lists them in the chronological order mentioned above *Ibid*, p. 4. Sivathamby dates these texts to the period of the early anthologies.

44. 1st C.B.C. - A.D. 2C: early poems of *Aiṅkuṟunūṟu, Kuṟuntokai, Naṟṟiṇai* and probably of *Akanāṉūṟu* and *Puṟanāṉūṟu* (i.e the poems of Ammuvaṉ, Ōtalāntai, Ōrampoki, Kapilar, the elder, Pē yaṉ etc.

2nd C.A.D- A.D. 3rd C: *Porunārāṟṟuppaṭai, Perumpāṇāṟṟuppaṭai, Paṭṭinappalaī Kuṟincipaṭhi*

A.D. 2ndc-A.D. 4 the : Mataipaṭukṭam. Maturaikkañci, Neṭuralvāṭkas and some poéms of Aiṅkuṟunūṟu, kuṟuntokai, Naṟṟunai, Patiṟṟuppattn, Puṟanāṇuṟu and Akanaṇūṟu (by poets like Paraṇar, nakkirar, the first, Māṅkusṭimarutih etc.)

A.D 3rd C- A.D 5th C : *Mullaippāṭṭu, Ciṟupāṇāṟṟuppaṭai* and poems of *Aiṅkuṟunūṟu, Patiṟṟuppattu, Puṟanāṉūru* and *Akanaṉūṟu* (by poets such as Nappūtaṉār, Nallūr Nattatṉār)

A.D. 4th C -A.D. 6th C : *Ciṟupāṇāṟṟuppaṭai*

Further the dates for the other texts are as follows:

5th-7th C.A.D. *Kalittokai* and *Paripāṭal* (Book III)

5th-6th C. *Cilappatikāram*

45. Earliest poems in the anthologies:
    Aiṅkuṛunūṛu Kuṛuntokai
    Naṛṛiṇai 1st. Century B.C. to 2nd Century A.D.
    Puṛanāṇūṛu
    Akanāṇūṛu
    Porunarāṛṛuppaṭai
    Perumpaṇāṛṛuppaṭai 2nd to 3td Century A.D.
    Paṭṭinappālai
    Kuṛiñcippāṭṭu
    Middle strata in the anthologies : new songs in the
    Pattuppāṭṭu
    Malaipaṭukaṭām
    Maturaikkāñci 2nd to 4th Century A.D.
    Neṭunalvāṭai
    Later Strata : new songs in the *Pattuppāṭṭu Mullaippāṭṭu* 3rd to 5th Century A.D.
    Ci*ṛupāṇāṛṛuppaṭai*
    Latest strata in the anthologies :
    4th to 6th Century A.D.
    Tolkāppiyam Book III (*Porulatikāram*)
    5th century
    Final version of the epic *Cilappatikāram* 5th of 6th century
    Kalittokai and *paripāṭal* 5th to 7th century *Tirumurukaṛṛuppaṭai* 7th to 9th century
    Hardy, Viraha Bhakti, 1983, p. 125.
46. Hart, 1975, p. 8; 1976 (a), p. 41.
47. Sivathamby, 1981, pp. 66-67. He dates the *Tirumurukāṛṛuppaṭai* also to this period.

    Vaiyapuri Pillai also dates the *Kalittokai* and *Paripāṭal* to a later period *A History of Tamil Language and Literature* Madras, 1956, pp. 29-30.

    Nilakanta Sastri states that the *Kalittokai, Paripāṭal* and *Tirumurukāṛṛuppaṭai* are considered post *Caṅkam* works because of the greater simplicity, evolved grammar and richer presence of Sanskrit words, 1972, p. 11.

    Zvelebil also agrees with this late dating (5th-7th C's A.D.) of *Kalittokai* and *Paripāṭal* on the basis of the metre used, new structural words and allusions to Sanskrit-Purāṇic legends. The poems of the *Paripāṭal* contain references to shrines and Purāṇic legends which point to a late date of composition. These poems may be regarded as a form of transition between traditional love poetry and emerging devotional literature, 1973, pp. 119-30.

    The Jesudasans also date the *Kalittokai* and *Paripāṭal* to 2nd half of the 4th Century A.D., 1961, pp. 40-41.

    Friedhelm Hardy dates the *Kalittokai* and *Paripāṭal* on the basis of the religious content to a period later than the anthologies. The *Kalittokai* is later than the anthologies because of the rustic style, vulgarisms in language and elements of folk culture, references to mythical episodes of Kṛṣṇa especially evident in the poems describing the bull fight and *Kuṛavai* dance. Similary the *Pāripatal* is taken to be a late text as it deals with a temple milieu (that of Viṣṇu). Hardy notices in this text a definite awareness of Viṣṇu as a transcendental absolute- something which becomes more clear in the Āḻvār hymns.

Hardy, 1983, pp. 127-28; 67-93.

48. Hart, 1975,, p. 9; 1976 (a), p. 41.

Jesudasans, 1961, p. 39.

Vaiyapuri Pillai in fact dates the *Cilappatikāram* as late as 9th C.A.D. and *Maṇimēkalai* to an age later than 5th C. on the basis of the internal evidence like reference to Pattini cult for the first time, reference to sacred places like Srirangam and Vēṅkaṭam which became important only around late peiod; description of the urban centres and social life which differs from that outlined in the anthologies; birth stories and the description of the systems of philosophy and language 1956, pp. 147-53.

Subrahmanian, however, assigns an early date for the two epics, 1980, pp. 27-30.

Sivathamby also settles for a date around late 5th or early 6th C for *Cilappatikāram* as indicated by lingustic, literary and social factors and states that *Maṇimekalai* was a later text than the *Cilappatikāram,* 1981, pp. 75-81.

While MGS Narayanan dates the *Cilappatikāram* to the 8th-9th Century A.D. on the basis of the inscription found at Kunavāyir Kōṭṭam which is dateable to that period. S. Hikosaka dates it to 750 A.D. on the basis of the text's indebtedness to Sanskrit in terms of words found in the text: concept of karma introduced by the Buddhists or Jains and not found in the *Caṅkam* literature, allusions to Nāyaṉmārs and Āḻvārs; descriptions of cities like Pukār (which is differently described in *Paṭṭinappālai,* Pattini and Sakti cult popularised by Iḷaṅkō Aṭikaḷ which was not popular in the *Caṅkam* period and the marriage of Kōvalaṉ and Kaṇṇaki in the Brahmanical style according to Vedic rites with chantings by a brahmin priest found for the first time in the *Cilappatikāram.* The *Maṇimēkalai* is placed between 890 A.D. and 950 A.D. by Hikosaka on account of the following factors. Text contains elements of Tantric Buddhism; reference to a Chola king as ruler of Kāñci and not a Pallava king. Hikosaka is of the view that Cāttaṉār would have composed it as an attempt to revive Buddism since it was on the decline "The Age of Cilappatikaram and Manimekalai", *Journal of the Institute of Asian Studies,* Vol. V. No.2 March 1988, pp. 91-114. It is difficult to accept the 9th Century dating of the *Cilappatikāram* put forth above. The text is definitely assignable to the Pre-pallavan period (5th-6th Centuries A.D.) on the basis of the style and contents. The text does not refer to the Pallavas of Kañci. Moreover, it still talks of the Cēra, Cōḻa and Pāṇṭiya kings which is an indicator of its being a pre-Pallavan text.

49. Subrahmanian, 1980, pp. 30-31.

50. Sivathamby, 1981, pp. 67-70.

S.N. Kandaswamy after an analysis of the language structure of the *Tolkāppiyam* and Tamil Brahmi inscriptions and contents of the text postulates that the major portion of the text was composed before 300 B.C. "The Age of Tolkappiyam" in *Journal of Tamil Studies* Vol. 20, Dec 1981, pp. 37-71.

The Jesudasans assign the work to about the first century A.D.

51. Hart, 1976(a), p. 41.

52. For a discussion on features of division etc of *Tolkāppiyam* see Zvelebil. 1973, pp. 130-49.
53. Sivathamby. 1981, pp. 68-70.
54. Vaiyapuri Pillai assigns the *Tolkāppiyam* to a period later than the 4th century A.D. - 1956, pp. 13-14, p. 65.
55. Hardy, 1983, p. 125.
56. *Periplus of the Erythraen Sea* is dated to the 1st Century A.D.

    Ptolemy's *Geography* was written in the middle of the 2nd Century A.D.

    pliny's work is dated to C.A.D. 77.
57. The burials excavated are more in number than the habitation sites. Data on the megaliths can be got from *Indian Archaeology :A Review* (brought out by Archaeological Survey of India) and books which have appeared over the years like:

    Leshnik, *The South Indian Megalithic Culture:* Pandukal Complex, Wiesbaden, 1974.

    B.K. Gururaja Rao, *The Megalithic Culture in South India,* Mysore, 1972.

    B. Narasimhaiah, *Neolithic and Megalithic Cultures in Tamil Nadu New Delhi*, 1980.

    N.R. Banerjee, *The Iron Age in India,* Delhi, 1965.

    K.S. Ramachandran, *Archaelogy of South India: Tamil Nadu* New Delhi, 1980.
58. Leshnik "Nomads and Burials in the early history of South India" in Leshnik and Sonthemer (re.) *Pastoralists and Nomads in South Asia,* Otto Harrasowitz, Weisbaden, 1975, p. 56.
59. Maloney, on the basis of the literary sources, has suggested potential areas where excavations could prove useful "Archaeology of South India: Accomplishments and Prospects" in B. Stein (ed.) *Essays in South India,* 1976, pp. 24-33. Dr. Champakalakshmi notes that there is need to attempt to relate archaeological evidence to literary tradition, to check the reliablility of historical tradition through excavated data or to indicate such possibilities. The problem of correlating literary evidence with archaeological material would require an investigation into and proper handling of the literary sources. The results of such an investigation for the Tamil region seems to be utterly discarded.The basic need seems to be systemmatic indexing of names of places, peoples, and regions mentioned in the concerned literature, identifying and mapping them out geographically and extending the assistance of archaelogy to such areas. A historical atlas of early sites known from literatrure would be the first essential step towards such attempts at correlation of archaeological and literary evidence "Archaeology and Tamil Literary Tradition" *Puratattva,* No. 8, 1975-76, p. 110.
60. *Ibid*, p. 117.
61. pioneering work has been done on the Tamil Brahmi inscriptions by I. Mahadevan. For details see "Corpus of the Tamil Brahmi Inscriptions" in R. Nagaswamy (ed.) *Seminar on Inscriptions,* Madras (1966) 1968, pp.57-63.

    "The Tamil Brahmi Inscriptions of the Caṅkam Age" in *Proceedings of the Second International Conference Seminar of Tamil Studies,* Madras 1968, Vol. I, pp. 73-106.

    Tamil Brahmi Inscriptions Lecture printed by the Tamil Nadu State Department of Archaeology, Madras, 1970.

62. 46 sites in Tamil Nad and 6 sites in Kerala have yielded Roman coins. In certain cases punch marked coins have been found with Roman ones. Coins with the tiger seal attributed to the Colas was found at Kaveripattinam. I am grateful to S. Suresh for information on coins.
63. Clarendon Press, Oxford, 1968.
64. See Chapters II, III, IV and V. Also see his article "Tamil Heroic Poetry. A comparative study" in *Art and Literature,* 1986, pp. 69-75.
65. Kailasapathy, 1968, p. 11; pp. 229-3.

    He suggested that the *Tolkāppiyam* is a bardic grammar or an aid to the instruction of young bards-Kailasapathy, *Ibid*, pp. 48-52.
66. Hart, 1976(a), p. 42.

    Hart, 1976(b), pp. 326-27.
67. J.R. Marr, 1985, pp. 453-55.
68. *Ibid*, p. 455.
69. *Ibid*, pp. 454-56.
70. K. Zvelebil, 1973, p. 12.
71. K Zvelebil, 1973, p. 30.
72. K. Zvelebil, 1974, p. 11.
73. G. John Samuel "literary Theories of Tamil Heroic Poetry" in *Studies in Tamil Poetry,* Madras, 1978, pp. 1-2.
74. Samuel, 1978, pp. 5-6.
75. *Ibid*, pp. 13-14.
76. Samuel, 1978, p. 18, pp. 19-27.
77. Samuel, 1978, pp. 7-8.
78. Sivathamby. 1981, pp. XXVI-XXVII.
79. For details see Sivathamby, 1981, pp.101-05.
80. Sivathamby, 1986, p. 23.
81. Hardy, 1983, pp. 167-93; pp. 202-21.
82. Hardy, 1983, p. 126.
83. These observations are based on the characteristics of heroic poetry out lined by Bowra : *Heroic Poetry,* London, 1961, pp. 5-77, p. 197, p. 254., p. 530, p. 404, p. 414. See also Vansina *Oral Tradition: A Study in Historical Methodology,* London, 1965 who states that veiled expressions and stock phrases are commonly found in oral Poetry: pp. 69-72; pp. 143-45.
84. Such a characterisation is done by Bowra, 1961, p. 60, pp. 132-33, p. 179, p. 502, p. 506.
85. Bowra attributes presence of miraculous elements to the primitive stage of heroic poetry. In the aristocratic stage, however, the heroes like Gilgamesh, Beowulf etc do not change shape. They arepowerful in themselves and do not need extraneous powers. We do not come across heroes of such stature like Gilgamesh, Hercules etc. in early Tamil literature.
86. R.Finnegan outlines that oral literature cannot totally be separated from written literature in any absolute sense. A poem may be orally composed and later transmitted in writing or

perhaps written initially and then performed by oral means. Oral poems do not usually have title-Finnegan, *Oral Poetry,* Cambridge, 1981 pp.1-6. Also oral poetry varies in size ranging from short plays to long epics-Finnegan, p. 1; Bowra, 1961, p. 330.

87. He gives an example for this 'when a Boshongo song about an event which took place during the reign of king Kot a NCE makes a passing reference to pearls. This is certainly not because there was any intention to convey the information that pearls had been introduced in the country in the 18th century. Nevertheless the fact has been conveyed. even if the informant was unaware that he was conveying it', p.48.

88. Vansina, 1965, p. 50.

89. Vansina identifies panegyric, poetry as one type of oral tradition—p.149. Books of Kailasapathy, Hart, Zvelebil provide more details regarding the *akam-puṛam* classification.

90. K.A. Nilakanta Sastri "Sanskrit Elements in Early Tamil Literature" in K.M. Shrimali (ed.) *Essays in Indian Art, Religion and Society* (Indian History Congress Golden Jubilee Year Publication Series), Vol.1, New Delhi, 1987, pp.45-48.

91. Hart, 1976 (a), p. 42.

92. These views are expressed in the Afterword of *Poems of Love and War,* 1985, pp. 271-73 A.K. Ramanujan, *Interior landscape,* London 1967.

93. R. Gurukkal, 1989(a), p. 162.

94. R. Gurukkal. 1989(a), pp. 162-63 also lists the books/articles which are helpful in such an analysis.

95. These words comprise ethical and love poetry. The love poems are smaller in size. They very between 3-6 and contain few details as compared to the earlier anthologies.

96. There are a few translations of the Tamil Texts. they are:

    A.K. Ramanujan, *The Interior Landscape: Love poems from a classical Tamil Anthology.* Bloomington Indiana University Press, 1987 (translation of select poems of *Kuruntogai*).

    A.K. Ramanujan. *Poems of Love and War: from the eight Anthologies and the Ten long poems of classical Tuamil* OUP, New Delhi 1985.

    P. Jotimuttu, *Ainkurunuru,* Translation and *commentry, Christian Literature Society, medras, 1984.*

    A.V. Subramanian, *The Ten Decades* (*Patirrupattu A Sangam poetical work*), Tamil Nadu Government's translation of classics: 5, Tamil Nadu Text Book Society, Madras, 1980.

    A.V. Subramanian, *Narrinai (An Anthology of Amour)*, Department of Tamil Development-Culture, Government of Tamil Nadu, Madras, 1989.

    David Ludden & M.S. Pillai, *The Kurunthogai, an anthology of classical Tamil love poetry, Madurai, 1976.*

    N.R. Balakrishna Mudaliar, *The Golden Anthology of Ancient Tamil literature.* 3vols. Madras 1959.

    J.V. Chelliah, *Pattupattu. Ten Tamil Idylls* South India Saiva Sidhanta Works Publishing Society, Madras, 1952.

    N. Raghunathan, *Six long poems from Sangam Tamil,* Vigneshwara Publishing House, Madras, 1978.

The *Cilappatikāram* has been translated by three scholars.

Alain Danielou. *Silappadikarm (The Ankle Bracelet)*, George, Allen and Unwin, London, 1967.

Kaa Naa Subramanian, *The Anklet Story,* Agam Kala Prakashan, New Delhi, 1977.

V.R.R. Dikshitar, *The Cilappatikaram,* South India Saiva Sidhanta Works Publishing Society, Madras, 1978.

Prema Nandakumar, *Manimekalai*,Tamil University, Thanjavur, 1989.

Ilakkuvanar, *Tolkappiyam, with Critical Studies,* Madurai, 1963.

E.S. Varadaraja Iyer, Tolkappiyam. Porulathikaram 1948 (He has translated only four *Iyals* of the text)

Quite a few translations of *Kural* are available.

V.R.R. Dikshitar, *Tirukkural of Tiruvalluvar,* Adyar Library, Madras, 1949.

G.U. Pope, *The Sacred Kurral of Thiruvalluvar Nayanar* (Rp) Asian Educational Services, New Delhi.

G.U. Pope, *The Nalatiyar,* South India Saiva Siddhanta Publishing Society, Tinnevelly, 1958.

CHAPTER - II

TAMIḺAKAM : THE REGION-GEOGRAPHY, ECOLOGY AND SETTLEMENT PATTERN

Tamiḻakam, as portrayed in the Tamil literary sources, is supposed to have extended from Vēṅkaṭam Hills (i.e the modern Tirupati hills) in the North to Cape Comorin[1] in the south and from Bay of Bengal in the East to the Arabian Sea in the West. The modern delineation of this region corresponds to present day states of Tamil Nadu and Kerala, though the northern boundary, namely the Vēṅkaṭam hills are now included in the modern state of Andhra Pradesh. Tamiḻakam, here, does not correspond to the present day state of Tamil Nadu. Hence, for the purpose of our study we shall refer to the region as delineated by the early Tamil texts.

A study of the geography and ecology of Tamiḻakam is taken up as it has been observed that the "geography of a region furnishes the essential baackdrop to the matrix of its cultural motivations[2]". This region[3] is taken up for study as it is distinct as a region from other regions on account of physiographic and ecological differences. Further, the region is taken up not only because it is distinctive, but also because it has a large corpus of texts providing evidence of a non-Vedic cultural context to study early societies in India which came under Vedic and "Aryan" cultural impact. In other words, the region under study evolved as a cultural unit with a long historical past and certain dominant linguistic, literary and cultural traditions, non-Vedic and non-Sanskritic in origin, and remained distinctive despite influences from other regions and cultures. Yet, as a unit of geographical study it is complex and full of variations. These variations would have influenced the development potentialities of the different parts of the region. Consequently the distribution and nature of settlements would have been different. Subsequently, the development of society in early Tamiḻakam was considerably determined and influenced by these geographic and physiographic variations. Some of the nuclear sub-regions of Tamiḻakam, such as the Cōḻa Pāṇṭiya and Cēra dominated river valleys carry the impact of these variations to this day to a remarkable degree within the larger unified Tamil macro region.

It has been pointed out that studies on historical geography in the past have largely made regions correspond to contemporary political boundaries.Some studies have identified regions based on linguistic boundaries. A major drawback in such studies has been that they have considered such regions as undifferentiated geographical and cultural units within which variations have been ignored[4]. However, for the purpose of our study the region and its diversity is understood by the delineations provided by the early Tamil texts and not on the basis of political or linguistic boundaries. A major drawback in such studies has been that they have considered such regions as undifferentiated geographical and cultural units within which variations have been ignored.[4] However, for the purpose of our study the region and its dirersity is understood by the delineatione provided by the early Tamil texts and not on the basis of political or linguistic boundaries.

A study of the present geography, geology, soil and climatic conditions of the region which can be made from gazetteers (all India and district ones) and books describing the geography of India[5] would help to identify the areas referred to in the texts and thereby bring out the historical geography of Tamiḻakam, its variations in ecology and topography.

The early Tamils classified their land into ecological niches or *tiṇaiṣ*.* Here we are dealing with the ecological situation. These were called *aintiṇai* as a whole[6]. The regions was also conceived of a whole as it is difficult to demarcate the area of a *tiṇai* as the *tiṇais* are interspersed with one another[7].

The *tiṇais* mentioned in early Tamil literature are the *Kuṛiñci* (mountainous tracts) *mullai* (pastures) *murutam* (riverine tracts). neytal (the coastal/littoral tracts) and *pālai* (and waste tracts). Palai was hot treated as a separate *tiṇai* as it was a seasonal ecological zone created at times on account of scarcity of rains or hot summer conditions. There are examples in the texts which show the transformation of *mullai* and *kuṛiñci* in a particular part of the year (seasonal) into *pālai* lands[8]. Sivathamby envisaged that the *pālai* was treated as a separate behavioural pattern presumably on account of two factors. First, because the poets felt the need to treat the theme of separation which took place during that part of the year. Second, because some groups of the hilly region took to highway robbery as a way of livelihood[9].

The *Tolkāppiyam,* which codifies the literary conventions, mentions that each *tiṇai* denoted by the name of a flower was marked by three major features namely *mutal, karu and uri*[10]. While *mutal* denotes space and time[11], *karu* refers to the typical features of landscape like deity, food, flora and fauna, water source, drums and a musical instrument[12] (See Chart 1). These five *tiṇais* were correlated with the different emotive cirucumstances or behavioural aspects in love and war (*uripporul*).[13] Therefore, *tiṇai* indicates an ecological region as well as an emotive situation.

Scholars have analysed the social and historical significance of the *tiṇai* concept in various ways. A unilinear development from pre-historic to early farming society is recognised in this concept by some scholars. P.T. Srinivasa Iyengar viewed this as

* Tiṇai literature means a situation, either behavioured love (akottiṇai) or war (purattīṇai) or physiographic/ecological situation.

illustrating the evolution of civilisation as "all these kinds of natural regions are found in the Tamil country, though on a small scale, and as the South Indian spread from region to region he developed the stages of culture which each region was calculated to produce"[14]. For Ramachandra Dikshitar the *tiṇai* concept provided a clue to the pre-history of South India since "South India in pre-historical days was peopled by a number of tribes, of whom five could be distinguished according to the geographical classification of the soil....The Tamil Social organisation which had its distinctive characteristics born out of environment, as anthropology holds, is unique in having realised the five different stages of human life in prehistorical times"[15]. Kamil Zvelebil interpreted the *tiṇai* concept as a unilinear evolutionist concept. He states it is possible that the division reflects the historical migration of pre-Dravidian and proto-Tamil population from the hills and jungles to the fertile plains and to the seaboard or in other words, the development from the neolithic hunter, through the intermediate stage of the keeper of the flocks, to the settled tiller of the soil and fisherman[16].

While theories of evolution per se are interesting, the region does not present a unilinear development. Instead we shall show in the course of this thesis that there was co-existence of different modes of subsistence and hence differences in social milieux.

We will view the descriptions of *tiṇai* (both as an ecological region and behavioural situation) as they are highlighted in the texts. This method in our view is more scientific. Moreover, the relationship between man and nature has to be probed in these eco-zones to have an idea of the development of the *tiṇais*.

The conception of the *tiṇai* as ecological zones was not just a literary convention but a geographical reality. The *Āṟṟuppaṭai* poems of the *Pattuppāṭṭu* describe the various regions the bard had to pass through before reaching the locality of the patron[17].

The *kuṟiñci* region, as portrayed in the Tamil texts extended over mountainous and hilly tracts. These regions would correspond to the western and eastern ghats, Anaimalais, Nilgiris, Palanis, Cardamom, Agastyamalai ranges, Varshanad hills and the Tamil Nadu hills (namely Javadis, Shevaroys, Kollimalai, Paccamalai)[18]. Most of these lay in Cēra territory with a few in Pāṇṭiya land[19]. The in habitants of these tracts were the *Kuṟavar* and *Kāṇavar*[20], and their economic activities were limited to hunting gathering honey[22], digging up edible tubers[23] and slash and burn cultivation[24]. The *kuṟiñci* regions were rich in natural products like pepper, ivory, teak, aromatic woods like sandalwood and *akil*[25] and some gems.[26] Even today the Malabar region is famous for its pepper. These tracts were areas of relative isolation inaccessible and generally far away from the main highways with simple forms of subsistence. Though poor in day-to-day resources, they were rich in natural products like pepper, woods, ivory etc which figured in the trading network outside Tamiḻakam[27].

The *mullai* regions were pastures, meadows and scrublands. Those areas which could be classified as *mullai* would be the forests and meadows on the lower slopes of the Tamil Nadu hills, Kerala hills and Coimbatore plateau. Cattle rearing was the dominant activity of this tract[28]. The pastoralists living in this tract were the *Iṭaiyar*

Iaiyar, Kōvalar and *Āyar* who domesticated cows, goats and sheep[29]. Some form of shifting cultivation was practised here. The main crop grown was *varaku* (a kind of millet). From descriptions in *Perumpāṇārruppaṭai* and *Maturaikkāñci*, we may surmise that these *mullai* lands were peripheral to the *marutam* lands[30]. These tracts were regions of expanding agricultural activities and we find slow transition from a pastoral to a agrarian economy. It is interesting to note that the major trans-peninsular route linking the western and eastern coasts of Tamiḻakam passed through the *mullai* lands of the Coimbatore plateau. These tracts seem to be involved in the trading activities and transmarine commerce as this region was rich in beryl and semi-precious stones which constituted one of the exports to the West, Hoards of Roman coins found here confirm the region's involvement in maritime commerce.

This division into *tiṇais* was not rigid and there are cases where they overlapped. Both *kuṟiñci* and *mullai tiṇais* had cultivable slopes where shifting cultivation or slash and burn cultivation were taken up by the *kuṟavar* as indicated earlier.

According to the *Tolkāppiyam,* the settlements of the *kuṟiñci* region were denoted by the use of the terms *ciṟukuṭi* and *kuṟicci*[31] and those of *mullai* tracts were known as cēri *and palli*[32]. The *ciṟukuṭi* were mostly small hamlets or small villages where the *kuṟavar/kāṇavar* lived. Besides, the term *kuṭi* found in the texts stood for the clan as well as the place of residence. For instance, we came across a Kōvalarkūṭi in the *Perumpāṇāṟruppaṭai*[33] and the Āykuṭi of Āy Aṇṭiraṉ near the Potiyil hills[34]. Further, mention is made of Iṭaikkāṭu[35] and Iṭaikkuṉṟūr[36]. The term *iṭai* could mean something between two zones or could denote the hamlets of the cowherds and shepherds. We come across references to chiefs of certain hilly and pastoral regions exercising socio-political control. Some of those chiefs constituted the Vēḷir. The Vēḷir of Kuṉṟūr (modern Coonoor in the Nilgiri hills), Āviyar of Aviṇaṉkuṭi (in the Palani hills of Madurai district), *Vēḷir* chieftains like Porunaṉ near the Kodaikanal region of Madurai, Pāri of Parampumalai, Pēkan of Vaṉamalai, Āy of Potiyil malai and Vaḷḷuvaṉ of Ñāñcilmalai are some of those mentioned in literature[37]. Further, certain groups like the *Vaṭukar* and a chieftain Pulli residing in the Veṅkaṭam hills (the northern boundary of Tamiḻakam) are mentioned. One also comes across references to *mūtūr* (old settlement) in the poems of the *Pattuppāṭṭu*[38]. They were presumably the centres of the chiefs of the *kuṟiñci* and *mullai*. In this connection it has been pointed out that the *mūtūr* as described in the *Ciṟupāṇāṟruppaṭai* and *Malaipaṭukaṭām* seem to have been merely camps of the chieftains of the hilly and pastoral tracts[39] although *mūtūr* would also indicate an old settlement and not a mere camp.

Other settlements on the hilly regions on the western coast include Kuṭalur, Māṅkāṭu, Pāmallur and Umpaṟkāṭu[40], Umpaṟkāṭu could denote a village surrounded by a forest, full of elephants (as umpar means elephants). This could have been in the Cēra country as that country was full of elephants. This was gifted to a poet (Kummaṭṭūr Kaṇṇaṉār-*Patiṟṟuppattu* II). Another place referred to is Ceṉkaṇmā (North Arcot

Dist.) of Naṉṉaṉ which also lay in a hilly tract[41]. Ceṇkaṇmā is modern Cengam (the headquarter of a taluk in North Arcot dist).

While singing the praise of Nalliyakkōṭaṉ the poet of *Ciṟupnaṟṟuppaṭai* also informs us of two important places in the *mullai* regions namely Māvilaṅkai and Vēlūr[42]. Kodumanal (in Coimbatore region) is an important centre of the *mullai* tract. It emerged as an important craft centre on account of its strategic location on the banks of a tributary of the Kaveri and on the route leading to the West coast. Its proximity to the beryl mines could have contributed to its development as an important manufacturing centre for beads. Considering the low technological development and the subsistence base consisting of hunting, food gathering, shifting cultivation and stock rearing of the *mullai* and *kuṟiñci* regions the social groups of this region could not have lived in large settlements. However, Kodumanal as a craft centre seems, from its archaeological remains,a fairly large settlement. These are distinct from the *pērūr* (big settlements) which emerged in the *marutam and neytal* tracts as we shall note in a later section of this chapter. However, there is a perur in Coimbatore district, evidently on important trade centre from very early times, which also seems to have emerged in a small agricultural pocket (Also see Appendix 1).

The river basins constituted the fertile agricultural tracts (*marutam*) with the main rivers flowing in this region being the Pālār, Peṇṇaiyār, Kāveri, Vaikai, Tāmraparaṇi-flowing into the Bay of Bengal and Periyar and Ponnani-flowing into the Arabian Sea. These fertile tracts were the main rice producing areas and the nuclei of the three kingdoms *viz* those of Cēra, Cōḻa and Pāṇṭiya lay in these areas.[43] They were evidently nuclear regions or areas of attraction.[44] It is evident from the Tamil texts that these were the most significant tracts as we shall see later. The inhabitants of these *marutam tiṇais were the* uḻavar and *toḻuvar*.[45] Fertility of the land, agricultural operations and irrigation facilities in *marutam* are vividly portrayed in the literature. The fertility of the land particularly in the *Cōḻa nāṭu* due to the river Kāveri is constantly referred to in the literary texts. Āvūr Mulaṅ Kiḻār in a short poem seems to deliberately exaggerate the importance of this land saying that the land was so fertile that a tiny piece where a female elephant might rest could produce enough to feed seven male adult elephants.[46] A *veli* (5 acres) of land is said to have produced a full thousand *kalams* (a measure) of paddy.[47] Poems of the *Puṟam* genre refer to the *Cōḻa nāṭu* as *nalnātu* or *puṉal nāṭu* (good, fertile).[48] In fact its fertility continues to be reflected even in later texts such as *Kaḻavaḻi Nāṟpatu* where the Cōḻa king is referred to as *puṉal nāṭaṉ* and *Kāviri Nāṭaṉ* Though these descriptions are sometimes symbolic or used as stock phrases, they are nevertheless indices of the fertility of land. Even today the Kāveri basin is one of the richest agricultural zones of South India.Soils of other river basins such as those of Vaikai Tāmraparaṇi and Pēriyāru must have also been fertile enough to support the crops. The tillers of the soil knew the technique of harnessing the bullocks (*erutu*) at their necks to a ploughshare (*mēḻi* or *nāñcil*) with a cross bar (*nukam*)[49]. Agricultural operations like harvesting of the paddy with sickles, threshing and storing of grain are mentioned in the texts. In this context, the *Porunarāṟṟuppaṭai* refers to:

> Farmers with their sickles bend to reap their harvest
>
> Pile rice sheaves in immense stackheap daily grains threshed out that look like hills|| and store it in large bins enclosed in straw|| that stand ranged close without a space between|| Each plot enclosed five acres (*veli*) in extent,
>
> produces paddy thousand *kalams* full
>
> This is the land that the Kaveri well sustains"[50]

Archaeological evidence for the agricultural implements is scanty. Buffaloes (*erumai*) were said to have been employed in ploughing operations[51]. Crops cultivated extensively in the *marutam* were rice and sugarcane[52]. Agrarian production seems to have increased with the provision of irrigation facilities. References to irrigation mainly consist of tanks and minor dams[53]. The *Porunarāṟṟuppaṭai* refers to tanks enclosed by bunds on the Kaveri river[54]. The Cōḷa king Karikāla is said to have constructed a dam[55]. Production of high yields of paddy crops may have been facilitated by such irrigation facilities.

Efforts were probably made to increase cultivation. In the *Paṭṭinappālai* it is mentioned that "where forests were, now hamlets rise, he (Karikālaṉ) deepens tanks (and) makes rich the land[56]." We are informed that "In the *kuṟiñci* tract are mountains high where grow the short stalked *thorai* rice on uplands sown from which the *akil* tree and the sandalwood have been well cleared[57]." In spite of the nature of the terrain which provided only limited areas for cultivation restricted to river valleys the surplus production of paddy is referred to in literary sources[58]. Miḻalai, Kuṉṟūr and Vīrai are indicated to be some of the rich rice producing centres. It is interesting to note that Vīrai and Miḻalai were Vēḷir settlements. These settlements are described to be overflowing with rice[59]. The *Perumpāṇāṟṟuppaṭai* also hints at surplus production as we are told that:

> "in fields that bring continued income great.
> The reapers cut the thick and hollow stalks
> of ripened rice whose large grains look like swarms
> of stinging wasps. They pile in large full heaps
> The sheaves in ample threshing grounds, where gifts
> Are offered to the gods beneath the shades
> of snake-infested marutham branches tall.
> They pull the large stacks down around which lie
> The Spider's silver web resembling much
> The white attire of demons going through
> The devil dance in ordered kindred crowds.
> Then they thresh out the grain with bulls.

Remove the chaff and Straw, and dry the grain
By shifting it in the west wind with their hands
The grain this heaped in marutham hamlets rich
Resembles Meru great, the northern mount"[60].

The *Porunarāṛruppaṭai* also refers to this surplus production and to heaps of paddy stacked up and stored in large bins[61]. In this context a burnt brick structure consisting of two closed almost square compartments with a front verandah excavated at Tirukkāmpuliyur has been identified by the excavators as a double granary. Since there was no opening for the compartments, the grain was probably poured into it from the top. The foundation was laid of brick bats, pebbles and hard earth with mudplaster as the binding medium[62]. The subsistence base of the *Mūvēntar* may have been facilitated by the production of a surplus in the *marutam* tracts. Clarence Maloney is of the view that this production of rice provided the economic basis for the emergence of more complex social patterns and made possible a life quite different from that of a culture dependent on millets, grains and pulses[63]. In the subsequent chapter we shall show the *marutam* as the most dominat *tiṇai* in which social complexity prevailed.

The *Tolkāppiyam* mentions that the settlements of the *marutam* were designated as *Ur*[64]. We come across quite a few places eding with the suffix *Ur* as well as other place names. To the north of the Kāveri Valley in the districts of Vriddhachalam and Chidambaram urn burial sites have been found indicating the sedentarisation of people. A number of settlements along the river Kāveri or in the deltaic region such as Aḻundur[65] (moderm Tiruvalundur near Mayavaram). Ātuturai[66], Kaḻār[67], Kuṭanṭaivāyil[68], Kuṭ avāyilṭ[69], Neṭuntēru[70], Piṭavūr[71], Pōr[72], mentioned in the texts indicate that this area was colonised (Also see Appendix 1). This is also supported by limited archaeological evidence. Excavations of sites in the lower Kaveri valley like Alagarai, Tirukkāmuliyur, Uṛaiyūr and Kiḻaiyur yielding material remains of the megalithic as well as early historical sites indicate that the lower Kāveri valley was one of the zones of attraction for the early settlers[73]. Habitation may be tracted back to the 4th-3rd Centuries B.C. Urn burial sites reported in the taluks of Nagapattinam, Tanjavur, Mayavaram, Kumbakonam, Orattanadu, Tiruchirapalli and Kulittalai taluks also lend credence to this early colonisation and settlement. All this is also reflected in the *Paṭṭinappālai* which referes to "rows of settlements (*Kuṛumpatūr*) of numerous families (*Kuṭi*) in the vast Cola land, who showed no enmity amongst themselves"[74].

Another river basin colonised from early times was the Vaikai-Tāmraparaṇi basin as evident from numerous urn burial sites in the Madurai and Tirunelveli districts. This region was also fertile and surplus production of paddy in the settlements of this region like Aḻumbil[75], Allūr[76] and Mutuveḷḷiḻai[77] are referred to in the sources. Vayalūr another place mentioned, was possibly full of cultivated fields of paddy[78] as the term *vayal* itself meant fields. Besides a radio carbon date of ± 95 B.C from Koṛkai situated at the mouth of Tāmraparaṇi suggests that the Tāmraparaṇi delta was inhabited from early times and was also producing rice. Maloney indicates that "small sections of many ancient bunds can be seen, rising up to twelve feet above the rice fields"[79].

Settlements in the Toṇṭai-nāṭu (northern part of Tamiḻakam which included the Pālār, Peṇṇaiyār deltaic regions) on the basis of archaeological evidence go back to the 3rd/2nd Century B.C. In the *Ciṟupāṇāṟṟuppaṭai*, Āmūr is mentioned as one of the fortified settlements of the *marutam* where the *antaṇar* (*brāhmaṇas*) resided[80].

Political centres of the three *Vēntar* i.e Uraiyūr, Vañci (Karūr) and Madurai are all situated o the banks of rivers in the *marutam* tracts (the first two on the Kāveri and the last on the Vaikai).

The coastal litoral tract or *neytal* was another area of attraction. Both the east and west coasts were studded with ports and centres of trade (*Paṭṭiṇams*) despite the fact that there were no natural harbours to accommodate large ships. In these tracts lived the fishermen (*paratavar*) and salt manufacturers (*umaṇar*). Traditionally this region was known for its fishing and salt manufacturing activities[81]. It is only in passages of later texts that one finds reference to the *parata* who were described to be merchants and shippers living in coastal cities, in the big mansions, engaged in trading in conches, pearls, tamarind, salt, horses and fish[82].

In the *Tolkāppiyam* the settlements of the *neytal* region were designated as *pākkam* and *paṭṭiṇam.*[83] While the *pākkam* may have been the hamlets/small villages where the fisherfolk (*paratavar*) lived, the pa*ṭṭiṇams* definitely indicated larger settlements or ports which emerged on the coast. On account of their strategic location they would have served as centres of trade (or trade enclaves) housing heterogenous populations. These *paṭṭiṇams* were the *emporia* described by foreign accounts. Some of the ports frequently mentioned in connection with trading activities in literature are Toṇṭi[84] and Muciṟi[85] on the west coast in the Cēra country, Nīrpēyāṟṟu[86], Eyirpaṭṭiṇam[87] and Vīrai[88] on the east coast in the northern part of the region, Pukār on the east coast in the Cōḻa country and Koṟkai and Maruṅgūr-paṭṭiṇam in the Pāṇṭiya country.[89] (Also see Appendix 1). The foreign classical accounts also furnish us with names of coastal centres and ports. Those mentioned in the writings are Tyndis (Toṇṭi of the Tamil texts equated with Ponnani), Muziris (Muciṟi of the Tamil texts equated with Cranganore), Naura and Nitra (identified with Cannanore and Mangalore)[90], Bacare (identified with Porkad/Varakkalai)[91], Nelcynda (identified to be very near modern Kottayam),[92] Khaberis (Kāverippaṭṭiṇam/Pukar)[93] and Kolkhoi[94] (Koṟkai). Archaeological excavations conducted at many sites on the east coast such as Vasavasamudram, Karaikkadu, Nattamedu and Vanagiri indicate a 1st/2nd century A.D date for the earliest levels indicating their emergence/efflorescence with the expansion of trading activities, while other centres such as Arikamedu, Korkai, Kaveripaṭṭiṇam and Alagankulam have pre-1st century levels indicating a habitation going back to 2nd century B.C. for Arikamedu, 8th century B.C. for Korkai and 3rd century B.C. for Kāveripaṭṭiṇam. No regular excavations were carried out in the ports on the west coast with the exception of Muziris where occupational deposits going back only to the eighth habitation on the coast lines where trade enclaves and ports emerged. It is through these ports which are mentioned in the foreign accounts that articles of trade were imported or exported. Clarence Maloney has argued that the early coastal trade was instrumental in the development of civilisation in South India and early Sri Lanka. His study is mainly confined to the development in the Pāṇṭiya region. Malone indicated the importance of the coasts in functioning as the diffusion centers of civilisation in the extreme south and Sri Lanka[96].

As mentioned earlier, the *pālai* tracts denoted the arid regions which included areas which experienced temporary drought due to the absence of rainfall or scanty rainfall. These tracts probably included some parts of the southern tip of the Indian peninsula, district of Ramanathapuram and in the state of Tamil Nadu which experiences drought sometimes even today. The people of these tracts *maṛavar, maḻavar, eyiṉar* etc., took to plundering and looting wayfarers as a way of life[97] for their sustenance as nothing much could be grown or was available in these areas.

Another scheme of division of land is referred to in the texts. Besides the division of land into *tinais* the land was divided into *meṉpulam (agrarian regions)* or *marutam* and *vaṉpulam*[98] (which includes mountainous regions, pastures and arid tracts). In the *vanpulam* regions shifting cultivation was practised and the crop was millet (*varaku*).

The above survey is indicative of the uneven development of the *tinais*. One finds the co-existence of diverse modes of economic activities being carried on in these *tinais*. Consequently, the development potential of each of these regions was different. It is the *marutam* region and the *neytal* to a certain extent which were the most developed and prosperous of the *tinais* and characterised by socio-economic differentiation as we shall show later. This was the region in which production of a surplus was possible an account of the irrigation facilities. Surplus production was not possible in the hilly areas owing to the inhibiting factor of geography. Land in the coastal littoral tracts was sandy, and hence not agriculturally productive[99].

Mc Adams has pointed out that "the areas in which independent civilisations originated seem to have been characterised by a series of specialised micro environments for which different equally specialised subsistence pursuits were appropriate. The existence of interdependent zones of this type fostered the formations of 'symbiotic regions' within which the complementary distribution of subsistence products could be effected[100]. This observation is particularly relevant to Tamiḻakam of the early historical period wherein the *tiṇais* or ecozones are spoken of as *ulakams* or worlds in themselves[101]. They must have been fairly self-sufficient units with the exception of the *neytal*. The inhabitants of *neytal* must have been dependent on the *marutam* lands for rice and millet[102]. However, there was some exchange of rice and salt. Poems attest to the symbiotic exchange of commodities between *tiṇais*[103]. A very interesting example of symbiotic exchange is furnished by the *Porunarāṛṛuppaṭai* which informs us about:

"The fishers on the sea-coast lands where grow
The bunchy coconut and the plantain tree
The *Kanthal* rich, and *naga* tree on which
The large owl shrieks, and where the peacocks dance
Well keeping time with the music of the bees
With plumage spread out on the sands as white
As bright moonlight. move out to forest lands
Those selling honey and roots eatable
Exchange them for the fish's fat and wine
They barter sugarcane and roasted rice
For toddy and deer flesh. The fisher folk
Sing hillmen's songs, while hillmen garlands wear
of fragrant blooms that grow along the coast.
The dwellers of the desert sing the songs
of those in fertile lands, and these in turn
Praise forest lands where grows the mullai blue
The wild fowl eats rice, while the domestic fowl
eats millet grain The hillside monkey rolls in
salty marsh While cranes that take a bath in briny
seawaves rest themselves on hills"[104].

The gradual expansion of the agrarian economy had a considerable impact on the nature of relationships between the various modes of economic activity in the different tinais. Symbiotic exchange and hostility[105] characterised the interactional relationships between *tiṇais*. Hostility was on account of contrasts in the productivity of the *tiṇais*. There were frequent predatory raids on *marutam* on account of its high level of productivity by people of non-agrarian regions which resulted in the destruction of crops and irrigation tanks[106]. Rulers of the three major chiefdoms also engaged in wars between themselves to gain control over resources of others.[107].

From the above survey of the *tiṇais* and their physiographic features and the nature of their settlements it is clear that they are micro envioronmental in character and could have developed specialised subsistence pursuits and established symbiotic relationships with the another. At the same time, the textual descriptions of the regions also point to the emergence of dense settlements visible particularly in the Kāveri and Vaikai-Tāmraparaṇi river basins. The fertire alluvial soils could have been instrumental in making the *marutam* lands as the mahor zones of attraction. Further, the nature of the settlements also varied on account of the Physiographic factors. In contrast to the small settlements of the hilly and pastoral regions the settlements of the *marutam* and *neytal* were bigger in size and accompanied by socio economic diversification.

At this stage a discussion of the term '*nāṭu*' is necessary. The term *nāṭu*[108] is used in the early Tamil texts in a generic sense to refer to an ethnic region and settled area distinct from non settled regions irrespective of the nature of economic activity. Scholars working on early medieval history have viewed the *nāṭu* (which was a micro unit) as an agrarian unit or peasant region.[109] The assembly of the micro region was also denoted by the term *nāṭu*. Another term *Kuṟṟam* has also been considered as equivalent to the *nāṭu*.

In Burton Stein's view most of these *nāṭu* units of the Kāveri and Pennar river basins existed before the reign of Rājarāja I-the Cōḻa king and "these units as the prime units for social and agrarian organisation provided the basis for the Chola political order". The location of villages within the *nāṭu* was influenced by the availability of water resources. Names of the earliest *nāṭus* indicate their association with things related to agriculture. Stein has furnished many examples of this such as Maṇṇi-nāṭu in Kumbakonam taluk (Thanjavur) is named after the Maṇṇiyar river, Iḍaiyāṟṟu nāṭu refers to land between the two rivers. Pulalerikkil nāṭu and Ambattūr ēri kiḻ nāṭu in Toṇṭai maṇḍalam region derive their name form a great lake or tank. The *nāṭu*, the basic peasant unit, was also an ethnic region as the peasant units are believed to be clan groups. In essence, the *nāṭu* was an agrarian unit.[110]

In the early medieval context, the term *nāṭu* came to be conspicuously and primarily associated with agrarian units as by the 7th century A.D. the dominance of agriculture over economic activities had become established, and hence came to serve as a convenient revenue (political) unit under the Pallava, Pāṇṭiya and Cōḻa rulers.

Some of these *nāṭus* may well have evolved as agrarian units from the early historical times. Hence, as Stein rightly holds, the *nāṭu* undoubtedly preceded the rise of the Cōḻa power. There are quite a few references to *nāṭu* in association with different ecological contexts in the *Caṅkam* texts (vide Appendix+2). However, in the early historical period as pointed out, *nāṭu* did not invariably mean agrarian unit. Sudarshan Seneviratne has pointed out that the *nāṭu* may indicate the movement by a people into or their settling down within a territory due to demographic growth and increase in agricultural activities. Further, it is suggested that the term *nāṭu* could have been derived from the root "*nad/ nada* to walk, go, pass, proceed, happen or *nadu* to walk, to enter, or probably to plant (the foot). This has an interesting parallelism with the *janapada* (Indo Aryan) which also means 'foothold of the folk/clan'[111]. In the *Caṅkam* texts the territories of the *Mūvēntar* (which are *janapada* like polities) are referred to as Kuṭanāṭu (Cēra), Cōḻa nāṭu (Cōḻa) and Pānti Nāṭu (Pāṇṭiya). All of them had pockets of fertile land, hilly or forested land and dry tracts. The Cēra, Cōḻa and Pāṇṭiya chiefdoms are also said to have comprised various *tiṇais* and not just the *marutam*. No doubt the nucleus of the three chieftaincies lay in the *marutam*.

Thus the *nāṭus* of the early historical times were not necessarily agrarian units. The *nature* of some *nāṭus* such as *puṉal nāṭu*, *nīrnāṭu*, Kāviri *nāṭu* would denote an agricultural association. Two *Kuṟṟams* which appear in the texts Muttūṟṟu Kuṟṟam and Miḻalai Kuṟṟam appear to be agrarian units as their surplus rice production is mentioned in the texts[112]. These two *Kuṟṟams* are known to have continued as important agrarian units under the early medieval Pāṇṭiyās (7th-10th centuries A.D.)[113]

Nāṭus could have developed as large habitational areas in course of time and could have included different ecological zones. For instance, the *nāṭus* of the Cēra, Cōḻa and Pāṇṭiya were large units covering various ecological zones comprising different production techniques, housing different social groups and under the hegemony of the chieftain. To state another example Parampunāṭu of Vēl Pāri was such a *nāṭu* covering fertile areas, hilly zones and forests. Another *nāṭu*, Nāñcilnāṭu literally ment the plough land. Since it was under the control of the Ays who were pastoral chiefs of the Velir clan the region could have been mainly pastoral. Seneviratne is of the view that in this *nāṭu* different production techniques could have co-existed viz pastoralism and agriculture. Therefore, the *nāṭu* stood for a large geo-political economic unit which covered different ecological zones and in which varied modes of subsistence prevailed.[114] In this context, it is interesting to note that an island is also referred to as *nāṭu* i.e. Yāṟṟunāṭu.

It appears that *nāṭus* were named after specific regions (such as Vēṅkaṭa nāṭu- the area around Vēṅkaṭam hills and Tulu Nāṭu - the Tulu country) or after the community residing in a particular *nāṭu* (such as Koṅkar nāṭu and ōymā) (vide Appendix 2).

Nāṭu could have denoted a small unit created politically by chieftanis for administrative purposes or to introduce cultivation in them. The Cōḻa king Karikāla is described to have cleared jungle tracts to create *nāṭus*[115] (or to intoduce cultivation?)

From the above it is clear that the term *nāṭu* could be traced back to the early historical period, but in a generic sense, because the *nāṭus* in the early texts were essentially not agrarian units. Some or them could have been associated with agriculture in the marutam region in the early historic period in juxtaposition to other *nāṭus* which were hilly or forested. As an agrarian unit the *nāṭu* came into sharp focus only by the 7th century A.D. with the pre-eminence achieved by agriculture as a major economic activity vis-a vis other economic activities. *Kōṭṭam* is a term known from this period which refers to a temple or a space kept apart for worship. *Kōṭṭam* is taken to be derived from *kōṭṭai* meaning fortified area. However, it appears that it should be derived from the Sanskrit term *Kōṣṭha* meaning a space kept apart for some purpose[116]. It is used in this sense in the early medieval inscriptional records as for example in the Kasakkuḍi Copper plates of the Pallavas[117]. In the early medieval period *Kōṭṭam* was used to indicate a large area pastoral-cum-agrarian. Within such *kōṭṭams* were established the *natus*[118] which were agrarian because by the 7th century A.D. the dominance of agriculture over other economic pursuits had been established. Against this background one can proceed to examine the patterns of settlements in Tamiḻakam on the basis of the archaeological material.

The proto historic and early historic periods are marked by the rapid growth of settlements in almost all the ecological zones. This is a fact attested by literary records also. Settlements before this period i.e. in the pre-historic period were scattered in various zones.

The settlements of Early Man were confined to the region around the river basin of the Korttalaiyār (Pālār) in the modern state of Tamil Nadu as indicated by the number of old stone age tools found there[119]. As Sankalia has pointed out no palaeolithic tools were found on the west coast either because of the inhibiting geographical factor of the recent formation of the coastal belt or because of the fact that no proper survey has been conducted here.[120] Early man was essentially a good gatherer and hunter,[121] as elsewhere.

Late Stone Age sites were mostly discovered on the coastal regions near modern Calicut[122] on the west coast and in Tirunelveli and Ramanathapuram close to the east coast. The economy of the Late Stone Age people was one of hunting and fishing and presumably they had temporary encampments on or near the coast.[123]

As the transition to Neolithic age occurred man gave up food gathering and started practising primitive agriculture along with domestication of animals, weaving and pottery making[124]. Neolithic man settled at the foot of hills (some of which had natural caverns) and terraces in close proximity to sources of water such as rivulets or streams[125]. The habitation sites of the neolithic man are mostly located in the districts of North Arcot and Dharmapuri in Tamil Nadu which correspond to the *mullai* tracts. Important sites of this neolithic culture are:

Paiyampalli (Distirict North Arcot)
Chandrapuram (District North Arcot)
Gollapalli (District Dharmapuri)
Togarapalli (District Dharmapuri)
Pannimaduru (District Dharmapuri)
Dailmalai (District Dharmapuri)
Mullikadu (District Dharmapuri)[126]

It is intriguing to note that unlike in southern Karnataka the neolithic folk in Tamil Nadu did not settle on the banks or rivers or in the plains.[127] The neolithic people did not settle on the west coast because of the thick forest growth there.[128]

The neolithic folk would have been semi-sedentarised people as evident from the nature of their economy. These people seem to have been pastoralists[129] (as evident from the tracts where the sites are found i.e. mostly pastures and at the foot of hills). They could have been agriculturists in a limited sense practising dry-farming. Varieties of mllet could have been the main crops which could have been grown in the foothills with minimum irrigation. Further, a greater sedentarisation is also evident from the huts in settlements noticed in a few sites. The beginnings of certain crafts like pottery can also be seen in this phase. In the Tamil region as a whole there are no vestiges of any chalcolithic cultures as found in some other parts of South India. The megalithic, which succeeded the neolithic, seems to be an intrusive one. In Paiyampalli and Sengamedu[130], however, one finds a overlap of the Neolithic and Megalithic layers.

The dissemination of Iron Age Culture in the peninsula was associated with burials known as megaliths. Most of the sites are burial sites except for example Kunnattur and Paiyampalli which are habitation sites as well. The geographical distribution of this culture is wider than any of the earlier stone age cultures. This is evident from the presence of a large number of megaliths in all the ecozones. In other words, in all the *tiṇais* known to the *Caṅkam* works, the archaeological culture uniformly attested is the mega lithic culture, with the two major diagnositc features viz., iron and Black and Red ware (henceforth BRW). To quote Leshnik "A significant aspect of Pandukal (he uses the term pandukal for the megaliths) geography is that the burials do not necessarily conform to the land use patterns inherent to agriculture. Unquestionably, there are cemeteries in, or near, cultivable tracts but in numerous instances they appear in forested hill ranges in remote valleys or in isolated wastelands"[131]. It would appear that in the proto historic i.e. early megalithic phase there was increasing sedentarisation of people[132].

The chronology of the South Indian megaliths is baffling and tentative dates have been put forth for the megaliths spanning a long period from 1000 B.C. to 300 A.D. Hence it would be more logical to postulate a proto historic phase in the spread of this culture and locate its end phases in the early historical period coinciding with the early Tamil culture or the *Caṅkam* and post-*Caṅkam* literature.

The introduction of iron in peninsular India is believed to be marked by Hallur, (located in the valley of the river Tungabhadra in the present day State of Karnataka), a site whose beginnings are dated to as early as 1105+ 100 B.C. to 955 + 100 B.C. on the basis of carbon dating[133]. If, as is generally believed, iron was introduced into peninsular India by 1000 B.C., it must have spread to other parts of the Deccan, Andhra Pradesh and Tamil region by 3rd century B.C. However, the dates given by archaeologists for different sites vary. On the basis of the evidence largely available from Brahmagiri, Wheeler assigned the megalithic culture to a period between 300 B.C. and 100 A.D.[134]. Leshnik provides a general time bracket of 3rd century B.C.-2nd century A.D. for the megalithic burials but also mentions that particular characteristics of the Tamil Nadu burials are more generally assignable to the end of this time span than to the beginning. For him this is indicated by the richer and more varied nature of the grave goods at such sites as Adichanallur (in Tirunelveli District) and Suttukeni (South Arcot). Further in Leshnik's opinion, the burials in Tamil Nadu and Kerala post date those of Karanataka and Andhra Pradesh[135]. This is contradicted by the evidence from Korkai. On the basis of the discovery of two burial urns and a radio carbon date of 785 B.C. from the lowest levels at Koṛkai at the mouth of the Tāmraparaṇi river in the Tirunelveli district Champakalakshmi suggests that "this would indicate an early occupation of the site by the urn burial folk earlier than other dated sites of the megalithic phase in the Tamil country"[136]. Judging from the Koṛkai evidence it is probable that the coastal region of the Tāmraparaṇi valley was colonised around 8th century B.C. Leshnik, on the other hand, does not accept such an early date. Strangely, he dates the urn burial site of Adichannallur to 4th 5th Centuries A.D.[137]. This is not acceptable as the evidence of the radio carbon date from the earliest strata at Koṛkai takes the site back to the 8th century B.C.

However, the protohistoric levels at all other sites in the region do not reveal occupational levels going as for back as 8the century B.C. On the basis of the Paiyampalli evidence it can tentatively be surmised that the people using iron, BRW and practising megalithism moved in and settled down in the North Arcot region by 4th-3rd B.C.[138]. For the Chingleput region Banerjee and Soundararajan have dated the megalithic burials to a period slightly later than 3rd/2nd Century B.C.[139]. We have the following dates for the protohistoric-early historic levels for some important sites in the Kāvēri valley.

Uraiyur: Dist Trichy 3rd to 1st century B.C. to 1st/ 2nd century A.D.-4th century A.D.

Tirukkāmpuliyūr: Dist Trichy 3rd century B.C.-3rd/4th century A.D.

Alagarai: Dist Trichy 3rd century B.C.-3rd-4th century A.D.

Kāveripaṭṭiṇam: Dist Tanjavur 3rd century B.C. 5th century A.D.[140].

The lowest levels of all these sites are characterised by BRW, urn burials and occasionally iron. So we can state, albeit tentatively, that Tamiḻakam was colonised by about 3rd century B.C. Many of the settlements which arose in this period subsequently developed into important early historic centres. Thus, differences in the dating of specific sites notwithstanding, the 3rd century. B.C. appears to be the terminus ad quem for the uniform spread of this megalithic culture all over Tamiḻakam.

Evidence for the presence not only of early settlers but also well established polities such as the Cēra, Cōḻa, Pāṇṭiya, and Satiyaputra in Tamiḻakam around the 3rd century B.C. is furnished by the Aśokan edicts[141]. They are said to be located on the borders of the Mauryan empire.

B.K. Gururaja Rao and S. Nagaraju are of the view that there is clear proof for the early and late age of the megaliths. However, according to them in the absence of any acceptable internal chronology of the megaliths either geographical or typological, it is not easy to differentiate between megaliths of the iron age and the later post-iron age survivals. The burials of the later phase are characterised by the occurrence of coins, particularly Roman coins and russet coated Kaolin painted ware in the Coimbatore megaliths[142]. Here, the coins found are a corroded bronze coin dated to 3rd-2nd centuries. B.C. on the basis of its similarity with an Eran coin; a silver coin of Augustus in association with a hoard of punch marked coins and a gold coin dateable to the beginning of the 4th century A.D. from a barrow in the Nilgiris[143].

The above survey is enough to indicate the difficulties arising in using the data of the protohistoric period for tracing the processes of change or the interface between protohistoriç and early historic cultures on account of its tentative chronology. What is clear is the fact that there was a movement of people into the Tamil coutry. Vestiges of settlements indicate the colonisation of various parts of the region at various points of time from 8th century B.C. to 3rd century B.C. and after. It would be logical to assume that these were the people who stimulated the rise of the culture portrayed in the ealy Tamil poems.

The above survey is also related to the discussion/debate on the authorship of the Megalithic culture and/or the BRW and iron. The intrusive character of the megalithic culture is generally accepted. There are scholars who advocate that the megaliths should be attributed to the Dravidian speaking people as the distribution zone of the megaliths in peninsular India covers exactly the areas occupied by them today. Both D.H. Gordon and Christoph Von Furer Haimendorf observe that these people migrated into this region around 700-400 B.C. and suggest that these people arrived on the West coast by a maritime route[144]. Though N.R. Banerjee agrees that the Dravidian speakers were the builders of the megaliths, he is of the view that the Dravidian speakers who were spread over the north-western part of India before the time of the composition of the *Rg Veda* (which is placed between 1500 B.C. and 1000 B.C.) were gradually pushed southwards by the Aryans. He has further postulated that on their way they must have picked up the use of iron and Black and Red ware pottery and also the megalithic strain, the triple characteristics of the early Dravidians either from the cairn burial folk or from the Aryans with whom such burials were becoming unpopular at the time or both. They could have borrowed the BRW from the Ganga plain where it occurs before 600 B.C. or with great probability from the central and west Indian chalcolithic folks. Further, he is of the view that some of the cairn burial folk may have accompanied the Dravidian speakers in their southward movement and accentuated the megalithic aspect[145]. This migration is placed by him in the ealy half of the first millennium B.C.

It has also been pointed out that "the uniform occurrence of the BRW in the lowest levels of all the excavated sites and the density of the distribution of megaliths with the dominant BRW would show that the BRW levels represent the earliest settlements of a widespread agrarian population or more correctly pastoral cum-agrarian population and as such form the earliest archaeological culture of importance in this region. Habitation and burial sites located side by side would also indicate that the basic elements in the evolution of the Tamil socio-economic organisation as presented in the Sangam works were provided by the authors of the culture"[146]. Further, it has been suggested that "the BRW is quite independent of the megalithic idea as seen from its occurrence in megalithic and non-megalithic context"[147]. Champakalakshmi has indicated that the sudden emergence and proliferation of megaliths in the southe would point to a fusion of several elements, the BRW and iron which came together to South India and the megalithic idea and cult, which were probably picked up during the course of the BRW movement from the north to the south or that the BRW and iron were adopted by an already established megalithic culture. The dominance of the intruding BRW culture was due to its advanced iron technology and hence its widespread and uniform character[148]. Incidentally, the megalithic structures vary considerably as seen on the surface and in the excavations, whereas iron and BRW are invariably present.

As for the authorship of the megalithic culture a majority of scholars like D.H. Gordon, Haimendorf, N.R. Banerjee, Balakrishnan Nayar[149] are inclined to associate them with Dravidian speakers. An exception can be made in the case of Asko Parpola who tries to relat teh early megaliths to a wave of Aryan speakers[149(a)].

In this connection it would be interesting to examine certain legends associated with Agastya, who in both the northern and southern traditions, is considered to be a great sage who introduced civilisation in the south. Proponents of the theory of Aryanisation (like Nilakanta Sastri) of South India interpret these legends as representing Agastya as the harbinger of Aryan civilisation in South India. At the same time it must be noted that in the southern tradition, particularly Tamil, Agastya is celebrated as the father of Tamil and is said to have organised the second Tamil *Caṅkam* and composed the earliest grammar of the Tamil language known as *Akattiyam.* He is also associated with the Potikai hill identified with the Bettigo of Ptolemy and located in the southern most part of the Western ghats[150]. According to a slightly later tradition recorded in the *Maṇimēkalai* the river Kāvēri flowed from his pitcher[151].

These traditions would point to an early colonisation of the South and the Tamil country in particular probably by a Dravidian speaking people who introduced agriculture and rapidly colonised the south. Attempts have been made by various scholars to correlate archaeological evidence particularly the BRW of the Megalithic culture with the literary traditions and thereby link the BRW with specific ethnic groups such as Dravidians, Aryans (Vrātyas)[152] Yadavas[153] and with a certain group of people like the Vēḷr[154] who were pastoral chiefs as well as agricultural communities. It has been suggested that the migratory pattern may be recognised early in the megalithic phase which probably followed the western coastal regions and branched off from Maharashtra towards the east into the Andhra region and southwards to Karnataka, Konkana, Kerala and to the Tamil regions, that a section branched off from Kerala to the Tamil areas moving gradually down the river valleys and northwards to the region of Kanchipuram (Toṇṭai nāṭu). It would be highly useful to work out the chronological position of the megaliths of different regions to see if the megaliths follow this movement in the order suggested above[155]. Working out a chronology of the megaliths is baffling and difficult. Even if a migration pattern is worked out it would be tentative and specultive.

Thus we notice that working out routes of dispersal of the megaliths is not an easy task. In this context it is worthwhile to remember the remarks made by the Allchins. "The South Indian graves appear as a developing complex with several streams of influence combining in them. First, some grave types are reminiscent of those of Central Asia, Iran, or the Caucasus and could well represent traits brought from these areas by Indo-European speaking immigrants. Next, some appear as developments of the indigenous neolithic-chalcolithic burial customs of the Deccan. A third series points to influences from outside India, and comparable types may indicate the source of the influences. Thus stone cist graves, with and without port holes, are found in the Levant and on the coasts of South Arabia. Pottery sarcophagi occur in Mesopotamia and the Persian Gulf region during the late centuries B.C. and legged urns identical to Indian types are reported from Yemen. The same regions provide evidence of rock cut graves with shaft like entrances, in form strikingly reminiscent of those of the Malabar coast. Strictly speaking not all these examples are dated with any precision, and therefore they can scarcely provide a firm basis for comparisons; but they suggest that during the 1st millennium B.C. India received them as influences by dint of maritime contacts with the Middle East. A fourth stream also cannot be exluded i.e. there being the possibility of local development in peninsular India itself, the stone alignments appear to belong to this class"[156].

Two facts emerge from the above survey and BRW, the two distinguishing traits of the proto historic phase, are indigenous traditions of the Indian Subcontinent. The third characteristic factor, that of the burials, has a definite foreign element which is not easily identifiable.

Clarence Maloney has tried to see this problem not only on the basis of archaeology but also in association with the literary traditions manifest in the *Caṅkam* poetry. In his opinion, the Iron age culture diffused through the south with militaristic people. These people had the distinct knowledge of iron weapons and knew the use of horse. Further, he points out that the *puṟam* category of early Tamil Literature idealises militarism, the horse, iron heads and spears and that such a militaristic tradition using iron tools and weapons listed above, plus the rather uniform diffusion of Iron Age Material culture and the larger population supported by irrigated rice cultivation explain the extension of a single language such as Tamil or Telugu over so wide an area[157].

Besides Maloney, there are other scholars who have earlier pointed out that the last phase of the megalithic culture was contemporaneous with the phase in which early Tamil texts were composed. K.R. Srinivasan has drawn our attention to several references to burials in the early Tamil Literary texts namely *Puṟānaṉūru, Naṟṟinai* and *Patiṟṟuppattu* which are equated with the megaliths. The general term used for the graveyard in these texts is *kāṭu* and *puraṅgāḍu* which means a waste land set apart for burials in the wilds near the village. Normally one notices that the megalithic burials are located away from the habitation sites. Srinivasan points out that later on one finds two different names *Iḍukāḍu* for burial grounds and *Suḍukāḍu* for cremation grounds[158]. There are reference to *tāḻi* (which are receptacles of dead remains) which generally connoted an urn in the *caṅkam* texts[159]. The Cera and Cōḻa kings seem to have been entombed in *tāḻis*[160]. Further "there is a reference to a vēḷir chieftain being buried in the burial ground where the red eared cock and *poguval* (a bird) sit on the heap (of stones) outside the lid that covered the red burial urn"[161]. On finding fragments of crushed or broken pots in a cairn filling in Sanur, N.R. Banerjee suggested that they are the relics of a ritual, probably of pot breaking, connected with entombment[162]. Further, the *Maṇimekalai,* a post-*Caṅkam* work, mentions five kinds of burials in areas adjacent to Kāveripaṭṭiṇam. These are cremation (*cūṭuvōr*), exposure and burial (*iṭuvōr*), pit burials (*totukulippātuppor*) burial in underground cists or cellars (tālvyiṇ *aṭaippōr*) burial inside receptacle (urn) (*tāḷiyiṛkavippōr*)[163].

The introduction of iron by the megalithic people into the region is seen as a revolutionary one i.e. as signifying a major step towards the development of a farming/ peasant society. Gururaja Rao noticed "the emergence of a vigorous iron based agricultural economy in South India revolutionising the life of the people in contrast to their bucolic neolithic predecessors"[164]. Soundararajan observed that the Iron Age cultural development was the most propitious event that happened in the history of Tamil Nadu because even more than the neolithic settlements in a few scattered centras in its north western fringes, it is this that brought enduring patterns of agricultural endeavour and semi-urban habitational growth to the bulk of Tamilnad[165].

Since iron was available in the magnetite, laterite, black magnetic sand in the Malabar and Travancore regions on the West coast and from magnetite, haematite, laterite in the areas of Tirunelveli, Madurai, Salem, Tiruchirapalli, Coimbatore, Nilgiris, Pudukkottai, Chingelput, North and South Arcot, its availability does not seem to have been a problem for these early megalithic settlers. There is evidence of pre-industrial smelting in these areas[166]. A rich repertoire of iron objects is visible in the burials. Out of these the iron weapons predominate over the agricultural implements. Weapons of war include arrow-heads, spear heads, daggers, knives, javelins and sword. Besides other objects like nails, adzes, chisels, blades wedges etc presumably used as tools in carpentry were recovered from the burials. One also comes across objects of domestic use such as bangles, bracelets, rings etc.

Agricultural implements found in the burials are very meagre. Adichanallur, a rich urn burial site, also yielded few agricultural tools[167]. Though the iron plough was not found in the archaeological remains (except at Tirukkāmpuliyūr where a plough tip was reported[168]) there are references to the use of the plough in the texts. On the basis of the predominance of weapons of war Maloney postulated that the Iron Age diffused throughout the South with a militaristic people as indicated earlier. References to the blacksmith (*kollaṇ*) and his workshop occur mainly in the *marutam tiṇai*. Here again they are mostly mentioned as sharpening weapons of war or making them. The Allchins have indicated that 'the range of identical tool types, repeated many times as at sites as far apart as Nagpur and Adichanallur that is to say some 900 miles apart must testify to the diffusion of a fairly tight knit group of iron workers"[169].

Archaeological excavations have revealed abundant iron slag at Paiyampalli[170] and Appukallu[171] where iron was probably melted and worked but no furnaces or kilns were reported. Simple techniques of iron working may have prevailed. The *Wootz* method of manufacturing iron and steel was prevalent from very early times according to Gururaja Rao[172]. It is not easy to determine the extent of utilisation of iron in agriculture. However, the absence of advanced agricultural implements like the plough should not be taken to indicate the minimal use of iron in agricultural practices. Certainly agriculture was not marginal to the megalithic economy as we shall show later that urn burials are mostly associated with the river valleys even though ploughs or other agricultural tools are not reported here. Literary references to agricultural activities are far too conspicuous to be overlooked. Excavations of the megaliths have divulged that the burials were of different kinds. These variations of grave types seem to present a confusing picture. Moreover, the terminologies used to denote the grave types differ from scholar to scholar[173].

There is no systematic and clear study of the typology of the megaliths. Writers like Gururaja Rao and Narasimhaiah use the term cairn circle to refer to an independent burial when it is just a surface feature[174]. Again the sarcophagus and urn burials are referred to by Narasimhaiah as though they are separate or independent burial types when it is just an internal feature.

As suggested by Leshnik the method of systemising this diversity is by grading these burials according to

(1) the narure of the receptacle used for the bones.

(2) the nature of the 'protector' for the ossuary.

On this basis the grades of burials are[175]:

1. Plain pit burial:

This consists of a pit closed by a stone slab in which the bones are placed directly on the floor or more often on a stone slab resting of the floor. There is no ossuary to hold the bones. Two examples of such burials in northern Tamil Nadu are Kunnattur (Chingleput district) and Odugattur (North Arcot district).

2. Pit containing ossuary:

In this burial type the ossuaries occurring on the floor of the pit are 1) urns or 2) sarcophagi. Within this category one generalisation that can be made is that generally the sarcophagus ossuary is limited to the Chingleput district of northern Tamil Nadu and the pit urn burial is the common type in the valley of the river Kāveri and the areas to the south of the Kāveri.

3. Protected ossuary and direct deposits:

Here the ossuary is placed in a vault which is either:

(a) a boulder cist,

(b) a slab cist, or

(c) a catacomb tomb

Within this protector, there would be an ossuary in the form of an urn or sarcophagus or there would be direct deposits of the bones rarely. While the Pudukottai district yielded slab cists containing urns, the terracotta sarcophagi was found in Panduvaram Deval, Devanur, Pallavaram, Suttukeni in the northern parts of Tamil Nadu, sites where the slab cists contained direct deposits would include Odugattur, Kunnattur in Tamilnadu and Porkalam, Eyyal, Muribetta, Fraserpet, Somwarpett in Kerala.

Catacomb tombs, the third sub category, was found only in Kerala. One particular site Feroke yielded both urn and sarcophagi in the tombs[176].

Even within these three grades enumerated variations occur and no two burials are really alike[177].

It is not clear which groups in the contemporary society resorted to this sort of burials. Leshnik is of the view that these burials were those of pastoralists confined to rural areas[178]. Looking at the long procedure and expenditure involved in their construction only well to do groups in society could have afforded such burials. References in literature indicate that rulers and probably persons of high rank were interred in urns[179]. Moreover, some burials, especially urns, have rich grave goods in the form of beads and gold (in some rare instances) which again testify to their association with groups of high status.

Soundararajan has made a beginning in working out the distribution pattern of the megaliths in Tamilnadu. He starts from the extreme southern parts of the region (Tirunelveli, Ramanathapuram and Madurai) where he notices a predominantly urn burial mode with large urns which were buried in a single pit generally close to a water source without any ring or stone circles around the grave. A good amount of copper or bronze utensils and objects and microliths (rarely) were found in the few excavated sites. Adichanallur was the most outstanding site of this area.

In the area from Pudukkottai and Tiruchirapalli onwards are seen slab cist tombs "forming a chamber often of an elaborate kind with side chambers and front chambers outside and provided with the post hole opening". Internally the urn was used for internment purposes. Cists with the sarcophagi coffin (s) are noticeable in South Arcot. Thus Soundararajan observes that the "carrier and the internment vary in the various zones and give us a broad indication of what is the resident part of the culture and what is the intrusive element." A few sites in the western part of Tanjavur district have the urn burials. From this it is clear that the urn burial is associated with the southeraly district while the cist (with or withour sarcophagi) are seen in the northerly districts. Therefore, Soundararajan feels that while the cist and the sarcophagus coffin would have entered TamilNadu as impulses from the north i.e. lower Deccan the large solitary non-megalithic urn should be considered indigenous in conception. These urns moved northwards and permeated into the cist tomb garb of these areas.

In Soundarara jan's opinion the main route of cist tomb from the Deccan would appear to have been taken through North West TamilNadu across North Arcot, Salem, Western part of S.Arcot, Western part of Tiruchirapalli and Pudukkotai, south of which it stops, not for want of suitable material for the cist because these are quite profuse and many of these hillocks have been excavated into rock cut temples by the early

Pandyas, but because the urn burial culture was far too dominant here and was not disposed to take in the megalithic garb"[180]. This distribution pattern of the megaliths worked out by Soundararajan is relevant even now.

It is very difficult to equate a particular burial type with a particular ecological zone[181]. A tentative attempt in this regard can be made (more or less on the same lines as Soundararajan). To a large extent urn burials are found in the river valleys and as Seneviratne has indicated there is a 'tendency for urn/cairns/stones circles/pit burials to be generally associated with areas more suitable for paddy cultivation'[182].

We notice a concentration of sites in the major river valleys. It is the lower Kāveri valley which has numerous vestiges of settlements some of which like Uṛaiyūr, Kāveripaṭṭiṇam, Tirukkāmpuliyūr became important in the subsequent early historic period. There are numerous urn burial sites in the taluks of Tancavur, Nagapattinam, Mayavaram, Kumbakonam, Orattanadu, Tiruchirapalli, Kulittalai and Muciri-all in the flood plains of the Kāvēri. Besides a few sites like Muttrapalion, Suttukeni and Perimbe on the flood plains of the Pennar in South Arcot and also Takkolam on the Coovam river and Nipatturai on Ponnaiyar in North Arcot contain urn burials. Further down south we come across urn burials on the upper fringes of the Vaigai valley i.e. around Madurai and T. Kallupatti[183].

The absence of settlements in the lower Vaigai valley may be due to the fact that the Vaigai being a non-perennial river had water only in certain pockets which was utilised. Another thing worth noting is the affinity between the urn burials/stone circles with areas suitable for agriculture even in hilly regions as evident from the urn burial at Thathanodaimedu located on the lower area below the Bodinayakkanur pass which overlooks the Kambam valley[184]. In the extreme south settlements can be noticed in the upper portions of the river valleys of Vaippar, Chittar and Tamraparani. Extensive urn burials on the upper Vaippar at the foot hills of Sankaranainar hills include Sivagiri, Panaiyoor, Vasudevanallur, Karuvanallur etc. On upper Chittar urn burials occur at Ilanji and Courttalam. Urn burials are seen at Sivasailam on the upper reaches of the Tāmraparaṇi at the foot hills of Agastyamalai, Koṛkai, Adichanallur and in their vicinities and the Tiruneleveli taluks[185].

All the principal river valleys show definite evidence of settlements. As indicated earlier settlements in the river valleys arose in various chronological periods. Most of these regions are predominantly agrarian regions and there is corelation between urn burials and agrarian regions[186]. Did the people practising agriculture in the *marutam* use the urn as a form of burial? It is necessary at this juncture to refer to the Vēḷir who could have been one of the earliest agrarian communities of the region. Some of the Vēḷir settlements are referred to in literature as over flowing with rice. This has prompted Champakalakshimi to state that megaliths occur at important Vēḷir sites which occasionally are both burial and habitation sites. Stretching the argument further is it possible to suggest a correlation between the urn burials and the Vēḷir settlements of the riverine areas?[187]

Though we notice a tendency for urn burials generally to be located in the riverine areas conducive to agriculture, there are exceptions. Two sites in South Arcot district on the river Ponnaiyār, Kollur and Deva nur yielded sarcophagi burials[188]. However, urn burials are also noticed in a non-agrarian context i.e. Kodamalaiputtur, Kunnattur etc[189]. Does this indicate the burials of the agriculturists who had close association with the pastoralists? A notable feature is the near absence of proto historic sites in Ramanathapuram and in the eastern portion of Madurai[190]: Could this be attributed to these tracts being the arid zones of *palaitinai* which according to the literature hardly had any settlements except those of *maṛavar/kaḷḷar* etc who took to looting, plundering and killing wayfarers passing through their tracts?

Moving on to the second major type i.e. the sarcophagus a, receptacle along with the cists we find that this occurs in the northen portion of the region mainly in Chingelput and North Arcot districts which are primarily non-agrarian regions[191]. Is this suggestive of a correlation between sarcophagi and non agrarian regions? Now the cists can be made only in hard stony areas and the sites like Odugattur, Panduvaram Deval, Paiyampalli etc. are located at the foot hills. These were the pastoral scrub lands. Is it possible to state that people practising pastoralism with some shifting agriculture used the sarcophagus cist as a mode of burial?

The Dharmapuri, Salem, Coimbatore regions are the dry farming areas of Tamil Nadu. There are a number of sites on the lower hills and the megalithic burials are of dolmenoid cist, port holed cist and cairn circles[193]. These were the *mullai* tracts and the high concentration of settlements in the area have been attributed to the strategic location of this area with the routes connecting southern Karnataka with Kerala passing through this area. Secondly, in environmental terms, the excellent pasture lands on the slopes of the hills were ideal for pastoral-cum-agricultural subsistence and thirdly, their proximity to raw material. The Salem district is said to possess the maximum variety and largest deposit of minerals[194].

All the major hills i.e Anaimalai, Palani, Cardamom are dotted with burials of different types[195]. Dolmens are generally noticed in the hilly regions (or the *kuṛiñci* tracts) mainly the Nilgiri and Palani Hills and also in the Bison Valley near Peria Kanal in the High ranges and in the Aryanad valley. Besides thousands of cairns are also reported in the Nilgiris. One of the reasons for this could be easy availability of stone in the hills which could have been used to erect the dolmens. Can these be attributed to the hill dwellers (*kuṛavar* and *kāṇavar*) who besides hunting and food gathering also practised shifting cultivation on the slopes of the hills?

An interesting feature is the discovery of rock-cut caves belonging to the protohistoric period in the Cochin and Malabar regions of Kerala. These caves are found in the strip of land between the mountainous tracts on the east and the coastal alluvial plans on the west and this strip of land is made up of lateritic plains[196]. It is difficult to ascribe these to any particular social group.

Regarding the settlements on the coastal (*neytal*) region we find that there are a few settlements of the megalithic context in certain pockets. Around Kāveripaṭṭiṇam, a group of sites roughly dateable to the period 3rd century B.C. to 1st century A.D. have been excavated. These would represent the early phases of occupation with evidence of their growth into a hinterland area for the urban centres or ports that developed by the 1st century A.D.. Similarly, Koṛkai (with urn burials) another coastal site in the Pantiya region, and Arikamedu, a coastal site in north TamilNadu, have early BRW levels dateable to pre Christian era. These centres became important centres definitly by the early historic period when trade became an important activitiy.

Trade contacts seemed to have also stimulated the rise of centres such as Karaikkadu, Nattamedu, Vasavasamudram (Nirppeyaṟṟu of the *Caṅkam* text) etc around the 1st century A.D. or even earlier.

It must also be added that urn burials are found in early historical sites situated on rivers, such as Kāñcipuram, Koṛkai and Kāvēripaṭṭiṇam, the last two being in the *neytal tiṇai*. Urn burials are also found in the vicinity of certain other historical sites. For example, not far from Karūr (located on a tributary of the Kāvēri) is the urn burial site of Malaikkovilur[197] and Adichanallur is not far from the site of Koṛkai. Besides, the habitation areas of the early historic sites of Alagarai and Tirukkāmpuliyūr are characterised by the use of black and red were and iron objects which are significant characteristics of Megalithic remains.

We have already stated that urn burials are associated with areas suitable for paddy cultivation i.e. mostly the riverine belts. Taken together with literary evidence on the three polities and the Vēḷir, a surplus in agricultural production must have been available to support large populations as is evident from the high density of urn burials in some parts of the agrarian belts. That the megalithic people developed agriculture is proved by the fact that "unproductive foot-nills rocky and gravelly lands were utilised for the location of their graves, while lower down, the plains were reserved for agricultural purposes"[198]. Good irrigation facilities are essential for intensive cultivation of crops especially rice. It has been contended by several scholars that megalithic folk introduced tank-based irrigation as is evident from the megaliths of Chingle put which are in the vicinity of such ancient tanks[199]. This has led Gururaja Rao to state that large irrigational tanks were often constructed by bunding the slopes of the hillocks and high grounds across the natural gradient of the high ground on which the rain waters were flowing down. These tanks supplied water for their household life and to their crops[200].

Other methods of irrigation could have been through rivers and wells. Ring wells have been discovered at the lowest habitation level at Kāñcipuram and Vasavasamudram[201].

All this would have facilitated the cultivation of rice as Maloney observed that irrigated rice provided the economic basis for the emergence of more complex social patterns and made possible a life quite different from that of a culture dependent on millets, grains or pulses[202]. Probably rice was cultivated in the lower Kāveri valley and certain pockets of the Pālār, Ponnaiyār, Vaigai and Tāmraparaṇi and Periyār. Excavations have yielded rice grains at Kunnatur and charred husks from Tirukkāmpuliyūr. Although there is meagre archaeological evidence to sustain this association, for the people living in the riverine belts agriculture must have been the main mode of economic subsistence. This could have been supplemented by fishing. The megalithic people presumably fished in the rivers by making a basket like split bamboo trap by nets of strong strings as no fish hooks have been found in the excavated graves[203].

Settlements in the Chingelput, North Arcot districts and a few in the Coimbatore region mostly lay in *mullai* region (or the forests and scrublands) where the main mode of subsistence would have been pastoralism which could have been supplemented by slash and burn cultivation and hunting. The presence of pastoralism is indicated by the bones of cattle, sheep and goat recovered from one of the burials at Sanur in Chingelput[204]. Some of the verses of the *Caṅkam* texts like *Puṟanāṉūṟu* 159 allude to slash and burn cultivation of millet (*varaku*). Paiyampalli yielded pulses, while traces of rice were found at Muttrapalion (in Pondicherry) and Panduvaram Dewal (N.Arcot).

Pestle and mortar and stone querns presumbly used for pounding grain were recovered from Odugattur, KodamalaiPuttur, Sanur and Perumbair. Agricultural implements found were also simple like hoes, axes and sickles which reflect the prevalence of slash and burn cultivation. Rice cultivated would have been of the dry kind. It is pointed out by Leshnik that 'pastoral nomads wherever they are maintain contact withe cultivators for they require grain. In some cases, the cultivators may be more or less settled segments of the pastoralist society itself, and it seems that an explanation of this sort is applicable here...'[205]

A sort of mixed economy seems to have prevailed with pastoralism, slash and burn agriculture and hunting. Location of certain sites at the foot of hills could have also provided opportunities for hunting game.

In the proto historic-period there was some sort of interaction between the Tamil country and other parts of India. Archaeologically, this is attested by the uniform repertore of iron tools and Black and Red ware. Besides articles of *chank* (conch) are found even in inland sites thereby indicating some sort of exchange. As *chank* was available mostly at sites such as Kanchipuram on the Vehka (Vegavati) and Alakankulam (at the mouth of Vaigai) where conch shell bangles in different stages of manufacture were found, they could have served as 'production' and 'distribution' centres because transportantion was possible through the river. There must have been some sort of trade contacts at a rudimentary level of 'drift trade' in this region between the various eco-zones where the sites are located. The *Caṅkam* texts also indicate a symbiotic exchange of articles though they mainly comprised food stuffs.

An understanding of the geographical features in Tamilakam has enabled us to view the development of cultures in the context of the sub-regional variations. As compared to the stone Ages, it is only in the megalithic phase that we notice a rapid increase in settlements. Most of the region was occupied by this time. Chronologically the beginnings of this period could be traced back to 4th/3rd centuries B.C. tentatively. The megalithic folk seem to have had the know how to exploit the potential of the river valleys as we find a large number of sites in these river basins which were the main agrarian belts. These nuclear regions ultimately become the nuclei of important urban settlements during the early historical period by about the 1st century A.D. It is these tracts which witnessed the production of agrarian surplus and the rise of three chiefdoms. This also attests to the unevenness of the various ecological zones, where different groups were at different levels of development, a fact which continues to be reflected in the early historic period through the *tiṇais* and their diverse economies.

The significant contributions made by the megalithic BRW culture to introduce elements of civilisation are aptly listed by Seneviratne as "a basic metal technology i.e. iron, potters wheel, the plough, paddy cultivation, dam and tank irrigation, a greater degree of craft specialisation, the ability ot harness the environment with greater efficiency, the establishment of new settlements and the definite beginnings of a sedentarised village culture, the emergence of petty exchange centres and the relative expansion in the exchange network, prelude to a greater demographic expansion, the emergence of petty chieftaincies, the introduction of the horse, new burial types (megaliths) and pottery types (characteristic BRW, all black ware, red ware and the russet coated painted ware)" All these basic elements of civilisation further developed in the early historic period and one sees greater sedentarisation, increased agricultural production, the emergence of major and minor chiefdoms, diversification of economic activities through craft specialisation and trade and social differentiation leading to the rise of an incipient urbanism in certain areas.

FOOTNOTES

1. *Puṟanaṉūṟu* 6: *Vaṭāatu paṇipaṭu neṭuvarai vaṭakkum Teṉāatu Uru Keḻu Kumariyiṉ teṟkkum*
   Puṟanāṉūṟu 17: *Teṉkumari Vaṭa peruṅkal kuṇa kaṭalā ellai*
   Cilappatikārm VIII: 1-2 *Neṭiyōṉ kuṉṟamun tōtiyōḷ pouvamum Tamiḻ varam parutta taṇpuṇal naṇṇdttu*
2. K.V. Soundararajan "Determinat factors in the early history of Tamil Nad", (Part I) *Journal of Indian History,* 1967, p. 648.
3. "A region has been understood as an area of specific location which is in some ways distinctive from other areas and which extends as far as that distinction extends" - Harm De Blij, *Geography: Regions and Concepts.* USA 1971, p. 5
   It has also been understood as a homogenous area with physical and cultural characteristics distinct from those neighbouring areas—*International Encyclopaedia of Social Sciences,* 1972 (Rp. Ed.) Vol. 13 pp. 377-78.
4. B.D. Chattopadhyaya: *A Survey of Historical Geography of Ancient India,* New Delhi, 1984, p. 42.
5. *Imperial Gazetteer of India*: Vols. XVI, XIX, XX, XXI (Rp. Editions), Today and Tomorrows Printers and Publishers, New Delhi.
   Madras District Gazetteers, Madras District Manuals

R.L. Singh, *India: A Regional Geography,* Varanasi 1971

O.H.K. Spate and A.T.A Learmouth, *India and Pakistan: A General and Regional Geography,* London 1972 (Reprinted with corrections)

6. *The Tolkāppiyam* mentions the word *aintinai* but only lists four *tiṇais.* *Tolkappiyam*: *Porulatikāram: Akattiṇai Iyal* 2; 5
7. R. Gurukkal "Forms of production and forces of change in Ancient Tamil Society" *Studies in History,* Vol. 5, No.2, 1989, (a), p. 164.
8. *Cilappatikāram XI* : 62-66; Sivathamby, "Early South Indian society and economy: The tiṇai concept", *Social Scientist,* December, 1974, p. 26.
9. K. Sivathamby, 1974, p. 27.
10. *Tolkāppiyam* : *Porulatikāram, Akattiṇai Iyal* 3.
11. *Tolkāppiyam* : *Porulatikāram, Akattiṇai Iyal* 4,6,7,8,9,10 mention the suitable time and the season for each *tinai.*
12. *Tolkāppiyam* : *Porulatikāram, Akattiṇai Iyal* 5 The commentator to the text Nacciṇārkiṇiyar provides a list of these. The *Karupporuḷ* comprises objects of the environment/nature. Two major works focussing on treatment of nature in the *Caṅkam* texts are M.Varadarajan's *Treatment of nature in Caṅkam literature,* Madras, 1969 and X.S Thaninayagam, *Nature poetry in Tamil: The classical period,* Singapore 1963.
13. *Tolkāppiyam* : *Porulatikāram Akattiṇai Iyal* 14. The *Uripporuḷ* of five *tiṇais* are

1. *Kuriñci*	*Puṇartal*
2. *Mullai*	*Iruttal*
3. *Marutam*	*Ūṭaḷ*
4. *Neytal*	*Iraṅkal*
5. *Pālai*	*Pirital*

Besides the *Tolkāppiyam Porulatikāram Akattiṇai Iyal* 20 mentions that the inhabitants of the *tiṇai* have two names. The commentator Nacciṇārkkiṇiyar states that they are *Kulappeyar* and *urippeyar* (see chart 2).

14. P.T Srinivasa Iyengar, *History of the Tamils* upto 600 A.D., Madras, 1929, p. 4. As quoted by K.Sivathamby, 1974, p. 23.
15. V.R.R. Dikshitar, *Studies in Tamil Literature and History,* University of Madras, 1936, p. 178
16. K. Zvelebil "Tamil Poetry 2000 years Ago" *Tamil Culture,* Vol. 10, Madras, 1963. Thaninayagam also agress with the evolutionary interpretation of the *tiṇai* concept as he states that this five-fold division throws light on human origins and the development of human culture *Landscape and Poetry,* London, 1966, p. 39.
17. *Cirupāṇāṟṟuppaṭai* 11 143-202 and *Perumpāṇāṟṟuppaṭai* 11. 46-392 describe the various *tiṇais* which the bard passed through along with the inhabitants, occupations and food habits for each *tiṇai*. So does *Maturaikkāñci* 11 238-326.
18. Selvanayagam "The Regional Concept in Geography and the classification of land in the Ancient Tamil Country", *Proceedings of the Second International Conference Seminar of Tamil Studies,* Vol. II, Madras, January 1968, p. 221.
19. *Maturaikkāñci* 11 287-90.
20. *Aiṅkuruṇūṟu* 298: 2; *Naṟṟiṇai 64:4.*
21. *Akanāṇūṟu* 132:7; 182:6 *Naṟṟiṇai* 85:9.

22. *Akanāṇūṟu* 322:12.
23. *Aiṅkuruṇūṟu* 208:1 ; 270:2.
24. *Akanāṇūṟu* 140:11 ; *Aiṅkuruṇūṟu* 284:2 ; *Kuruṇṭokai* 82:4.
25. *Paṭṭinappālai* 1. 186; *Kuruntokai* 339:1; *Naṟṟiṇai* 64:5 ; 5:3 Burning of logs of sandalwood and *akil* show that the *kuriñci* tracts abounded in this sort of vegetation *Naṟṟinai* 282:2; Akānānūru 172 : 6-13. Pattinappālai 1188 mentions the sandalwood and *akil* of the Cēra country arriving in Kāveripaṭṭiṇam.
26. *Kuruṇtokai* 379:2; *Akanāṇūru* 282:2-5; *Naṟṟiṇai* 169:7 ; 142: 4; 221:4 *Puṟanāṇūru* 331:5; *Akanāṇūṟu* 14:7 ; 54:10; *Naṟṟiṇai* 69:8; 364:9
27. R. Sumathi, *Trade and its impact on the early Tamils: The Cola Experience,* unpublished M.Phil dissertation Hawaharlal Nehru University, New Delhi, 1984, pp. 34-35.
    These articles figured as export items from ports on the West Coast. Tyndis and Muziris in *Periplus* 56. The *Periplus* 56 mentions that pepper grown around Kuttanatu (Cottonara region between Quilon and Kottayam) was exported. The early Tamil literature also contains references to the export of pepper- *Akanāṇūru* 149; *Puṟanāṇūru* 343.
28. Zvelebil "Pastoralism as reflected in the classical Tamil theory of landscapes" in Leshnik and Sonthemier (ed.) *Pastoralists and Nomads in South Asia,* Wiesbaden, 1975, p. 36.
    Selvanayagam 1968;, p. 222.
29. *Puṟanāṇūru* 390:1 *Perumpāṇāṟṟuppaṭai* 1. 193. *Maturaikkāñci* 11. 271-85.
30. K. Sivathamby "An analysis of the anthropological significance of the economic activities and conduct code ascribed to the Mullai tiṇai", *Proceedings of the First International Conference Seminar of Tamil Studies,* Madras, 1966 (1968), pp. 324-26.
    Padiyur (in Coimbatore) and Vaniyambadi (in Salem) were two famous beryl mines- Warmington, *Commerce between the Roman Empire and India,* New Delhi, 1974, pp. 250-51.
    Excavations at the site of Kodumanal near Karur have revealed lot of semi-precious stones and rock crystals indicating it to be a factory site. R. Nagaswamy "Roman sites in TamilNadu : Recent discoveries", *Madhu,* New Delhi 1981, p. 338.
31. *Tolkāppiyam* : *Porulaṭikāram: Akattiṇai Iyal* 18 Nacciṉārkkiṉiyar commentary.
32. *Tolkāppiyam* : *Porulaṭikāram: Akattiṇai Iyal* 18 Nacciṉārkkiṉiyar commentary.
33. *Perumpāṇāṟṟuppaṭai* 1.166.
34. N. Subramanian, *Pre Pallavan Tamil Index,* Madras, 1966, p. 85.
35. Poet Iṭaikkāṭaṉār, author of some of the *Caṅkam* verses belonged to the village. *Akananūru* 139, 194, 274, 284, 304, *Kuruntokai* 251, *Naṟṟiṇai* 142, 221, 316 *Puṟananūṟu* 42. There is now a place of that name in the Pattukkottai taluk of Tanjore District.
36. *Puṟanāṇūru* 76. It was the place to which Iṭaikkuṉṟūr Kiḻār belonged.
37. See R.Champakalakshmi "Archaeology and Tamil Literary Tradition", *Puratattva* No 8, 1975-76, pp. 121-22.
    Also R. Gurukkal "Social Formation and Political Process in Early Tamilakam" Paper presented at teh Seminar on *The State in Pre-Colonial South India,* Jawaharlal Nehru University, 1989 (b) pp15-19.
38. *Ciṟupāṇāṟṟuppaṭai* 1. 201
    (Kanci is described as *mutur* in the *Perumpāṇāṟṟuppaṭai* 1.411)

Mullaippāṭṭu 1.7

Neṭunalvāṭai 1.29

39. R.Sumathi 1984:, p. 53 fn. 23

R.Champakalakshmi 1986, p. 5 fn. 25

40. Is Kudalur on the western hills now Gudalur on the Nilgiris?

N.Subramanian 1966:, p. 311

Pamalur is mentioned as a place in the Cēra land which was conquered by Neytalaṅkāṉal Ilañceṭ ceṉṉi *Puṟanāṉūṟu* 203: Subramanian 1966:, p. 554.

Maṅkaḍu is also referred to as a town along the Western Ghats in the probably named after mangroves which existed there. 1966:, p. 666.

Umpaṟkāṭu was the village to which the poet Ilañkaṇṇanār belonged - Also see G.Manoharan, *Place Names and territorral divisions in Sangam literature;* unpublished M.Phil Dissertation, Madras, 1986, p:91.

41. *Malaipaṭukatām* - colophon - It is in the region of North Arcot district.

42. *Ciṟupāṇāṟṟuppaṭai* 1.120, 1.173.

43. Cēra: *Patiṟṟuppaṭṭu* 28:7-10;88: 25-?8.

Cōḻa: *Puṟanāṉūṟu* 35: 8-11.

Pāṇṭiya: *Puṟanāṉūṟu* 71:9-11.

44. These unclear regions in B.Subba Rao's scheme of classifications corresponded to the major river systems, were areas which were colonised and occupied and could sustain large communities - *The Personality of India,* Baroda, 1958, p. 12.

45. *Uḻavar* denoted cultivators or tillers and the use of plough

Akanāṉūṟu 30:8 ; 41:6 ;211:5

Naṟṟiṇai 60:2 ; *Puṟanāṉūṟu* 13:11

Toḻuvar Puṟanāṉūṟu 24.

46. *Puṟanāṉūṟu* 40.

47. *Porunarāṟṟuppaṭai* 11 246-48.

48. Puṟanāṉūru 61: 12; 67; 8; 68; 10.

49. *Nāñcil* see *Akanāṉūṟu* 42:5 ; 141:5

Puṟanāṉūṟu 19:11 ; 20:11 ;56:4

Meḻi-Paṭṭinappālai 1.205

Uḻupatai denotes ploughshare - *Puṟanaṉūṟu* 35:25

The *Perumpāṇāṟṟuppaṭai* provides an interesting description - 11 225-46

50. *Porunarāṟṟuppaṭai* 11. 242-48; J.V. Chelliah (Tr.) 1962, p. 75.

51. *Pakatu* ḍenoted buffaloes—*Perumpāṇaṟṟuppaṭi* 1.198; *Cirupānāṟṟuppaṭan* 11 189-90

Akanāṉūṟu 56:3 ; 91:5

52. *Porunarāṟṟuppaṭai* 1.193: *Puṟanāṉūṟu* 28:11-14 ; 29:13.

53. Denoted as *āyam* and *Cirai* in the texts *Ayam-Akanāṉūṟu* 68:2

Ciṟai Ibid 76:11; 200:9; 208:19; 346:9 Rajan Gurukkal "Aspects of Early Iron Age Economy: Problems of Agrarian Expansion in Tamilakam "*Indian History Congress,* Proceedings, 1981, p. 72.

For further details see T.M. Srinivasan "A brief account of the ancient irrigation Engineering systems prevalent in South India" (Rp) from *Indian Journal of History of Science,* Vol.5, No.2, 1970, pp.315-25 and "Water Lifting Devices in Ancient India : Their origin and mechanisms (from the earliest times to C.A.D. 1000)" (Rp.) from *Indian Journal of History of Science,* Vol.5, No.2, 1970, pp. 379-89.

54. 1.240.
55. *Paṭṭinappālai* 11 283-84 refers ot construction of tanks by Karikāla.
    There is a reference in the *Cilappatikāram* to Karikala's construction of sluices and canals to distribute water X: 108-11.
56. 11.283-84; J.V. Chelliah (Tr.)1962, p. 47.
57. *Maturaikkāñci* 11 286-7; J.V.Chelliah (Tr.) 1962, p. 247.
58. *Akanāṉūṟu* 6:5; 201:12-13; *cilappatikāram X* : 150-52 *Puṟanāṉūṟu* 353: 8-9; 376:5-6; 396:19-20.
    In fact in *Puṟanāṉūṟu* 396 the poet states that once the food vessel is opened it is not closed. In other words, the chieftain goes on serving.
59. Miḻalai :*Puṟanāṉūṟu* 24.
    Virai : *Akanāṉūṟu* 206.
    Kuṉṟūr: *Naṟṟiṇai* 280.
60. 11.228-42; J.V. Chelliah (Tr.) 1962, pp. 119-21.
61. 11. 243-46.
62. T.V. Mahalingam, *Excavations in the Lower Kaveri Valley,* 1970, p. 111
    Rice husks and charred paddy grains are reported at Tirukkampuliyur. Singaravelu has pointed out the following sub species of paddy - *vennel, aivannel, torai, cennel* and *putunel.* While the *vennel, aivannel* and *torai* were found in the mountainous regions in wild and cultivated forms, the *cennel* and *putunel* were cultivated in the riverine tracts. Further, he postulates two phases of development of agriculture - the first stage occurred in the mountainous *mullai* regions where little effort was put in to grow the cereals specially paddy i.e. *vaṉpulam* regions. From here the paddy cultivation would have spread to the semi-arid or arid regions and finally to the riverine and to an extent in the coastal regions -1966, p. 42.
63. C.Maloney, 1976, p. 8.
64. *Tolkāppiyam*: *Porulatikāram Akattiṇai Iyal* 18 Naccinarkkiniyar commentary.
65. *Akanāṉūṟu* 246:14 Identified by Subramanian 1966, p. 64.
66. Manogaran, 1986, pp. 81-82.
67. *Naṟṟiṇai* 281:3.
68. N. Subrahmaniam 1966, p. 282.
69. *Ibid*, p. 284.
70. Was a town in the Cōḻa country- *Naṟṟiṇai* 161:5 Subrahmanian 1966, p. 507.
71. Poet Paraṇar belonged to this place in the Kāveri region -*Akanaṉūṟu* 186:16; N. Subramanyam 1966, p, 621.
73. See the later section of this chapter.
74. 11.26-28; R.Champakalakshmi 1975-76, p. 113.
75. *Maturaikkāñci* 11 344-45. Ruled by Manalviralvēl. *Akanāṉūṟu* 44:1-5 alludes to surplus paddy production here.

76. Now situated in Sivaganga taluk in Ramanathapuram district - Manogaran 1986, p. 69.
77. *Maturaikkāñci* 1.119; Subrahmanyan 1966, p. 705.
78. Must have existed close to paddy fields as *vayal* in Tamil means paddy fields *puṛanaṇūṛu* 58 mentions the death of Pāṇṭiyaṉ king here. Manogaran, 1986, p. 79.
79. Maloney 1976, p. 12.
80. *Ciṛupaṇāṛṛuppaṭai* 11 187-88.
81. *Paṛatavar:Ainkuruṇūṛu* 180:1-2; 60: 1-3 *Naṛṛiṇai* 74: 1-4; *Akanāṇūṛu* 187:22 ; 300:1-2.
82. *Perumpāṇāṛṛuppaṭai* 11.319-23.
    Muturaikkāñci 11. 315-26.
83. *Tolkāppiyam* : *Porulatikāram Akattiṇai Iyal* 18 - Naccinarkkiniyar commentary.
84. Toṇṭi mentioned by Ptolemy as a city-VII 1.8 - situated at the mouth of the river Ponnani - identified with Ponnani by Schoff (Tr.) *Periplus of the Erythraen Sea,* New Delhi 1974 (Rp.), p. 204. Toṇṭi harbour here referred in *Puṛanāṇūṛu* 290 : 12
86. *Perumpāṇāṛṛuppaṭai* 1.319.
87. *Ciṛupāṇāṛṛuppaṭai* 11 152-3 - identified with Marakanam—R. Champakalakshmi 1975-76, p. 122 *Periplus* 60 refers to it as Sopatma.
88. *Akanāṇūṛu* 206:13-14. Identified as Viıampattinam (Arikamedu) south of Pondicherry.
89. *Naṛṛiṇai* 358:10 - Identified with Alagankulam.
90. While Schoff identifies it with Cannanore 1974, p. 204, McCrindle identifies with Mangalur - J.W.McCrindle *Ancient India as described* by Ptolemy (ed.) Ramachandra Jain, p. 46.
91. Schoff identified it to be Porkad 1974, p. 211. McCrinde identified it to be near Workallebarrier, p. 53.
92. Schoff 1974, p. 205.
93. Author of *Periplus* classified it as a 'market town'—*Periplus* 60, while Ptolemy elevated it to the status of an emporium - Ptolemy VII 1.13.
94. Ptolemy describes it to be an emporium VII-1-10.
95. K.V. Raman "Tamil Nadu and Kerala: Archaeological Investigations in the Recent Past" B.K. Gururaja Rao (Ed.) *A Decade of Archaeological Studies in South India,* Dharwar, 1978, pp. 9-10.
96. Maloney "The beginnings of civilization in South India", *Journal of Asian Studies* Vol. XXIX, No.3, 1969, pp. 606-14.
97. *Akanāṇūṛu* 89:10; 169:4;121:11; 79:14;127:15.
    Aiṅkuṛuṇūṛu 352:1 ; 363:2
    Kuṛuṇtokai 283:5 ;12:3
    Naṛṛiṇai 33:6; 387:4.
98. *Puṛanāṇūṛu* 395;
    Perumpāṇāṛṛuppaṭai 1.206.
99. K. Sivathamby 1974, p. 29.
100. R. McAdams "The Natural History of Urbanism" in Possehl (ed.) *Ancient cities of the Indus* New Delhi, 1979, p. 21.
101. *Tolkāppiyam* : *Porulaltikāram Akattiṇai Iyal: 5.*
102. K. Sivathamby 1974, p. 28

103. *Puṟanāṉūṟu 33: 11-5;* Aiṅkuṟuṉūṟu 48: 2-3 *Akanāṉūṟu* 140:5-8.

104. 11.214-25; J.V. Chelliah (Tr.) 1962, pp. 73-75.

105. *Akanāṉūṟu* 366: 1-11.

106. *Puṟanāṉūṟu* 15, 16, 57.

107. The Cōḻas mode attempts to again access to the pearl fisheries of the Pāṇṭiya coast and the rich pepper areas of Cēra territory .R.Champakalakshmi, 1986, p. 5.

108. *Pre Pallavan Tamil Index* defines *nāṭu* as county, territory and kingdom, 1966 pp. 488-4489.

Etymological meanings of *nāṭu* would be country, district, province, locality, situation, earth, land, world, kingdom, state, rural tracts, open place agricultural tract. *DED* 3012, p. 242.

109. Pioneering work on the *nāṭu* was done by. Y. Subbarayulu - *Political Geography of the Cola country,* Madras, 1973. In fact Stein's work *Peasant State and Society in Medieval South India,* 1980 is based on Subbarayulu's analysis of the *nāṭū*.

110. See chapter III of *Peasant, State and society for more details.*

111. Sudarshan Seneviratne 1989, p. 22.

112. Miḻalaikuṟṟam : *Puṟanāṉūṟu* 24:19.

Muṭṭuṟu Kuṟṟam : *Puṟanāṉūṟu* 24:22.

113. Rajan Gurukkal; *The Agrarian System and Socio - political organiation under the Early Pandyas* C.A.D 600-1000 unpublished, Ph. D thesis, Jawaharlal Nehru University, 1984, Appendix 1.

114. Sudarshan Seneviratne, 1989 pp. 23-24.

115. *Paṭṭinappālai* 11. 283-84.

116. R. Champakalakshmi 'The Study of Settlement Patterns in the Cōḻa period: Some Perspectives'. *Man and Environment,* Vol. XIV, No. 1, 1989, p. 96.

117. T.N. Subramanian (ed.) *Thiry Pallava Copper Plates,* Madras, 1966, Sanskrit portion 1.98.

118. R. Champakalakshmi, 1989 (b), p. 96.

119. K.S. Ramachandran *Archaeology of South India: Tamil Nadu* Delhi, 1980 pp. 18-24.

Habitation sites of early stone age man were located in this area as it was rich in quartzite. besides water was readily available her - F.R.Allchin and B.A.llchin *The Rise of Civilisation in India and pakistan,* New Delhi, 1983, p. 42.

120. H.D. Sankalia, *Pre History and Proto History of India and Pakistan,* 2nd ed. Poona, 1974, p. 69.

121. H.D. Sankalia "beginnings of Civilisation in South India", *Proceedings of the Second International Conference Seminar of Tamil Studies*, vol.II, Madras, January, 1968, p. 28.

122. B. Allchin *The Stone Tipped Arrow,* London, 1966, p. 114

123. F.U. Zeuner and B.Allchin "The Microlithic sites of Tinnevelly District, Madras State", *Ancient India, No. 12, pp. 4-20.*

124. An idea of the neolithic way of life can be got from a type site namely Paīyampatti in North Arcot district which has been extensively excavated. Two phases are seen by the excavator. Pottery comprised of pale grey and burinished grey wares and a small amount of red ware

Tool types include bone tools, short blades of jasper, agate and chert and stone axes, querns, mortars, pestles, pounders and pebble polishers made of stone were found. People probably lived in pits of different sizes and depths which were roughly circular and oblong. Partitions were noticed in some pits. The second phase is indicated by a predominant use of red ware pottery (though grey ware was also seen, absence of bone tools and an increase in stone blades and presence of grains (horse gram, green gram and ragi). People probably lived in huts over pits as indicated by post holes on the ground levels. K.S. Ramachandran, New Delhi, 1980, pp.35-37.

125. B.Narasimhaiah *Neolithic and Megalithic cultures of Tamil Nadu,* New Delhi, 1980, p. 30. K.S. Ramachandran 1980, p. 33.
126. B.Narasimhaiah 1980, pp. 28-30
     K.S. Ramachandran 1980, pp. 32-33.
127. B. Narasimhaiah 1980, p. 30.
128. C. Maloney, 1976, p. 3.
129. Animal bones of bovines, sheep, deer and fowl, pig, cat etc have been discovered-*IAR* 1967 - 68: 27-28. Besides clay figurines of long horned cattle apparently used as symbols of fertility were also found. -R. Sumathi *The Proto History of Northern Tamil Nad : assessment of the potentialities and processes of change,* Seminar paper, Jawaharlal Nehru University, p. 12.
130. K.S. Ramachandran 1980, p. 43.
     R. Champakalakshmi, 1975-76, p. 119.
131. L.S. Leshnik "Nomads and Burials in the early history of South India" in Leshnik and Sonetheimer ed. *Nomads and Pastoralists in South Asia,* Weisbaden, 1975, p. 58.
132. Gururaja Rao postulated that there was an increase in the size of the population in this period as a large amount of labour must have been needed to organize and transport huge blocks of stone in the construction of megaliths or in erection of bunds across water for storing up rain water for irrigation of crops - *The Megalithic Culture in South India,* Mysore, 1972, p. 298. Demograpic increase, however is not visible in archaeological records.
133. M.S. Nagaraja Rao *Proto Historic Cultures of the Tungabhadra valley,* New Delhi, 1984 (2nd ed.), p. 15.
134. R.E.M Wheeler *Early India and Pakistan,* (Rev. ed) London, 1968, pp. 62-63.
135. L.S. Leshnik *The South Indian Megalithic Burials : The Pandukal complex,* Weisbaden, 1974, p. 246.
136. R. Champalakshmi 1975-76, p. 115.
137. Leshnik 1974, p. 193.
138. R. Sumathi -Seminar paper, p. 8.
139. Banerjee and Soundararajan "Sanur 1950 and 1952: A Megalithic site in Chingelput district", *Ancient India,* vol. 15, p. 9.
140. *IAR* 1964-65:25 ; *IAR* 1965-66 : 37
     Mahalingam, *Excavations in the Lower Kaveri Valley,* Madras, 1970, pp. 14-16 ; 65
     R. Champakalakshmi 1975-76, p. 113.
141. The 2nd major rock edict, Romila Thapar, *Asoka and the Decline of the Mauryas,* Delhi 1973, p. 251.

142. S. Nagaraju and B.K. Gururaja Rao "Chronology of Iron Age in South India" in D.P. Agarwal and D.K.Chakrabarti (Ed.) *Essays in Indian Proto History,* New Delhi, 1979, p. 328.
143. K.R. Srinivasan and N.R. Banerjee "Surveys of South Indian Megaliths" *Ancient India* No. 19, 1953, p. 112.
144. As mentioned in N.R. Banerjee *The Iron Age* in India, New Delhi, 1965, p. 55, 61.
145. *Ibid*, p. 62.
146. R. Champakalakshmi 1975-76, p. 118. It has been subsequently pointed out by the author that the uniform occurence of BRW represents the earliest settlements of widespread pastoral cum agrarian population.
147. *Ibid*.
148. Ibid p 118.
149. *The Problem of Dravidian Origins:A linguistic, Anthropological and Archaeological Approach,* Madras, 1977, pp. 54-135.
    (a) *Arguments for an Aryan origin of the South Indian Megaliths,* Madras, 1973.
150. R. Champakalakshi 1975-76
151. Maṇimekalai Patikam-1.11
152. Asko Parpola in his work *Arguments for an Aryan origin of the South Indian Megaliths,* Madras, 1973 argues for an association of the megalithic culture with the Vratyās. These Vratyās belonged to waves of Aryans who came earlier than the Rg. Vedic people They arrived much earlier than the later waves of Aryans and introduced iron.
153. R. Thapar "Puranic lineages and Archaeological Cultures", *Puraṭaṭṭva,* No. 8, 1975-76, pp. 86-98.
154. R. Champakalakshmi, 1975-76, pp. 110-22.
155. *Ibid,* p. 120.
156. F.R. Allchin and B. Allchin, *The Birth of Indian Civilisation,* Penguin, 1968, pp. 229-30.
157. Clarence Maloney 1976, p. 11.
158. K.R. Srinivasan "The Megalithic Burials and Urn Fields of South India in the light of Tamil Literature and Tradition" *Ancient India,* No.2, July 1946, pp. 11-14.
    Also "Megalithic monuments of South India - Literature and Tradition", *Transactions of the Archaeological society of South India,* 1958-59, pp. 4-8.
159. *Puṛanāṇūṛu* 228: 256.
160. *Paṭiṟṟuppaṭṭu* 44: 22-23
    Puṛanāṇūṛu 228:1-15.
161. *Puṛanāṇūṛu* 238: 1-15.
162. M.R. banerjee "The Megalithic Problem of Chingelput in the light of recent exploration" *Ancient India,* No. 12, 1956, p. 31.
    R. Champalakshmi, 1975-76, p. 119.
163. *Maṇimēkalai VI* : 67-68.
164. B. K. Gururaja Rao, 1972, pp. 267-68.
165. K.V. Soundararajan, 1967, pp. 660-61.
166. D.K. Chakrabarti "Beginnings of iron in India" *Antiquity,* Vol. L, 1976, p. 117.

167. Leshnik 1974, p. 63.
168. Mahalingam 1970, p. 109.
169. Allchins 1968, p. 227.
170. *IAR* 1964-65 : 23.
171. *IAR* 1976-77, p. 47.
172. B.K. Gururaja Rao 1972, pp. 300-04. He states that Roman traders in the Cera country in the first Century A.D were attracted by this steel. Probably the swords from India mentioned by Ktescas and swords of Quintus Curtius were manufactured by the Woetz process by the megalithic folk.
173. See V.D. Krishnaswami "Megalithic types of South India", *Ancient India* Vol.5, 1949, pp. 35-46
    L.S. Leshnik 1974
    K.S. Ramachandran, 1980
    Narasimhaiah *Neolithic and Megalithic Cultures in Tamil Nadu,* New Delhi, 1980
    B.K. Gururaja Rao 1972.
174. Leshnik 1974, p. 226.
175. *Ibid*, pp. 226-27., p.
176. *Ibid*.
177. *Ibid*, p. 232.
178. *Ibid*, p. 246.
179. *Puṛanāṇūṛu* 228.
180. Soundararajan, 1967, pp. 661-62.
181. R. Champakalakshmi has given suggestions for carrying out such an exercise 1975-76, pp. 110-23. In this she has highlighted the fact that megaliths occur at important Vēḷir sites which occasionally are both burial and habitation sites.
182. S. Seneviratne "*The Social Base of Buddhism: South East India and Sri Lanka*" unpublished Ph. D. thesis Jawaharlal Nehru University, New Delhi, 1985, p. 27.
183. *Ibid*, p. 49.
184. *Ibid*, p. 49 1985, p. 49.
185. *Ibid,* pp. 50-51.
186. R. Sumathi seminar paper, p. 19.
187. A table of the Vēḷir settlements and the form of burials there is indicated in S. Seneviratne "Pre-State to State Societies: Transformations in the political Ecology of South India with special reference to Tamil Nadu" paper presented at the seminar on the *The State in Precolonial South India,* Jawaharlal Nehru University pp. 16-17.
188. Leshnik 1974, p. 33.
189. R. Sumathi, seminar paper, p. 20.
190. R. Seneviratne 1985, p. 51.
191. Narasimhaiah 1980, pp. 122-25.

192. R. Sumathi, Seminar paper, p. 19.
193. Narasimhaiah 1980, pp. 113-17.
194. Seneviratne 1985, pp. 32-33.
195. *Ibid*, p. 48.
196. B.K. Gururaja Rao, 1972, p. 50; pp. 50-58.
197. B.K. Gururaja Rao "The Megalithic culture in Tiruchirapalli District" in *Professor K.A.M Sastri Felicitation Volme,* Madras 1971, pp. 203-04.
198. B.K. Gururaja Rao, 1972, p. 299.
199. *Ibid*

   Srinivasan and Banerjee "Survey of South Indian Megaliths", *Ancient India* No. 15, p. 5.

   Seneviratne 85, p. 47.

200. *IAR* 1953-54 : 12; *IAR* 1970-71: 33.
201. *Ibid*
202. Maloney 1976, p. 8.
203. Ramachandran, 1962, p. 62.
204. As quoted by R. Sumathi—Seminar paper, p. 48.
205. Leshnik, 1974, p. 43.

CHART - 1

THE *AINTIṆAI* AND THEIR CHARACTERISTICS

Typical flower (=name of region and poetic theme)	LOVER' UNION *Kuriñci*	PATIENT WAITING *Mullai*	LOVER'S UNFAITH-FULNESS *Marutam*	ANXIETY, SEPARATION *Neytal*	ELOPEMENT, SEPARATION *Pālai*
Landscape	mountains	forest, pasture	cultivated countryside	seashore	wasteland
Season	cold season early frost	rainy season	all seasons	all seasons	summer, late dew
Time	night	evening	dawn	sunrise	midday
Hero	poruppaṉ, *verpaṉ, cilampaṉ, nāṭaṉ*	*nāṭaṉ tōṉral*	*ūraṉ, makiḻnaṉ*	*cērppaṉ pulampaṉ*	*viṭalai, kāḷai, mīḷi*
Heroine	*Kuṟatti, koṭicci*	*maṉaivi, kiḻatti*	*kiḻatti maṉaivi*	*nuḷaicci, paratti*	*eyiṟṟi*
People	*Kuṟavar, kāṉavar*	*iṭaiyar, āyar*	*uḻavar, kaṭaiyar*	*nuḷaiyar, paratar, aḷavar*	*eyiṉar, maṟavar*
Occupation	guarding millet fields, honey-gathering	pastoral occupation, some cultivation	agriculture	fishing, drying fish, selling salt	wayfarers, robbery, fighting.
Pastime	bathing in waterfalls and streams	bull-fight *kuravai* dance	bathing in ponds, festivals, arts	bathing	dancing, fighting
Settlements	*ciṟṟūr, ciṟukuṭi, kuṟicci*	*ciṟṟūr, pāti cēri palli*	*pērūr, mūtūr*	*pākkam, paṭṭiṉam*	*kuṟumpu*
Waters	Water-fall hill-pond	pond, rivulet	river, pool, well	well, sea, saltmarshes	waterless stagnant water
Beasts	monkey, tiger, bear elephant, pig	deer, hare	buffalo, freshwater fish, otter	crocodile, shark	wild dog, tiger, lizard, elephant
Birds	peacock, parrot	jungle hen, sparrow	heron, stork, swan	sea-gull, marine crow	dove, eagle, kite, hawk
Trees/Flowers	teak, *vēṅkai* sandal,	koṉṟai, water lily, red	mango, lotus	puṉṉai, taḻai-shrub	uḷiñai, ōmai cactus

Typical flower (=name of region and poetic theme)	LOVER' UNION *Kuriñci*	PATIENT WAITING *Mullai*	LOVER'S UNFAITH-FULNESS *Marutam*	ANXIETY, SEPARATION *Neytal*	ELOPEMENT, SEPARATION *Pālai*
	bamboo jack fruit	kāntaḷ piṭavam		tāḷaishrub, muṇṭakam, aṭampu	
Food	millet, (*tiṇai*) mountain-rice	*Varaku tuvarai*	rice	fish	
Instrument	*toṇṭaka paṛai-drum, mountain lute*	*ēṛṛu-drum forest lute*	*maṇapaṛai* (drum) field-lute *nelari kiṇai*	*pampai*-drum vilari lute	*uṭukkai*-drum desert-lute
Melody-type	*kuṛiñcippaṇ*	*cātāri*	*marutappaṇ*	*cevvaḷi*	*curam*
God	*Murukaṇ*	*Māyōn* (Tirumāl)	*Intiraṇ*	*Varuṇaṇ*	*Koṛṛavai* (Kali)

Note : *kuṛiñci* : conehead, *Strobilanthes*; various S. and *Barleria* species; said to grow at an altitude of 6000 ft. and flower only once in 12 years; flower is bluish, *mullai*: *Jasminum sambac*; Arabian jasmine, *marutam*: *Terminalia tomentosa*, *neytal*: white Indian water lily, *Nymphaea lotus alba*: blue nelumbo, *pālai*: silvery-leaved ape-flower, *Mimusops kauki;* grows in barren tracts; is evergreen; blossoms small, white.

Based on Nacciṉārkkiṉiyar commentary on *Tolkāppiyam Porulatikāram* 18 and K.V. Zvelebil (1973;, p. 100).

CHART - 2*

TIṆAIS : ASSOCIATIVE NOMENCLATURE FOR PEOPLE

KULAPPEYAR

Kuṛiñci	*Mullai*	*Neytal*	*Marutam*
Kāṉavar	*Kōvalar*	*Nuḷaiyar*	*Kaḷamar*
Vēṭṭuvar	*Itaiyar*	*Timilar*	*Uḻavar*
Iṛavuḷar	*Āyar*	*Paratavar*	*Kaṭaiyar*
Kuṉṟavar	*Potuvar*	*Nuḷaittiyar*	*Uḻaittiyar*
Vēṭṭuvittiyar	*Iṭaicciyar*	(other female names may be there)	Kaṭaicciyar
Kuṛattiyar	*Kōvittiyar*		(other female names can also appear)
Kuṉṟuvittiyar	*Potuviyar*		
(other female names also may be there)	Āycciyar		

URIPPEYAR

Kuṛiñci	*Mullai*	*Neytal*	*Marutam*
Veṛppaṉ	*Aṇṇal*	*Koṇkaṉ*	*Makiḻnaṉ*
Cilampaṉ	*Toṉṟal*	*Tuṛaivaṉ*	*Ūraṉ*
Poruppaṉ	*Kuṛumpoṛaināṭaṉ*	*Cērppaṉ*	*Maṉiyōḷ*
Koṭicci	*Maṉaivi*	*Mellampulampan* (other names may also occur)	

* Based on Nacciṉārkkiṉiyar's commentary of *Tolkāppiyam Porulatikāram* 20.

CHAPTER III - A

EARLY HISTORICAL TAMIL SOCIETY : CLAN, KIN AND LINEAGE

In the earlier section while discussing geography, ecology and settlement pattern it has been pointed out that the archaeological (megalithic) culture of the proto-historic period and the early historic periods coincide with the early and end phases of the megalithic culture. The overall developments of these two periods is summed up in the following statement:

"By the beginning of the Early Historic period, there was an essential synthesis of the following structural developments viz the natural selection of the lower plains as areas of attraction, greater sedentarization, demographic expansion, an emphasis on intensive agriculture and surplus production, the harnessing of organic and inorganic sources of energy i.e. draught animals and water, for agriculture, technological innovations associated with iron and hydraulic control, the evolution of chiefdoms and social ranking, the beginnings of new forms of specialization and organization of labour, the development of new forms of exchange patterns-all hitherto unknown during the Early proto Historic period"[1].

While the above statement is generally correct, it is necessary to distinguish between two broad phases of socio-economic development even on the basis of early Tamil texts of the *Caṅkam* and correlate it with archaeological evidence. It would then become clear that the above statement applies directly to the *marutam* or riverine plains whereas the other eco-zones show uneven development.

As noted in the earlier chapter, the ecological factors compelled the inhabitants of the *tiṇais* to practise different modes of subsistence. Man-nature relationship varied from *tiṇai* to *tiṇai* conditioned by the physical environment. This was instrumental in the emergence of various kinds of subsistance patterns, religious beliefs and social institutions in the different *tiṇais*[2]. Early *caṅkam* poems throw light on the ways of adaptation to environment by the inhabitants of a *tiṇai*. The inhabitants of different *tiṇais* seem to be lineage groups dispersed in various segments practising different modes of subsistence. The existence of various modes of subsistence did not preclude craft specialisation at a rudimentary level more conspicuously in *marutam* and *neytal tiṇais*. Tamil texts reflect rudimentary craft specialisation. There are also references to other social groups which may have lived off the agrarian surplus.

The social organisation of the Tamils cannot be explained in terms of a monolithic structure. Uneven levels of development of the *tiṇais* on account of ecological constraints accounted for the presence of varied forms or organisation in the *tiṇais*. For example, at the level of the *kuriñci* and *mullai tiṇais* the 'tribal' basis of social norms and organisation persisted, while the *marutam* and *neytal* emerged as the important regions of activity characterised by socioeconomic deversification. In other words, an incipient stage of urbanism set in in *marutam* and *neytal* tracts. At the level of polity one can discern a ranked hierarchical structure. In a sense a sort of pyramid emerged with the *Mūvēntar* (three kingdoms of Cēra, Cōḻa and Pāṇṭiya) at the top with other chieftains like *vēḷir, non-vēḷir* and *ūrkiḻār* below following them in this order.

In the sphere of religion one finds the absence of a dominant ideology and priestly class. On the whole, a study of the source material indicates that society was in a stage of transition from a tribal and fairly egalitarian one to a peasant or farming society with an incipient urbanism all of which marked a growing differentiation in certain enclaves within certain *tiṇais*.

Firstly, the social groups of each *tiṇai* will be discussed separately in the initial part of this chapter. This would facilitate an understanding of the social formations in the region under study.

I. THE ECO-ZONES AND ETHNIC GROUPS :

Taking the *kuṛiñci* (the hilly and forest tracts) first, the *kuṛavar* and *kāṇavar* are mentioned as the inhabitants of the hilly tracts and forests[3] and practising different modes of subsistence like hunting, shifting cultivation and removing honey from bee hives. While womenfolk of the *kuṛavar* were referred to as *koṭicci, kuṛatti* and *kuṛamakaḷ* the young ones were known as *kuṛakkuṛumākkaḷ*.

The *kuṛavar* generally lived in and around the hills/ hillocks in small settlements[4] having trees like sandalwood *akil, vēṅkai* and jackfruit[5] and different types of flowers which their womenfolk plucked[6]. Besides, the flora comprised trees like *akil* (eagle wood), *vēṅkai* (pterocarpus marsupium), jackfruit etc. and fauna which included flowers like *kuṛiñci* and animals like monkeys, elephants and birds like peacock[7]. Their huts were generally small in size and built of dried grass[8]. They are described to be hunters wielding the bow and arrow to kill animals like deer, elephant and porcupine[9]. Removing honey from beehives seems to have been another occupation of the *kuṛavar*[10]. These *kuṛavar* also practised slash and burn cultivation[11] as the hills had cultivable slopes. They harvested crops of millet like *eṇal, tiṇai*[12] etc. and also grew *avarai*. Their *tiṇai* fields were normally guarded against parrots and birds by young girls (*koṭ icci, kuṛamakaḷ, kuṛavar maṭamakaḷ*) who drove these birds away by using instruments like *taṭṭai* and *kuḷir*[13]. This indicates the direct participation of women in the production process. Interestingly, most of the poems of the *kuṛiñci* describe the hero's meeting with the heroine when she is guarding the *tiṉai* fields Once the family came to know of her clandestine love affair, the heroine was kept under strict guard and supervision, A few poems also record the *kuṟavar* chasing elephants and protecting the *tiṉai* fields from being trampled by shouting and making noise[14] or by burning sticks of wood at night[15]. Guarding of the *tiṉai* fields against ravages by birds and animals was an important task. In one instance, however, the *kuṟavar* are stated to be sozzled after drinking toddy that they forgot to guard the *tiṉai* fields from being trampled by the elephants[16].

One poem describes the *avarai,* a pulse, a creeper also growing with the *tiṉai*[17]. The *kuṟavar* in that case may have grown it as a second crop.

The others involved in *tiṉai* cultivation and its protection are *cēṉōn* and *punavan*. In fact, the poems are not explicit on the nature of the relationship between the *punavan Cēṉōṉ* and *kuṟavar.* While the *puṉavaṉ* is described to be growing *tiṉai*[18] at night by holding or burning flaming torches and setting on *machans*[19] (platforms erected on a height to enable them to get a full view of the field). In our view the *cēṉōṉ* seems to be working or employed by the *kuṟavar* as he is usually mentioned to be guarding the *tiṉai*.

The *kuṟavar* seem to have been a fairly egalitarian group bound by ties of kinship. There is only one poem which alludes to some sort of differentiation among the *kuṟavar.* Poem 276 of *Naṟṟiṇai* describes the *tōḻi* talking to the hero (as indicated in the colophon) where she tells him that they were not daughters of *vēṭṭuvar* (hard hearted hunters who hunted with dogs) nor *kuṟava* girls (who were daughters of hunters) but *koṭicci* (who belong to the clan of *kuṟavar* who cultivate) thereby implying that they were higher in status than the other two. Within the *kuṟavar* community or tribe itself there would have been some practising hunting and others practising shifting cultivation. Those practising shifting cultivation would have been better off in economic terms than those who practised hunting, and therefore, the former were presumably higher in status It is important to note that a chieftain of the *kuṟavar* is mentioned as Ēṟaikkōṉ.

The term *kuravar* is used interchangeably with *kāṉavar* also (for forest dwellers) in some poems. the *kāṉavar*[20] are more or less described in the same way as the *kuṟavar* practising hunting, food gathering and shifting cultivation. Perhaps their hunting skills were better than the *kuṟavar* as is suggested by the poems. They are depicted to have strong hands and using the bow and arrow and at times a catapult to hunt and kill animals like pigs and porcupine or laying traps[21]. At times they were assisted in their hunting activities by dogs[22]. Besides they also dug out tubers from the ground[23]. In the course of such diggings they came across precious stones and even gold[24]. Like the *Kuṟavar* they also took up slash and burn cultivation[25]. guarding of the *tiṉai* was done by erecting *machans* with lamps[26] or by lighting fires of sandalwood and *akil*[27].

Slash and burn cultivation did not require advanced agricultural implements. irrigation facitilies. draught animals used in agricultural operations. Implements like hoe, sickle and axe would have been sufficient for this. Moreover, crops like millet or wild rice were of the dry farming type which required little water.

The *Kuṛavar* and *kāṇavar* were clans bound by kinship ties practising primitive form of subsistence like hunting and food gathering and slash and burn cultivation. All the members of the household cooperated in the shifting cultivation. The heavier tasks of clearing the forests and ploughing with hoes was presumably done by the men folk while guarding the millet crops during the day from the ravages of birds was left to the women folk. Although all the *Kuṛavar* had access to resources, there would have been some (especially those practising shifting cultivation) who would have been better off. Though on the whole they seem to be an undifferentiated community some sort of differentiation may have existed as is evident from the poem 276 in *Naṟṟiṇai*.

Pastoralism was mainly practised in the *mullai* lands though a few pastoralists must have existed in pockets in other areas such as *marutam*. The pastoral groups referred to in literature are *aṇṭar, āyar. iṭaiyar* and *kōvalar* and they domesticated the cow, goat and sheep. Terms such as *āy, āyaṉ, āytti, āyi, āycci,* refer to the cowherd community[28] and male herdsman and female herdswomen/ cowherdess. *Āymakaḷ* also denotes the cowherdess. The pastoralists who would have been nomadic in the protohistoric period would have become sedentarised by the early historical period. Once they settled in a region they could have moved about within the region or their nomadism could not have taken them over long distances. However, the early Tamil poems are not explicit on this aspect.

The *aṇṭar* must have lived off the milk products of the cows as reference to the ghee made out of cows milk is found in a poem[29].

The *iṭaiyaṉ*, in most cases, referred to the shepherd who had a flock of goats[30]. At night they are described as shielding the goats against foxes by keeping them together and burning logs of wood to provide light[31].

They usually carried a stick, a mattress and some sort of an umbrella made of mat[32]. These *iṭaiyar* (shepherds) brought milk to the house and also sold it by shouting the price of milk[33]. They *iṭaiyaṉ* was generally not economically well off. He wore soiled clothes and lived in houses with leaking roofs[34].

The *kōvalar* were the cowherds. A typical *mullai* scene portrayed in the *akam* poems describes the *kōvalar* to be taking the cows to graze in the morning and return in the evening playing the flute[35] which was probably made of *koṉṟai*[36]. They had sticks in their hand (*kōl*) and their cows had bells which tinkled. the sitck was probably used by them to dig out water to quench their thirst as well as that of their cattle[37]. That they were fond of flowers is evident from the poems. They strung garlands of various flowers which adorned their hair[38]. These *kōvalar* distributed food to all hungry wayfarers who passed on their route[39]. They are said to have lived in small settlements (*kurumpuṇam*).

Nothing much is known about the relationship between the different pastoral groups. Only a poem of the *naṟṟiṇai*[40] gives an indication of some sort of a difference between a *kōvalar* and *iṭaimakaṉ*. This poem states that the *iṭaimakaṉ*, one who grazes goats, keeps the flowers grown in the small settlement of the *kōvalar* (who grazes cows). The *kōvalar* could well be higher than the *iṭaimakaṉ* as the *kōvalar's* settlement is specifically mentioned. This would imply that the *kōvalar* was higher in status on account of cows being more important as wealth than the goats kept by the *iṭaiyaṉ*.

There may have been some chieftains belonging to the pastoral community of *Aṇṭar* who exercised hegemony over the people in their areas. The *Patiṟṟupattu* mentions one such chieftain Kaḻuvuḷ who fought with the Cēra ruler Kuṭakkō Iḷañcēral Irumpoṟai and was defeated[41]. Mention is made of a poet by the name of Aṇṭarmakaṉ kunivaḻuti : *Aṇṭar* was a name of the Pāṇṭiyan ruling elite. *Aṇṭarmakaṉ* meant descendant of the *Aṇṭar* who were cowherd/shepherds. Vaḻuti was a title of the Pāṇṭiyaṉ ruler. In the words of Sudarshan Seneviratne, "it appears that sections of cowherd/shepherd were subjugated by the Pandyas and probably their chieftains were absorbed into the political hierarchy of the Pandyas. Like the Mauryan epithets taken in the south the subordinate group of the *mūvēntar* may have also taken up title, names, epithets etc. as a means to imitate the overlord[42]" and in this case they took the title of Vaḻuti. Certain chieftains of the *Vēḷir* category such as *Pēkaṉ, Eyiṉaṉ, Aṇṭiraṉ* had epithets like Āy, Āvi, Āviyar which indicate pastoral connections/affiliations[43]. Texts also mention the Koṅkar, another group of people other than the *iṭaiyar/kōvalar* etc. or the *mullai tiṇai* groups who were pastoralists living in the pastures of the Coimbatore, Salem districts.

One of the lays of the *Pattuppāṭṭu* provides a fairly detailed description of the pastoral community living in the *mullai tiṇais*. The settlement consisted of huts with doors, tied by strong ropes and was fenced by a thorny hedge, Inside the settlement the cattle, goats and sheep were tied. The *āymakaḷ* (cowherdess) with smooth bamboo like shoulders and hair, churned butter from the curds in the morning. Later, she took this buttermilk in a pot and sold it. From the proceeds she fed her kin (*kiḷai*[44]). By selling ghee she acquired good buffaloes and cows. The *kōvalar's* food consisted of *tiṇai,* rich and milk.

These pastoral groups seem to have been bound by ties of kinship. We find a combination of different modes of subsistence like hunting, stock rearing and slash and burn cultivation in the *kuṟiñci* and *mullai* eco-zones. The people essentially did not rely on one mode of subsistence alone. If differences existed among the people of *vaṉpulam* (*kuṟiñci* and *mullai*) it must be attributed to economic factors i.e. differential access to resources. Also differences would have been prevalent between the chieftains and the general populace. The chieftains accumulated prestige goods like gold, pearls etc. either by plunder raids and wars with other chieftains which they redistributed.

Martial groups like *maṟavar*[45], *maḻavar* and *eyiṉar* were generally those who lived in the *pālai* areas. (*pālai* was an arid region created on account of hot summer conditions and scarcity of rain). Out of these the *maṟavar* or *maḻavar* (terms which are frequently used as synonyms) performed diverse activities like robbing and killing wayfarers who passed through their tracts, fighting for chiefs and lifting cattle or recovering stolen cattle.

These groups are described to be ruthless people who took to plundering, robbing and killing people passing through their areas[46]. This was one of their means of subsistence as the *pālai* tracts had practically little Vegetation and water. Moreover, scarcity of food made the *maṛavar* resort ot robbery. Most of the poems mention the hero crossing the dangerous tracts of the hostile *maṛavar* who do not spare anything that came their way. besides they also killed and ate the flesh of animals like cow and deer. They lived in small settlements[47].

The *maḻavar* and *maṛavar* were depicted as brave, valiant warriors with fierce looking eyes and the force of tiger[48]. Their weapons included bow and arrow, spears and swords[49]. The *maṛavar* generally fought for chiefs/ kings. They would have served as warriors[50] possibly on account of their physical prowess. Further, they are stated to be fearless warriors who do not run away from the battle field even when wounded[51]. They usually took oaths before they went to fight[52]. Besides, the *maṛavar* and *maḻavar* also indulged in cattle raids either stealing or recovering cattle for themselves or some chieftain[53].

In the *Pattuppāṭṭu* there are similar descriptions of the *maṛavar* as in the anthologies. They are described to be brave warriors who could withstand the arrows of enemy soldiers. and in the service of the Pāṇṭiyan ruler[54]. In the *Malaipaṭukaṭām* they are described as brave warriors who guard the palace gates of Naṉṉaṉ[55].

The *maṛavar* and *maḻavar,* though inhabitants of the *pālai* areas, may have lived in other eco-zones where they functioned as warriors. In a society dominated by war the *maṛavar* as soldiers may have played important roles. These warlike tribes were instrumental in cattle lifting, which according to M.G.S. Narayanan, was not a prelude to warfare but a separate act. According to Narayanan, these *maṛavar* may have been used by kings to their advantage in return for which they were assigned whole villages for personal loyalty and military service[56]. In fact these *maṛavar* seem to have recognised the advantages of wet land or cultivable land and a poem mentions a warrior as lord of such land.

Judging from the references in the later texts like *Patiṛṛuppattu* and *Pattuppāṭṭu,* the *maṛavar* may have served as warriors for the chieftains in their raids against their enemies. Once they were ensured of their daily subsistence through gifts of land, these people could have given up plundering and looting.

Another martial group referred to in the anthologies are the *mallar*. They are warriors with immense strenght who fight valiantly and do not run away from the battlefield even when they are losing a battle[57]. In one context they are referred to as wrestlers their strength being compared to that of a buffalo[58].

Yet another group which figures in the *pālai* situations is that of the *eyiṉar*[59]. The *eyiṉar* also practised hunting, looting and killing wayfarers for their sustenance. The womenfolk were known as *eyiṛṛi*. They *eyiṉar* are depicted in the poems as those who wield the bow and arrow and who waited for people to pass through their areas (mostly in the *pālai, tiṇai*[60]).

One poem refers to the *eyiṇar* as warriors living in *Kuṭanāṭu* (Cēra country). They could have been inducted as warriors on account of their valour and martial character. They killed wild boars and brought the flesh mixed with white rice and served it to people who passed through their areas[61].

Descriptions of the *eyiṇar* settlements are furnished by the *Perumpāṇarruppaṭai*. One of these descriptions woul indicate that it was that of the ordinary *eyiṇar* folk. The *eyiṇar* are said to be living in huts thatched with leaves of *īntu* palm along the spacious forest paths. The roofs of the houses looked like the backs of the porcupine and helped to keep the rats and squirrels away. While some of the *eyiṟṟi* lay on the skins of deer with their children, some dug the ground and removed the rice from below the ground. Then, this rice was pounded with short pestles and cooked. The bard of this poem informs another bard that he and his kinsmen would be served this rice along with salted meat on teak leaves by the *eyiṇar*[62]. The *Ciṟupāṇarṟuppaṭai* also mentions the *eyiṟṟi* feeding rice, tamarind curry and hot meat of deer to the bards[63]. Food served to people would comprise red rice and flesh of iguanas[64].

The description of another settlement (*Perumpāṇāṟṟuppaṭai* 11.118.31) shows that it was of an important personage probably a chief as it is described to have spacious houses where one finds spears, bows, quivers or arrows and shields. Hounds are chained inside the settlement. The settlement looked like a fort with a door and fencing all around.

It is interesting to note that while the *maṟavar* and *maḻavar* were warlike groups engaged in robbing or fighting. The *eyiṇar* figure as more hospitable groups serving whatever was available in their settlements to bards or others who passed by their settlements.

Another group mentioned in the texts are the *vēṭṭuvar* who were hunters[65] or fowlers. They may have lived in the *kuṟiñci*_tracts where game was easily available. Poems of the early anthologies describe the *vēṭṭuvaṉ* as hunters with dogs, hunting birds and animals[66]. They are said to live in small settlements[67]. In fact *Puṟanāṉūṟu* 320 depicts the life of a *vēṭṭuva* settlement. The *tiṇai* is dried outside on deer skin and the settlement has deer playing about. These people ate meat cooked on fire of sandalwood logs along with fish[68]. Another poem refers to the *Vēṭṭuva* exchanging deer meat and ivory for toddy [69].

Thus we notice that the inhabitants of the *tiṇais* discussed above were clan groups bound by kinship ties essentially living in the *vaṉpulam* regions practising primitive modes of subsistence for their sustenance. Most of these clans were self sufficient and managed to live out of the resources available in their zones of habitation except for exchanging a few prouducts by barter. Differentiation amongst these groups was between the chiefs and the general folk.

In the *marutam tiṇai,* we find that agriculturists who were the main producers of cereal crops were denoted by a number of terms such as *uḻavar*[70], *toḻuvar*[71], *kaḷamar*[72], *arinar.* The *uḻavar* and *toḻuvar* were those who ploughed, sowed, transplanted and harvested paddy[73]. At times bullocks/buffaloes used by them for ploughing are mentioned[74]. There were some who were engaged in removing weeds and other unwanted plants from the paddy fields. While doing the agricultural operations like ploughing, transplanting, watering or harvesting paddy or sugarcane these farmers probably sang songs as different sounds made by these farmers are recorded in literature[75]. For threshing the paddy it appears that they allowed a buffalo to trample the sheaves of crop[76]. The *kaḷamar* are mentioned to have had a weakness for toddy[77]. They are mostly described to be drunk with toddy[77]. They are mostly described to be drunk with toddy. Were they labourers who worked in the fields? If they were labourers then they could have drunk toddy after their work, and hence, they could have been mentioned as having a weakness for toddy. The *Arinar/Arivānar* were those who cut paddy against the sound of the beats of the *taṇṇumai*[78] (drum). Were they also labourers who were involved in harvesting paddy? The *Perumpāṇāṟṟuppaṭai* supplies interesting information on the settlement of the *uḻavar* as well as the agricultural operations involved in the production or rice[79]. The *uḻavar* also indulged in serving food to the bards[80] who passed by their settlements.

It is difficult to establish the relationship between these various groups. All the groups are mentioned as indulging in various operations. Would they have functioned collectively in these operations?

From the terms used for these people doing various kinds of agricultural operations it appears that they refer to the different functions associated with agriculture rather than different social groups. However, the nature of these functions would point to some of them at least being employed by the householders or *kiḻār* who controlled land and got them cultivated. The *kaḷamar* and *arinar* would seem to belong to this category although the *uḻavar* may refer to peasants cultivating their lands or perhaps occasionally working in other people's lands. The *kiḻār* in general refers to those who control land (owned land?) and were probably householders similar to the *gahapatis* of the north (see Chapter III Section B). Some of them emerged as important local chiefs and perhaps got their lands cultivated by others.

The term *kiḻār,* as occurring in the *Caṅkam* texts, seems to refer mainly to the non-*brāhmaṇā* agricultural householders, although when *brāhmaṇās* were given lands by the ruling families, they also came to be known as *kiḻār. Kiḻār* thus came to mean those who possessed land. While some of the *kiḻār* emerged as chiefs/important personages and their glories were sung by poets, some of the *kiḻārs* themselves were poets (vide Appendix 3). The medieval commentators' attempt to distinguish between superior and subordinate *vēḷāḷās* could well we a result of such a interpretation/ understanding of the terms used in the *Caṅkam* texts for those who controlled land and for those who were involved in the various stages/functions in the agricultural operations. However, it is noteworthy that the term *vēḷāḷā* does not occur in the early anthologies although the *Tolkāppiyam* in the *Poruḷatikāram* assigns the *vēḷāḷās* to the fourth category in the fourfold social order[81].

The *Parata Paratavar/Valaiñar* were inhabitants of the littoral tracts. (*neytal*[82]) The fishermen are also known by other terms such as *Iṇamīṉ Vēttuvaṉ*[83], *Valaiñar*[84], *Mīṉ Kōlpavar*[85]. These *paratavar* (fishermen) are portrayed in the poems as living in small settlements (*ciṟukuṭi*) which are said to be noisy and stinking of fish on the shores of the high sea[86]. They used to fish in the seas mainly at night using nets in small boats (*timil*) with lamps of fish fat in them[87]. However, there are two references to them fishing during the day. The technology used in the catching operations was simple and limited to nets, (which were well fastened) fish hooks and some sort of hammers[88]. The poems also mention the *paratavar* repairing the boats and fishing nets[89]. While part of the fish caught was distributed among their community a part of it was dried in front of fishermen's houses[90] and some of the fish was sold[91] or exchanged for rice[92]. Sometimes, toddy also figured in the exchanges[93]. The fishermen generally drank toddy and indulged in playing the *taṭa* instrument and dancing the *kuravai*[94]. The *Perumpāṇāṟṟuppaṭai* gives us an insight into the settlements of the *Valaiñar*. The *paratavar* are said to be living in

"short-roofed huts
With *vanchi* and white *kanchi* branches built.
Across the beams are ordered bamboo laths
Well bound with *thalai* strings. these huts are thatched
With *tharpai* grass. Fish baskets lie in front of sheds with *bent-stemmed punnai* branches built And paved with sands upon which fruit vines creep.
Here fishers old and young sit with their kin.
They with their children go to fish in pools
Quite deep and dark, where red-steaked *kayal* fish
And prawns move mixed like bows and arrows sharp
That smell of flesh. They watch the banks of pools
Which e'en in summer long remains so deep
That shoulders of the men who bathe in them
Cannot be seen. If thou dost wish to stay
In homes of men who use their knotted nets,
Thou wilt be served with drink made with the paste
Of rice unpounded, cooled in large, wide pots,
And, mixed with it, fine powdered sprouts of rice

That look like white ants nests where serpents live;
And toddy that's stirred with the fingers well
And then matured by being kept in jars
That have wide mouths for two full days and nights
To Sweeteb it. All this thou will receive
Along with fresh fish fried, when thou art tired"[95]
"Further, the *Paṭṭinappālai* informs us
In the centre nets are spread
To dry on sandy yards that seem
Like gloom with moonlight patches mixed.
Here red-haired fishers garlands wear
of blossoms, cool and white, and vines
beneath the pines with hanging roots.
They plant the sword of the gravid shark
To seat their sea-god great, for whom
They wear the bloom of sheath-ed pine,
And toddy drawn from rugged plams
They drink. Their women dark are clad
In green leaf garments, and with these
On full moon days, neglecting work,
Not fishing on the wide cold sea,
These men who live in sandy groves
That smell of fish do eat and play"[96].

Even amongst the *Paratavar* there may have been some sections who were affluent and not just fishermen. Some poems refer to the *paratar* as traders fishing conches, shells and pearls and selling pearls and conch bangles[97]. The *paratar* may have realised the advantage of trading in these luxury items and may have channelised some parts of it out of the region as pearls figure as one of the exports to the Western World. On account of this trade they may have accumulated wealth and presumably started to live in bigger settlements and even in urban centres[98], while the ordinary fisher folk would have continued to live in small settlements on the sea coast. One poem alludes to this sort of differentiation among them. In this interesting poem, the female companion of the heroine tells the hero that the heroine's life is not comparable to that of the hero's as the heroine hails from a small settlement near the groves on the sea shore. She is said to stink of fish as she dries the *sura* fish. Further the *toḻi* tells him that their life depends on what they get from the sea. Whereas the hero of the poem is described to be belonging to a *mūtūr* (old settlement) and travelling about in a chariot[99].

A section of the *Paratavar* probably rose to be small chieftains in the southern Pāṇṭiyaṉ territory. The *Teṉ paratavar* are said to have troubled the Cōḻa king Ceruppāḻiyerinta Iḷañcētceṉṉi and were in turn defeated by him[100]. They were also defeated by Neṭuñceḻiyan the Pāṇṭiya ruler[101]. Apart from this, nothing much is known about them. Clarence Maloney opines that the Pāṇṭiya and Cōḻa monarchs relied on the *paratavar* to import horses for them. Later these *paratavar* on the Cōḻa coast, according to Maloney were absorbed or evolved into *ceṭṭi* castes[102] by the 7th century A.D.

The other social group of the *neytal* tract were the *umaṇar* who were manufacturers and traders of salt[103]. There are numerous references in the poems to these *umaṇar* who transported salt on the backs of animals and carts[104] (mostly wooden) drawn by buffaloes and bullocks travelling through rough, beaten dangerous and hostile paths[105] and through forests[106]. Normally, they travelled in groups or *cāttus*[107] cooking on the way[108] and shouting the price of salt as they went[109]. Examples of salt sellers from the texts show that they sold the salt of *neytal* in the hilly regions[110] and exchanged it for paddy presumably from the *marutam*[111]. That salt was in great demand is reflected in one poem which shows that people were waiting for the salt sellers and their carts[112]. The lays of the *Pattuppāṭṭu* also describe the salt sellers travelling in bullock carts in groups with children and their pet monkeys.

Thus in the *neytal* region, the fisherfolk who fished and traded conches and pearls would have definitely been better off then the ones who fished. Differentiation seems to have prevailed presumably on account of the economic factors. Certain sections of the pastoralists seemed affluent compared to the others on account of access to resources or sucessful exploitation of such resources. In the *kuṛiñci* the *kuṛavar* practising shifting cultivation may have been better off than the ones who took up hunting and food gathering.

There are survivals of some of these groups till recent times. Such groups/tribes do not seem to have been brought into the mainstream of societal organisation which dominated the *marutam* region. Those which survive as anthropological relics and exist in cetain pockets of the region are the *kuṛavar, iṭaiyar, kaḷḷar, maṛavar, paratavar,* and *vēṭṭuvar.*

The *kuṛavās* divided into a number of branches are described to be living in the Travancore region (Kerala)[113]. *Iṭaiyans* are reported to be living in the Coimbatore region which constituted one of the *mullaitinai* of the early historic period. Some of the *Kuṛumba* or *Kuṛumaṉ* were shepherds and are found in the Nilgiri hills, Wynad (in Kerala) and Nilambur-Attipadi hills in Malabar[114].

The *Kaḷḷar* are now said to be living in the districts of Tanjore, Tiruchirappalli, Madurai and Pudukottai[115]. The *Maṛavaṇs* are found in the Madurai and Tirunelveli districts where "they occupy the tracts bordering on the coast from Cape Comorin to the northern limits of the Ramnad zemindari"[116]. It is appropriate to note that some of the areas in the districts of Ramnathapuram where the *maṛavar* live even now were part of the *pālai* zones where the *maṛavar* would have lived in the early historical period. *Vēṭṭuvaṇs* live in the districts of Salem, Coimbatore and Madurai as well as in Malabar (Kerala)[117]. Thus we notice the *paratavar* also survive today[118] as one of the important *śūdra* castes.

Thus we notice remnants of early historical clan or ethnic groups living in certain areas of Tamil Nadu and Kerala which formed part of ancient Tamilakam. The *eyiṉar* and *umaṇar* do not exist today. The agriculturists who are now known as *vēḷālar* have been referred to as *vēḷalar* in the early medieval records, while in the *Caṅkam* texts[119] the term occurs only in the *Tolkāppiyam Porulatikāram* as a generic term.

All these clan groups were bound by ties of kinship which is also reflected in the production relations[120]. The stock expression *Ilaiyarum, Mutiyarum, Kiḷai* appear in the poems to denote the labour processes of any *tiṇai* or any lineage[121]. While mutiyar denoted the elders, *iḷaiyar* the youngsters, *kiḷai* denoted the other kin members, (*kiḷai* literally means a branch[122]). Could *iḷaiyar* and *mutiyar* correspond to junior and senior members of a lineage? Most of the production process was shared by the kin members in the different eco-zones and even in *marutam* the services of those outside the clan lineage were generally not required for agricultural operations. The family/extended family was the unit of labour. Essentially, the kin groups functioned in a complex system of co-operation. It is only when land was granted to groups such as *maṛavar* and *antaṇar* (*brāhmaṇās*) that the householding economy[123] appeared and the extended family may have employed labour to cultivate their lands. By doing so they would have transcended kinship ties, leading to differentiation within the clan or lineage. The term *kuṭi* is used in the texts to denote clan as well as the place of residence. Small settlements of *maṛavar,* hunters and cowherds are referred to as *ciṛukuṭi*[124].

The kinship basis of organisation is also reflected in the terms used for the kin in early Tamil texts. Generally, the terms used for the kin in early Tamil texts are the father (*tantai*), mother (*tāy or aṉṉai*) and the brothers (*taṉṉaiyar, taṉṉaimār, taṉṉaiyum and eṉṉaiyar*). In some instances, a girl's husband (*kāṇavaṉ*) son (*makaṉ*) and children (*cirār*) are mentioned. The foster mother (*cevilittāy*), the female companion of the heroine (*tōḻi*) also figure in the poems though one does not know whether they were actually kin members. Normally it is the girl's (heroine of the poems) relatives such as father, mother, brothers, etc. who are referred to in the context of a love/war situation involving the girl. It is interesting to note that the *Tolkāppiyam* lays down that only mother, foster mother (both in certain cases) and *tōḻi* could speak in the poems and not the father or brothers[125]. George Hart is of the view that other relatives of the woman are not mentioned as they were "not part of the unit which is created by the union of man and woman[126]". There do not seem to be any terms to denote the grandparents, uncles, aunts ot cousins in the texts. Normally, the term *kiḷai* was used to denote the kin of the social groups discussed above and the term *okkar* was used in the context of the relative of the bards and poets.

The early Tamils recognised the natural coming together of a man and woman in all the eco-zones especially the *kuriñci* and therefore, their conception of marriage was very simple. In other words, free mixing was prevalent and the marriage celebrations/rituals do not seem to have been formalised or systematised. With the exception of the *marutam* there is no influence of the brahmanical or dharmasastraic forms of marriage even in the *marutam* and *neytal*, the most advanced *tiṇais* in the early Tamil texts.

Scholars like George Hart try to see the cross cousin form of marriage prevalent in Tamilakam possibly on account of the importance given to kinship in those times. Marriages in the period of the anthologies could have been between kin members or between strangers. An important feature of the kinship system of the Dravidians was cross cousin marriage[127]. This is linked up by Hart with the sacred power of a woman and the necessity to keep that power under control[128]. Hart traces the origins of such ideas concerning women to the "megalithic Dravidian society" which flourished in the Deccan in the latter part of the first millennium B.C. Further he points that "several elements like woman's chastity as a source of power for her husband, sati, widow asceticism, impurity during menstrual periods and others relating to women came from this culture. Significantly, Hart noted that the cross cousin marriage is found in parts of India where the megalithic culture flourished[129].

Hart is of the view that the woman is thought to be possessed by a sacred force (*aṇaṅku*). This force has to be kept under control and if not kept under control it would be dangerous. Hence, great restraint has to be practised by the woman in controlling her sacred power to maintain harmony of her family (of her kin as well as her husband and son). So the woman had to maintain her chastity and marry within her kin. Therefore, attempts were made by her brothers and fathers to keep her within the family so that they could retain the benefit of her power. As mentioned earlier this is linked with the concept of cross cousin marrige. By marrying her cross cousin the woman's beneficial power would be within the kin as the cross cousin would already have been part of the protective relationships as brothers[130].

Hart has laid inordinate emphasis on the sacred powers of a woman[131]. A poem of the *kuṟuntokai* is construed by him to show marriage between kin (i.e. between cross cousins) as well as marriage between strangers[132]. There are no direct or expilicit references to cross cousin marriage in early Tamil literature. Also, we do not come across references to attempts (with the exception of one poem) made by brothers or fathers of the girl to get her married within the kin. Wherever the brothers are referred to in the poems they are mentioned as warriors fighting wars[133] and not as trying to control the sister's (woman's) marriage. In one instance the father of the woman is described to be reluctant to get his daughter married to anybody who asks for her hand[134]. In fact there are no direct references to either cross cousin marriage or marriage between strangers. Marriages to strangers would have implied the breaking up of kin ties, and hence, kinship factor would have determined the Dravidian cross-cousin marriages althought Hart states that it would imply the breaking up of the protective relationship between man and woman.

Early Tamil poems describe the love between hero and heroine (could have been kin or strangers) which may have ended in marriage and to the practice of arranged marriages and where suitors came to see the girl. Consent of the girls parents was necessary for marriage. In some cases, the poems of the *pālai* situation refer to elopment of the heroine with the hero when there was no other alternative or choice. Poems are also silent on the aspect of dowry but some of them mention a bride price[135]. Perhaps the hero's journey to acquire wealth which is a theme of some poems could have been to pay for the bride price. One poem mentions that the father will not get his daughter married even if he received wealth equal to the city of Muciṟi[136]. Bride price seems to be a feature of the *paraiyaṉs* [137] and other low caste communities even today.

We get a good idea of the marriage ceremony from two poems of the *Akanāṉūṟū*. Poem 86 says (At dawn), When the curved white moon was not affected by inauspicious planets... four girls with pure bangles, whose spotted stomachs have given birth to sons said together, "May you have love so that you care for the man you receive (as husband), and so that you, not slipping from chastity, are a help to him. After that, the guests take flowers and rice, dip them in water (according to the modern commentary, turmeric water) and throw them at the bride so that they adhere to her hair" In *Akanāṉūṟū* 136 we are told that:

"With unrestrained generosity they honored eminet guests giving them white rice flowing with ghee and full of faultless meat

As omens fell together favourably as the vast sky shone with clear light and as there was an unjeopardised conjunction of the moon and cakatam (the wagon, a constellation) they readied the marriage house and worshipped the god

Then, as the great kettle drum roared with the loud marriage drum and the girls who had washed her for marriage looked unwinking with their flower eyes and then quickly hid themselves, her relatives put on her a white thread with fragrant cool buds brought forth in the first rain by roaring clouds from arukai a tuber with black petals like polished sapphires spread in valleys where alomost grown calves graze on the forked, dull backed leaves of soft flowered vakai

And they made her resplendent with pure garments.

Then they came arousing my desire and they gave her to me lovely with ornaments and wiped off her to me lovely with ornaments and wiped off her sweat in that pandal where the sound of marriage was like rain"

It is interesting to note that both these poems describe the marriage cermony in the *marutam tiṇai*. Could it be suggested that some sort of formal procedures of marriage existed only in the *marutam tiṇai* and not in the others where free mixing was prevalent?

Another cermony mentioned was the anklet ceremony which preceded a wedding. It appears that the girls' anklets would be taken off before marriage possibly at the girl's house[138].

It is interesting and important to note that in the above descriptions there is no circumambulation of the fire and no presence of brahmans chanting *mantras*. Both these two features are noticeable in the *Cilappatikāram*.

By the time of the *Tolkāppiyam* (i.e. the *Porulatikāram*) marriage seems to have been institutionalised and systematised. Marriage rituals were created by the *Aiyar* (Aryans?, *Brāhmaṇās?*) when dishonesty and insincerity prevailed[139]. Further the influence of the Dharmasastraic forms is also evident from a *sūtra* of the *Tolkāppiyam, (Porulātikaram)* which mentions eight forms of marriage[140]. Comnenting on the *sūtra* Nacciṇārkkiṇiyar lists the eight forms of marriage as *piramam, pracapatyam, aritam, teyvam, acuram, rakcacam, paicacam and kāntarvam.* Out of these eight forms the *Kāntarvam* could have been the widely prevalent form in ancient Tamil country on account of free mixing between men and women.

II. ECONOMIC DIVERSITY AND PROFESSIONAL FROUPS:

(a) Craft Groups

Kinship did nor preclude the development of craft specialisation however in the fields of metal working, weaving, pottery etc[141] although craft specialisation was at a tudimentary level.

Kollar is the name generally used for blacksmiths/iron smiths. They are usually referred to in the poems in the *marutam tiṇai.* The blacksmith is referred to in the early texts quite frequently along with the techniques employed in shaping iron/steel. His workshop was called *kolturai* or *ulaikkalam.*[142] He is said to have used bellows to heat the metal and the pincers[143].

In a society dominated by war ideology and heroism, the function of the blacksmith was to make weapons of iron like spears and axes or sharpen arrows for the ruling lineages, warriors and rulers[144]. Besides, they also helped other social groups by making sharp hooks for the fisherman[145] or assisting the farmers in tilling operations[146]. A rich repertoire of iron objects have been found in the megalithic sites. The role of the blacksmith in a society dominated by warfare may thus have been a significant one. One is, however not sure about whether they were itinerant blacksmiths. The terms *kammiyaṇkammiyar* seems to have denoted the artisans in general. In the poems they are described in various capacities as workers in copper or bronze[147], weavers, carpenters, ship builders and goldsmiths.

Weaving must have been an important occupation and weavers must have woven cloth for internal consumption as well as for export, The *Arthaśāstra* refers to cotton fabrics from Madura[148] and the author of the *Periplus*[149] refer to Argaritic muslins (from Uṛaiyūr) which constituted one of the important items of export. Besides, the *Porunāṛāṛruppaṭai* refers to cotton cloth resembling the slough of a snake[150]. Archaeological evidence, however, is quite meagre on the production of textiles.

Exacavation at Uṛaiyūr and Arikamedu have yielded dyieng vats though Madurai and Kāñci, the principal centres of textiles have not yielded similar archaeological evidence. Spindle whorls were excavated from Kunnattur and Odugattur which are mainly megalithic sites and also from some megalithic and early historical sites such as Tirukkampuliyur and Kodumanal. At Kodumanal the spindle whorls noticed were made of iron. A bunch of silk threads was reported at Tirukkampuliyur, piece(s) of cloth are reported also from Kodumanal and traces of cloth were found on several bronze objects at Adichannallur.

The *kammiyar* are frequently described as goldsmiths and jewellers making beautiful ornaments[151]. Nothing much is known about the workshop of the goldsmith or the type of tools he used. Goldsmithy of those times was supposed to be a delicate fine work as evident from the term which conveys the above meaning (*Ñuṇviṇai*[152]). Epigraphic evidence attests to the importance of goldsmiths. Tamil Brahmi inscriptions mention the *poṉkolavaṉ*[153] (goldsmith) *poṉvāṇikaṉ*[154] (gold merchant) besides a lapidary[155]. Gold could have been procured from the Kolar hill regions in Karnataka as that region is reputed for its goldmines. These goldsmiths must have essentially catered to the urban, and ruling elite and must have been independent specialists not under the control of any one or patronised by the ruling authority. Articles of gold were redistributed gifts to bards and poets by chieftains. Texts also mention the accumulation of gold in the hands of chieftains. The *ton mutir veḷir*[156] are said to have hid their gold in mount Pali[157]. Others like Naṉṉaṉ Veṇmaṉ[158] and Titiyaṉ[159] are described to have possessed gold and ornaments of gold.

There are references to the *taccaṉ* or carpenter who was essentially involved in making chariots and wheels with spokes attached to chariots[160] presumably for chieftains and kings. Only in one instance in the carpenter indirectly mentioned to be making plough and plough shares[161]. An inscription from Mamantur describes the *taccaṉ* as a stone mason[162] who in later times came to be specified as *kal taccaṉ*. The carpenters must have catered essentially to the ruling elite. Specialisation in the field of pottery was another feature. The potter referred to as *vēṭko* or *kalañcey kōvaṉ* in the texts made vessels (*kalam*) as well as urns for burials mostly for domestic consumption[163].

There were poets who belonged to artisan/craftsman groups by profession as attested by the poems. At times the place of residence and the nature of craft is indicated in their names. (Vide Appendix 4).

All these specialists seemed to have worked independently without being attached to any ruling authority or being dependent on any particular patron or group of patrons[164]. Most of the articles except for cloth was geared for domestic consumption.

There is no clear evidence of special relationship or economic interdependence between craftsmen and traders as many producers of goods were themselves sellers or traders.

However, an exception could be made in the case of *aṟuvai vaṇikaṉ* who seems to be a specialised trader because textile was an item of export. Royal control of production of commodities was absent with the exception of pearls. The Pāṇṭiyās exercised control over the pearl fisheries worked by condemned criminals in the Gulf of Mannar[165].

(b) *Traders and Merchants*

Expansion of trading activities within the region led to the growth of a mercantile community. the early Tamil poems refer to *umaṇar, paratavaṛ, vampalar, vaṇikar, vilaiñar and pakarnar*[166] mostly in the context of the *marutam* and *neytal tiṇais*. The *paratavar* were one of the most important of the mercantile groups. The *umaṇar* were a category of itinerant traders who travelled long distances to sell salt in the hinterlands. Of the *umaṇar* and *vampalar* who may have been traders, the *Perumpāṇāṛṛuppaṭai* states:

> "The men that trade in salt adorned with wreaths of woven leaves with large, fine shoulders strong. Andpowerful viry frames protect the cart By walking by the side of bulls well hitched. The small-hold yoke.
>
> They take with them spare bulls
>
> And go through hamlets reached by lengthy roads Announcing the sale of salt. Bold strangers sell
>
> To those who rest from the jurney of a day
>
> Rare, useful things obtained from hills and seas Their chests are marked with wounds received
>
> In fights from arrows sharp. They wear tight clothes
>
> To which are swords attached. Their shoulders strong
>
> Are wide, and bear the cruel bow. They are Like the god of death they strongly wield the spear.
>
> They wear white-handled shining swords that look
>
> Like snakes that crawl on hills. Hung on their sides
>
> By ribbons striped. They wear shoes on their feet
>
> To guard their soles, and on their bodies, coats
>
> The erect-eared ass that has a scarred, strong back
>
> Which bears the burden of a pepper bale
>
> That looks like a large jackfruit with scanty pulps
>
> Is driven on wide paths"[167].
>
> There were also peddlars (*tiri vilaiñar*) who operated in the urban centres

moving from house to house selling goods. Thus the *Maturaikkāñci* refers to

"Old dames who tie their well combed hair go about from house to house with rare attractive things,

and fragrant blooms in large well made trays"[168]

Besides these there were *pakarnar* who seem to have been traders selling goods in the market places (*ankaṭis*). About the *pakarnar* of Madurai we are told that:

"They buy the product of the hills, the plains

And the sea and other things of wealthy lands

Games, pearls and gold and trade in them"[169]

This is interesting as the *pakarnar* seem to have moved from one zone to another for procuring goods. Unlike the peddlars/ hawkers, the *pakarnar* must have been formally organised in order to procure goods from various zones. The peddlars/ hawkers must have sold mostly simple commodities/ articles of daily subsistence while the *pakarnar* may have sold luxury goods like pearls, gems and gold in addition to daily necessities. Moreover, they seem to have sold goods from a fixed centre at the market place.

Commercial activities had increased to such an extent that the *Maturaikkāñci* refers to specialist traders selling particular wares in the urban centres at the market places. These were *Pūviṇar* (sellers of flowers), *kotaiyar* (sellers of garlands), *cuṇṇattar* (sellers of aromatic powders probably used in bathing), *ilaiyiṇar* (Seller of betel leaves and arecanuts) koṭu euṭṭu-nūṟṟinar (sellers of lime), *kaṭainar* (sellers of conch bangles), *maṇi kuyiṇar* (those who made jewellery from gems), *poṇ-cūṭar-Iḷai puṇainar* (goldsmith who made jewellery), *Kaliṅkampakarnar* (traders in Kalinkam fabric from Kalinga-orissa), *vampuniṛaimuṭinar* (makers and sellers of fine cloths) and *cempuniṛaikoṇmarum* (manufacturers of copper articles[170]). From this it is apparent that the manufacturer of the product was also the seller[171].

Among the various groups the specialist merchants involved in trading activities seem to have functioned in commercial centres which had market places. About the evening bazar (*ālaṅkāṭi*) at Madurai the text *Maturaikkāñci* furnishes the following information

"The bustle of the evening market place

Sounds like the din heard in a seaport town

To which are brought so many diverse goods

By merchants who rare jewels took for sale

To distant countries wide, and now return

In vessels large that do at flood time come

From the deep ill smelling sea into
shallows dark At Midnight"[172]

The markets/market places were a feature of the commercial centres located in *marutam* and *neytal tiṇais*. In the *tiṇais* barter prevailed where the residing communities exchanged their articles with others. Presence of the mercantile community or the market place is not attested to in these areas. Merchants seem to have lived in spacious streets in the urban centres especially Pukār. This also reflected in the later epic *Cilappatikāram*.

Epigraphic evidence attests to merchants and traders who were prosperous enough to make donations of caves and beds to monks of heterodox sects. Those who made such donations include Viyakaṉ Kaṇatikaṉ - the *upuvāṇikan*[173] (salt merchant), Neṭumal (i) aṉ *pāṇitavāṇikaṉ* (sugar merchant[174]) Elacantaṉ—krṭunanikaṉ (iron merchant). Eḷa(v)a Aṭaṉ *-aṟuvai-vaṇikan* (cloth merchant[176]), Vēni Ātaṉ - Vanikan[177] (merchant) Atti-*poṉvāṇikaṉ* (gold merchant)[178], Tēvaṉ cāttaṉ *-maniyvannakkan* (dealer in precious stones/lapidary[179]).

In contrast to the widely prevalent guild system rampant in North India and Western Deccan, we find that there are very few references to guilds or guild organisations in the Tamil country[180]. They early Tamil inscriptions from Mankulam refer to donations by the *nigama* (mercantile guilds) of Tiruvellarai and to a Kāviti (a guild chief[181]). Early Tamil poems refer to salt sellers *(umaṇar)* travelling in caravans to the interior areas (*cāttu-* derved from Sarthavaha?) which we have mentioned earlier. The title Mācattuvan of Kōvalaṉ's (hero of the epic *Cilappatikāram*) father itself suggests that he was a sarthavaha or caravan leader. This is the only indication we have to the organisation of traders into some sort of formal body.

Since we have very little information on the guilds in Tamilakam it is difficult to comment on their functions and their nature. The relationship between the merchants and the ruling authoriry is not clear. However, the situation in contemporary Deccan was different where close ties existed between the ruling elite, merchants and the Buddhist order[182]. In Tamilakam individual merchants made donations to Jain and Buddhist monks. members of the ruling families also donated caves to the members of the 'heterodox' sects i.e. Buddhism and Jainism[183]. Merchants and huseholders of Tamil origin are also mentioned in the epigraphic records of Sri Lanka and vice versa. The inscriptions found in Periya-Puliyan Kulama in Vavuniya district in Sri Lanka record the donations of a Buddhist Cave and a flight of steps by Visakha, a householder and merchant from Tamil country[184]. An inscription of 1st-2nd century A.D. from Tirupparaṅkuṉṟam cave outside Madurai refers to a householder probably a merchant from Sri Lanka making a donation[185]. Another inscription from Muttuppatti mentions one Caiy-aḷaṉ a person of Ceylonese origin[186].

The presence of merchant/trading groups in ports and urban centres and the mention of the *vaṇikan* in the Tamil Brahmi records suggest the emergence of this community in the urban centres as part of the affluent elite of the urban centres. The Tolkāppiyam also takes cognisance of this fact and includes them as the third category under the (*vaicikaṉ*) under the four fold classificatory scheme[187]. It seems relevant to note that some of the poets of the anthologies belonged to the mercantile community. Their names invariably comprise the major commercial centres as a prefix and the nature of their trade (vide appendix 5).

One of the important consequences of Tamilakam's transmarine commerce with the Roman West[188] was the arrival of merchants (*Yavaṉās*) from the West in the commerical centres. The term *Yavaṉa* derived from Ionia (for Ionian = Greeks) also came to refer to anyone coming from the west i.e. Mediterranean and West Asian origin. References to the Yavaṉa merchants in the *Caṅkam* poems[189] occur in the *marutam* and *neytal* context. The *yavaṉās* could have comprised merchants and others (probably boatmen) who travelled in the ships with them. Poems record that the *yavaṉās* came with gold and wine in their ships and returned with pepper and visited the port of Muciṟi frequently[190]. Lamps of fine workmanship was another item brought by them[191]. Some of the *yavaṉās* were enlisted into service and served as bodyguards to rulers[192] and palace guards[193] at night possibly on account of their fearsome looks and physical prowess.

The *yavaṉās* had their settlements at the ports of the region namely Kāveripaṭṭ iṉam, Arikamedu, Alagankulam and Muciṟi, and they visited the ports frequently. Roman antiquities like pottery, coins have been recovered from the excavations conducted at these sites.

The *Paṭṭinappālai* mentions that in the port of Pukār (Kāveripaṭṭiṉam) were seen

> "people speaking diverse tongues that come from great and foreign homes
> Mix freely in friendly terms with those
> who occupy this glorious town"[194].

One can infer from the above descriptions that *yavaṉās* would have been one of the groups which would have settled here. This diversity of the population at Pukar is also reflected in the *Cilappatikāram* as we shall see later. In fact there is a settlement known as Veḷlaiyaniruppu (literally the abode of white men), a site near the present day Kāveripaṭṭinam. However, excavations at this site have not revealed any large scale settlement but only show a deposit going back to the 9th century A.D.[195]. The port of Kāvērippaṭṭiṉam would have been frequented often by the foreign merchants on account of its strategic location at the mouth of the river Kāveri. The classical writings (foreign accounts) have classified it as a market town and an emporium[196]. At Kiḷaiyur (another sector of Pukār) a wharf excavated[197] also lends credence to Pukār functioning as an important port. Roman contact at this site is testified by the discovery of Rouletted ware at two sites around Kaveripaṭṭiṉam viz Manigramam and Pallavaneeswaram[198].

Arikamēdu is said to be Vīrai of the *Caṅkam* texts[199] and Poduca/ Podouke[200] of the Graeco-Roman texts. Extensive excavations carried out at this site have brought to light remains of an 'Indo Roman trading station[201]'. Excavations were conducted at two sectors here the northern and southern. Diggings in the northern sector have revealed remains of a warehouse, arretine and rouletted ware and amphorae while in the southern sector dyeing vats were exposed by the diggings[202]. On the basis of the structures and objects recoverd it can be suggested that the northern sector housed the *yavaṇās* or foreigners and the southern housed the local population. The textile 'industry' was also located in the southern sector.

Roman contact at Alagankulam (Unur-Marunkurpattinam of the *Caṅkam* texts) situated at the mouth of the Vaigi river (was it Perimoula the largest emporium mentioned by Pliny?[203]) is attested by the presence of the rouletted ware, amphorae and Roman coins (of the reigns of Valentine II - 383-95 A.D., Theodesius I (383-393 A.D.) and Arcadius (395-408 A.D.[204])

Settlements of the *yavaṇās* could have come up in Muciṟi (Muziris of the foreign accounts) on account of their frequent visits to this place for procuring pepper. A temple of Augustus was said to be built at Muziris[205]. Those *yavaṇās* coming initially as merchants/traders may have in course of time settled down at Muziris. Mention of a temple of Augustus indicates the presence of *yavaṇās* at Muziris.

Apart from this we have little information on the foreign merchants, their settlements and relationship with the local people/ruling elite. At this stage it would be useful to contrast Tamiḻakam with the situation in Western Deccan and north India. The *yavaṇās* ruling over western Deccan and north India, worshipped Brahmanical deities, adopted Buddhism or Jainism and indigenised their names i.e. bore Sanskrit names[206] and thereby acquired legitimation and acceptance. They also made donations on a large scale in western Deccan. It has been suggested that the donations made by the *yavaṇās* bearing Sanskritised names in Western Deccan may indicate that efforts were made by these 'foreigners' to be absorbed into indigenous social system[207]. These *yavaṇās* were brought into the cast ehierarchy and *yavaṇā* rulers in India were assigned a low *kṣatriya* status.

However, the influence of the *yavaṇās* over the native population in Tamiḻakam was minimal. None of them became rulers in Tamiḻakam unlike in the north or western India in the same period. They were not part of any social order as no efforts were made by them to indigenise. Only in one instance are the *yavaṇās* referred to as *milecca* and that too in the sense of an alien[208]. There are no donations by foreigners in Tamiḻakam with the exception of one where an inscription refers to an individual from "Īḻam donating a cave to Jain monks"[209]. Does such an absence of records of donations imply that the *yavaṇās* did feel the need to acquire legitimation and acceptance? The *yavaṇās* seem to have come to Tamiḻakam mainly for trading purposes as there was great demand for Roman wine, lamps and gold coins and a few of them, as we have seen, were employed by the ruling families as palace guards and bodyguards.

Hostility between the indigenous population and the foreigners is not attested in the records of this region.

Coins (indigenous and Roman[210]) would have been used by merchants and traders in transactions at the market place in the urban centres. It is interesting to note that early indigenous coins have been found in association with the Roman coins[211]. Perhaps these coin types were used by two categories of people, the foreign one by high level traders and the local coins of small value by common people presumably at places where markets existed. Coins may not have had a wide circlation among social groups dependent on hunting, plundering or stock rearing.

Early Tamil poems refer to *kāṇams* and *kācu* which were conferred as gifts to poets. The *Patiṟṟupattu* mentions that Aricilkiḻār received a gift of 900,000 (gold) *kāṇams* and Kākkaippāṭiṉiyār Nacceḷḷaiyār received 100,000 gold *kāṇams*[212]. Since no indigenous gold coins of the period have been discoverd could *kāṇams* conferred to bards taken to be Roman coins[213]?

Due to the ramification of trading activities urban enclaves developed in the *marutam* and *neytal*. In the urban centres heterogeneity in population and complexity in economic activities are indicated. One can get an idea of the port of Pukar i.e. the urban layout from the *Paṭṭinappālai*. On the shore of the port area were the King's warehouses which were guarded by the ruler's agents and the wharf front with pegs to which boats were tied. The fishermen's settlement or quarters (*puraccēri*) are found in the outskirts of Pukār probably near the seashore. The street of the merchants a *paḷḷi* (of Jains?) and the place where items like toddy, fish and meat were sold are referred to in the *Paṭṭinappālai*[214]. Besides, Pukār housed all the people speaking different languages[215].

One comes across a more detailed description of the lay out of Pukār in the *Cilappatikāram* thereby indicating its development into a big urban centre Although we do not have much information on the layout of other centres (ports and royal centres), we can presume that their spatial organisation was similar to that of Pukār.

III. PATRONAGE AND RECIPROCITY : THE BARDS AND POETS

There were certain groups of singers, dancers, bards and poets who appear to have been supported by the ruling elite or certain *tiṇai* inhabitants. In other words, they were non-producing groups. Groups such as the *pāṇar, viṟali, kōṭiyar, vayiriyar, pulavar* etc were associated with all the *tiṇais*. Some *pulavar,* however, belonged to different professional groups. Basically they were people wandering about in search of patrons who liberally showered them with gifts. Besides, there were others like the *iravalar* and *paricilar* who also visited the courts of king/chieftains and asked for gifts. Gifts given to these groups comprised food and luxury items such as gold, horses, chariots.

The *pāṇar* were bards who sang songs to the accompaniment of the *yāḻ*[216] (a type of lute). They played the *taṇṇumai* drum during the battle[217]. They are depicted in the poems to be travelling in search of patrons as their poverty made them do so. Normally a large body of kinsmen (*okkar*) accompanied them. In most cases they went to kings/chieftains' court and sang their praise[218]. For this they were given gifts in the form of flowers of gold[219], gold necklace[220] elephants, horses, chariots[221], toddy[222], food[223] and in one instance small settlements (*ciṟūr*[224]) from rulers as well as others. They also moaned the death of the patrons/chieftains[225].

In most of the *akam* poems they are depicted as messengers acting on behalf of the hero and the friends of the hero who mediated in the love affairs and domestic quarrels between the heroine and the hero[226]. The *Tolkāppiyam* categorises the *pānan* as a *vāyil*[227]- one who is attached to the hero or heroine or a spokesman.

Evidence suggests that these minstrels were wandering about from place to place in search of munificient patrons. Only one description in the *Maturaikkāñci* indicates that these minstrels probably lived in small settlements (*cēri*)[228] although it is not clear whether such *cēris* were located in the outskirts of cities, and hence indicate isolation from other social groups. The *pāṇaṉ* was however held in high esteem in the period of the early anthologies. Patronage and generosity towards them is highlighted in the *Caṅkam* poems especially of the *Puṟanāṉūṟū*. It is only by the early medieval times that word *pāṇaṉ* denoted a low caste[229]. By the time of the Āḻvār devotional poetry the *pāṇaṉ* was definitely looked down upon as a low caste. In most cases they were singers and messengers and appear not to have carried on other occupations. There is only one reference to a *pāṇaṉ* catching fish in *Akanāṉūṟū*[216].

The *Viṟaḷi/Viṟaliyar* were artists skilled in singing, dancing[230] and playing musical instruments[231].

The poverty of the *viṟaliyar* made them search for patrons mostly munificent rulers. They followed the *pāṇaṉs* in search of such patrons[232]. A special theme in the *Puṟanāṉūṟū* known as *Viṟaliāṟṟuppaṭai* directs the *viṟali* to a patron[233]. In *Puṟanāṉūṟū* 105.1 the *viṟali* asked to go to the court of chieftain Pārivēl so that she would get jewels and gifts. Another poem states that if the *viṟaliyar* palying *yāḻ* went dancing and singing/Pāri would even give away his land (*nāṭu*) and hill[234]. Gifts to the *Viṟaliyar* include flowers of gold[235]; ornaments and garlands of gold, pearl[236], female elephants[237], horses and gold chariots[238].

However, in one song they are mentioned in an unusal capacity. Here the smiling ornamented *Viṟaliyar* who arrange their hair in five different ways are asked by the king to help in cooking food for people to be fed[239]. In all the above mentioned instances the *viṟaliyar* are described in a non-religious context. Mention is made of the *viṟaliyar* in the *Malaipaṭukaṭām* in a different context[240] associated with the worship of a deity and this seems to be an invocation before singing. They had to praise/pay obeisance to God (*kaṭavuḷ* though it is not clear which one) in accordance with established music rules before singing.

By the time of the *Paripāṭal* (5th-6th centuries A.D.) the *viṟaliyar* seem to have been entrusted with other duties. The colophon to *Paripāṭal* gives an indication of their role as a messenger on behalf of the hero, a role which the *pāṇaṉ* performed. There are hardly any and references to the *Viṟaliyar* in their capacities as singers and dancers in the *Kalittokai* and *Paripāṭal*. The *iyavar*[241] were another group of musicians who played some muscial instruments[242] made of bamboo[243]. Two poems describe the *iyavar* playing the instruments in the battlefield. One poem states that the *iyavar* played the *āmpal paṇ* on the flute when the Cēra ruler Utiyaṉ went to fight[244]. Another mentions that the soldiers and kings rushed forward in the battlefield when the *Iyavar* played musical instruments[245]. They must have inspired warriors to fight in the battlefield. In return they may have been served well fermented toddy[246] along with other warriors.

Groups like *Kōṭiyar and vayiriyar*[247] were those who sang, danced, acted and played musical instruments. Tamil texts refer to them synonymously with the *kūttar*. The *kōṭiyar* are described to be playing some sort of trumpet[248] and drum[249]. They are said to have participated in *viḻās*[250]. Like all other bards, they traversed long distances in search of patrons along with their retinue of relatives (*okkar*[251]). The lays of the *Pattuppāṭṭu* give us some details of the patronage granted to the *kōṭiyar* by chieftains[252]. They were given gifts by chieftain Ōri[253]. The *vayiriyar* like the *kōtiyar* played drums[254], (probably *paṟai*) the *tivaviṉ yāḻ*[255] and other instruments apart from singing and dancing[256]. They also went to munificent patrons who distributed gifts generously[257]. *Puṟanāṉūṟū* 164 praises chieftain Kumaṇaṉ for removing the poverty of these *Vayiriyar*. The *Vayiriyar* are said to have been given gold by the Pāṇṭiyaṉ king Kuṭumi[258] and horses, (used by warriors wielding the sword or spear) chariots and ornaments by the Cēra king Cēlvakkaṭuṅkō Vāḻiyātaṉ[259] as mentioned in the colophon of the text.

Besides the hunger of the relatives (*okkar*) of the *vaiyiriyar* was totally wiped out. Toddy was another item served to these *vayiriyar*[260]. The *Maturaikkāñci* refers to these *vayiriyar* as dancers who danced in the festival and were showered gifts by the Pāṇṭiyaṉ ruler[261]. Even in the *Paripāṭal* the *vayiriyar* (whose songs are faultless) were stated to be beneficiaries of gifts from the Pāṇṭiyaṉ ruler[262].

There were other groups like *āṭunar/āṭuvar, āṭumakaḷ and pāṭunar* (singers and dancers) who like all others frequented the court of kings[263]. The *āṭumakaḷ* seems to have been an acrobat as she is mentioned to be walking on a twisted rope when the musical instruments were played. The *āṭunar* and *pāṭunar* got gifts from kings and chieftains like Kōpperuñ Cōḻan and Āy Aṇṭiran[264]. It is difficult to establish the status of these singers and dancers and their relationship (if any) with others like *pāṇar, kūttar* etc who also sang and danced.

By the time of the *Paripāṭal*, there seems to have been a change in the context of their role as singers and dancers. In the *Paripāṭal* they are mentioned to be singing at the shrine of Paraṅkuṉṟam[265]. So the locale shifted from the court of the chieftain to the shrine/temple when the temple became an important institution.

There were certain other groups of drummers mentioned in the texts, who do not seem to be of the same category as the singers and drummers.

The *kiṇaiyaṉ* was one who played the *kiṇai* drum (also known as *taṭāri*) and *parai* generally during battles. They were also recepients of gifts from kings which mainly comprised food[266]. A reference to the *kiṇaiyaṉ* (in the *Puṟanāṉūṟu* 379) going to the king's place in the early hour of the morning suggests an association with the ruler and the court.

The *Akavunar*[267] also played the *kiṇai* drum though we do not know the relationship they had with the *kiṇaiyaṉs*. Normally these people are associated with prophesies and foretelling the future[268].

Another drumming group was that of the *tuṭiyaṉs* who beat the *tuṭi* drum to announce a battle or during battle[269]. Like other groups the *tuṭiyaṉ* must have gone to persons who gave them gifts[270]. The *tuṭiyaṉ* is generally mentioned as low born *iḻiciṉaṉ*[271].

The *iravalar/ irappōr/ iravaṉ mākkaḷ* were generally those who begged or asked for alms[272]. They do not seem to have had any talent in either singing glories of the ruling elite or dancing.

Asking for alms/begging seemed to be their way of life. They are also portrayed in the poems as people who travelled to the courts of chieftains. *Puṟanāṉūṟū* 203:12 mentions that even if there was poverty, famine etc the Cōḷa ruler Iḷañcēticeṉṉi gave to people who asked even if they had taken enough from him on previous occasions. Āy Aṇṭiraṉ is said to have given well built chariots to those who asked[273]. In some cases the chiefs/kings offered protection to those people by acting as a *puravalar* (protector) and prevented them from going away from their place by giving good food etc[274]. When the person (protector) died his praise was sung. Some poets advocate the giving of alms by patrons. In *Puṟanāṉūṟū* 359 Aṇṭuvan Kīraṉ is asked by the poet (Kāvaṭṭ aṉār) to give golden decorated horse drawn chariots to those who ask (*Iravalar*) and thereby earn their praise.

They got gold jewels and fragrant wine of the *yavaṉās* served by ornamented girls[275]. Another poem conveys that a chieftain gave *varaku* and *tiṉai* to those who asked even when the stocks were almost depleted[276].

In this context, it may be interesting to note that chieftain ruled over a non-*marutam* land most probably *mullai* as the fact that rice is not cultivated in that region is mentioned. Such chieftains ruling over *vaṉpulam* lands were also as generous as their counterparts ruling over *meṉpulam.*

In addition to all these groups there were poets (*pulavar*[277]) who sought patronage and gifts (*paricilar*) in return for singing the glory of the patrons. The *pulavars,* unlike the bards (*pāṇaṉ* and others), were of high caste according to Hart[278]. These *pulavars* adopted the bardic traditions when they eulogised the patrons/rulers. In addition to this, Hart states that these poems of the *pulavar* (who were both men and women) modelled these composition on those of the illiterate and low class performers particularly the *pāṇaṉs*. Like the bards, they went about in search of patrons whose praise they sung. George Hart is of the view that the anthologies comprised poems of the *pulavaṉs* which were collected together[279]. Some of these *pulavar* were rulers (like Ollaiyurtanta Pūtappāṇṭiyaṉ, Nalaṅkiḷḷi, Kulamuṟṟattuttuñciya Kiḷḷi Vaḷavaṉ etc.) while others like Kapilar, Māmūlaṉār, Peruṅkaucikanār etc. were *antaṇar* (*brāhmaṇās*) and were held in high esteem by the kings. On the death of Pāri (a chieftain) his friend Kapilar (the *antaṇaṉ pulavan*-brahmana poet) took the responsibility of looking after Pāri's daughters and made attempts to get them married. For this purpose he went to the court of chieftain like Irunkōvēḷ and Viccikkō[280]. It appears that the status of the *pulavaṉ* was higher than that of the *pāṇaṉ* (minstrel).

Quite a few poems of the *Puṟanāṉūṟū* mention the poets going to chieftains/ kings. *Puṟanāṉūṟū* 120 and 107 sing the praise of Pari. The *Pulavar* praise Pāri for his generosity and principles. Poet Uṟaiyūr Ēṇicceri Mutamōciyār states in *Puṟanāṉūṟū* 375 that Āy Antiran is the resort of poets. In *Puṟanāṉūṟū* 27 the poet Uraiyur Mutukaṇṇaṉ Cāttaṉār praises the Cōḷa king Nalaṅkiḷḷi by stating that there are only a few kings with name and fame and the rest just live and die. The kings also did certain deeds or won battles in order to prove their generosity and valour to earn recognition from the poets. In *Puṟanāṉūṟū* 72 the Pāṇṭiyaṉ king Talaiyālāṅkaṉattu Cēru Veṉṟa Netuñceḻiyaṉ states that the academy of poets headed by Maṅkuṭi Marutaṉ need not sing his glory. if he did not defeat in the battlefield those kings who spoke mean words of him.

In *Puṟanāṉūṟū* 12:1-3 poet Nettimaiyar says that the poets were honoured and made to sit on the decorated chariots along with elephants. One epoem shows how the chieftain Malaiyamāṉ Tirumuṭikkāri knew how to differentiate the poets and treated them accordingly instead of treating everybody alike.

The respect shown to poets is evident from a poem of the *Puṟanāṉūṟū*. The poem states that the poet slept on the *muracu* (drum) of a chieftain. Instead of being angry with the poet for this act of sacrifice, the chieftain began to fan the poet.

The poets seem to have had close personal relationships with their patrons. They lamented the death of their patrons. *Puṟanāṉūṟū* 240: 12-15 mentions how many poets with their relatives sought the patronage of Āy Aṇṭiraṉ and only on his death left his court to search of another benefactor. In another poem the poet Aiyur Muṭavaṉār asks a potter on the death of king Kiḷḷivaḷavaṉ whether he could make an urn (*tāḻi*) out of the wheel of the world with the mud of the Meru moun tain which can be sung by the *pulavar*[281]. Poetess Auvaiyar on the death of Atiyamāṉ Neṭumāṉ Añci sings that the spear which killed Atiyamāṉ left the learned poets speechless[282].

The fame of the king (*pukaḻ*) lived beyond his death in the songs of the poet. This fame was determined by the poet. In Puram 282 poet Cēramāṉ Pālaipaṭiya Peruṅkaṭ uṅkō praises the valour of a warrior/ hero and states that even though he is dead and his body is cut into pices he lives in the poems recited by the poets.

Like the *pulavar* the *paricilar*[283] were generally poets who went to kings/chieftains in search of gifts. In one of the poems the poet on hearing the death of chieftain Vēl Evvi sang the glory of this chieftain who gave big legged elephants without counting[284]. A poet Taṅkar Porkilloṇār mentions that a chieftain entertained him and later gave as gifts gold coverings of the elephants killed in battle[285]. When the poet Peruntalai Cittiraṉār met the chieftain Kumaṇaṉ who he had nothing to give to the poet asked the poet to behead him and take the head to his brother so that he could get the gift which the brother had announced as reward for killing Kumaṇaṉ[286].

There are a few poems which describe the delying of the gift to the poet by the king/chieftains in order to detain the poets at their courts for a longer time[287]. Some of the *paricilar* could have also been a high status group.

Thus we notice that most of the references to the *pulavar/paricilar* occur in the *Puṟanāṉūṟū* as this text on war and heroism has eulogies on kings/chieftains, Patronage and generosity to the poets and bards by the rulers seems to be crucial to the legitimisation of their rule[288]. Moreover their fame depended on the eulogies sung by these poets and as David Shulman states these kings were as dependent on the *pulavar* as the *pulavar* were on them[289]. The patron poet relationship was an important feature of those times.

FOOTNOTES

1. S. Seneviratne "Pre state to state societies, Transformation in the Political Ecology of South India with special reference to Tamil Nadu." Paper presented at the seminar on *The State in pre-colonial South India,* Jawharlal Nehru University New Delhi 1989.
2. Relation between the physical environment and human activities was taken note of by Daryll Forde to study the various communities ranging from food gatherers, cultivators and pastoral nomads in different regions. In other words, the relations between habitat, economy and society were explored in his book *Habitat, Economy and Society,* London, 1971 (Rp.).
3. *Tamil Lexicon P.* 1046
   Tamil Lexicon P. 1134.
4. *Aiṅkuṟuṇūṟu* 298:2 ; *Naṟṟiṇai* 64.4 :
   Kuṟuntokai 339 : 3 At times they are referred to as *kunṟakuṟavaṉ.*
5. *Kuṟuntokai* 339:3; *Naṟṟiṇai* 5:3 ; 64:4;
   Akanāṉūṟu 12:9 - 10.
6. *Kuṟuntokai* 208:3; 95:3;
   Akanāṉūṟu 52:3; 78:7.
7. *Aiṅkuṟuṇūṟu* 298:2; 277:1.
8. *Aiṅkuṟuṇūṟu* 252:1; *Akanāṉūṟu* 12:9 - 10.
9. *Akanāṉūṟu* 132:7 ; 182:6 ; *Naṟṟiṇai* 85:9; *Kuruntokai* 272.

10. *Akanāṉūṟu* 322:12.
11. *Akanāṉūṟu* 140:11; *Naṟṟiṇai* 209:2; *Puranāṉūṟu* 231:1.
12. *Aiṅkuṟunūṟu* 284:2; *Kuṟuntokai* 82:4; *Naṟṟiṇai* 44:8; 209:2; 373:3; *Puṟanāṉūṟu* 168:5.
13. *Aiṅkuṟunūṟu* 281:3 ; 282:2 ; 288:3 ; 290:3 ; 296:1 ; *Akanāṉūṟu* 188:13-14; *Kuṟuntokai* 214:3; 360:6; *Naṟṟiṇai* 22:1; 102:8; 13:4; 204:11; 306:3.
14. *Kuṟuntokai* 346:2; *Naṟṟiṇai* 108:3; *Akanāṉūṟu* 348:111-12.
15. *Akanāṉūṟu* 73:14-15.
16. *Akanāṉūṟu* 348.
17. *Kuṟuntokai* 82:4.
18. *Kuṟuntokai* 105:1 ; 133:1; *Naṟṟinai* 119:1.
19. *Akanāṉūṟu* 73:14-15 ; *Kuṟuntokai* 375:5; *Naṟṟiṇai* 276:5.
20. *Pre Pallavan Tamil Index* defines them to be foresters and hunters-p. 272.
21. *Akanāṉūṟu* 34:3 ; 132:5 ; 172:6 ; 231:5 ; *Kuṟuntokai* 333:1 ; 335:6 ; 385:2 ; *Naṟṟiṇai* 75:6 ; 82:11 ; 85:8 ; 285:3 ; 336:3.
22. *Akanāṉūṟu* 248:6.
23. *Aiṅkuṟunūṟu* 208:1 ; 270:2.
24. *Kuṟuntokai* 379:2 ; *Akanāṉūṟu* 282:2.
25. *Akanāṉūṟu* 368:1 ; *Kuṟuntokai* 214:1 ; *Naṟṟiṇai* 386:2; *Puṟanāṉūṟu* 159:15.
26. *Akanāṉūṟu* 88:5 ; 102:2.
27. *Naṟṟiṇai* 282:7 ; 393:5 ; *Puṟanāṉūṟu* 247:2.
28. *DED* 283, p. 25.
29. *Kuṟuntokai* 210.
30. *Naṟṟiṇai* 169:7.
31. *Akanāṉūṟu* 94:4.
32. *Naṟṟiṇai* 142:4 ; *Akanāṉūṟu* 274:8 ; *Kuṟuntokai* 221:4.
33. *Kuṟuntokai* 221:4 ; *Naṟṟiṇai* 142:4.
34. *Puṟanāṉūṟu* 54:11; *Akanāṉūṟu* 274:8.
35. *Akanāṉūṟu* 14:7 ; 54:10 ; 74:16 ; 124:14; 214:12; 219:15; 354:5; *Naṟṟiṇai* 69:8; 364:9; 371:8 *Mullaippāṭṭu* 1.15 ; *Netunalvāṭai* 1.3; *Kuṟiñcippāṭṭu* 11. 221-22.
36. *Naṟṟiṇai* 364:9.
37. *Akanāṉūṟu* 155:8 ; 327:7 ; *Aiṅkuṟunūṟu* 304 : 1.
38. *Puṟanāṉūṟu* 339:2.
39. *Akanāṉūṟu* 311:1.
40. 266.
41. *Patiṟṟuppattu* 88:9.

42. S. Seneviratne, *The Social Base of Buddhism: South East India and Sri Lanka*. Unpublished Ph.D. Thesis, Jawaharlal Nehru University, New Delhi, 1985, p. 215.
43. *Ibid.*, p. 358.
44. *Perumpāṇāṟṟuppaṭai* 11. 160-80.
45. The *DED* (3900, p. 317) describes *maṟavar* as inhabitant of desert tracts, of hilly tract, one belonging to caste of hunters, person of *maṟavar* caste, warrior, hero, commander military chief, cruel, wicked person.
46. *Akanāṉūṟu* 121:11 ; 337:11 ; *Naṟṟiṇai* 387:4; *Akanāṉṟu* 89:10; 169:4; 363:10 ; *Aiṅkuṟunūṟu* 352:1; *Kuṟuntokai* 283:5; 297:1; 333:1; *Naṟṟiṇai* 33:6 ; 48:6 ; 148:6.
47. *Akanāṉūṟu* 284:8 ; 297:6.
48. *Akanāṉūṟu* 101:5 ; 129:12 ; 131:6

    Akanāṉūṟu 87:7; 75:6 The *Kalittokai* continues to refer to the *maṟavar* living in *pālai* as fierce looking, with eyes like a tiger, having curly hair, twisted beards, and deft in handling the bow and harassing the people who passed through their tracts-4:3; 5:2; 15:7.
49. *Naṟṟiṇai* 86:1; 84:7; *Patiṟṟuppattu* 30:41; 40:8; 69:8;

    Puṟanāṉūṟū 31:9; 270:9; 274:2; 332:2; 336:5.
50. *Puṟanāṉūṟū* 55:8; 72:5; 227:4; 351:1-5;

    Naṟṟiṇai 18:6; *Patiṟṟuppattu* 36:4.
51. *Puṟanāṉūṟū* 97:11; *Patiṟṟuppattu* 49:10 ; 28:4

    Patiṟṟuppattu 37:1.
52. *Puṟanāṉūṟū* 369:3; *Patiṟṟuppattu* 58:4.
53. *Puṟanāṉūṟū* 259:3; 260:17; 345:5;

    Akanāṉūṟu 35:6; 63:12 377:4; 101:5; 129:12; 131:6

    Akanāṉūṟu 269:4; 309:2
54. *Maturaikkāñci* 1.396; 1.726; 1.396; 11.687-88.
55. 1.489.
56. M.G.S. Narayanan 'Cattle Raiders of the Sangam Age,' *Indian History Congress,* Proceedings, Bhubaneshwar 1977, pp. 70-82.
57. *Patiṟṟuppattu* 81:34. In fact *Patiṟṟuppattu* 66:14 states that the *millar* do not like to die anywhere else except on the battlefield. They are described to be observing *vaṭakkiruttal* with Kōpperuñcōḻan - *Puṟanāṉūṟū* 219:2.

    The chief Toṇṭaimān Iḷañtirayaṉ is described as *Maḷḷar Maḷḷa* (warrior of warriors) - *Perumpāṇāṟṟuppaṭai* 1.455. The *Maḷḷar* continue to be described as brave warriors who fight on the battlefield in the *Kalittokai*- 106:10.
58. *Puṟanāṉūṟū* 84:5; 89:6; *Akanāṉūṟu* 227 :11;

    Aiṅkuṟunūṟu 400:1 Generally the term *maḷḷar* denoted a warrior who could be a hero of a poem (*Puṟanāṉūṟu* 251:3) or kings/chiefs - *Puṟanāṉūṟu* 254:3; *Patiṟṟuppattu* 38:10; *Aiṅkuṟunūṟu* 94:1.
59. *The Pre Pallavan Tamil Index* describes *eyiṉars* as hunters -, p. 161; *Aiṅkuṟunūṟu* 364:1-2; 365:3.
60. *Akanāṉūṟū* 79:14; 127:15; 319:3; *Ainkuṟuṇūṟu* 363:2;

    Kuṟuntokai 12:3.
61. *Puṟanāṉūṟu* 177:13.

62. *Perumpaṇāṟṟuppaṭai* 11.81-100.
63. *Ciṟupanāṟṟuppaṭai* 1.175.
64. *Perumpāṇāṟṟuppaṭai* 11.118-31.
65. *DED* 4547:, p. 382.
66. *Naṟṟiṇai* 189:7; 276:1-4;
    Akanāṇūṟu 28:8; 318:13; 387:9
    Puṟanāṇuṟu 19:5; 33:1; 144:21; 150:7; 202:1; 205:9
    One of the *vēls Ōri* (who is also called Valvil Ōri as he wielded the bow very well) is described to be a suc cessful hunter. *Puṟanāṇūṟu* 152 mentions that when the poet told the chieftain that there was no hunter like him or gave the meat of the deer hunted by him and the gold found in his hill.
67. *Puṟanāṇūṟu* 324.
68. A poem indicates that the *vēṭṭuva* caught fish - *Akanāṇūṟū* 36:5-6.
69. *Patiṟṟuppattu* 30:9.
70. *Uḻavaṉ* is described to be ploughmen agriculturist, ploughman Tamil Lexicon, p. 467.
71. *Toḻuvaṉ* is also cultivator, husband men, *Tamil Lexicon* , p. 2102.
72. They are mentioned to be inhabitants of an agricultural tract, husband's men and even *śūdras* in the *Tamil Lexicon,* p. 812.
73. *Akanāṇūrū* 30:8; 204:10; 236:4;
    Puṟanāṇūṟu 348:1; 379:3;
    Aiṅkuṟunūṟu 33:4; *Puṟanāṇūṟu* 13:1;24:1 209:2;
    Perumpāṇāṟṟuppaṭai 1.211; *Naṟṟiṇai* 95:6; 340:7.
74. *Akanāṇūru* 41:6-7 *Puṟanāṇūṟu* 289: 3-5.
    The *uḻavar* are referred to as *ēraḷar* who plough *Patiṟṟuppattu* 76:11.
    Kuṟuntokai 131:5; 181:4; 213: ; 309:1 *Akananuru* 314:4.
75. *Kuṟuntokai* 155:1-3; *Maturaikkāñci* 1.89; 1.262
    Porunarāṟṟuppaṭai 11.193-95; *Perumpāṇāṟṟuppaṭai* 1.213 *Akanāṇūṟu* 184:13. They also played the drum - *Patiṟṟuppttu* : 90:41.
76. *Akanāṇūṟu* 37:2.
77. *Akanāṇūṟu* 366:3; 346:5 :*Puranāṇūṟu* 212:2
    Maturaikkāñci 1.260.
78. The *Arinar/Arivānar* are mentioned in some instances to be cutting the paddy - *Naṟṟiṇai* 275:1; 350:1; 8:6; 400:3.
79. *Perumpānāṟṟuppaṭai* 11.355-62 mentions jack fruit, tender coconuts and bananas.
80. *Ciṟupāṇāṟṟuppaṭai* 11.190-94 states that the sisters of the *uḻavar* served the bards pounded white rice with crab curry. In *Puṟanāṇūṟu* 375:4.7 the poet Uṟaiyūr Ēṇiccēri Muṭamōciyār initally laments that he has to ask those who earned a living by ploughing (*Ēriṉvāḻnar*) to give him something as he has nothing else except bark and tender plamyra fruits.
81. *Tolkāppiyam Porulatikāram Marapu Iyal,* Sutras 625-639.
82. *DED* 3263;, p. 266. while the *paratar* are said to be fishermen and merchants the *paratavar* are described as fishermen - *Pre Pallavan Tamil Index,* 1966:, pp. 531-32.
83. *Akanāṇūṟu* 270:3.

84. *Aiṅkuṟunūṟu* 180:2.
85. *Akanāṉūṟu* 100:7.
86. *Akanāṉūṟu* 140: 1-5; 270: 1-3; 330:15; *Naṟṟiṇai* 4:1; 63:1; 87:8; 101:8; 219:6 *Paṭṭiṉappālai* 1.112.
87. *Aiṅkuṟunūṟu* 180:1-2; 60:1-3; 65:11; 100:7; 240:5-6 *Naṟṟiṇai* 74:1-4; 111:2-3: 175:1-4; 199:5-8; 372:11-13.
88. *Akanāṉūṟu* 187:22; 300:1-2.
    Kuṟuntokai 184:5-6; *Akanāṉūṟu* 303:8-11; 250:11; 210:1.
    Kuṟuntokai 304:3-6. *Naṟṟiṇai* 388:4-6.
89. *Akanāṉūṟu* 10:9-10; *Naṟṟiṇai* 207: 7-10.
90. *Akanāṉūṟu* 70:1-4; *Naṟṟiṇai* 63:1-4; *Kuṟuntokai* 320:1-4;
    Akanāṉūṟu 20:12.
91. *Maturaikkāñci* 1.256: *Akanāṉūṟu* 30:3.
92. *Akanāṉūṟu* 340:17-19.
93. *Naṟṟiṇai* 38:1-5.
94. *Naṟṟiṇai* 239:1-4; 249:2-3.
95. 11.263-82; J.V. Chelliah (Tr.), pp. 121-23.
96. 11. 82-97; J.V. Chelliah (Tr.), p. 35.
97. *Akanāṉūṟu* 280:11-14; 350:11-15
    Akanāṉūṟu 296: 8-9; *Aiṅkuṟunūṟu* 195-1-2;
    Maturaikkāñci 11.315-26.
98. *Perumpāṇāṟṟuppaṭai* 11.319-23, *Maturaikkāñci* 11.315-26 The *Perumpāṇāṟṟuppaṭai* mentions the *Paratavar* to be living in different streets.
99. *Naṟṟiṇai* 45.
100. *Akanāṉūṟu* 378.
101. *Maturaikkāñci* 11. 139-51.
102. Clarence Maloney: "The Paratavar: 2000 years of culture dynamics of Tamil Caste," *Man in India* Vol.49, No. 3, 1969, pp 230-35.
103. *Akanāṉūṟu* 159:1; *Naṟṟiṇai* 331:2.
104. *Puṟanāṉūṟu* 307:7.
105. *Akanāṉūṟu* 30:5; 17:13; 173:10; 303:17; 296:9; 329:5 388:4.
106. *Puṟanāṉūṟu* 313:5.
107. *Akanāṉūṟu* 39:10; 167:7; 291:15.
108. *Akanāṉūṟu* 119:8; 169:6; 191: 4-8; 337:5;
    Kuṟuntokai 124:1.
109. *Naṟṟiṇai* 4:7; *Akanāṉūṟu* 390:3.
110. *Naṟṟiṇai* 138:3; 386:17.
111. *Naṟṟiṇai* 254:6; 183:5
    Akanaṉūṟu 390:3.
112. *Puṟanāṉūṟu* 116:7.
113. For all the survivals see 'Thurston *Castes and Tribes of Southern India* 1987, (Rp.). *Kuṟavar* Vol. IV, pp. 122-25.

114. *Iṭaiyar* Vol.II, pp. 352-55
Also see *kurumba* or *kuruman* (some of whom are shepherds) Vol. IV, pp. 155-57.
115. *Kaḷḷar* Vol. III, pp. 53-91.
116. *Maṛavar,* Vol. V, pp. 22-48
117. *Vēṭṭuvar Ibid.,* Vol. VII, pp. 394-404.
118. *Paratavar* Maloney, 1969, pp. 230-35 Also see R. Gurukkal, 1989, p. 165.
119. *Ibid.,* p. 165. The term *Vēḷaḷar* occurs for the first time in *Paripāṭal* which is a late text and subsequently in some of the Eighteen minor works.
120. For details see E. Terray, *Marxism and Primtive Societies,* New York, 1972.
B. Hindess and P. Q. Hirst *Precapitalist modes of Production,* London, 1975, pp. 73-78.
121. Akanāṉūṟu 348: 11-12; *Naṟṟiṇai* 207:9.
122. The *Tamil Lexicon* furnishes the following meanings for term *Kiḷai* - to ramify, branch out, to multiply, increase in number, as families, branch, bough, kindred, relations, section, divisions, family etc., p. 941.
123. For details of the householding economy see R. Thapar *From Lineage to State,* 1984, pp. 38-39.
The *maṉaikaḷamar* are people who work in the house and also plough the land and are given food and shelter. These people are also gifted with either objects such as horses, elephants, cattle and paddy by Ceraman Celvakkaṭuṅkōvāḻiyātaṉ-*Puṟanāṉūṟu* 387:25. The *toḻuvar* in one instance are mentioned as persons who do odd jobs in the house. *Neṭunalvāṭ ai* 1.49. Did they help in cultivation activities?
124. *Kuṟuntokai* 95:3; *Akanāṉūṟū* 330:5; *Naṟṟiṇai* 4:1; 219:6; *Perumpāṇāṟṟuppaṭai* 1.157, Also S. Seneviratne, 1989, pp. 7-8.
125. *Tolkāppiyam Porulatikāram* 42.
126. Hart, 1974, pp. 30-31.
127. Under this concept a boy married either his mother's brother's daughter or father's sister's daughter - see Thomas R. Trautmann *Dravidian Kinship,* 1987.
128. For such notions see his article on "Some aspects of kinship in ancient Tamil literature" in Thomas R. Trautmann (ed.) *Kinship and History in South Asia,* Ann Arbor 1974, pp. 29-57.
129. *Ibid.,* p. 44.
130. *Ibid.,.,* pp. 32-42.
131. For a critique of Hart's notion of the sacred see K.Zvelebil "The Dravidian concept of the Sacred" in *Tiru Murugan,* Madras, 1981, pp. 13-26
132. *Kuṟuntokai* 40. Hart translates it thus
My mother and yours,
What were they to each other?
My father and yours
how were they kin?
I and you
How do we know each other?
And yet
Like water that has rained on red fields,
Our hearts in their love
Have mixed together.

133. *Puṛanāṉūṛu* 337; 342; 350; 352; 353.
134. *Puṛanāṉūṛu* 346.
135. *Naṛṛiṇai* 234.
136. *Puṛanāṉūṛu* 343.
137. Bride price prevalent among the Paraiyans - G. L. Hart, *The poems of ancient Tamil; their milieu and Sanskrit counterparts,*
Berkeley, 1975, p. 48.
138. *Ainkuṛunūṛu* 399.
139. *Tolkāppiyam Porulatikāram Karpu Iyal* 145.
140. *Tolkāppiyam Porulatikāram Kaḷavu Iyal* 92.
141. See Hindess and Hirst, *Pre-Capitalist Modes of Production,* London, 1979, pp. 51-69.
142. *Puṛanāṉūṛu* 95:5; 170:17.
143. *Akanāṉūṛu* 202: 5-6; 224:2 *Naṛṛiṇai* 133:9; 125:3. The metal was heated to a high temperature and then beaten by the blacksmith till sparks flew from the metal *Akanāṉūṛū* 72:6; *Naṛṛiṇai* 13:5.
Koṭiru is the term used for the pincers which resembled the crabs- *Perumpāṇāṛṛuppaṭai* 1. 207.
144. *Puṛanāṉūṛu* 36:6; 170:15; 180:12; 312:3; *Akanāṉūṛu* 9:1.
145. *Kuṛuntokai* 304:1.
146. *Kuṛuntokai* 172:5.
147. They made shining vessels of copper-*Naṛṛiṇai* 153:2. Bronze vessels were found at Adichannallur-*Archaeological Survey Reports,* Madras 1899-1900, 1904-05 Nos. 747 and 749, 22nd July, 1901, pp. 4-5. *Kammiyar* were skilled in making gapless joints- *Neṭunalvāṭ ai* 1.85.
148. *Arthaśāstra* (Tr.) R. P. Kangle II, XI, 114-15.
149. *Periplus* :59.
150. *Porunarāṛṛuppaṭai* 11. 82-83
In the *Maturaikkāñci* weavers were described to be selling small and big pieces of cloth- 1.521.
151. *Naṛṛiṇai* 313:2; *Puranāṉūṛū* 353: 1-2
The goldsmith also polished pearl.
Naṛṛiṇai 94:4.
152. *Naṛṛiṇai* 138.
153. I Mahadevan "Corpus of the Tamil Brahmi Inscriptions" in R. Nagaswamy (ed.) *Seminar on Inscriptions, Madras,* (1966), 1968
Alakarmalai Insc. No. 30.
154. Pukaḷūr Insc. No. 66.
155. Araccalūr Insc. no. 62.
156. K. V. Raman "Some Ancient Crafts and Technology in Tamil-Nad as revealed in Excavations" *Proceedings of the Second International Conference Seminar of Tamil Studies",* Vol. II, 1968, p. 399.
Also *Paṭṭinappālai* 1.7 refers to gold from northern hills being imported into Kāveri-paṭṭiṇam. Could this be the Kolar area?

157. *Akanāṉūṟū* 372:3.
158. *Ibid.*, 173: 16.
159. *Ibid.*, 331: 2.
160. *Kuṟuntokai* 61:1
He is said to have made 8 chariots in a day-
Puṟanāṉuṟu 87:3; 290:4-5.
161. *Puṟanāṉūṟu* 206:11,
162. I. Mahadevan, 1966, Insc. No. 71.
163. *Puṟanāṉūṟu* 32:8; 228.
164. Independent specialists are those who "produce goods or services for an unspecified demand crowd that varies according to economic social and political conditions", whereas attached specialists "produce goods or provide services to a patron, typically either a social elite or a governing institution" - For further details see E.M. Brumfiel and T.K. Earle "Specialisation, Exchange and Complex Societies: An introduction", in E.M. Brumfiel and T.K.Earle Ed. *Specialization, Exchange and Complex Societies,* Cambridge, 1987, pp. 5-6.
165. *Periplus* 59.
166. Meanings of these words are furnished by the *Tamil Lexicon.*
Vampalaṉ :itinerant, newcomer, wayfarer *Vol.* VI, p. 3492.
Vāṇikaṉ : merchant, trader, Vol. VI, p. 3586.
Viḷaiñaṉ : seller, Vol. VI, p. 3715.
Pakarnar : hawkers, Vol. V, p. 2380.
167. *Perumpāṇāṟruppaṭai* ll. 59-80; J.V.Chelliah (Tr.) 1962, pp. 109-11.
168. *Maturaikkāñci* ll. 407-09;
J.V. Chelliah (Tr.) 1962, p. 253
169. *Ibid.*, ll. 503-06; J.V. Chelliah (Tr.) 1962, pp. 260-61.
170. *Ibid.*, ll. 379-401; ll. 511-21.
171. K.K. Pillay, *Social History of the Tamils,* Madras, 1975, p. 247.
172. *Maturaikkāñci* ll. 537-44; J.V. Chelliah (Tr.) 1962, p. 261.
173. I. Mahadevan (1966) 1968
Aḻakarmalai Insc. No. 34.
174. Aḻakarmalai Insc. No. 37.
175. Aḻakarmalai Insc. No. 38.
176. Aḻakarmalai Insc. No. 43.
177. Pukaḷūr Insc. No. 63.
178. Pukaḷūr Insc. No. 66.
179. Araccalūr Insc. No. 72.
180. R.Champakalakshmi, 1986, p. 8 X 11.
For guild organisation in North India See G.L.Adhya's *Early Indian Economics,* Bombay, 1966.
R.Thapar "The Impact of Trade C. 100 B.C.-300 A.D. in India in *K.M. Ashraf Memorial Volume,* New Delhi, 1969, pp. 30-38.

For guild organisation in Western Deccan see H.P. Ray's *Monastery and Guild : Commerce under the Sātavāhanās* New Delhi, 1986.

181. I. Mahadevan 1968, Insc. Nos. 3 and 6
Ibid., Insc. No. 3.
182. R.Champakalakshmi 1986, p. 11.
183. Pukaḷūr Insc. Nos 56 and 57 where the Cēra Iḷaṅkaṭuṅkō made such a donation.
184. S. Paranivitana *Inscriptions of Ceylon,* Vol. I, 1970, Insc. Nos. 356 and 357.
185. I. Mahadevan 1968, Insc. No. 57.
186. *Ibid.*, Insc. No. 52.
187. *Tolkāppiyam* : *Porulatikāram Marapu Iyal* 629; 631; 632.
188. REM Wheelar et al 1946, pp. 17-124
"Roman contact with India, Pakistan and Afghanistan" in Grimes (Ed) *Aspects of Archaeology, Essays presented to O.G.S Crawford,* London 1951, pp. 345-81 *Rome beyond the Imperial Frontiers,* London, 1954.
Warmington: *Commerace between the Roman Empire and India,* New Delhi, 1974. (Rp.)
Vimala Begley "Arikamedu Reconsidered", *American Journey of Archaeology*", Vol. 87 pp. 461-81.
R. Nagaswamy : *Vasavasamudram,* Madras 1978
"Roman sites in Tamil Nad :Recent Discoveries "*Madhu* New Delhi, 1981, pp. 337-39.
K.S. Ramachandran, *Archaeology of South India*: Tamil Nadu, Delhi, 1980.
N.Kasinathan : Alagankulam: A Preliminary Report, State Department of Archaeology, Madras, 1992.
For Kodumanal See the newspaper reports (as a full report has not been published) Excavations yield precious artefacts, *The Hindu,* 30-11-90.
189. *Akanāṇūṟu* 149; *Puṟanāṇūṟu* 56; 343.
190. *Akanāṇūṟu* 57; 149; *Puṟanāṇūṟu* 343.
191. *Neṭunalvātai* 11. 101-02;
Perumpāṇāṟṟuppaṭai 11.316-19.
192. *Mullaippāṭṭu* 1.66.
193. *Mullaippāṭṭu* 1.61.
194. *Paṭṭinappālai* 11. 214-17.
195. *IAR* 1962-63, p. 13.
196. *Periplus* 60 classifies it as a market town Ptolemy calls it an emporium-VII; 1.13.
197. *IAR* 1962-63, p. 13. Radiocarbon date of this structure from a wooden samples is 315 B.C.
198. *IAR*: 1963-64, p. 20
IAR: 1964-65, p. 25.
199. *Akanāṇūṟu* 206: 13-14.
200. Poduca - *Periplus* 60
Poduke Ptolemy VII : 1-14.
201. R.E.M. Wheeler 1946.
202. *Ibid.*, pp. 24-114.
203. Perimoula was referred to by Pliny and mentioned by Maloney, 1976, p. 32.

204. N.Kasinathan: Madras, 1992, 14-15.

205. E.H.Warmington, 1974, pp. 37-38.

206. For example the Besnagar Pillar Inscription of Heliodorus which indicates that he was a worshipper of Viṣṇu-D.C.Sircar: *Select Insçriptions Bearing on Indian history and Civilization,* Calcutta, 1942, pp. 90-91. Also Suvira Jaiswal, *The Origin and Development of Vaisnavism,* Delhi 1987, 2nd ed., p. 28.

For example Usavadata the son-in-law of Nahapāna in Western Deccan-See inscriptions of Uṣavadāta found at nasic-J. Burgess, *Report on the Buddhist Cave Temples and their inscriptions,* Varanasi, 1964 (Rp.), p. 99; Also H.P.Ray, 1986, p. 38.

207. R.Sumathi, 1984, p. 121.

208. *Mullaippāṭṭu* 1.66.

209. I. Mahadevan 1968, Insc. No. 51.

210. Indigenous issues of coins comprise: Hoard of 1128 silver punch marked coins from Bodinayakkanur (Madurai district) with a fish symbol on them (could have been a Pāṇṭiyaṇ state issue). Ceṅgam hoard from Andipatti in the North Arcot District assigned to chief Naṉṉaṉ of Cengam referred to in the *Malaipaṭukaṭām* (also a dynastic issue)- R. Champakalakshmi, 1968, p. 52 ff. (Square copper coins, many of which are highly corroded, have been excavated from the early levels at Vanagiri, Neidavasal, Manigramman, Sayavanam and Pallavaneesvaram (part of Kaveripattinam) and Kanchipuram-*IAR* 1961-62:, pp. 26-27; 1963-64:p.20; 1964-65;p.25; 1971-72:, p. 43. Coins from Kāvēripaṭṭiṉam are reported to have the figures of a standing tiger with up lifted tail on one side and an 'elephant' or a fish on the other. Since tiger was the insignia of the early Cōḻas it has been suggested that these coins were issued by the early Cōḻa State. Besides, coins of the Cēras (Mākōttai) have also been found-See R. Krishnamurthy's

"Mākkōtai Coins" in A.V. Narasimha Murthy (ed.).

Studies in South Indian Coins, Vol.II

Madras, 1992, pp. 89-93. Punch marked coin hoards are found in Tamiḻakam at the follwing places (based on P.L.Gupta "A bibliography of the hoards of punch marked coins of Ancient India" - *Journals of the Numismatic Society ofAncient India,* Vol. XVII, pp. 15-19.

Alampalayam	Dist. Coimbatore	Silver 63nos
Bodinayakkanur	Dist. Madurai	Silver 1138nos
Chavadipalayam	Dist. Coimbatore	Silver exact nos. not known
Coimbatore	Dist. Coimbatore	Silver 3 nos.
Coimbatore	Dist. Coimbatore	Silver large no.
Eyyal	Dist. Cochin	Silver 12 nos.
Kaun iakuttai	Dist. Salem	Silver 17 nos.
Mambalam	Dist. Madras	Silver 770+nos.
Penar	Dist. Coimbatore	Silver a pot full
Tondamanathan	Dist.South Arcot	Silver 27 nos
Veerasikhamani	Dist. Tirunelveli	Silver 287 nos
Venbavur	Dist. Trichy	Silver 991 nos
Venbavur	Dist. Trichy	Silver 1375 nos

Besides this stray finds are reported at Keyedi (Chingelput), Madurai, Mahabalipuram and Srivaikuntam (Tirunelveli).

211. The following places have yielded hoards of punch marked coins with Roman coin hoards - Mambalam (Madras), Chavadipalayam (Coimbatore) Tondamanathan (South Arcot) and Pennar (near Coimbatore). Cera Makkotai coin was found with Roman ones as surface find at Karur. Some gold and silver coins (no details available on this) found with Roman coin at Kallakinar (Coimbatore). I am grateful to S. Suresh for this information.
212. *Patiṟṟuppattu* VI *Patikam* ; VIII : *Patikam;* IV: *Patikam.*
213. In primitive societies it has been noticed that "often precious objects.. have a dual nature, they are both goods and non goods, 'money' and gifts according to whether they are bartered between groups or circulate within the group "M. Godelier" Salt money and the circulation of commodities among the Baruya of New Guinea" *Prespectives in Marxist Anthropology,* Cambridge, 1977, pp. 128-29.

   Roman coins could have been precious objects performing dual functions serving as money used in ciruculation and objects conferred by kings/chiefs as gifts to enhance their social status.
214. *Paṭṭinappālai* 11. 40-55; 11. 59-74; 11. 116-171, 11.183-212.
215. *Ibid.,* 11. 213-18.
216. *DED* 3351, p. 272 describes the *pāṇaṉ* to be an ancient class of Tamil bards and minstrels. Hart indicates that the *Pāṇaṉ* took his name from the word *Paṇ,* a generic name for modes of music, somewhat similar to the modern raga, 1975, p. 138.
217. *Akanāṉūṟu* 106; *Naṟṟiṇi* 310.
218. *Puṟanāṉūṟu* 138. *Pāṇa* was asked to go to Nāñcil Vaḷavaṉ;

   Puṟanāṉūṟu 69:4, 70:1 - *Pāṇa* is asked to go to Kiḷḷivaḷavaṉ; *Puṟanāṉūṟu* 68:4 - *Pāṇa* is asked to go to Cōḻaṉ Nallaṅkiḷḷi; In certain instances, poets also made the patrons donate generously.
219. *Puṟanāṉūṟu* 364: 1-9 (Flowers of gold, toddy and a chutney made of meat).
220. *Puṟanāṉūṟu* 12:1; 11:15 (golden chain and gold lotus)

   Puṟanāṉūṟu 361: 13.
221. *Puṟanāṉūṟū* 135: 16 (Āy Aṇṭiraṉ gave to *Pāṇar paricilar*).
222. *Puṟanāṉūṟu* 334:6.
223. *Puṟanāṉūṟu* 34:14 (Cōḻa Kulamuṟṟattuttunciya kiḷḷivaḷavaṉ fed Pānar with good rice, milk and honey.)

   Puṟanāṉūṟu 319:9-10 *Pāṇa* got rabbit meat

   Puṟanāṉūṟu 328:6-11 (*Pāṇa* is given curd, fruits, well cooked meat, rice with ghee)

   Puṟanāṉūṟu 326:9-11 (*Pāṇa* is given meat, curds and rice)

   Puṟanāṉūṟu 327 (*Pāṇa* is given *varaku*)

   Puṟanāṉūṟu 115:2; 170:13 Poverty and hunger of *Pāṇar* is removed.

   Puṟanāṉūṟu 141:1; 239:17.
224. *Puṟanāṉūṟu* 302.
225. *Puṟanāṉūṟu* 242; 15:9.
226. *Aiṅkuṟunūṟu* 43: 4; 82:1; 422:7; 473; 474; 477; 478; 479.

   Kuṟuntokai 85:127

Naṟṟiṇai 167
Akanāṉūṟu 50:244.

227. *Tolkāppiyam, Porulatikāram* 193.
228. *Maturaikkāñci* 1.269.
229. They were degraded to lower caste later and not in this period. One of the Āḻvārs Tirupāṇāḻvar is said to have hailed from the *Pāṇa* caste.
230. *Puṟanāṉūṟu* 172:3; 32:4; 109:16; 60:5.
231. *Akanāṉūṟu* 151:9; *Puṟanāṉūṟu* 132:3.
232. *Puṟanāṉūṟu* 135:4; 139:4 that the kings of that age devoted time for encouraging such fine arts is brought out in a poem where the poetess warns a Cēra king not to spend too much time with the *Viṟaliyar* as it would give scope for people to think of him as a person who spends time for the fine arts even though he was a brave warrior- *Patiṟṟuppattu* 51:21.
233. *Puṟanāṉūṟu* 64:2; 133:1.
234. *Puṟanāṉūṟu* 109:16.
235. *Puṟanāṉūṟu* 302: 2-3; *Malaipaṭukaṭām* 1.569; *Perumpāṇāṟṟuppaṭai* 1.486.
236. *Puṟanāṉūṟu* 170:11.
237. *Patiṟṟuppattu* 43:22.
238. *Perumpāṇāṟṟuppaṭai* 11. 487-90.
239. *Patiṟṟuppattu* 43:22.
240. *Malaipaṭukaṭām* 1. 536.
241. *The Pre Pallavan Tamil Index* 1966 defines *Iyavar* (derived from *Iyam* a musical instrument) as bards who sang the glory of the hero in the battlefield., p. 108.
242. *Puṟanāṉūṟu* 336:6.
243. *Aiṅkuṟunūṟu* 215:3.
244. *Naṟṟiṇai* 113:10.
245. *Ainkuṟunūṟu* 425:2.
246. *Patiṟṟuppattu* 27:5.
247. They are described in the *Pre Pallavan Tamil Index* as dancers and those who played the bent or horned' musical instruments. Kailasapathy is of the view that the word *kōṭiyar* is derived from *kōṭu* blowing horn-*DED* 824, p. 146; Kailasapathy, *Tamil Heroic Poetry* 1968, pp. 107-08. *Pre Pallavan Tamil Index* identifies the *Vayiriyar* as *pāṇar* and dancers. Kailasapathy is of the opinion that the word *vayiriyar* is derived from *vayir* 'bamboo bugle' *DED* 4514, p. 378 and hence they are buglers and trumpeteers- Kailasapathy, 1968, p. 108.
248. *Naṟṟiṇai* 212:3.
249. *Kuṟuntokai* 78:2.
250. *Akanāṉūṟū* 352: 4. They are described to be beating the drum during the festival -*Patiṟṟuppattu* 56:2; Also *Paṭṭinappālai* 1.253.
251. *Akanāṉūṟu* 309:9 mentions them going to Cēra chieftain Vāṇavaṉ These *Kōṭiyar* sang the glory and achievements of a chieftain when they saw him.
252. Nalliyakōṭaṉ did so - *Cirupāṇāṟṟuppaṭai* 11. 125-26.
253. *Cirupāṇāṟṟuppaṭai* 1. 109.
254. *Akanāṉūṟu* 328:1; *Naṟṟiṇai* 100:10.

255. *Patiṟṟuppattu* 29:8
256. *Akanāṉūṟu* 155:13.
257. *Patiṟṟuppattu* 23:6.
258. *Puranāṉūṟu* 9:9.
259. *Patiṟṟuppattu* 64:8.
260. *Patiṟṟuppattu* 43:34.
261. *Maturaikkāñci* 750.
262. *Paripāṭal* X : 130.
263. *Puranāṉūṟu* 221:1-2
Puranāṉūṟu 128:6.
264. The *Pāṭunar* are said to have got horses, male elephants, chariots- *Paṟanāṉūṟu* 240 These singers used to mourn the death of their patrons, like for example, their sorrow at the death of chief Veḷimāṉ is described to be like the sorrow of the wife of the king—*Paṟanāṉūṟu* 238:7.
265. *Paripāṭal* VIII: 1. 109.
266. *Puṟanāṉūṟu* 79
Patiṟṟuppattu 75.9
According to Hart, "it was the ritual duty of the *kiṇai* player to go to the palace and wake the king with his drumming"- 1975, p. 144.
267. *Akanāṉūṟu* 249
Akavunan are described by the *Pre Pallavan Tamil Index* as *pāṇar,* dancers, singers, p. 21.
268. The *Akavunan* and *Akavanmakal* foretold the future-vide *Kuṟuntokai* 23; Also Hart 1976, pp. 144-46.
269. *Pyṟanāṉūṟu* 260, 269, 287, also Hart 1975-, p. 146.
270. *Puṟanāṉūṟu* 269, 280.
271. *Puṟanāṉūṟu* 287, 170.
272. *DED* 400:, pp. 35-36; *Tamil Lexicon,* p. 315. *Irappu* according to the *Lexicon* means begging/asking alms.
273. *Puṟanāṉūṟu* 241:1.
274. *Puṟanāṉūṟu* 250:2.
275. *Puṟanāṉūṟu* 56:17.
276. Another poem *Puṟanāṉūṟu* 313 refers to the hero telling the *iravalmākkaḷ* to take elephants and chariots from enemy lands even before his gaining possession of them.
277. The *Pre Pallavan Tamil Index* 1966 gives the following meanings for the word; wise men, men of knowledge, poets-p. 579. The *Tamil Lexicon* gives the following meaning wise men, sages-p.2786.
Paricilar were solicitors of gifts according to the *Tamil lexicon, p. 2512.*
278. Hart 1975, p. 148.
279. *Ibid.*, pp. 148-58.
280. See poems 201, 202 of *Puranānuru.*
281. *Puṟanāṉūṟu* 228.
282. *Puṟanāṉūṟu* 235.

283. *Pre Pallavan Tamil Index*, 1966, p. 533.

284. *Puṟanāṉūṟu* 233.

285. *Puṟanāṉūṟu* 326.

286. Naḷḷiyakkōtaṉ also distributed to the *paricilar* according to their merit - *Ciṟupāṇāṟṟuppaṭai* 11.214-20.

287. *Puṟanāṉūṟū* 205, 206, 208, 211.

288. R.S.Kennedy "The King in South India as Chieftain and Emperor", *Indian Historical Review,* Vol.III, July 1976, p. 3.

289. David Shulamn "Poets and Patrons in Tamil literature and literary legend" in B.Stoller Miller (ed.) *The Powers of Art: Patronage in Indian Culture,* Delhi, 1992, pp. 91-94.

CHAPTER - III-B

EARLY HISTORICAL TAMIL SOCIETY : FROM KINSHIP TO CASTE— THE IMPACT OF *VARṆA*

The above survey of *tiṇai* groups based on kinship/ lineage organisation is clearly indicative of the dominat feature in the society of the earlier phase of the early historical period. Against this background, the idea of the *varṇa* could be taken up for discussion.

A *varṇa* based organisation of society is not clearly discernible in the region. The *Tolkāppiyam* in a section, dateable to a later period, refers to a four-fold division of society[1]. It appears that the author of this work on grammar, which is also a normative text, was influenced by the northern Brahmanical ideas regarding the four-fold division and tried to apply the concept to Tamiḻakam though with a difference. In Tamiḻakam there is no one to one correspondence with the Vedic-Brahmanic concept of *varṇa*.

The *brāhmaṇās* as a group are described in the early anthologies as an educated knowledgeable class reciting the Vedas (*maṛai*) and occasionally performing *vēḷvi* or sacrifices which could have included *yajna* or the Vedic sacrifices in which they officiated as priests. As a group, the *brāhmaṇās* would have been respected. In this period, unlike in the later periods, they did not hold positions of social eminence. The *vaiśya varṇa* comprised the mercantile community and the artisans and craftsmen were not brought into the orbit of *vaiśya varṇa*. The *vēḷāḷa* is a late term which did not correspond to the *śūdra* of the north, although they are mentioned as the fourth category[2]. The idea of *dvija* or twice born is used only for the *brāhmaṇās* (*antaṇar*) who are referred to by the term *irupiṛappāḷar* in the *Caṅkam* texts. The *antaṇar* could have hence been considered as twice born. Besides, there are quite a few references to the low born such a *iḻiciṉaṉ* or *iḻipiṛappaṉ* (low born) in the *Caṅkam* anthologies. The people who were considered low born were the drummers (*tuṭiyaṉ* and *paṛaiyaṉ*). The *pulaiyaṉ* was also considered low born presumably on account of their menial work or their involvement in funerary rites (as known from *Puṛanāṉūṛu* 360 and 363). It is interesting that the *iḻipiṛappāḷaṉ* figures in the anthologies and not in the *Tolkāppiyam*.

Another high status group mentioned in the *Caṅkam* anthologies are the *Cāṉṛōr*.

The ranks of *Cāṉṟōr* may have included wise, educated, elderly people who were given respect. They need not have necessarily been *antaṇar.* It has been pointed out that the principal past times of the *Cāṉṟōr* or *uyarntōr* (the noble ones) would have been fighting, feasting, hunting and partaking in games[3].

The picture of society one gets from the early anthologies is one where the elite had crystallised. The dominant position would have been held by high status groups such as rulers, chiefs and noblemen. In fact the *Caṅkam* poems themselves reflect the life of the elite. the terms used *kiḻavaṉ, kiḻāṉ, tataivaṉ, kiḻatti, entai* suggest their high status[4]. Even amongst the inhabitants of the *tinai* there must have been elite elements not necessarily engaged in production activities for daily subsistence.

The populace below the elite could have been engaged in eking out their daily livelihood. As pointed out, the inhabitants of the *tiṇais* were carrying out occupations determined by their environment.

Essentially therefore, the four-fold division referred to in the *Tolkāppiyam* seems to have been an occupational division or an attempt to fit into the four-fold (*varṇa)* framework the major occupational groups. By the time the *Porulatikāram* of the *Tolkāppiyam* was composed, a division between *Uyarntōr/ mēlōr/* (higher ones / wise ones) and *kiḻōr* (low ones) seems to have crystallised.

This is evident from the customs of marriage prescribed in the text. Marriage rituals seem to have been created by the *Aiyar* (learned- were they *brahmanas?)* when dishonesty and insincerity became common in the conduct of love[5]. Further, writing in about 13th-14th centuries, Nacciṉārkkiṉiyar, the commentator of the *Tolkāppiyam,* stated that the *mēlōr* and *kīḻōr* had different rites[6]. The *uyarntōr* were consulted when doubts arose on the girl's choice of a partner[7]. Writing in the context of the 13th century when the *vēḷāḷas* were dominant Nacciṉārkkiṉiyar stated that the four *antaṇar, aracar, vaṇikkar* and *uyarnta vēḷḷāḷa* (higher *vēḷḷāḷas*) could go for acquisition of wealth and knowledge[8]. From this it is clear that at least certain sections of the *vēḷāḷas* were treated on par with the higher echelons of society. Again, the text is not clear on who the *kīḻōr* were. Were they people who practised pottery, smithy, weaving and other menial occupations? Although there is reference to the four groups along with certain privileges, one ins not clear as to whether the notion of untouchability or restrictions on interdining, rigidity of professions, emphasis on high birth all associated with a 'caste' structure prevailed in any form. One thing which is clear is that the *brāhmaṇās* by this time could have emerged as high status group on account of their high birth and knowledge. Hence, they could have been categorised as *uyarntōr* along with the ruling elites and traders/merchants. In the *Tolkāppiyam* and in the eighteen minor works, as we shall see in the ensuing section, the *brāhamṇās* are definitely looked upon with respect and their high birth or high association is emphatically stated.

Brāhmaṇās[9] are conspicuously referred to in the *marutam* and *neytal tiṇais.* They are mentioned in various capacities *viz* as scholars well versed in the Vedas, performing six duties, out of which officiating at sacrifices was one and receiving gifts was another as *pulavar* (poets), as *dūtās* (envoys) and occasionally indulging in other occupations such as making conch bangles. Generally, they are portrayed in the texts as people learned in the *Vedas* (*maṟai*) due to which they are also known as *nāṉmaṟai mutalvar, nāṉmaṟaiyōr* and *maṟai-kāppaḷar*[10]. The *Ciṟupāṇāṟṟuppaṭai* describes the *antaṇar,* who recite the Vedas, to be living at Āmūr[11] (a fortified centre). Besides, they were supposed to perform six duties/acts such as reciting (*Vedas*), sacrificing, making others recite and perform sacrifice, giving and accepting gifts[12]. Even amongst the *antaṇar* there could have been some who were possibly sages as some *antaṇar* are mentioned to be carrying a staff and vessel (*kamanṭalam*) in their hands besides wearing clothes dipped in saffron colour water[13].

Their involvement in various kinds of rites and sacrifices is clearly explained in the texts. A notable feature of this period is that the *brāhmaṇās* do not figure as temple priests. References to *brāhmaṇās* functioning as priests occur only in the late poem *Tirumurukāṟṟuppaṭai* by which time the temple emerged as an important institution.

A poem of the *Puṟanāṉuṟu* presents a picture of their involvement in funerary rites. As we are informed:

> "Who is left to defeat in battle advancing as the strong-thonged drum roars out?
>
> Those who came could not prevail before your vanguard but scattered and ran
>
> The mean kings there died and so escaped the rite that would have rid them of their infamy:
>
> When they had died in bed,
>
> their bodies would have been taken.
>
> and, all love for them forgotten to purge them of their evil.
>
> Brahmins of the four Vedas and just principles
>
> Would have laid them out on green grass prepared according to ritual would have said"
>
> "Go to where warriors with renowned anklets go who have died in battle with manliness their support,"
>
> and would have cut them with the sword.
>
> They died there, great one.
>
> while you received a fine wound as you attacked, making battle scatter and bringing down on the field of killing elephants whose rut hummed with striped bees as it trickled into their mouths"[14]

The *brāhmaṇas* also performed sacrifice (*vēḷvi*) with sacrificial posts. *Puṟanāṉūṟu* 166 descibes that a *brāhmaṇa* Kauṇiyaṉ Viṇṇantāyaṉ who perfomed 21 sacrifices without omission used much *ghī* in his sacrifices. Further, the *brāhmaṇas* are described by another term *Irupiṛappāḷar* (twice born). They performed sacrifices where there were three fires (*muttī*[15]). Officiating at the *Rācacūya* ceremonies performed by the Cōḻa king Perunaṛkiḷḷi or other *vēḷvis* (Vedic sacrifices) performed by Cōḻa kings would have been mandatory for these *brāhmaṇas*. As part of *dānā or dakṣina* not necessarily after a *vēḷvi* they would have got gold and land[16], to which references are few in the early anthologies.

It is interesting to note that some of the poets (*pulavar*) of the *Caṅkam* poems hailed from this community of *antaṇar* (vide Appendix 6).

A facet of their character was their morality. *Brāhmaṇās* were reputed for their morality. This is testified by Kapilar. After the death of Pāri, Kapilar was saddled with the responsibility of looking after Pāri's daughters and finding suitable grooms for them. When he went to the court of kings he emphasised the fact that he was a *brāhmaṇa* and a *pulavaṉ,* and therefore, there was no need to fear that he might have spoiled the girls or tainted their character[17]. At times the *brāhmaṇas* were sent as envoys as can be inferred from a poem where:

> "A young Brahmin his withered waist like a *vayalai* creeper creeping sadly along,
>
> came at night, entered the camp without pausing, and said a few words.
>
> At that they gave up their ladders and bolts and bells were taken from the elephants of many wars"[18].

Not all the *antaṇar* were learned or taught the Vedas even in those times. One poem mentions *antaṇar* not performing rituals but making bangles of conch[19]. So even in this community, there would have been the privileged ranks engaged in reciting and imparting the *Vedas* while the under privileged may have taken to other occupations such as making bangles of conch. Could this be attributed to economic necessity?

The *Perumpāṇāṟruppaṭai* provides an interesting account of the settlement of the *antaṇar*

> "The house are with cow dung smeared, In which are idols. Fowls and dogs are banned.
>
> Here live the guardians of the Veda truths Who teach e'en bent-billed parrots to utter them.
>
> Fair bangled Brahmin dames that are as chaste
>
> As the one whose name the northern star doth bear
>
> That lights the wide bright sky, will serve to thee
>
> At sunsed well-cooked rice that bears the name of a bird, with slices of the citron fruit with fragrant leaves and pepper flavoured well
>
> And boiled in butter taken from the milk of red-skinned cows, and also pickles made of fragrant soft fruits of the mango tree"[20].

These settlements of the *brāhmaṇās* are said to be clean without the presence of dogs and chickens[21]. George Hart is of the opinion that *brāhmaṇās* lived apart like today and refused to keep animals like dogs or chicks lest they become polluted[22].

The *brāhmaṇās* seem to have gained respect and importance from the rulers as the *Patiṟṟuppattu* mentions that the Cēra ruler Celvakkaṭuṅko Vāḻiyātaṉ bowed only to the *antaṇar*[23]. In another instance, poet Kāri Kiḻār in *Puṟanāṉūṟu* 6 states that the coronet of Pāṇṭiyaṉ ruler Pal yakācālai Mutukuṭumi Peruvaḻuti should bow before the *antaṇar* of the four Vedas. Also, in another poem the poet "advises women, cows and Brahmans to leave a city before it becomes a battle field"[24].

Geoge Hart accounts for the presence of various kinds or categories of *brāhmaṇās* in ancient Tamil Nadu. According to him, the first Brahmins who came to Tamil-nad from the north encountered a society which was totally alien to them and their way of life in which there were no plethora of gods or even if they were, they did not resemble the Aryan ones, and they had no complex mythology, "The priests (of Tamiḻakam) were of low caste and were thought to contaminate others by their presence". The only alternative for the *brahmanas* was to associate themselves with royalty. While some of them may have had to participate in unbrahmanical activities as cutting up the bodies of those who died in bed, some served as envoys and advisors to "kings" and some became *pulavar* (poets). By such acts they carved out a place for themselves in Tamil Nadu. As other brahmins came in later to Tamil Nad they found that they were accepted and did not change their way of life as the earliest ones did. Thus there were different kinds of brahmins in Tamilnadu. In his words "some were very much Tamilized, while others resembled in most respects their northern counterparts"[25]. Further, he is of the view that this distinction exists even today among the Tamil brahmins especially the *Aiyankars* (the Tamil Vaiṣṇava brahmins[26]).

Brāhmaṇās also became a part of the redistributive network. Land seems to have been conferred as gifts on the *brāhmaṇās* though the references to this are few. This had a considerable inpact on production processess in the region. Since *brāhmaṇās* did not cultivate the land themselves they had to hire working families to do it. Kinship ties were transgressed while employing such labour. This also heralded a change and led to the growth of a householding economy with the growth of private ownership of land in a limited way. Such a *brāhmaṇa* household is referred by *Puṟanāṉūṟu* 166. It is quite likely that the term *Kiḻāṉ*[27] (*Kiḻār*) was used to denote even *brāhmaṇa* householders (owning land).In the epigraphic records of the early medieval period the land owning *brāhmaṇās* of the *brahmadeya* are called *brahmadeya kiḻavar* (*kiḻār*[28]).

Generally the *brāhmaṇās* were identified by *gotra*[29]. The concept of *gotra* as a particular form of kinship had not really taken root in Tamiḻakam. It has been pointed out that the *gotra* was an exogamous clan where exogamy was emphasised in the prohibition on marrying *sagotras* and marrying those related up to seven generations on the father's side and five on the mother's[30]. In Tamilakam, the concept seems to have had marginal applicability. We come across *gotra* names only from the names of a few poets (vide appendix-7). In only one instance do we hear of a brahman household and the name of Kauṇiyaṉ Viṇṇan Tāyaṉ (of *kauṇtinya gotra*) of Pūñcāṟṟūr celebrating *vēḷvis* (sacrifices[31]). Thus it is clear that the gotra seems to have been used to identify descent groups of a high status like the brahmans and remained essential to brahman identity. Perhaps the Vedic notion of *gotra* was slowly seeping into the region. Only in one isolated context do we come across the *gotra* used for a group other than the *brāhmaṇa*. A grafitti inscribed potsherd from Arikamedu refers to an individual called Ātiraiyan who calls himself a descendent of the lineage (*gotraja - gotra*) of Cāttan Āvi. Accrding to Seneviratne, Atirayan recorded his lineage affiliation with Āvi or Āy who were a clan of the Vēḷir[32]. The Vēḷir were pastoral-cum-agrarian communities ruling over different parts of Tamiḻakam.

The *Aracar* constituted the ruling groups comprising the *Vēntar,* Vēḷir and non-Vēḷir. chieftains[33].

The emergence of a mercantile community in Tamilakam has already been highlighted earlier. This would have warranted their inclusion in the four-fold division. Here again, it is interesting to note that only the *vaisikaṉ* (*vaṇikaṉ*) (trader/ merchant) is mentioned as the third in the four fold order[34]. Artisans and craftsmen are not given any position in the four-fold hierarchy.

It has already been indicated that the *vēḷāḷa* did not correspond to the *śūdra*. Nacciṉārkkiṉiyar, the medieval commentator, recognises two divisions within the *vēḷāḷa* community the superior (*uyarnta vēḷāḷār*) and inferior, the superior *vēḷāḷā* enjoying a position of social eminence along with the *antaṇar* and *aracar.* Were the inferior *vēḷāḷās* agricultural labourers and those engaged in menial tasks for eking out their livelihood?

So from all this it is clear that *varṇa,* per se, had not become the basis of social organisation and the region did not develop a caste structure. Essentially, the four-fold division referred to in the *Tolkāppiyam* seems to be an occupational division. At this point it would be relevant to take into account two poems of the *Puṛanāṉūṛu* highlighting a four-fold division. *Puṛanāṉūṛu* 183 mentions four *pāls* or orders (though one does not know what they were) but states that people from the lower orders could rise to the higher ones by education suggestive of social mobility. Another poem of the same text (335) mentions four *kuṭis* namely *Tuṭiyaṉ, Paṛaiyaṉ, Pāṇaṉ and Kaṭampaṉ* and only one God worthy of being worshipped with paddy strewn before him, namely, the hero stone. There are misconceptions in the interpretation of this poem. Scholars like Nilakanta Sastri and K.K. Pillay[35] have equated four *kuṭis* with four castes. Nilakanta Sastri goes on to say that "these castes and this worship were of very great antiquity, perhaps survivals from pre-Aryan times"[36]. Such misconceptions are not warranted. The poem actually describes a settlement (probably *mullai*) where the four groups (of singers and drummers) resided. Hart takes all the four to be of low status because of the sacred power they came into contact with in their occupations. Evidence, however suggests that the *pāṇar* were held in high esteem in the period of the anthologies and it is only by the early medieval times, they were really condemned as low castes.

The idea of ritual pollution may have have been prevalent as there are references to *pulaiyaṉ*. It has been observed that the term *pulaiyaṉ* is derived from *pulai* which is the ancient Dravidian word for pollution[37]. There are numerous references to low born people such as the *iḻiciṉaṉ* or *iḻipiṟappāḷaṉ* (one of low birth). A low man who stitches a cot (beds) for a woman is called an *iḻiciṉaṉ*[38]. *Puṟanāṉūṟu* 170 refers to the man who plays the *tuṭi* (drum) in a village as an *iḻipiṟappāḷaṉ*. Similarly, the person playing the *tuṭi* when soldiers go to fight a battle is addressed as a *pulaiyaṉ*[39]. So also is the man, who plays the *taṇṇumai* (drum) to summon persons to fight, referred to as a low man and a *pulaiyaṉ*[40].

It is hard to find any reference to restrictions (if any) imposed upon these groups. Even though the idea of pollution may have been prevalent, the practice of untouchability had not taken root. Though the *pulaiyaṉ* was spoken of as *iḻipiṟappāḷaṉ*, degraded or low born, there is no indication that he was an untouchable[41]. There were no commensual taboos or restrictions on inter dining as chieftains dined with warriors during *uṇṭāṭṭu*. Therefore, *varṇa* as an ideology or framework for social hierarchy/ stratification had not taken root in Tamiḻakam in the early phase except in its incipient form in the *marutam* region. The explanation for this phenomenon must be sought in the prevalence of different forms of production with a kin based organisation of the production process. The forms of production were different in different *tiṇais* and the processes of change or development were also uneven. However, in the *marutam,* agriculture as the major economic activity is not only attested but is seen to be consciously promoted and organised by the ruling elite. Hence, when such agricultural activities expanded and a systematic agrarian organisation became necessary, especially due to the concept of the gift of land to *brāhmaṇās* and others who were in royal service, an ideology which could integrate different people into the agrarian organisation also became essential. This, the *brāhmaṇās* provided through their *varṇa* framework.

FOOTNOTES

1. *Tolkāppiyam*: *Porulatikāram* śutras 623-639.
2. It occurs first in the *Paripāṭal* 20:63 and in a minor didactic work *Nāṉmaṇṇikaṭikai*.
3. R. Sumathi, 1984, p. 182.
4. Kailasapathy: 1968, pp. 11-13.
5. *Tolkāppiyam*: *Porulatikāram* 145.
6. Nacciṉārkkiṉiyar states that the *kīḻōr* could not love secretly (*kaḷavu*)-*Tolkāppiyam Porulatikāram* 145. The rites and customs of marriage applicable to the higher and lower folk were common till a point of time (though one is not clear about the date/period)- *Tolkāppiyam*: *Porulatikāram, Kaḷavu Iyal* 117. Could it have changed with the change in material conditions?

7. *Tolkāppiyam*: *Porulatikāram* ; *kaḷavu Iyal*: 117.
   In Nacciṉārkkiṉiyar's view, the *Uyarntōr* were the *brāhmaṇas*. Both the lovers (girl and boy) had to be equal or the hero could be superior in status—*Tolkāppiyam*: *Porulatikāram* , *Kaḷavu Iyal* : 93.
8. *Tolkāppiyam*: *Porulatikāram* ; *Akattiṇai Iyal*: 31; 33.
9. They are referred to as *antaṇar/pārppāṉ*. Etymological meanings of *antaṇar* and *pārppāṉ* are *brāhmaṇās* and seers/*brāhmaṇās*. *DED* 126:p. 12; *DED* 3366:, p. 273.
10. *Perumpāṇāṟṟuppaṭai* 1 301; 1 315
    Puṟanāṉūṟu 26, 122. 2.
    Paṭṭinappālai 1. 202.
11. *Ciṟūpāṇāṟṟuppaṭai* 1.187, 1.204 indicates that they could always go to Amūr palace where the gates were open always.
12. *Aiṅkuṟuṉūṟu* 4:2 ; 387:2
    Puṟanāṉūṟu 1:6 ; 361
    Maturaikkāñci 11.468-75; 1.656
    Paripāṭal 1:13; 3:14
    Kalittokai 36:25; 119:12
    Patiṟṟuppattu 24:8.
13. *Mullaippāṭṭu* 1.37
    Kuṟuntokai 156.
14. *Puṟanāṉūṟu* 93; Hart (Tr.) 1975, p. 41.
15. *Puṟanāṉūṟu* 367: 12-13.
16. The *patikams* of the *Patiṟṟuppattu* mention gifts of land.
17. *Puṟanāṉūṟu* 201; 202. Also Hart, 1975, p. 53.
18. *Puṟanāṉūṟu* 305 Hart (Tr.) 1975, pp. 52-53
    Another one alludes to the *brāhmaṇa* acting as a *dūta-Naṟṟiṇai* 321.
19. *Akanāṉūṟu* 24: 1.
20. 11.299-311, J.V. Chelliah (Tr.) 1962, p. 123.
21. *Perumpāṇāṟṟuppaṭai* 1.297.
22. Hart, 1975, p. 53.
23. *Patiṟṟuppattu* 63: 1-2.
24. *Puṟanāṉūṟu* 9.
25. Hart, 1975, pp. 55-56.
26. *Ibid.*, p. 56.
27. An interesting comparison between the *Kiḻār* (n) with the North Indian counterpart *gahapati* can be made. The *kiḻāṉ* as well *gahapati* were heads of households. Both were wealthy (atleast the *kiḻār* of *meṉpulam*). Some of the *kiḻār* were/became chiefs and distrubuted gifts. Non kin labour may have been employed by the *kiḻāṉ* in cultivation. So we see the emegrence of a householding economy in few parts. For *gahapati* see R. Thapar. 1984, pp. 36-42.
28. I am grateful to Dr. Champakalakshmi for this information.
    Also see *Karandai Tamil Sangam plates of Rajendra Chola I,* Memoirs of the Archaeological Survey of India No.9 (Ed.) K.G. Krishnan, New Delhi, 1984, p. 33:, p. 77.

29. For a discussion of the *gotra* see G.S. Ghurye *Two Brahmanical Institutions Gotra and Charana*, Bombay, 1972.

    T.R. Trautmann definess *gotras* as "exogamous patriarchal clans from an emponymous ancestor who is a *ṛṣi* primeval seer or more strictly a hearer of part of the eternal Veda which he transmits to mankind ot its inestimable benefit"—*Dravidian kinship*. 1987, p. 244.

    Trautman states that only brahmins have true gotras. The main function of these gotras was regulation of marriage, p. 244.
30. R.Thapar, 1984, p. 45.
31. *Puṛanāṇūṛu* 166.
32. Seneviratne, 1985, p. 356.
33. The attributes associated with the *aracar* (*vēntar/mūvēntar?*) with a sceptre (cenkol) are army, flag umbrella drum, horse, elephant, car (chariots?) garland and crown. *Tolkāppiyam* : *Porulatikāram, Marapu Iyal* 626.

    The attributes of the petty rulers are bow, lance, anklet, flower, garland wreath, car and sword-*Tolkāppiyam*: *Porulatikāram, MarapuIyal* 638.
34. The *Tolkāppiyam* also mentions that the *vaicikaṉ* will lead a mercantile life -*Porulatikāram, Marapu Iyal* 632.
35. K.K. Pillay "Land marks in the History of Tamilnad", *Proceedings of the Second International Conference Seminar of Tamil studies,* Madras 1968, Vol. I, p. 18.
36. Nilakanta Sastri *A history of South India*: *from Prehistoric times to the Fall of Vijayanagar,* Madras, 1958, 2nd ed., p. 126.
37. *DED* 3714: Hart, 1975, p. 199.
38. *Puṛanāṇūṛu* 82.
39. *Naṛṛiṇai* 77.
40. *Puṛanāṇūṛu* 289.
41. K.R. Hanumanthan "Was there untouchability in early Tamil society?" *Indian History Congress, Proceedings of the 38th session,* Bhubaneshwar, 1977, p. 96.

CHAPTER - III-C

THE LATER PHASE : SOCIAL TRANSFORMATION

The society of the later phase of the early historical period as gleaned from the epics *Cilappatikāram* and *Maṇimēkalai* and the eighteen minor works may now be taken up for discussion. This distinction between the early and late phase of the early historical period is necessitated by the varying chronological time span of the *Caṅkam* corpus as well as the difference in ideas and contents between the earlier anthologies and the later epic and didactic works.

The anthologies and Ten songs portray a society which was conditioned by the natural/physical environment. All aspects of life were envisaged against the backdrop of nature. In this society elements of change were noticeable in some zones. Within the *marutam* there was agrarian expansion. Differentiation recognisable in the *marutam* was on account of economic factors. A survey of the settlement pattern also indicates change. Dense settlements are seen particularly around the river valleys and in the coastal regions. In these areas emerged the higher levels of polity and possibly *varṇa* differentiation on account of the presence of *brāhmanās*. The 'urban' centres which arose in the *marutam* and *neytal* were characterised by socio-economic diversification and hierarchy. The northern influences are also visible in these *tiṇais* and a merger of the northern ideas with the southern ones can be seen particularly in the fields of religion and polity. Complexity in the religious sphere is attested by the presence of the Brahmanical, Buddhist and Jain ideologies and the absence of a single dominant one. The inscriptions talk of donations to followers of Buddhism and Jainism. New elements crept into the tribal/kinship basis of organisation thereby making way for the rise of a peasant society marked by incipient urbanism.

It is such a society in transformation which produced the minor didactic works. These works are normative and ethical possibly on account of the influence of Jainism and Buddhism. These texts provide clues to indicate the transformation which was setting in. Even the *Tolkāppiyam* which standardised or formalised the existing norms would belong to the category of normative texts although it can be dated to the earlier phase in general (*Eḻuttuatikāram* and *Collatikaram*) whereas its third section *Poruḷa-tikāram* is clearly late and may be co-eval with the minor didactic works. Hence, it reflects a socially differentiated society influenced by the brahmanical ideology of *varṇa* which was adapted to the Tamil social milieu. Thus, most of the elements of change had made their appearance even in the first phase of the early historical period. In the later phase features such as agrarian expansion, growth of urban settlements and marked social differentiation between the high born and low born gained more ground in the fabric of the social formation.

The *Kiḻkkaṇakku* works seem to provide clues to the transition of the existing social formation into a predominantly agrarian one. War ideology which played an important role in the society of the earlier period could not be conducive to agriculture as plundering raids led to destruction of crops and possibly vandalism causing damage to settlements. As a result, there was no possiblity of the evolution of an agrarian base for a more stable political structure. This is also attested by the decline of the major ruling families of the Cēras, Cōḻas and Pāṇṭiyās, once maritime trade declined and the flow of prestige goods on which the three chiefdoms mainly depended for their dominance, ceased. There was no alternative resource base such as an agrarian base with institutional means to appropriate a regular revenue to fall back on.

It is only in the Cōḻa region that such a resource base was just beginning to emerge under the early rulers like Karikāla and perhaps also Perunaṟkiḷḷi who performed the *Rācacūya*. The expansion of agriculture and its dominance over other forms of economy must have been a long process for it is only by the late sixth or early seventh century A.D. that such a development is reflected in the Tamil epigraphic records pointing to the transformation of the tribal/ethnic socio-economic forms towards a predominantly land based agrarian economy.

The earliest recorded evidence indicating this change to a new socio-economic formation comes from a non-*marutam* zone i.e. Pulāṅkuṟicci in the present Ramanathapuram district. The Pulāṅkuṟicci inscription dateable to the 5th century A.D. records the grant of land for the creation of a *brahmadeya* (an agrarian settlement under the *brāhmaṇās*), and lays down the rights, privileges and obligation of land holders, lease holders and actual tillers[1]. This is seen as the "earliest attempts to introduce large scale agriculture in non-marutam areas or drier localities"[2].

In this context, the *Kuṟaḷ*, the most notable among the eighteen didactic works, becomes significant. The *Kuṟaḷ* extolls agriculture. It reflects the existing conditions of those times and emphasises the importance of agriculture in a whole section as agriculture had emerged as an important economic activity. This is evident from the following couplets:

"Husband men (*uḻavar*) are the sheet anchor of the world; for on them depends the lives of others"[3], "Even saints who have forsaken the world needs must cease from spiritual pursuits, were farmers to sit idle with folded arms"[4].

Further, it states that even if one pursues other things one has to return to the plough[5]. "That country which has a peasantry whose fields rustle with thick waves of corn becomes the refuge of several other countries"[6]. To show how crucial the rains were to agriculturalists Vaḷḷuvar, (author of the *Kuṛaḷ*) states that "the cultivators would cease to plough where the clouds free supply of water failed"[7]. Again to show the independence of this occupation, the *Kuṛaḷ* says that "the ploughmen alone live as the freemen of the soil; the rest are mere slaves that batten on their toil"[8]. The peasant is one who toils "in the sweat of his brow, begs not at other men's doors, but ungrudgingly shares his bread with those that beg for alms"[9]. Again, he reiterates the position of the peasant when he states that those who ploughed and ate truly lived, while others were subservient and ate what those, who ploughed, gave.

In addition to all this Valluvar also delineates the agricultural techniques and practices right from ploughing, manuring, weeding, irrigation facilities and guarding of the crop. Besides, he takes note of the measures for control of natural calamities like flood, hail and diseases and pests which are harmful to the crops[10]. For him, there was nothing like land unfit for cultivation as he says that "Dame Earth seems to smile regretfully at the idle sons of the soil who put in no efforts and plead poverty"[11].

In the earlier period it was pointed out that efforts were made to increase cultivation by deforestation by certain rulers like Karikāla. They also provided facilities for irrigation. With land grants (though few in number) the cultivated area definitely increased. The *marutam* along with neytal emerged as the most advanced tiṇas is indicative the increased agrarian expansion in this period a change can be perceived in the *tiṇais*. It was the *marutam* which further grew in importance. The importance of agriculture can be judged from references in another text *Tirikaṭukam*. In fact one of the verses states that one must have the desire to lead the life of a farmer[12] and a farmer will bring about his own downfall if he did not protect his fields when the grain was ripe[13].

Land grants to *brāhmaṇās* led to the formation of a new system of production which transcended kinship ties as the *Brāhmaṇās* not being agriculturists got the lands cultivated by others. In this social formation plough agriculture emerged as the dominant mode of subsistence. All this is indicative of the development of an agrarian society and at the end of this period i.e. by about 6-7th centuries A.D., the dominance of agriculture over all other economic activities was established. The *nāṭu* which was not essentially an agrarian unit in the earlier part of the historical period, emerged as an agrarian peasant unit or a settled area where agricultural operations took place by the end of this period. Further, the *Kōṭṭam* which was a larger unit, pastoral-cum-agricultural also became an agrarian one with many *nāṭus* emerging within it.

It was pointed out that the ruler's right to tax had not been firmly established. Wealth acquired through plunder, loot and tribute could have been the source of revenue to the rulers[14].

The practice of payment of tribute to the ruler continued in the later part of the early historical period. References in the *Cilappatikāram* to tributes paid to the Pāṇṭiyaṉ and Cēra rulers by certain communities are detailed in the chapter on Polity. It is also possible the rulers recognised the importance of a regular source of income from the peasants in the form of land tax with increased agrarian expansion during the later period. The literature takes cognisance of the increase in the dues paid to the king (tax or tribute). Perhaps Vaḷḷuvar's couplet reflects such a situation when he states that "the king who extorts money at the point of the bayonet is like a highway man who waylays the benighted traveller with his threatening cry stand and deliver"[15].

In the later phase of the early historical period there is a change in emphasis from war ideology to moral and ethical basis of kingly authority. Most of the texts (mainly the *Kuṛaḷ*) advocate just or righteous rule by a king, which will benefit his subjects. This is clear from the following couplets.

"The unrighteous king who oppresses his subjects is more cruel than one who leads the life of a murderer"[16].

"That country will perish any day whose monarch does not administer justice by day"[17].

"The people who live under a graceless king suffer like the earth unvisited by drops of rain"[18].

"Victory is won not by the spear but by the unswerving sceptre of a monarch"[19].

"Where people possess a king, who does not enforce justice, wealth does not confer more happiness than poverty"[20].

The northern influences are reflected in certain couplets of the *Kuṛaḷ* which prescribe what a king should have, —in other words, —an administrative machinery. A king's strength lies in a good strong army, territory, wealth, fortress, allies and ministers[21]. Again, there is repeated emphasis on the qualities of a minister and his duties. It is said that a minister (*amaicca*) must have tenacity of purpose, birth in a respectable family, welfare of the people in mind, profound learning and perseverance[22]. Further, the minister should be one who finds out the means, the time, the deed/act and accomplish it[23]. The minister should be capable of strenghening the monarch and earning his praise[24]. A well organised espionage system, in which the King is kept well informed by the spies, is necessary[25].

The epics also talk of two institutions *Aimperuṅkuḻu* and *Enpēr āyam*[26] which helped in the discharge of administrative duties.

All this is suggestive of the presence of or an awareness of the need for an organised administrative apparatus something which was absent in the earlier phase of the early historical period.

Although we hear of an elaborate administrative machinery in the texts such as the *Kuṛaḷ* none of the records throw any light on the political situation of the times after the decline of the three chiefdoms of the Cēra, Cōla and Panṭiya. It has been argued that their decline was due to the withdrawal of the western trade and also due to the "lack of an institutional coherence and resource base to fall back upon in a crisis"[27]. There are no records except for the *Kaḷavaḷi Nārpatu* which sings of the glory of a Cōḷa chieftain defeating a Cēra one. Besides, there is no clear evidence on the political configuration of those times. The only possible reconstruction of this period is made on the basis of later brahmanical records of the Pāṇṭiyas and the Pallavas particularly the Vēḷvikkuḍi grant of the Panṭiyas[28] which refer to the Kalabhras as occupying the political centre of Madurai as *Kaliarasar* or evil kings. It seems that the Kalabhras occupied the Cola region as recorded in a Tamil literary tradition in *Tamiḻ Nāvalar Caritai*[29]. A revival of the Pāṇṭiya authority is claimed to have been made by Katuṅkōṇ (late 6th century A.D.) the first Pāṇṭiya ruler of the early medieval period.

With the dissolution of the heroic society the processes of redistribution and gift giving also underwent a change. No longer did the bards and minstrels play an important role as they did before. While the other singing and dancing groups seemed to have gone into oblivion the *pāṇa* seems to play a less significant role in the patron-client or chieftain-bard relationship which was crucial to the early polities in the first phase. He is more often a mediator of domestic quarrels between the hero and heroine[30]. It has been postulated that the *viraḷi* also had by this time changed into *kaṇika*[31] (courtesan). Presumably the gift and reciprocity between chieftain and bard were not essential to a society transforming itself into a predominantly agrarian or farming one.

Inhabitants of the *tiṇais* who were clan/lineage groups continued to live in dispersed segments in the *tiṇais* although the references to them in the epics and minor didactic works are few. Groups like *maṛavar, maḻavar, eyiṇar, kōvalar, paratavar* and *kuṛavar* continued to inhabit their eco-zones. While, some of them like the *maṛavar, maḻavar, paratavar* are referred to as living in the 'urban' centres, others like *eyiṇar, kōvalar, vēṭṭuvar* etc., lived on the fringes of the urban settlements or in the forests. All this is evidenced by the eighteen didactic works and the two epics.

Among these the love poems such as *Aintiṇai Aimpatu, Aintiṇai Eḻupatu, Kainnilai, Kar Nārpatu, Tiṇaimālai Nuṛraimpatu* etc. described the social groups living in the *tiṇais* more or less on the same lines as the anthologies. The *kōvalar* of *mullai* are mentioned to be playing the flute[32]. The *kuṛavar* girls are said to live in the hills[33] and the *kāṇavar* are said to grow the *enal*[34]. While the *eyiṇar* of *pālai* are portrayed as hunters wielding the bow, the *kalvar/kaḷḷar/kaṇaiyar* of the *pālai* are described as robbers who looted and killed travellers passing through their tracts[35]. These groups were still bound by ties of kinship.

As for the *pālai* the *maṛavar* and *maḻavar* may have moved away from *pālai* to the *marutam* and *neytal* areas. They are described to be soldiers/warriors who fought gory battles[36] in the capital cities. There are no references. in the epics to these people harassing wayfarers/travellers. While some of them may have given up looting and heinous practice of killing people, some would have settled for fighting in the armies on account of their physical prowess.

The fact of the fish mongers selling fish on the seashore and fishermen fishing in the *timil* (boat) is highlighted in the *Cilappatikaram*. Songs on the seashore (*kānal vari*) sung by Kōvalaṉ and Mātavi as described by the *Cilappatikāram* provide facets of the fishermen's lives-their living in small huts, catching and drying of fish on the lines of the earlier anthologies. Such a transformation showing considerable overlaps is attested by the fact that the kinship basis of organisation continued even in the later phase of the early historical period. The *tiṇai* groups were still bound by ties of kinship. Terms used for the kin are *emar*[38] and *eṉṉaiyar*[39] (probably included the closed kin i.e. father, mother, brothers etc.) The eighteen minor works are emphatic on the maintenance of relationship between the kin members/ relatives (*cuṟṟam, cuṟṟattār, kiḷaiñar*). Kinsmen are said to be the source of fortune and wealth[40]. It is apparent from a verse that some sort of division may have existed among clans as it mentions that it is not good to marry into a clan/ lineage/ community (*kulam*) of lesser status[41].

As for the *marutam* region, signs of change are more conspicuous and indicative of greater complexity. As for the inhabitants of *marutam* the description in the *Cilappatikāram* is interesting. On the route to Madurai, Kōvalaṉ, Kaṇṇaki and Kavunṭi Aṭikaḷ heard the songs of the *uḻavar* (*ērmankalam*), of the *kaḷamar* (who were presumably labourers) while they threshed the grain and the drums played by the *porunar*[42]. Besides, they saw more settlements of the *uḻavar* who were responsible for supporting the people[43].

Regarding the bards who travelled about in search of patrons the only referred to is the *pāṇa*. The *pāṇa* is mostly mentioned in the context of the *marutam*. He seems to have become the spokesman and mediator between the heroine and the hero's quarrels over the hero's visits to the *parattai* (harlot). Only in one instance is a *pāṇa* stated to be singing a hymn on the war dance of Durga (Koṟṟavai[44]). Did the *pāṇa* start to sing of the Gods (deities) instead of singing glories of the chieftain/ ruler and would this indicate the change?

The institution of harlotry seems to have become entrenched by this period particularly in the marutam *tiṇai* on account of the leisure the people had in the agricultural regions. Moreover, the control of land would have also made them wealthy enough to indulge in certain practices like visiting the harlots. There are references to *kaṇikai* (courtesans) in the epics who lured wealthy men by their charming methods[45]. On the other hand, the *Kiḻkkaṇakku* works on account of their ethical nature and influence of the heterodox sects look down upon such women who are called by a variety of names such as *poruṭ peṇṭir, taṉṉēri peṇṭir, ceykai makaḷir, vēcaiyar and kaṇika* and condemn associations with them[46].

There is some indication of the impact of *varṇa* from the didactic texts. The *brāhmaṇās* emerged as a superior group by this period. *Brāhmaṇās* (*antaṇar, pārppāṉ*) are generally portrayed in the epics as well versed in the four Vedas. They are referred to by different terms such as *Māmaṛaiyāḷaṉ, Nāṉmarai-antanar, naval antanan* and *irupirappalar.* In the minor didactic works, the *brāhmaṇa* is generally defined as one who recites the *Vedas* and fully understands it, one who leads a virtuous and righteous life[47]. It is good for the *brāhmanās* to live without forgetting the *Vedas*. Even if he forgot them he could learn anew. But the *brāhmana* should not fall from his status[48]. Respect towards the *brāhmaṇas* is advocated[49]. In fact the texts maintain that one should follow the path of the person well versed in the *Vedas*[50]. Donations to the *brāhmaṇas* in the form of cattle and gold is considered beneficial[51]. Their settlements are said to be clean, without the presence of dogs and hen[52]. The *brāhmaṇas* knowledge of astronomy is also hinted at[53]. Further, one text even stresses the fact that there is no birth like the *brāhmaṇa's* birth[54].

What is interesting is the fact of the *brāhmaṇas* being treated well even in the texts some of which were authored by Jains and Buddhists. Could this have led to the slow emergence of *brāhmaṇas* both as controllers of land and as ideologues? The Brahmanical knowledge of the calendar and astronomy may have further helped in the extension of cultivation in non-agrarian areas also[55]. By this time they seemed to have emerged as a superior group Therefore, in this context the respect shown to the *brāhmaṇas* or the emphasis on their high birth is more meaningful.

These didactic texts laid emphasis on high birth and advocated association with the high born[56]. Thus society of this period was characterised by marked social differentiation between the high born and the low born. Those of low birth are generally looked down upon. People of high birth (born in a good *kuṭi*) are said to do their duty, be principled and offer aid to others even when they are poor[57]. Besides, they are said to possess good conduct, dignity and excellence. Even if others have acquired wealth they do not possess these qualities[58]. Further, the high born never lose their self respect and utter words of abuse even when they have been abused[59]. Association and friendship with the high born *(periyavar, cāṉṟōr periyār)* is emphasised. Texts explicitly state that the low born could ally or become friendly with the high born[60] who are supposed to have good, pleasant speech, liberal hand and purity of mind. Such associations with the high born are compared to treasure troves[61]. Further, the high born are said to be those who value or honour their reputation and rear a blot on this[62]. However, a high birth without lofty aims / ideals is also useless[63]. On the contrary the low born *(kiḻmakkaḷ, kaṭaiyāya makkaḷ, kayavar)* are spoken of in derogatory terms.

These low born are spoken of in such derogatory terms[64] that even stones are stated to be better than low men. The low born do not understand decorum, do not give even when they can, do not perform good deeds that well born do even when things do not go well with them; and speak low words unlike the high born *(mēṉmakkaḷ*[65]*)* The *Ācāra kkōvai,* one of the eighteen texts, states that the *kiḻmakkaḷ* will not be talked of highly[66].

Although the texts seem to denounce the *kiḻmakkaḷ* per se, they state that these *kiḻmakkaḷ* could not be done away with altogether[67]. In other words, were the services of the *kiḻmakkaḷ* essential to the highborn?

The influence of *varṇa* is also suggested by the idea of ritual pollution, the restriction on the low born from learning the *Vedas*[68] and the denouncement of the low born.

Some of the texts are emphatic on the highborn avoiding contact/relation with the low born (*kiḻmakkaḷ*[69]). A verse advises those born in a high / good *kuṭi* not to live with the *kiḻmakkaḷ*[70]. Another verse from the same text (3) states that *kiḻmakkaḷ* should not be brought into the house. The presence of ritual pollution is suggested by a verse which stresses on bathing when touched by a low born[71]. It is interesting that medieval commentators like Arumpatavuriāciriyar interpreted the epic in *Cilappatikāram's* reference to the goldsmith walking at a distance from others to mean that being a member of a low caste, he kept himself at a respectable distance from members of higher castes[72]. This, however, can be attributed to the commentator's background or the context in which he was writing when the caste distinction had become well established.

The above survey is enough to indicate that by this period social differentiation had set in between the high born and the low born. The texts do not specify who the low born are or which are the categories of people to be classified this way. Whoever they were, their nature and deeds were frowned upon by the authors of the text. The text *Ācara Kkōvai* which talks of the concept of purity/ pollution and the restrictions on the low born seems to represent the view of the orthodox elements of the period.

Did the concept of purity/pollution gain ground on account of the impact of Sanskritic influence or because of the tribal moorings? The idea of pollution is not unknown to tribal societies. At this juncture it is not so easy to find answers to these issues as the texts to not provide direct evidence.

The texts are more concerned with ethics and morality. They are more intent on defining the *cāṉṟōr/ cāṉṟōṉ* ideal/wise men/man. Emphasis on this could possibly be attributed to the influence of the 'heterodox' sects. The *cāṉṟōr* (who could be the *uyarntōr*) are said to have the qualities of modesty, humility, good conduct, virtuousness and truthfulness[73]. They are supposed to be balanced[74] in times of adversity or prosperity, feed the hungry and give gifts[75]. In fact they are not supposed to stray from the path of virtues, as the texts state that it is better to be poor than gain wealth by committing sin[76]. Again another verse states that the truly great people scorn the riches acquired through slaughter[77]. The *cāṉṟōr* are grateful for any favours done[78]. To be called a *cāṉṟōr* in the society of that period carried a lot of importance and this is aptly reflected in a couplet of the *Kuṟaḷ* which says that a mother experiences more joy on hearing of her son being called a *cāṉṟōr* than at his birth[79]. Maintenance of good conduct and virtues was necessary[80].

Complexity of social organisation is further indicated by the increasing trade and commerical activities and the incipient urbanism stimulated by external trade due to which urban centres rose in certain restricted areas namely, *marutam* an *neytal*. It has been argued that decline of trade in the 3rd century A.D. synchronised with the decline of towns in north India[81]. As far as Tamiḻakam is concerned, the epics *Cilappatikāram* and *Maṇimēkalai* described the three main centres of Pukār, Madurai and Kāñcipuram in considerabel detail. From these descriptions the urban character of these settlements is evident. In fact the story of the epics is set in the main centres of those times. Although the story of the *Cilappatikāram* begins in Pukār (Kāvēripaṭṭiṉam) with an elaborate description of it, it also acquaints the readers with that Madurai and Vañci though the descriptions of these centres is hardly on the lines of Pukār. The description of Kāñcipuram found in *Maṇimēkalai* tallies more or less with of *Kāvēripaṭṭiṉam*. In the early historical period these urban centres in the *marutam* and neytal tracts housed heterogenous populations. The prosperity of these centres is reflected in the epics. However, this prosperity did not spread to the hinterlands and rural areas and there was a certain dichotomy between the 'rural' and 'urban'.

Pukār was strategically located at the mouth of the Kāveri. That it was a major centre involved in commercial activities is supported by the evidence in *Cilappatikāram*, which mentions:

"The untold wealth of the seafaring merchants of the rich city (Pukar) made even far famed monarchs covet it. The varieties of foreign merchandise rare commodities brought to the city by ships and caravans, were so vast that even if the whole world encircled by the roaring seas flocked into it, its wealth would not become diminished"[82].

The spatial organisation and social diversification of Pukār is very well highlighted in the *Cilappatikāram*. It was said to have distinct areas or localities. Two main areas of the city were *maruvūrpākkam* and *paṭṭinapākkam*. The *Maṇimēkalai* (I.72) also refers to the residential area as *Akaṇagar*. Separate areas were earmarked for the market place, the occupational/craft groups, the palace, army, port and shrines.

Kāvēripaṭṭiṉam housed the *Yavaṇās* (merchants from the west, who had their abodes) and sailors from distant lands[83]. In the streets of the city could be seen hawkers (*pakarvāṇar*) who went around with paints, bathing powders and cool pastes, flowers, incense and fragrant scents. Some places had the weavers selling fine fabrics made of silk, fur and cotton[84].

The market place at Pukār is discussed in the *Cilappatikāram*. Mention is made of people practising various trades starting their work in the early hours of the morning. Thus we are told of the cries of the sellers of foodstuffsk *kāḻiyar* (seller of *piṭṭu*) and *kūviyar* (seller of *āppam*); of toddy sellers (*kaṇṇōtai yāṭṭiyar*); of fishergirls (*mīṇvilaip-paratavar*); sellers of salt, (*veḷḷaiuppupakarunar*) sellers of meat (*paṇṇiṇ vilaiñar*); oil merchants (*ōcunar*); sellers of betel leaves (*pācavar*); sellers of perfume (*vācavar*); workers in bronze and copper (*Kañcakārar, cempuceya tarunar*); carpenters (*maraṅko *taccar*); blacksmiths (karuṅkai kollar); painters (*kaṇṇul viṇaiñar*), makers of dolls in clay (*maṇṇīttāḻar*); goldsmiths (*poṇceykollar*); workers in gems (*naṇkalan taruna*); tailors (*tuṇṇakarar*), workers in leather (*tōliṇtuṇṇar*); tailors (*tuṇṇakarar*), workers in leather (*tōliṇtuṇṇar*); musicians (*perumpāṇa*) and small artisans (*ciṛukuṛuṅkaiviṇai*). Further the epic states that these traders and workers had their own alloted quarters in the city with each living in a street[85]. This area of the place was known as *maruvūrpākkam*. All the specialist traders, craft groups lived in one area of the city which indicates that a separate area was exclusively earmarked for them. This, however, does not suggest their segregation or isolation from other communities and other parts of the urban centre. Presence of many craftsmen is indicative of a certain degree of craft specialisation. these sepcialists mainly living in urban centres like Pukār would have catered essentially to the urban elite/ruling families.

The *Cilappatikāram* furnishes information of another area in the city. Thus we are told about "the King's street, the car (chariot?) street with flying flags, the bazaar street, the broad highway where high born merchants (*peruṅkuṭi vāṇikar*) lived on either side in the turrented houses, the Brahmana street (*maṛaiyōr*), the street of physicians and astrologers (*āyuḷ vētar and kālak-kaṇitar*) respectively and of agricultural communities, and the broad street having the residences of those who desterously bored holes in gems and pearls (*tirumaṇi kuyiṛṛunar*) and mounted them and of those who polished the shells and the conches that were worn as ornaments (*valai-pōḷunar*). There were also separate quarters where dwelt *sūtas* and *māgadhas* , religious dancers (*aṇaṅke untāṭi*), astronomers mock dancers, prostitutes (*kāvaṛkṇikaiyar*), actresses (*ātaṛ kūttiyar*) maidens bearing flowers and betels (*puvilai-maṭantaiyar*), maid servants, bagpipe musicians, drummers of different sorts, buffoons and jesters (Nakaiveam-par)"[86].

About the *pattiṇapākkam,* we are told that "in an extensive open space, on the outskirits of the city were quarters occupied by cavalrymen with swift horses (*kaṭ umpari kaṭavunar*), elephant warriors (*kaliṛṛiṇ pākar*), charioteers with lofty chariots (*Neṭuntērūrunar*) and infantrymen with fearsome looks (*kaṭuṅkaṇ maṛavar*)"[87].

Further, the portion of the city between the *maruvūrppākkam* and *paṭṭiṇappākkam* was open and looked like a battlefied where the armies of two great kings could meet[88]. The market place (*naḷaṅkāṭi*) had permanent stalls where the noise of the buyers and sellers could be heard throughout the day[89].

As many as five *maṉṟams* (open places) are mentioned in the texts. The *veḷḷitaimaṉṟam* was the place where bundles of goods with names of owners were kept[90]. After this was the *ilañcimaṉṟam* with a miraculous lake. By bathing in this lake and going around it the hunchbacks and cripples, the dumb, the deaf and the lepers were cured of their deformities and gained health and grace of form[91]. The open place which had the shining stone was the *neṭuṅkālniṉṟamaṉṟam*. This shining stone also is said to have had healing powers and cured all those who had been bitten by snakes and those that had gone mad[92]. The *pūta* stood at the meeting place of four roads (*pūtacatukkam*[93]). There was another place (*pāvaimaṉṟam*) where there was a statue which would not open its mouths but would weep when the king deviated from the path of justice[94]. These open places could have served as the meeting ground of people from all walks of life.

Besides these, a number of temples (brahmanical and Buddist) are also mentioned. A discussion of this will be taken up in the later part of this section (vide Map 1).

Describing the coastal areas and the seashore, the text informs us that one could see different kinds of goods brought in ships by foreign merchants (*pulam peyar mākkaḷ*) who had left their homes and settled here. Light emanating from the lamps of probably hawkers and vendors who sold dyes, sandalwood, flowers, scents and sweets; the goldsmith (*ceyviṉai kammiyar*), of the *kḷiyar* and *kūviyar* (sellers of fooodstuffs like *piṭṭu* and *āppam*), of the shops of girl vendors of the fishmongers (*miṉvilai pakarvōr*), beacon lights erected to guide ships on the seashore (lighthouses?) of the fishermen (*paratavar*) who went fishing in their *timil*, of the foreigners speaking different languages (*moḻipeyar tettōr*) and lastly of the guards of the warehouses containing merchandise (*Paṇtaṅ kāvalar*[95]).

The author of the *Periplus* classified Pukār as a market town[96] while Ptolemy elevated it to the status of an emporium[97]. The fact that it served as an entrepot is reflected in the literature[98]. The harbour facilities and storehouses/ lighthouses in the coastal area have already been referred to in the earlier section. Foreign merchants and traders also settled here. In this context, it is interesting to note that one of the numerous sites excavated in the Kāvēripattiṇam complex is called Veḷḷaiyan Iruppu (white man's settlement). However, excavations here have shown occupational deposits going back only to the 9th-12th centuries A.D.[99]

Pukār was also probably a manufacturing centre of jewellery as several beads of semi-precious stone like agate, carnelian, chalcedony and jasper in various stages of manufacture have been unearthed from the early historical levels[100]. The presence of various crart specialists have already been referred to.

From the above it is evident that Pukār was one of the most important and vibrant 'urban' complex of those times.

We get acquainted with Madurai, a pērur (big settlement) situated on the river Vaikai, the capital of the Pāṇṭiyaṉ kingdom[101], from the *Cilappatikāram* when Kōvalaṉ enters it. The layout of this city was of a pattern different from Pukār. After passing through the fertile paddy fields the travellers (Kōvalaṉ and Kaṇṇaki) entered the suburbs of the fortress (surrounded by a moat) where lived the men practising *dharma* and which had residential quarters intersected by streams of fresh floods, lakes of expansive waters, fruit bearing coconuts, plantain trees, areca palms and bamboo sheds (rest houses?) for supplying water[102]. Kovalan entered through a street above a narrow passage (tunnel-*curaṅ*) leading from the moat encircled by defence forests guarded by *Yavaṉa* swordsman. Next he went through this forest gate and saw the interior part of the city. He saw courtesans in a street. After this he went through a highway which had double row of beautiful buildings which were the residences of courtesans and dancers[103]. The market place (*aṅkāṭi*) which Kōvalaṉ passed through had covered carts and vehicles, medicines, ornamented chariots etc. besides workers in copper and bronze, garlandmakers, saws made of steel, instruments for ivory cutting. Other streets passed by Kōvalaṉ were those of the diamond dealers, goldsmiths (the street which had flags) of cloth merchants (where several kinds of bundles of cloth were piled up) of the dealers of grain and black pepper. He also passed through the termini of four streets, streets of petty shops, *maṉrams*, lanes and broad streets before going beyond the ramparts[104]. Kōvalaṉ is reported to have felt pleased after seeing this big city of the Pāṇṭiya ruler. Though such an evidence is meagre compared to that of the descriptions of Pukār and Kāñci, it nevertheless provides interesting information of the spatial organisation at Madurai.

Madurai was an important centre of textiles as evident from the references in the *Arthaśāstra* to cotton fabrics from this place which has been pointed out in the earlier section.Archaeological excavations have not yielded anything connected with textiles at this site. In fact no systematic excavations could take place due to the continuous occupation of the city and the lack of potential areas for digging[105].

A description of Kañci (stituated on the river Vegavati a tributary of Pālar) is provided by the *Maṇimēkalai* when the work narrates the episode of the heroine Maṇimēkalai entering the town through the fort gate which was beautifully made. The description of the layout of Kañci given in the *Maṇimēkalai* is similar to the *Cilappatikāram's* description of Pukār. Maṇimēkalai saw the broad street that housed the soldiers (*Kāvalaḷar*) who guarded the other city limits. The streets where lived fish vendors, (*paṇmīṉ vilaiñar*) the sellers of white salt (*veḷḷaiuppu pakarunar*), saleswomen or wine pedlars (kaṇṇotaiyāṭṭiyar) sellers of *piṭṭu* and *āppam* (*kāḷiyar and kūviyar*), sheep's meat hawkers (*Mainniṇa vilaiñar*) sellers of betel leaves (*pācavar*) and perfumes (*vācavar*), coppersmiths and bronzesmiths (*cempuceyññar and kañcakārar*), goldsmiths (*poṇceykollar*) and metalworkers, carpenters (*maraṅko taccar*), painters (*ōviyamākkaḷ*), workers in leather (*toliṇ tuṇṇar*), tailors (*tuṇṇaviṇaiñarun*), garland makers (*mālaikkārar*), astronomers (*kālakkaṇitar*), musicians (*pāṇa*), workers in gems (*ilaṅkumaṇi viṇaiñar*), dancing women adept in dancing (*kūttiyar*), the bazaar street where heaps of grains were seen, street of minstrels like *māgatar, sūtar* and *vētāḷikar,* street of courtesans, street of weavers who weave finely (*nuṇṇuṛ kaiviṇai*), street of sellers of various gems (*panmaṇi pakarvōr*), street of *brāhmaṇās* (*maṛaiyor*) doing their work, street of officials and ministers (*amaicca*) the street of those who are in high professions (in administration?), public halls, assemblies, junction of streets and square (*maṉram, potiyil, canti, catukkam*) streets where elephants were trained and horses decorated with gold beads. Further after crossing them Manimekalai saw artificial hills and woodlands with waterfalls flowing that could even bring the gods from heaven down to the earth. Then she saw roads and rooms. glittering assembly halls and painted halls. Finally she entered the Indra *Vihāra* where the ascetics praised the Buddha and where she met Kovalan's father[106].

These were the various streets where the administrative and occupational groups lived. Presence of craftsmen from places outside Kanci and abroad are also recognised. The text states that jewellers from Magadha (*Makata viṇaiñar*), goldsmiths from Marāṭ ṭa (*Marāṭṭa kammar*), blacksmiths from Avanti, carpenters from the West (yavaṇa taccar) along with Tamil artisans (*Taṇtamiḻ viṇaiñar*) worked together to create the throne (of the Cōḷa king) which had coral legs, and bejewelled pillars[107]. Judging from this literary evidence, Kañci seems to have become a big urban centre from a *mūtūr* (old settlement) which had market places and buildings Since bangles of shell in various stages of manufacture have been profusely found in excavations at a locality in the vicinity of Kāñci locally known as Pallavamedu it can be deduced that Kāñci was a manufacturing centre of conch bangles[108]. Procurement of shell must not have been a problems as Kāñci had access to the coastal area through the port of Nīrppeyaṟṟu (Vasavasamudram?).

Morever, Pukār and Kāñci seem to have been occupied from an early period as attested by the urn burials and black and red ware discovered here. All the three centres rose to prominence in the early part of the historical period. Neither the decline of the three kingdoms nor the decline in trade seemed to have arrested the growth of these urban centres by the time of the epics. They must have been big centres to warrant such descriptions in the epics. The heterogenous character of the population of these centres is testified by literary sources. Archaeological excavations have not revealed monumental differentiation. Therefore, the textual and limited archaeological evidence seem sufficient to denote these centres as urban. From these descriptions it is evident that the *marutam* and *neytal* continue to be the most advanced *tiṇais* characterised by the presence of urban centres and soci-economic diversification.

FOOTNOTES

1. R.Nagaswamy "An outstanding Epigraphical Discovery in Tamil Nadu", *Fifth International Conference of Tamil Studies,* Madurai, 1981, Section 2, pp. 67-72.
2. R.Champakalakshmi, 1986, pp. 13-14.
3. *Kuṛaḷ* 1032.
4. *Kuṛaḷ* 1036; B.Natarajan (Tr) 1971, p. 81.
5. *Kuṛaḷ* 1031.,
6. *Kuṛaḷ* 1034; B.Natarajan (Tr) 1971, p. 81.
7. *Kuṛaḷ* 14

   So crucial were the rains to life which made Valluvar say that neither life nor right conduct can exist without water-*Kuṛaḷ* 20, He devotes a whole section to the discussion on rains: 11-20.
8. *Kuṛaḷ* 1033; B.Natarajan (Tr.) 1971, p. 81.

9. *Kuṛaḷ* 1035; B.Natarajan (Tr.) 1971, p. 82.
10. *Kuṛaḷ* 1038; B.Natarajan (Tr.) 1971, p. 82.
According to the *Cirupancamulam,* the farmer will protect his land, loosen the soil, add manure and then will plough it with a *kalappai* 58.
11. *Kuṛaḷ* 1040; B. Natarajan (Tr.) 1971, p. 82. A land abandoned by her owner is as sulky as a woman abandoned by her lord-*Kuṛaḷ* 1039.
12. *Tirikaṭukam* 42.
13. *Tirikaṭukam* 59.
It was necessary for the farmers to have bullocks. According to the *Nānmaṇi,* a *vēḷaḷaṉ* (farmer) is one who has bullocks-5.
To the farmer without bullocks scanty water also entailed suffering- *Iṉṉā Nāṟpatu* - 4.
14. *Kuṛaḷ* 756 mentions that the revenues of ruler are unclaimed wealth, tolls, and tributes.
15. *Kuṛaḷ* 552 B.Natarajan "Economic Ideas of Thiruvalluvar", Thirumathi Sornammal endowment lectures on Tirukkural, 1959-60 - 1968-69, University of Madras, 1971, p. 2.
16. *Kuṛaḷ* 551; Ramachandra Dikshitar (Tr.), p. 115.
17. *Kuṛaḷ* 553; Ramachandra Dikshitar (Tr.), p. 115.
18. *Kuṛaḷ* 557; Ramachandra Dikshitar (Tr.), p. 115.
19. *Kuṛaḷ* 546; Ramachandra Dikshitar (Tr.), p. 113.
20. *Kuṛaḷ* 558.
Also see *Kuṛaḷ* 558; 548; 545; 542; 561; 556, 564.
Besides the *Iṉṉā Nāṟpatu* states that living under a cruel king is suffering and to prostrate before a king who does not deserve it is not good - 3 and 13. Further, two more couplets of the *Kuṛaḷ* may be taken into account: The sceptre of the king is the standing proof of the *brāhmaṇās* and their teachings. Another one indicates that the *brāhmaṇās* who perform six duties will forget the Vedas and the yield of the cows will go down if the protecting King fails in his duties *Kuṛaḷ* 543 and 560.
Qualities such as fearlessness, liberality, wisdom, grace, energy, love for his subjects and protection and working for the welfare of the subjects are prescribed -*Kuṛaḷ* 390; 544; 382; 388.
21. *Kuṛaḷ* 761; 381; *Tirikaṭukam* 100
In fact Vaḷḷuvar mentions that a king who is not guarded by men of firm counsel will be ruined even if he has no enemies *Kuṛaḷ* 448
Could such notions be based on the '*Saptanga*' theory of the state propounded by Kautilya in his *Arthaśāstra?* The *Arthaśāstra* defines the seven elements as *svami* (ruler) *amatya* (minister) *janapada* (territory and population) *durga* (fortress), *kōsa* (treasury), *danda* (coercive, power) and *mitra* (ally). For details see R.S.Sharma's *Aspects of Political Ideas and Institutions in Ancient India,* Delhi 1991, pp. 31-48.
The difference between the two texts is that the *danda* or coercive power is mentioned in the *Arthaśāstra* but in the *Kuṛaḷ* the army is listed instead of danda.
22. *Kuṛaḷ* 632.
23. *Kuṛaḷ* 631; 634.
24. *Kuṛaḷ* 665.
According to the *Kuṛaḷ,* a treacherous minister of the king is equivalent to seventy crores of enemies - 639.

25. *Kuraḷ* 582, 583.
26. *Cilappatikāram* XXV: 11. 38-81.
    Maṇimēkalai I: 17
    For details regarding the composition of these two administrative institutions see N.Subramanian's *Sangam Polity,* Madurai, 1980, pp. 95-101.
27. R.Champakalakshmi "Urbanisation in South India: The Role of Ideology and Polity", Presidential Address, Section I, Ancient India, *Indian History Congress,* Proceedings of the 47th session, Srinagar, 1986, pp. 12-13.
28. Burton Stein holds that the "Kalabhra interregnum; as it is sometimes called may mark a point where non peasant people made their strongest bid to control some, at least of low land peasant population...." The Kalabhra rulers favoured Jainism
    Peasant State and Society in Medieval South India, New Delhi, 1980, p. 77;, pp. 76-81.
29. Nilakanta Sastri, 1958, p. 139.
    Nilakanta Sastri, *The Cōlas,* 1975 (Rp.), p. 102, fn.8.
30. *Aintiṇai Eḻupatu* 45; 46; 48; 49.
    Aintiṇai Aimpatu 21; 22; 23.
    Kainnilai 42, 45, 46, 47, 48.
    The *Tolkappiyam* mentions the *pāṇa* as a *vāyil* (spokesman).
31. S.C.Kersenboom Story "Virali (Possible sources of the Devadasi tradition in the Tamil Bardic period)" *Journal of Tamil Studies,* Vol. 19. June 1981, pp. 32-35.
32. *Aintiṇai Eḻupatu* 22; *Kainnilai* 10; *Kuraḷ* refers to the *ayar* playing the flute 1228. *Aintiṇai Aimpatu* 7 refers to the *ayaṉ* playing the flute.
33. *Tiṇai Moḻi* 4; 8.
34. *Kainnilai* 13; *Tiṇaimoḻi* 20.
35. *Kainnilai* 22; 23
    Aintiṇai Aimpatu 35; *Aintiṇai Eḻupatu* 36.
36. *Cilappatikāram* XXVI : 163; 170; 181.
    The *Kaḷavaḻi Nārpatu* which provides a description of the gory battle between the Cōḻa ruler and the Cēra ruler refers to the *maṛavar* as warriors who fight with weapons, who do not run away from the battlefield and who constitute the cavalry - 16; 22; 24; 28; 31.
37. *Cilappatikāram* XXII :13.
    Maṇimēkalai I:68; XXVI;86;
    XXVI:42.
38. *Tiṇai Moḻi* 5.
39. *Kainnilai* 54.
40. *Kuraḷ* 522; 524, *Nalatiyar* 179.
41. *Iṉṉā Nārpatu* 19.
42. *Cilappatikāram* X:11,125-26; 11.135-39.
43. *Cilappatikāram* X:11. 153-55.
44. *Cilappatikāram* XIII:11. 104-05.
45. *Cilappatikāram* XIV:71
    Maṇimēkalai XXIV: 2; XVI: 6;9 VII:50

Terms such as *parattai, kaṭaikaḻi makaḻir* are also used to denote the courtesans/harlots.

46. *Kuṛaḷ* 913; *Nālaṭiyār* 378; 375; 371; 354.

    Tirikaṭukam 81; 24 (words of the *parattai* land a person in great pain). One does not come across a *Kaṇikai* who says that she has no interest in wealth-*Tirikaṭukam* 76.

47. *Kuṛaḷ* 30; *Tirikatukam* 70; 98

    The *Nānmaṇikatikai* states that the *antaṇar's* mind should think of good thoughts. There are certain days on which *brāhmaṇās* do not read the Vedas i.e full moonday, new moon day, during rains and earthquake and on *ashtami* day - *Ācarakkōvai* 47.

48. *Iṇiyavai Nāṟpatu* 7; *Kuṛaḷ* 134.

49. *Ācarakkovai* 61; *Tirikatukam* 42.

    The *Ēlati* 54 states that those who help the *brāhmaṇās* will live longer.

50. *Iṉṉā Nāṟpatu* 2.

51. *Tirikaṭukam* 2.

52. *Iṇiyavai Nāṟpatu* 23.

53. The *Ācarakkōvai* 92 states that if people consult *antanar* about good days and do the things they want to do then they will be successful. *Antaṇar's* knowledge of the almanac would have been helpful in this.

54. *Nānmanikaṭikai* 35

55. R. Champakalakshmi 1986, p. 15.

56. *Nālaṭiyār* 146; *Tirikaṭukam* 92 indicates that a poor person who is not born in a good gamily need not have been born.

57. *Nālaṭiyār* 150: G.U Pope (Tr.), p. 68; 148; G.U Pope (Tr.), p. 67; 147; G.U Pope (Tr.), pp. 66-67; 141; G.U. Pope (Tr.), p. 64.

58. *Nālaṭiyār* 142: G.U. Pope (Tr.), pp. 64-65.

59. *Nālaṭiyār* 156; G.U. Pope (Tr.), p. 70

    Nālaṭiyār 69 states that those born in a good *kuti* are good towards even those who injure them.

60. *Nālaṭiyār* 125; G.U. Pope (Tr.), p. 54; 175, G.U. Pope (Tr.), p. 78; 177, G.U. Pope (Tr.), p. 79.

    Nālaṭiyār 172 advises that pople should gain from the words of the great men (*Periyār*).

61. *Nālaṭiyār* 160, G.U. Pope (Tr.), p. 160.

62. *Kuṛaḷ* 957.

    Nālaṭiyār 151, G.U. Pope (Tr.), p. 68.

63. *Nālaṭiyār* 199, G.U. Pope (Tr.), p. 88.

64. *Nālaṭiyār* 334; G.U. Pope (Tr.), p. 147.

65. *Nālaṭiyār* 143; G.U. Pope (Tr.), p. 65.

    96; G.U. Pope (Tr.), p. 42; 70 G.U. Pope (Tr.), p. 32.

66. *Ācarakkōvai* 80.

67. *Paḻamoḻi* 356.

68. *Paḻamoḻi* 229 restricts the *Cāṉṟōr* from teaching Vedas to the low born.

69. *Ēlati* 4 and 19 prescribe avoidance of relations with the low born.

    Tirikaṭukam 51 urges one to be away from the *kayavar* (*kiḻmakkaḷ*).

70. *Tirikaṭukam* 77.
71. *Ācarakkōvai* 10; *Ācarakkōvai* 86 orders people not to ask what the low born ate.
72. As quoted in V.R.R. Dikshitar, 1978, p. 257.
73. *Kuṛaḷ* 299; 982; 985; 1014.
74. *Kuṛaḷ* 115; 118.
75. *Nālaṭiyār* 184: G.U. Pope (Tr.), p. 82; 190; G.U. Pope (Tr.), p. 84.
76. *Kuṛaḷ* 657.
77. *Kuṛaḷ* 328; Also *Nālaṭiyār* 275, G.U. Pope (Tr.), p. 121.
78. *Nālaṭiyār* 344.
79. *Kuṛaḷ* 69.
80. Abstinence from drinking is advocated as a drunkard can never command the homage of the great - *Kural* 922, 923.
81. R.S.Sharma, "Decay of Gangetic Towns in Gupta and Post-Gupta times", *Indian History Congress* Proceedings of the 33rd Session, Muzaffarpur 1972, pp. 92-104.
82. *Cilappatikāram* II: 1-8, V.R.R. Dikshitar (Tr.) The *Cilappatikāram* 2nd ed. Madras 1978, p. 99.
83. *Cilappatikāram* V.11. 10-11.
84. *Cilappatikāram* V 11. 15-22.
85. *Cilappatikāram* V 11.23-39.
86. *Cilappatikāram* V, 11.40-53; V.R.R.Dikshitar (Tr.) *Cilappatikāram* 1978, p. 122.
87. *Cilappatikāram* V. 11. 54-56.
88. *Cilappatikāram* V. 11. 57-60.
89. *Cilappatikāram* V. 61-63.
90. *Cilappatikāram* V. 115-17.
91. *Cilappatikāram* 11.118-24.
92. Excavations at Vanagiri in the vicinity of Kāveripaṭṭiṉam have reveald a brick structure semi circular in plan with 2 metre high walls and an internal diameter of 8 metres and seems to have been fed by a 83 cm wide inlet channel from the Kaveri. The structure has been dated to the first-second century A.D. on the basis of Black and Red ware and Rouletted Ware-*IAR* 1963-64, p. 20. In the view of Dr. R.Champakalakshmi this could be one of the publick tanks of baths referred to in the literature (Could it have been the *Ilañcimaṉṟam?*) "Archaeology and Tamil Literary Tradition". *Puratattva,* No. 8 1975-76, p. 114.
92. *Cilappatikāram* V 11.125-27
(Could it have been a megalith a menhir or dolmen which was worshipped?)
93. *Cilappatikāram* V. 11. 130-34.
94. *Cilappatikāram* V 11. 135-40.
95. *Cilappatikāram* VI 11. 130-44.
96. *Periplus* 60.
97. *Ptolemy* VII. 1.13.
98. Pukar has been evaluated as a 'gateway city' spatially and a 'port of trade' functionally. For further details see R.Sumati, *Trade and Its impact on the Early Tamils: The Cōḷa Experience,* M.Phil dissertation, Jawaharlal Nehru University, 1984, pp. 198-200.

99. *IAR*, 1962-63, p. 13

Roman contact at Kāveripaṭṭiṇam is testified by the discovery of Rouletted Wares at Manigramam and Pallavaneeswaran-*IAR* 1964-65, p. 25.

100. K.V. Raman "Some Ancient Crafts and Technology in Tamil Nad as revealed in Excavations", *Proceedings of Second International Conference Seminar of Tamil Studies* , Vol.II, Madras, Janauary 1968, p. 397.

101. *Ptolemy* VII 1.89.

102. *Cilappatikāram* XIII 11. 178-96.

103. *Cilappatikāram* XIV 11. 65-72.

104. *Cilappatikāram* XIV 11. 170-84.

105. R. Campakalakshmi, 1975-76, p. 117.

106. *Maṇimēkalai* XXVIII 11. 42-84.

107. *Maṇimēkalai* XIX: 11. 107-16.

108. *IAR* 1953-54; p. 12.

CHAPTER - III - D

FEMALE ROLES : TRIBAL BEGINNINGS AND THE CHANGING CONTEXT

It is customary in conventional research to deal with the role of women in a society as a separate issue as if it is an isolated aspect of society. Here, the role of women is being discussed speparately not with the above view but for the purpose of highlighting that their roles in the different *tiṇais* needs to be placed in the perspective of the different economic milieu and also that their roles changed significantly in the context of certain eco zones.

Women in early Tamiḻakam seem to have performed diverse roles, as those involved in the production process, as housewives and as poetesses, singers and dancers.

Women in those days were involved in the production process. In the different *tiṇais* they participated in various ways in collecting, producing and feeding their kin. The girls of the *kuṛavar/kāṉavar* in *kuṛiñci* helped to guard the crops of millets against the *ravages* by birds. Women of the *āyar* folk made clarified butter (*ghī*) and sold butter, milk and *ghi*. Girls of the *paratavar* community in *neytal* helped in the drying of fish and selling it. The women folk of the *eyiṉar* dug out rice from the ground and pounded it and served it to the bards. Women of the *antaṇar* community do not seem to have participated in the production process but are described in the text to be feeding the bards who passed through their settlements.

Women in their role as mothers and foster mother are mentioned in the *kuṛiñci* and *pālai* poems. The meeting of a boy and girl and their clandestine love (*kaḷavu*) is the theme of the *kuṛiñci* poems. On hearing the love affair and noticing changes in the heroine's body due to love sickness the mother arranged for the *vēlaṉ* (the priest) to perform the *veṛiyāṭal* and pronounce the reasons for the sickness. In some instances, the girls were kept under surveillance at home under the mother and not allowed to go anywhere.

In the *pālai* poems, the main theme was elopement of the girl with the boy. When the girls eloped with their lovers the mother/foster mother (*cevilittāy*) are depicted to be Pining for the girl and worrying about her.

All this is indicative of the fact that these two *tiṇais* being relative zones of isolation were characterised by tribal basis of organisation, where free mixing would have been the socially accepted norm and practice.

George Hart has considered the woman as a holder of sacred power which had to be kept under control lest it would cause destruction. The cross cousin marriage, as an important feature of the kinship system of the Dravidians, is linked up by Hart to the sacred power of a woman. A woman was made to marry within her kin as it was necessary for her father and brothers to retain the benefit of her power. As stated in section A, Hart has oversfressed the role of the sacred power of a woman.

In the *marutam,* women played an important role in the ceremonies of marriaage where the *brāhmaṇa* participation in marriage ceremonies is not attested as seen in the anthologies. It is only when marriage is institutionalised and influenced by the Dharmasastraic traditions that *brāhmaṇās* played an important role in solemnising marriage. This formalisation of marriage is recorded in the *Poruḷatikāram* of the *Tolkāppiyam* and later described in some detail in the *Cilappatikāram.* Cross cousin marriage was not the norm of northern Aryan traditions but marriages between kin members may have continued in early Tamiḻakam among most ethnic groups despite Sanskritc influences which may well have been confined to the elite in society. It is also interesting to note that dowry (*stridhanā*) is not attested to in literature but the Tamil poems mention a bride price (see Chapter III Section A).

It has been stated that according to the brahmanic theory the ideal for a woman is to be a *pativrata* (a wife who is devoted to the husband, unquestionably loyal and submissive to the husband), its concomitants are virginity at marriage, chastity as the wifely goal, unassertiveness and submissiveness and unquestioning loyalty to the husband[1]

As the *marutam, neytal* (and to an extent *mullai*) were the *tiṇais* where the brahmanic influence was prevalent in various degrees, such ideals of virginity, chastity, in a woman may have been considered important.

Chastity was an important virtue in those days. A woman had to be chaste and in some cases her chastity is compared with that of the star Arundhati[2] (the wife of the sage Vaṣiṣta). Arundhati was well known for her chastity and made into a star. A chaste woman was expected to tolerate the wayward behaviour of men and their frequent visits to the *parattai/kaṇika* (harlot, courtesan). Most of the poems of the *marutam tiṇai* portray the sulking of the woman (*ūṭal*) on the man's (husband's) visits to the harlots. In most cases, the women were forced to reconcile and patch up with their husbands, thereby presumably maintaining chastity and wifely devotion.

This is in fact explicitly reflected in the epic *Cilappatikāram* wherein the heroine (Kaṇṇaki) accepts her husband Kōvalaṇ cheerfully even after his affair with the accomplished courtesan Mātavi. Not only is Kaṇṇaki a virgin and married at an early age (barely 12 years)[3] (as an essential feature of virginity) she is depicted as a chaste wife (*pativratā*). In fact even when she is advised to go to bathe in the sacred tanks dedicated to the sun (*Cūryakuṇtam*) and the moon (*Cōmakuṇtam*) and then worship the God of love (Manmathā?) to enjoy the company of her husband in this world Kaṇṇaki is said to have said that it is not proper[4]. In other words, married women who are chaste worship no other Gods but their husbands. Descriptions of her chastity is carried to such heights that Kaṇṇaki is said to have turned aggressive at the unfair execution of her husband Kōvalaṉ by the Pāṇṭiyaṉ ruler and burnt the city of Madurai. Details of this are too well known to be reiterated here. In the epic she is consecrated as Pattini in a shrine built by Cēra ruler Ceṅkuṭṭuvaṉ and by this came to be considered sacred[5]. This cult of the Goddess Pattini seems to have been prevalent only in the Cera region and later spread to Srilanka after the 7th-8th centuries A.D.[6]

Chastity as an important virtue may have been emphasised for the *mēlōr* or higher groups such as the householder's wife (*kiḻatti*) in the *marutam* and the women of the ruling groups, as the poems are mainly concerned with the affluent or higher groups of the society. There are few references to women of the lower groups of society. Descriptions of one group of low born women who were presumably agricultural labourers (*kaṭaiciyar*)[7] in the *Cilappatikāram* do not seem to depict them as chaste women. In the *kuriñci* and *pālai* chastity may not have been important as free mixing of men and women was the norm. Closely related to chastity were the norms for widowhood. Since widow remarriage was not allowed the chaste woman who did not want to lead a widowed life even burnt herself after her husband's death[8]. A poem also describes a wife asking a potter to make a huge urn (*tāḻi*) which would hold her, apart from her husband[9]. This sentiment is also echoed Pattini in a shrine built by Cēra ruler Ceṅkuṭṭuvaṉ and by this come to be considered sacred[5]. This cult of the Goddes Pattini seems to have been prevalent only in the Cera region and later spread to Srilanka after the 7the-8th centuries A.D.[6]

Chastity as an important virtue may have been emphasised for the *mēlōr* or higher groups such as the householder's wife (*kiḻatti*) in the *marutam* and the women of the ruling groups, as the poems are mainly concuerned with the affluent or higher groups of the society. There are few references to women of the lower groups of society. Descriptions of one group of low born women who were presumably agricultural labourers (Kaṭaiciyar)[7] in the *Cilappatikāram* do not seem to depict them as chaste women. In the *kuriñci* and pālai chastity may not have been important as free mixing of men and women was the norm. closely related to chastity were the norms for widowhood. Since widow remarriage was not allowed the chaste woman who did not want to lead a widwed life even burnt herself after her husband's death[8]. A poem also describes a wife asking a potter to make a huge (*tāḻi*) which would hold her, apart from her husband[9]. This sentiment is also echoed in another poem where the wife of the Pāṇṭyaṉ ruler Putapāṇṭiyaṉ is contemplating *Sati* or burning herself on the husband's pyre[10]. Normally the son performed the funerary rites. However, in one instance, the women offering *piṇṭams* (balls of unsalted rice) for their dead husbands is referred to in a poem of the *Puṟanāṉūṟu* (234). Even in the later *Cilappatikāram* the Pāṇṭiyaṉ queen is stated to have fainted immediately after her husband's death by saying that a woman can never survive a husband's death[11]. Either, the women ended their lives after their husband's death or as widows probably took up spinning for a livelihood[12].

Most of the women possibly perferred to die as the difficulties in leading a widowed life is brought out in a poem

> "Listen, all of you good men with your wicked schemes who would hinder me with words of restraint and not urge me to go. Listen, you good men! I am no woman to suffer austerities, eating for food *vēlai* leaves boiled with tamarind with white sesame paste and a squeezed ball of rice untouched by fragrant ghee whose light color resembles the seeds of a curved cucumber with chipmunk lines split with a sword, and to sleep on a bed covered with stones without even a mat. Go ahead, spurn the pyre of black wood heaped on the burning ground To me, since my great-armed husband is dead, that fire and a large pond of lotuses that have loosed from buds rich petals are the same"[13].

Women played important roles as mothers. This facet has already been highlighted in the *kuriñci* and *pālai* context particularly in relation to their daughters. Their role in bringing up the son is evident from poem of the *Puranāṇūṛu* (312) which states that it is the duty of the mother to give birth to a son and bring him up. Even among the martial groups (warriors) a poem of the *Puranāṇūṛu* mentions a woman (who is brave *Mūtilmakalir*) getting her son ready and sending him to the battlefield despite losing her father and husband in the battle[14]. In fact these courageous warrior women rejoiced when they heard that their sons had died in battle[15].

Harlots constituted another category of women who are mentioned only in the context of the *marutam tiṇai*. There were many kinds of harlots[16] who enticed men and indulged in activities such as singing, dancing and bathing in the river. In some cases, the men seemed to be attracted by the beauty and youthfulness of the *parattai* and went to them when their wives had given birth to children and consequently lost their vigour and beauty[17]. Another factor in the establishment of harlotry could be attributed to economic reasons Due to surplus production in the *marutam tiṇai* men would have had ample leisure which could have given men enough, scope to indulge in such activities and the surplus could have been used to pay for the harlots services. In the *vaṇpulam* regions it may have been necessary for the inhabitants to work continuously (either hunting, digging up roots, shifting cultivation) for their survival and this could have taken much of their time.

Further, a free mixing of men and women in pre-Marital stages and perhaps even post-marital stage would have acted as a counter to the development of a class of *parattai*. Although harlotry was well established even by the period of the anthologies, the harlots did not seem to have good reputations and were frequently looked down upon or ridiculed. These *parattaiyar* were said to be devoid of the sense of shame and modesty and were determined to keep the men within their clutches[18] and prevent them from going to their wives. As seen earlier, even the later *Kīḻkkaṇakku* works denounce the harlots and condemn associations with them[19].

As for the Buddhist and Jain attitudes towards harlots it seems to have been less harsh and more sympathetic. Even though the epic *Cilappatikaram* talks of Mātavi as the other woman i.e harlot or courtesan, it hardly denounces her character but rather praises the virtue of the chaste woman Kaṇṇaki. At the same time Mātavi herself is extolled as one who renounced worldly/material aspects and her daughter Maṇimekalai is made into an ideal and respectable nun in the other epic *Maṇimēkalai*. This indeed shows the acceptance of women within the monastic order (as nuns) which acted in direct opposition to the denial of Vedic learning to women in the brahmanical fold at a time when brahmanical order was becoming an increasingly noticeable feature of Tamil society especially in the context of the agrarian regions and urban centres.

The presence of a number of women poetesses (vide Appendix 8) would indicate that at least some sections of the women would have been learned enough to compose poems on various themes (i.e *marutam, mullai, pālai, kuriñci, neytal*[20]) and by this could have been counted among the ranks of the *Cāṉṟor* (wise). In fact one of the poetesses Auvāiyār was attached to a royal court that of Atiyamāṉ Añci. She is also said to have gone in her personal capacity to the court of Toṇṭaiman chieftain as ambassador. Like the poets, these poetesses could also criticise actions of the kings. One of these poetesses Naccel̤l̤aiyār also requested the Cēra King Āṭukōṭpāṭṭu Cēralātaṉ not to spend time with the dancers and singers as it would tarnish his reputation even though he was a fine warrior[21].

Besides these poetesses, there were *viṟaliyar* who were skilled in singing, dancing and playing musical instruments and who sang praises of the king/Chieftain for which they were given gifts. Some of the women were also good acrobats.

Thus we notice that the role of women in early Tamilakam was dependent on the economic milieu. Although women may have participated in economic activities or the production processes in *kuṟiñci, neytal* and *mullai,* there were some like the woman of the *antaṇar* community or the wives (*kiḻatti*) of householders (*kiḻāṉ*) and poetesses who may have been kept away from the production process. The brahmanical concepts of the ideal woman as chaste wife and mother are noticeable in the two advanced *tiṇais, marutam* and *neytal* and to an extent in the *mullai.*

FOOTNOTES

1. G.Obeyeseskere, *The cult of the Goddess Pattini,* Chicago, 1984, p. 430.
2. *Puṟanāṉūṟu* 122; *Akanāṉūṟu* 16.
3. *Cilappatikāram* I: 1.24; 1.27.
4. *Cilappatikāram* IX: 11. 59-64.
5. Ibid: contos XXVII and XXVIII.
6. Obeysekere.
7. *Cilappatikāram* X 11. 127-31.
8. *Puṟanāṉūṟu* 246.
9. *Puṟanāṉūṟu* 256.
10. *Puṟanāṉūṟu* 247.
11. *Cilappatikāram* XX: 11.78-81.
12. *Naṟṟiṇai* 353.

13. *Puṛanāṇūṛu* 246.
14. Ibid 279.
15. See the songs of *uvakkai kaluḷcci tuṛai* of the *Puṛanāṇūṛu*..
16. V.T.Manickam "Harlots in Ancient Tamil Literature", Proceeding of the First International Conference Seminar of Tamil Studies, Kuala Lampur, 1966, pp. 338-48.
17. *Akanāṇūṛu* 6:26; 56.
18. See poems 276 and 396 of the Akanāṇūṛu.
19. *Kuṛal* 913; *Nālaṭiyār* 378; 375; 371; 354 *Tirikaṭukam* 81; 24.
20. For a detailed discussion of the themes discussed by Tamil poets see L.Gloria Sundaramathy's "The women poets of Cankam Age", *Journal of Tamil Studies,* Vol.8, pp. 62-79.
21. *Patiṛṛuppattu* 51: 21-24.

CHAPTER - III - E

RELIGION (I) : THE *TIṆAI* DEITIES-FOLK FORMS AND SANSKRITIC TRADITIONS

Moving on the religious beliefs and modes of worship one finds the absence of a dominant religion or a universal religious system or mode of worship and a priestly class. Instead, the territorially segmented people in each tiṇai worshipped deities prescribed for that tiṇai. Modes of worship were mostly tribal marked by sacrifices to certain deities. Besides, other facets of religion include the cult of memorial stones and worship of totems. The spread of Puranic religion and its impact on folk forms is also seen in a few instances although not to a substantial degree.

The concept of a deity specific to an ecological niche (*tiṇai*) is found in the *Tolkāppiyam*. The *Porulatikāram* of the *Tolkāppiyam* defines the *tiṇai* deities as Māyōn (*mullai*), Ceyon (*kuriñci*), Vēntan (*marutam*), Varunan (*neytal*[1]). All these Gods are known from their basic Tamil forms and by Tamil names[2]. While the *tiṇai* deities Murukan, Māl and Korravai (assigned to the *pālai tiṇai*) continued to be worshipped in the later phase *i.e.* post *Caṅkam* period, the worship of Varunan disappeared. The references to Vēṉtaṉ and Varuṇaṉ as the gods of the *marutam* and *neytal* indicate the first attempts to establish equivalence with northern deities.

Murukan was God of Love as well as God of War. The name of Murukaṉ is derived from Muruku which means tenderness, tender age, Youth and beauty[3]. He is portrayed to be living under a *Kaṭampā* tree, wearing a garland and said to reside in the hills[4], Murukan inflicted love sickness on young girls of the *kuriñci tiṇai*. It was in this *kuriñci tiṇai* that clandestine love took place between the hero and heroine. On account of the love sickness (*kāmanoy*) changes occurred in the heroine's body. The mother or foster mother of the heroine on noticing the heroine's paleness or weakness called for the *Vēlan* without knowing the real cause of the condition. *Vēlan*[5] was the priest who officiated at the worship of Murukan. Normally the *vēlan* performed the ecstatic frenzied dance and acted as a soothsayer to pronounce the reasons for the heroine's condition. Invariably the causes of her condition were attributed to Murukaṉ though it was actually due to love sickness. We come across a number of poems in the *akam* anthologies which mention the *vēlan* doing the *veriyātal*[6]. The *velan* is said to wear a *Kaṭampa* garland like Murukaṉ and carry a *vēl* which was bright and shiny like lightening. The *vēlan's* ecstatic and frenzied dance is described in the texts. To take one example:

> "women who utter ancient truths, skilled at lying, spread out rice in a winnowing fan to discover the truth and say", "It is the presence of Murukan hard to bear".
>
> Mother believes them,
>
> in a house so well made it could be a picture, she prays:
>
> "may may daughter's loveliness, as lovely as a doll's return"
>
> The sweet instruments are played together, the floor is prepared a large pandal is decorated with ornaments for the dance,
>
> they put on katampu and white pieces of palmyra leaves, the sweet drone sounds behind a compelling beat they cry out the great name of the god throwing up their hands and the priest makes the large floor resplendent with his frenzied dancing,
>
> moving like a puppet
>
> manipulated by a skillful puppeteer"[7].

The worship involved putting up of a special structure (at times) and singing and dancing to the accompaniment of musical instruments. As part of the worship, sacrificial offerings were also made to Murukaṉ which were in the form of different varieties of grain (rice or millet), goat and blood[8]. At times the *vēlan* as soothsayer also rolled the *Kaḻaṅku* (molucca beans) at the girl's house to confirm that Murukaṉ was the cause of her condition[9]. This nature of worship of Murukaṉ by the *vēlaṉ* through ecstatic dancing, singing and animal scrifices has all the elements of a folk or popular religion with typical folk structure in which the sensual aspects pre-dominate. While dancing and singing continue to figure when Murukaṉ as is enshrined in the brahmanical temple (attested by the *paripātal*) animal sacrifices seem to go into oblivion. Dancing, singing and the *Kāvaṭi* and other self mortifying rituals which survive even today may be the remanants of the earlier folk traditions of Murukaṉ worship. The *vēlans* as a caste survive today and are mostly found in the state of Kerala. They are described to be sorcerers, devil dancers and quack doctors[10].

Murukan, also called *Cēyōn* (the Red one), is described in the anthologies as a fine warrior. The anger of a King going to war is often compared to Murukaṉ's anger in war[11]. In another verse of *Akanāṉūrū* he is referred to as *Neṭuvēl,* who is said to have destroyed those who did not bow to him[12]. A shrine of this deity existed at Tiruchiralaivāy (which is also Centil or Tirucceṇdūr[13]). Though he was said to reside on the hills the shrine at Tirucceṇdūr was on the sea where the "white crested waves could be seen[14]". One noticeable fact is the absence of reference to brāhmaṇās officiating in the shrine or in the specially designed place for the ritual in the early anthologies.

Thus we find that Murukaṉ symbolised love and heroism. He was the 'Tamil'

God par excellence in whom the Tamils of the classical *Caṅkam* age envisaged the divine in a personalised form and who at the same time represented their human ideals on a divine plane[15]. It is only in the *Paripāṭal* and *Tirumurukāṟṟuppaṭai* that this deity's descriptions emphasise his equation with Skandā/Subrahmanyā/Kārtikēyā and he is clearly located in the context of the temple as a house of God and a place of worship with the image in the temple as symbolising the manifestation of the divine (see following Section E-2). In other words, the Purāṇic associations are clear and more complete in the later phase.

References to Māyōn are scattered in the *Puranānūrū* and *Pattuppāttu* but are few in comparison to that of Murukaṉ. Māyōn (which means a person of dark complexion) as he figures in the texts could be identified with the brahmanical (Vedic/ Epic/ Puranic) deity Visnu/ Narayana/ Kṛṣṇa.

In *Puranāṉūrū* 56 Krsna is noted for his fame as destroyer of enemies and Balarāma for his strength. While Māyōn is said to have a body like blue sapphire and a bird on his banner (presumably Garudā), Balārama is said to have a body like the colour of a conch, have a plough for his weapon and a palmyra on his banner. Again in *Puranāṉūrū* 58 the colour of Kṛṣṇa and Balarāma is contrasted with Kṛṣṇa's body being black and balarāmā's body being like milk. Further Kṛṣṇa is said to wield the discus. One of the verses of the *Akanānūrū* 59 refers to Māl's (Kṛṣṇa's) dalliance with the gopis on the banks of the river Yamunā. Both Kṛṣṇa and the river Yamunā are denoted by Tamil names Māl and Toḻunai.

In the poems of the *Pattuppāttu* Māl/ Māyōn is referred to as reclining on the serpent conch[16], whose colour is like that of the ocean, whose chest is marked with Sri (Lakshmi) and who transcended the earth[17] and as the dark blue God who gave birth to a person with four faces (Brahma[18]). In another instance, the birthday of Māyōn, (who has defeated the numerous demons) celebrated on *Sravana* day by people of that age is recorded[19]. There is only on reference to a shrine in *Perumpāṇāṟṟuppaṭai* of Māyōn on the Veṅka (Vegavatiriver) in Kañcipuram (hence it is called Tiruveṅka). The reference here is to Visnu-Narāyana, the brahmanical deity. Early references to Māyōn would indicate his association with the royal courts at Madurai and Kañci[20]. Moreover, the origins of Toṇṭaimaṇs (who ruled over Kañci) are traced back to Māyōn[21].

If the Veḷir were pastoral-com-agrarian chiefs it would be logical to assume that they brought with them the worship of Balarāma and Kṛṣṇa, two of the five Vṛṣṇi Vīras (the pañca vīras) whose worship was a prominent feature in the Mathura region-the region of the Yadava[22]. It is significant that some of the Velir claimed descent from the Yadavas[23].

As compared to Murukaṉ, according to Hardy, Māyōṇ was not integrated into the *akam* traditions. It is only by the time of the *Porulaṭikāram* of *Tolkāppiyam* was Māyōṇ given a well defined position in the general frame of reference of *akam* poetry and given a place in the *mullai tiṇai*[24].

All the above references are essentially concerned with providing descriptions of Māl/Māyōṉ. We hardly know anything about the patterns of worship except for the fact that his birthday was celebrated. This is intriguing as at least some information regarding the patterns of worship can be gleaned from the texts for other deities.

Koṟṟavai is known by names other than Koṟṟavai in the texts. Koṟṟavai is assigned to the *pālai tiṇai*. Koṟṟavai, like Murukaṉ, was also said to be residing in the hills and was known as *Ayiraiyiṉ Kaṭavuḷ* (or the god residing on the hills[25]). In another poem she is called as *Kāṉamar celvi* (as she lived in the forest[26]). She was the goddess of victory. In the *Netunalvāṭai* the consorts of the warrior are described to pray to this goddess of victory for the victorious return of their warrior husbands from war[27]. This goddess also bestowed her blessings due to which a *pulavan* is said to have got horses[28]. The Cera King is said to have worshipped her[29]. In *Kuṟuntokai* 218 the goddess known as *Cūli* (holder of a trident) is mentioned and she is identified with Koṟṟavai the goddess of victory. She resided in the hills and was a recipient of a sacrifice offered by a woman whose lover had left on a journey. Further she was also given the blood from the bodies of the victorious warriors[30].

From this it appears that Koṟṟavai was an indigenous goddess of war and victory. The sacrificial offerings given to her also seem to indicate tribal practices. Only in one context is she referred to as *Cūli* (derived from Sanskrit sūla) which is indicative of the northern influence. However, it is only in the epics is she identified with Durga/ Parvati, the consort of Siva and as the mother of Murukaṉ and thereby becomes a goddess of the Puraṉic pantheon.

In the early anthologies there are very few references to Vēntaṉ who is equated with Intiraṉ. The *Tolkāppiyam* describes him to be the god of *marutam tiṇai*. Since the cultivators would have been dependent on the rains for the growth of their crops they could have worshipped Ventan or the God of Thunder. In the *Puranānūrū* there is one reference to the shrine (*Kōyil*) or the deuty (Netiyōn) holding a *vajra* indentified with Intira/ Ventaṉ[31].

Worship of Lord Intrira seems to have become prominent by the time of the epics and festivals (Intiraviḻa) were held in the port town of Kavēripattiṇam.

There is no reference to the term Varunan in the anthologies though the *Tolkāppiyam* mentions him to be the God of *neytal*. As discussed earlier the *Pattinappālai* informs us that the *paratavar* gathered around the sea on a full moon day and planted the horn of the *sūra* fish and worshipped, which appears to be a typical folk form, whereas Vedic Varuna, the cosmic deity who controlled the seas, is referred to only in the *Porulatikāram* of *Tolkāppiyam*.

There are references to the three-eyed god but nowhere is he denoted by the name Siva or associated with a specific region or *tiṇai*. Apart from the invocatory verses of a few anthologies, references to this god are incidental in the *Caṅkam* works. He is mentioned to be the three-eyed deity[32]; sitting under a banyan tree[33]; who has matted locks[34]; with a blue scar on the throat[35]; who rides a bull[36] and who has a crescent moon on the head[37]. Further, he is said to have destroyed the three forts of the *asurās*[38]. The *Malaipatukatām* refers to the god taking poison[39]. It mentions a shrine dedicated to the god who swallowed poison in the area of Naviraimalai which was under the sway of Naṉṉaṉ, one of the minor chieftains[40]. A reference to a temple (*nakar*) of the three-eyed god (Mūkkatcelvar) worshipped by sages (*munivar*) and circumambulated by the kins occurs in the *Puranāṇūrū* 6. Could this be a temple to Siva? It is interesting to note that Korravai is described in the later epic *Cilappatikāram* to be wearing a crescent moon on her head, wearing the hide of an elephant as garment and to have swallowed poison-all features usually attributed to Siva, the Puranic deity. Perhaps Siva, acquired all these attributes of Koṟṟavai when she was transformed into Parvati the consort of Siva.

Kūṟṟuvan (or death) is also mentioned in the texts as one who carries an axe or a club and takes people away at the appointed time[41].

Other figures mentioned are Parasurāma and Kubēra. The story of Parasurāma with an axe killing the warriors is mentioned once in *Akanāṇūrū* 200. Kubēra, the lord of wealth is not referred to as Kubēra but as Manitikiḻavaṉ in a poem where the hero going to see his courtesan, wearing new ornaments is said to look like Maniti-kiḻavaṉ—the lord of great treasure[42].

Arundhati also figured in the poems where the women are compared to be as chaste as Arundhati[43]. Hart is of the view that Arundhati is mentioned in the texts on account of her chastity which had important value in ancient TamilNadu. Another deity mentioned is the god of Kolli hillside. A figure of this God (Kollippāvai[44]) was carved on the hillside and the heroine is compared to this image or Kollippāvai[45].

There are stray references in the *CAṅkam* texts to episodes or stories from the *Mahābhārata, Rāmāyana* and *Kṛṣṇa Carita*. The Praise of King Ceramāṉ Peruṅcōṟṟutiyaṉ Cēralātaṉ feeding fice to the hundred (Kauravas) and five (Pandavas) is sung[46].

Two incidents of the Ramayana figure in the poems. *Puranāṇūṛū* 378 describes how a bard's family puts on ornaments given by the King, comparing this to the monkey's putting on Sita's ornaments which they found when she had dropped them while being carried away by Ravana. The poet sings:

> "Me (the King) gave wealth of excellent precious stones,
>
> Letting them fall down without end many more thean I was fit for
>
> When they saw that,
>
> my large family, burnt by the sun, put the ornaments meant for fingers on ears; those meant for ears they squeezed on fingers; those for waists they made fit their necks; and those meant for necks they put on their waists,
>
> So that,
>
> like the red-mouthed family of monkeys all decked out

When they took the lovely ornaments fallen on the ground the day the mighty demon (arakkan from Sanskrit raksasa)
abducted Sita
who had been joined to Rama of great destruction.
We laughed happily and unceasingly"[47].

Another poem of the *Akanāṉūṟū* refers to (Dhanus) Kōṭi where the gossip prevalent in the settlement which stopped after the marriage of the hero and heroine, is compared with the banyan tree with many roots which hushed while Rama slept and the ocean roared at Kōṭi (Dhanuskōṭi)[48].

These episodes, although not many, may be said to be early indications of the spread of early Epic/Puranic stories in Tamiḻakam.

Despite the evidence relating to such formal religious systems emerging due to Northern influences through Puranic structures, the predominance of folk forms of worship in this early phase is indisputable. This has been shown in the worship of Murukaṉ and Koṟṟavai particularly. To this may be added the rituals performed by various social groups like the *uḻavar* of *marutam*[49]. at various stages of agricultural activities.

In this context, it can be stated that the potter (*Kuyavaṉ*) who wore the garland of *nocci* flowers, forecast festivals in the settlements and also performed certain religious rites like feeding the Gods in the *manṟam* (commona place) of the settlements[50].

The cult of the memorial stones was prevalent during this period. The *Tolkāppiyam* refers to the six actions (or stages) connected with the hero stone ritual namely:

Kāṭci (Finding the stone)
Kalkol (the initial ceremony of chiselling)
Nīrppaṭai (Bathing the sotne)
Naṭukal (Erecting it)
Perumpaṭai (Engraving the name and fame of the warrior)
Vāḻttu-(paying homage[51])

These hero stones were located in dangerous *palai* tracts[52]. They were erected for eminent men, who were probably warriors who died fighting a battle or while stealing or recovering cattle. It was venerated as the spirit of the dead man was thought to reside in the stone. A verse of the *Puṟanāṉūṟu* 263 mentions that one should not fail to bow when one passed the stone that belongs to a hero. *Puṟanāṉūṟu* 335 while describing a warrior settlement mentions that the Gods of this region are stones (*naṭ ukals*) worshipped with offerings of paddy. These *naṭukals* were worshipped by the *maṟavar.* The *naṭukals* were decorated with garlands and peacock feathers and some of them even had a spear on them[53]. Names and achievements of the hero were often inscribed on the stone[54]. However, such *naṭukal* inscriptions of this period have not been recovered so far, although later hero stone inscriptions from the 6 iṇ century on wards are found[55]. Sometimes offerings of rice and toddywere made[56]. It has been suggested that the worship of the *naṭukals* may have gradually developed into present day folk deities such as *Aiyanār.* In other words, the origin of the Aiyanar deities may be seen in the *naṭukals*[57].This, however, does not seem plausible. Hart has suggested that "the concept of divinity actually residing in the stone was transferred later to the *Sivalingam* which seems to have taken over many of the functions of the *naṭukal.*[58]

Certain symbols of a totemic character were given a special place in the socio-political sphere. For instance, the royal emblems of the three major chiefdoms such as the carp of the *Pāṇṭiyas,* the tiger of the Cōḷas and the bow of the Cēra were totemic symbols. In addition to these the tutelary tree and the *muracu*[59] (royal drum) were also considered sacred to the Kings.

With the rise of trading activities, the spread of non-brabmanical sects can be seen in Tamiḻakam. The *Maturaikkāñci* records the existence of monasteries (paḷḷis) of the Jains[60] and Buddhists. In the text the Buddhist *Paḷḷi* is portrayed as a place where:

"young pretty women wearing jewels bright
Escorted by their husbands take with them
Their children bright whose lovely faces look
Like pollened lotus blomms: a comely group
They go with flowers and incense to the shrine"[61]

The fact that these "heterodox" faiths had devotees from the mercantile community is testified by the Tamil Brahmi inscriptions which record the donations they made.

Ramains of a baked brick structure[62] at the premises of Kāmakōti Matha in Kāñcipuram have been identified to be those of a Buddhist stupa[63] and assigned to the Mauryan period on the basis of Hiuen Tsang's (7th century A.D.) references to the existence of Mauryan stupas when he visited Kāñcipuram. Excavations revealed only four courses of bricks and nothing of shape and plan of the structure can be made out to be associated with a stupa.

An inscribed potsherd with the words "Puta lasita" from Kāñcipuram was taken to be the name of a Buddhist monk Buddharakshita[64].

Some of the poets or literary men of the *Caṅkam* anthologies belonging to the Buddist and Jain sects are also known (Vide Appendix 9).

Thus we find the prevalence of *tiṇai* cults, folk elements of worship and non-brahmanical faiths in the society of the early period. Tribal practices such as sacrifices, frenzied dancing persisted in the worship of the *tiṇai* deities. Places of worship were more in the nature of small shrines.Sanskritic/Puranic influence was minimal. There are hardly any references to *brāhmaṇas* functioning as priests in the shrines of this period. An ideology capable of integrating all the diverse elements of religion (*tiṇai* deities, patterns of worship) was absent in Tamiḻakam unlike the Deccan[65] where the spread of Vedic and Puranic religion are well attested and also the dominance of Buddhism particularly in the context of the trading and commercial groups.

The main change attested by the *Kalittokai,* an *akam* text, later than the six anthologies (as pointed out earlier) is in the sphere of religion. The imagery of the *Kalittokai* is interesting on two accounts. First the text shows the continuance of the folk forms of worship. Second, an evolved form of Kṛṣṇa worship penetrated / influenced by Kṛṣṇaite myths is seen in the text[65]. The *Kalittokai* is specially notable for the influence of the *Mahabhārata and Harivamsa* stories/episodes.

There are about seven references in the *Kalittokai* top Māyōṉ Māl which mention him by name. Besides, references to Māyōṉ are scattered in the texts. Such references outnumber the references in the earlier anthologies. Reference is made to the episode where Māl broke the strength of the wrestlers and made them run away[67]. Further the discus (*nēmi*) is mentioned thrice where the sunset on the mountain is compared with the discus of Māl, who broke the strength of the wrestlers, the discus which cut or struck the forehead of the elephant, where the darkness is similar to the complexion of Māl who has the discus, where he who has the discus is described as mighty in battle[68]. In another poem an allusion to *neṭiyōṉ makaṉ* is made and identified as Kṛṣṇa's son Pradyumna and also Kāma[69]. Another poem mentions Sri (Lakshmi) united to the chest of Māyavaṉ[70]. One reference to Māl has been interpreted by Hardy to indicate Viṣṇu as a transcedental deity[71].

Friedhelm Hardy notes on the basis of the analysis of references to Māyōṉ three elements from the *Kṛṣṇa carita.*

The *mullai kali* contains a group of poems (101-08) dealing with the theme of bull fight. Bull baiting or subduing a bull was necessary for a man of the *āyar kuṭi* to prove his valour if he wanted to marry a girl. This bull baiting event was probably held in an arena and watched by the *āyar* folk. Verses describing this custom contain interesting comparison of the colour of the bulls with the deities such as Kṛṣṇa, Balarāma, Siva and Murukaṉ and the actual scenes of the bull baiting with some episodes of the *Mahābhārata*[72].

The bull fight and *Kuravai* and mentioned as part of *mullai tiṇai* only in the *Kalittokai.* Again mention is made of the Pāṇṭiyās and Māyōṉ indicating the association between the two[73]. In Hardy's view, in the *kalittokai,* a folk custom (bull fight and *Kuravai*) is penetrated by Krsnaite symbolism. Further, we notice an awareness of the episodes from the *Mahābhārata* in the songs of *Kalittokai.*

Thus we notice a marked influence of northern ideas in the *Kalittokai.*

As part of the discussion on religion mention must be made of the invocatory stanzas composed in praise of Śiva, Viṣṇu and Murukaṉ. These stanzas were definitely composed at a later period (around 7th century A.D.). They are seen as an attempt ot brahmanise/puranise the Tamil classics and their religion.

In the initial period of the anthologies we notice only a minimal Sanskritic influence. The folk elements of worship continue even when the Sanskritic influence was considerable as evident from the *Kalittokai.*

FOOTNOTES

1. *Māyōṉ mēya Katurai ulakamum*
   Cēyōṉ mēya māivarai ulakamum
   Vēṇtaṉ mēya timpuṇal ulakamum
   Varuṇaṉ mēya perumaṇal/ulakamum
   Mullai Kuriñci marutam neytal ena
   Tolkāppiyam, Porulatikāram 5.
2. Hart, 1975, p. 56 although Hart states differently that they are not given Sanskrit names but Tamil equivalents.
3. *DED* 4081, p. 336.
4. *Malaipaṭukaṭām* 1.293; *Akanāṇūṟū* 266:1
   Kuṟiñcipaṭṭu 1.207; *Aiṅkuruṇūṟu* 243:1
   Puṟanāṉūṟu 14:19.
5. Vēlaṉ derived from root *vēl* accordign to *DED* (4555, pp. 383-84) refers to Skanda and a priest
   Worshipping Skanda.The *Pre Pallavan Tamil Index* also refers to vēlaṉ as Murukaṉ and a priest (who carried a spear) who officiated at Murukaṉ worship who is said to carry a staff in his hand 1966, p. 797.
6. *Akanāṇūṟū* 22:1, 98: 16-20; 182-16; 232;14; 242;10; 388:19.
   Kuṟuntokai 53;3; 111:1; 360:1
   Naṟṟinai 34:9; 51:6; 268:9; 273:5; 282:5;
   Aiṅkuṟunūṟu 241-50 (Songs are called *veṟi pattu* as these 10 songs refer to the *vēlaṉ* performing *veṟiyāṭal*).
7. *Akanāṇūṟū* 98; Tr. Hart, 1975, pp. 28-29.
8. *Akanāṇūṟū* 22, 242; 292.
   Kuṟuntokai 362.
9. *Aiṅkurunūṟū* 245; 249; 250.
10. Thurston 'Castes and Tribes of Southern India' Vol. VII, pp. 342-59.
11. *Puṟanāṉūṟū* 16; *Akanāṇūṟu* 1.
    Perumpaṇāṟṟuppaṭai 1.75.
    Porunarāṟṟuppaṭai 1.131;
    Maturaikkāñci 1.181.
12. *Akanāṇūṟu* 22.
13. Ibid 226.
14. *Puṟanāṉūṟū* 55:18.
15. F. Hardy *Viraha Bhakti,* 1983, p. 134.
16. *Perumpāṇāṟṟuppaṭai* 11.372-73.
17. Ibid, 11.29-32.

18. Ibid, 11.402-05.
19. *Maturaikkāñci* 11. 590-91.
20. For details of such an association see F. Hardy, 1983, pp. 155-57.
21. *Ibid.*
22. *Ibid.*
22. I am grateful to R. Champakalakshmi for this information.
23. A Vēḷir Iruṅkōvēḷ is said to have traced his ancestry from the Yadavas - *Puṟanāṉūṟū* 201.
24. F. Hardy, 1983, pp. 157-67.
25. *Patiṟṟuppattu* 79:17-18; 90:19.
26. *Akanāṉūṟū* 345.
27. 1.168.
28. *Akanāṉūṟū* 345.
29. *Patiṟṟuppattu* 90:19.
30. *Kuṟuntokai* 218.
31. *Patiṟṟuppattu* 79:17-18.
32. *Puṟanāṉūṟū* 241:2-3.
33. Referred to as Mūkkatcelvaṉ in *Akanāṉūṟū* 181:6 and as Mukkannan in the invocatory stanza of *Kolittokai.*
34. *Akanāṉūṟū* 181:16-17.
    Puṟanāṉūṟū 198:9 where he is referred to as *ālamar katavul.*
35. *Puṟanāṉūṟū* 1:13.
36. Ibid, 55:4.
37. Ibid, 1:3.
38. *Akanāṉūṟū* invocatory stanza.
39. *Puṟanāṉūṟū* 56:2.
40. *Malaipaṭukaṭām* 1.83.
41. Ibid, 11.81-83
    Naviramali is situated in the North Arcot district and the Siva temple there is called Kālakaṇtheśvara even now.
    —See A. Ekambaranathan's *Iconographic Concepts and Forms of Śiva in the Tamil country : As revealed by literature and epigraphs upto 9th century A.D.*, Unpublished Ph.D. Thesis, University of Madras, 1981, 78ff.
42. *Puṟanāṉūṟū* 145; 42; *Kuṟuntokai* 267
43. *Akanāṉūṟū* 66.
44. In one poem the chastity of the wife of a King is compared to that of the star in the north (*vaṭ amīṉ*) or Arundhati who was probably made into a star - *Puṟanaṉūṟū* 122.
    A poem of *Aiṅkuṟunūṟu* (442) mentions the hero praising his wife as being chaste as Arundhati.
45. *Akanānūṟu* 209; 62.
46. Ibid; *Kuṟuntokai* 89.
47. *Puṟanāṉūṟū* 2.
48. (Tr.) Hart, 1975, pp. 60-61.
49. *Akanāṉūru* 70.

50. *Perumpaṇāṟṟuppaṭai* 11.230-34.
51. *Naṟṟiṇai* 200: 1-4; 293:1-4.
52. *Tolkāppiyam, Porulatikāram* 60.
53. Carts of *umaṇar* went over *naṭukals* in *pālai* tracts-*Akanāṇūṟu* 343:4.
54. *Puṟanāṇūṟu* 264; 232, 329.
    Akanāṇūṟū 35.
55. *Akanāṇūṟu* 131, 179; *Aiṅkuṟunūṟu* 352
    Malaipaṭukatām 11. 387-88.
56. For details of hero stones of later period, see R. Nagaswamy's *Seminar on Hero Stones*, Madras, 1974.
57. *Akanāṇūṟr* 35;6-9.
58. Vittianantaṉ, *Tamiḻar Cālpu*, Madras, pp. 125-26.
59. Hart, 1975, p. 26.
60. The sacred status of the drum is described in *Puṟanāṇūṟu* 50. The poet after travelling came to the palace and lay down on the drum which was taken out to be cleaned (or given a bath). Instead of scolding the poet. the king fanned the poet while he slept. The enemy's drum was taken by a victorious king - *Puṟanāṇūṟu*, 26. Similarly a victorious king cut down his enemy's tutelary tree *Akanāṇūṟu* 46; *Puṟanāṇūṟu* 23; 57.
61. *Maṭuraikkāñci* 11.475-88.
    Pattinappālai 1.53.
62. *Maṭuraikkāñci* 11. 461-67.
    J.V. Chelliah (Tr.), 1962, p. 257.
63. These courses of bricks (size 56 X 23 X 8 cm and 40 X 18 X 6 cm) were revealed in period I B (1st century B.C. -to 4th century A.D.) *IAR* 1962-63, p. 12.
64. I.K. Sarma "Archaeological Evidences pertaining to Buddhism in Tamil Nadu" paper presented at an *International Seminar on "Buddhism in Tamil Nadu"* Madras, 1992, p. 6.
65. Ibid.
66. R. Champakalakshmi "Ideology and the State in South India" Mamidipudi Venkata Rangaiah memorial Lecture, 1989 published in the *Andhra Pradesh History Congress* proceedings of the 13th Session, Srisailam, 1989, p. 279 For a comparison of the situation in Western Deccan See H.P. Ray *Monastery and Guild: Commerce under the Satavahanas*, New Delhi, 1986.
67. Hardy, 1983, pp. 183-93.
68. *Kalittokai* 52:5; 134:1-4.
69. *Kalittokai* 134: 1-4; 119:3; 127:4.
70. Ibid 140:8.
71. Ibid 145:64.
72. *Kalittokai* 123 is interpreted so by Hardy 1983, p. 185.
73. *Kalittokai* 104; 105. Some scenes of bull baiting are compared to some episodes of the *Mahābhārata* like Dushasana pulling Draupadi to the court, Bhima killing Dushasana, Dhristadyumna killing Drona - 101. Reference is also made to Karna, Surya's son-108.
74. For details see Hardy, 1983, pp. 189-91.

CHAPTER - III-E

RELIGION (II) : NORTHERN SANSKRITIC TRADITIONS AND EMERGENCE OF FORMAL RELIGIOUS SYSTEMS

In the first phase of the early historical period as pointed out in an earlier section there was an absence of a dominant religious ideology but the presence of predominantly folk forms of worship as seen in the worship of deities of the *tiṇais,* sacrifices to some of them and minimal Sanskritic/Puranic influence. The northern brahmanical/Puranic influence was clearly beginning to be felt in all spheres but the emergence of a formal religious system as in the early medieval Saiva and Vaishnava sectarian religions, is not attested and the northern Puranic myths figure only in a limited sense.

The later phase of the early historic period is marked by a clear cut transformation in the religious sphere which is reflected in the *Paripāṭal* and *Tirumurukāṟṟuppaṭai* as well as the epics. Therefore, it is proposed to discuss this in a separate secton. Folk elements in the pattern of worship get adapted or merge with the Sanskritic elements thereby resulting in the transformation of certain deities under the Puranic/Sanskritic influence, while certain folk practices continue in conjunction with the northern elements. Moreover, the temple, shrine as a place of worship emerges as an important institution. Thus, an institutional form is given to religion and the milieu shifted from the court of the ruler to the shrine/temple of the deity. There are references to a number of shrines of both brahmanical and non-brahmanical sects. The patterns of worship differed.

The *brāhmaṇās* started to function as temple priests-a role which they did not perform in the earlier period. The idea of envisaging a deity as a transcendental absolute is something new as encountered in two texts - the *Paripāṭal* and *Tirumurukāṟṟuppaṭai* - a feature not known in the earlier anthologies. The deities, especially Murukaṉ and Viṣṇu were viewed as transcendental absolutes (something beyond the comprehension of the worshippers). Also there were attempts at the universalisation of the *tiṇai* deities Māyōṉ and Murukaṉ into important deities with a transcendent character and special attributes.

There is in this phase a conscious attempt to adapt the folk traditions with the Sanskritic elements. For the information on the worship of Murukaṉ we are dependent on the *Paripāṭal* and *Tirumurukāṟṟuppaṭai*. In the *Tirumurukāṟṟuppaṭai* a devotee who has received blessings from Murukaṉ directs other devotess to reach his shrine and obtain his grace. A discussion of Murukaṉ on the basis of this text is taken up here on account of two factors-worship of Murukaṉ in six shrines outlined in the text which indicates the importance of a shrine/temple as a place of worship. Second, this text contains allusions to stories of Murukaṉ (myths) found in the later text *Kaṇtapurāṇam* (such as the birth of Murukaṉ, his war with the *asurās*) and an attmept is made to blend the character of Murukaṉ, the war God of the Dravidians with Skaṇdā (Subramaṇyā) the God of the northern Puranic religion. The descriptions of Murukaṉ shifts to a new locale i.e the temple shrine. The shrines of Murukaṉ are generally located on hills which is evident from the fact that Paraṅkuṉṟam[1]. Tiruvāviṉaṉkuti[2] (Paḻani), Tiruvērakam[3] (Swāmimalai) and Paḻamuṭircōlai[4] (Aḻakaramalai) mentioned in the *Tirumurukāṟṟuppaṭai* are hill shrines. Hence, it is significant the *Tirumurukāṟṟuppaṭai* talks of Kuṉṟutōrāṭal, i.e dancing on the hills or God's play on the hills which fits in line with the evidence from the *Tolkāppiyam* assigning Cēyōṉ (Murukaṉ) to the *kuṟiñci* or mountainous tracts[5]. Of these shrines Paraṅkuṉṟam is the one referred to in the *Paripāṭal*[6] also. The *Cilappatikāram* in Conto XIV also mentions shrines of Murukaṉ at Ceṉtil (Tiruccentūr), Ceṅkōṭu (Tirucceṅkōṭu ?) and Ērakam. Various modes of worship of Murukaṉ can be gleaned from the *Tirumurukāṟṟuppaṭ ai* and *Paripāṭal*. Animal sacrifice offered to the God is evident from Canto 6 (Paḻamutircōlai). On festival days the devotess offer to Murukaṉ, who is installed with the flag that bears the image of the cock, gifts of *tiṉai* and flowers and the flesh of rams[7]. Various other oblations offered to this deity at Paraṅkuṅṟam included flowers, leaves, gems, spears, silk clothes, sandalwood and incense, lighted lamp, drums, peacocks, axes and elephants[8]. Murukaṉ was worshipped in the morning as well as evening[9]. Music and dancing as essential components of the worship of Murukaṉ are highlighted in the *Paripāṭal*[10].

Such references to music and dance in the *Tirumurukāṟṟuppaṭai*[11]. are not on the same scale as in the *Paripāṭal* Three forms of dances are mentioned by the poet along with the place in which they were performed namely *tuṇaṅkai* performed by the *pēymakaḷ* ('she devil') at Paraṅkuṉṟam, the *Kuravai* by the *Kuṟamakaḷ* at Kuṅṟutōrāṭal and *veṟiyāṭal* at Paḻamutircōlai. They are essentially suggestive of folk forms of worship. A dance of the young girls is mentioned in the canto on Paraṅkuṅṟam whereby the girls praised, blessed and glorified the banner of God (Murukaṉ) which had the image of the cock. They danced and sang so loudly that echoes of their songs could be heard on the slopes of the hills. The poet provides a vivid description of the girls beautifying themselves with flowers, sandalwood paste and jewels[12]. Another dance form treated in the text is the *tuṇaṅjkau* of the *pēymakaḷ* (she devil) where the devil after eating the flesh danced the *tuṇaṅkai* and sung the songs or warriors and battlefield, a song which induced terror and fear.[13]

A *kuravai* of the *kāṇavar,* the hill folk who dwell in small settlements, is portrayed in the section on Kuṅṟutōraṭal. Here the *kāṇavar* (who wield the bow), who are happy with their kin, dance the *kuravai* to the beat of the *toṇṭakam* while the damsels whose walk is similar to that of the peacock are with them. The Red God descended down, danced with them, embraced them and hugged them and accepted offerings. By doing this Murukaṉ showered his grace on the devotees i.e all the hill folk who danced[14]. This was essentially a tribal dance involving the hill folk. Viewed in this light the *Tolkāppiyam's* reference to Cēyōṉ as the god of *Kuṟiñci* seems apt and meaningful. Unlike the *Kuṉṟakuravai* of the *Cilappatikāram* praise of a king is not sung here.

Lastly in the Paḻamutircōlai, the *veṟiyāṭal* in Canto 6 (Paḻamutircōlai) is described. The *kuṟamakaḷ* scattered the flowers and spread the *tiṉai* mixed with blood on the *āṭ ukaḷam* (the field of the frenzied dance) and while they danced in frenzy, songs were sung, horns blown and bells were rung[15].

These three dances were different modes by which the people propitiated Murukaṉ. Tribal/folk components are visible from the offerings of sacrifices, the dancing of the *kuravai* and *tuṉaṅkai* and singing and the ecstatic/frenzied dancing of the *vēlaṉ*.

Before the *veṟiyāṭal* is performed we are informed about the rites performed by the *Kuṟamakaḷ* (woman of the *kuṟavar* tribe). She is described to be wearing two types of garments. After unfurling the flag which has the cock's design which is sacred to Murukaṉ, the *kuṟamakaḷ* applied a paste of white mustard and ghee (probably on the pole) and scattered flowers and prayed quietly. Then they scattered pure white rice mixed with the blood of strong rams and puffed rice (*veṇpoṟi*) As small offerings (*cilpali*) she placed food (rice?) of various kinds and sprinkled fresh turmeric and perfume. Afterwards they hung garlands (of *kaṇavira*) and blessed the shrines on mountain slopes. This was followed by buring of incense and singing of songs set to *kuṟiñci* tune accompanied by musical instruments[16].

The *Cilappatikāram* refers to three dances. "While the *vēṭṭuva vari* (Koṟṟavai) and the *āycciyar kuravai* (Māl) were performed in the Pāṇṭiya country, the *kuṉṟakuravai,* the dance of the *kuṟavā* girls, was done in the hilly part of the Cēra country. The call for this *kuravai dance* was given when some *kuṟavā* girls told their story of meeting kaṇṇaki and her ascent to the heaven. They urged their people to accept Kaṇṇaki as their goddess and offer oblations.

The initial part of the dance consisted of the call for bathing and bathing itself. (Later the *Tiruppāvai* a text part of the *Nalāyira Tiviyapirappaṇtam,* uses this idea of ritual bathing in the worship of Viṣṇu.) This was then folowed by singing and dancing. The start of this ritual drama was marked by a prayer to the *vēl* (spear) of Murukaṉ. The theme of the dance is about the love sickness (*kāmaṇoy*) of a girl. The mother of the girl had called for a *vēlaṉ* to diagnose the problem. This *vēlaṉ,* who was of the view that the illness of the girl was due to possession is ridiculed in the songs. Next are sung the songs in which requests are made to Murukaṉ (for marriage to the hero) if he appeared in the *veṟiyāṭṭu*. In the following section the girl tells another girl about what she said to the lover (who has arrived on the scene). Also she mentions about the likelihood of, an early marriage. In ensuing songs praises of Kaṇṇaki are sung. The dance ended with the *Kuṟavā* girl's wish (of the lover coming) being fulfilled and the wishing of prosperity and victory to the Cērā king[17]. The folk elements i.e bathing, singing, dancing, reference to the *vēlaṉ* are predominant in this Kuṉṟakuravai. This appears to have been a folk dance not influenced by the Sanskritic elements.

What is noteworthy in all the three dances is that prayers are offered for the victories of the kings (Pāṇṭiya and Cera). By this the dances assume political and religious significance. It is interesting to see how the folk/tribal culture is penetrated by Sanskritic influences (in the case of the *vēṭṭuva vari*) and the Kṛṣṇa myths (in the case of the *āycciyar kuravai*). In other words, both the folk elements and Sanskritic elements are recognisable from the descriptions given by the author of the *Cilappatikāram.*

Evidence in the *Tirumurukāṟṟupaṭṭai* seems to suggest that *brāhmaṇās* (*antaṇar*) may have functioned as priests in the shrines. This is an indication of Sanskritic influence. In the section on Tiruccīralaivāy in the *Tirumurukāṟṟupaṭṭai* when the six faces of Murukan are discussed the poet states that one face of the god guards the sacrifices performed by *brāhmaṇās* who adhere to the Vedic rites[18]. Canto 4 of *Tirumuru-kāṟṟuppaṭai* on Tiruvērakam throws light on the *brāhmaṇās* and their activities in the shrine. The *brāhmaṇās*(*irupiṟappāḷar*), who were born to parents from esteemed *kuṭ is* (can this be taken to refer to *gotra?*), are said to perform their six duties, earn their wealth by tending three fires (*muttī*), wear the sacred thread "consisting of nine threads, pray at proper hours, bathe and wear wet clothes, and praise God by singing softly but with precision the mystic formula of six letters and offer fragrant flowers to Murukaṉ[19]. These descriptions seem to provide proof of the *brāhmaṇās* acting as priests and performing rituals at the two shrines of Tiruccīralaivāy and Tiruvērakam.

Another interesting and noteworthy feature was the fusion of Murukaṉ, the war God of Dravidians with Skaṇda, the Aryan war God. This is clear from numerous references in the *Tirumurukāṟṟuppaṭai* and *Paripāṭal* where there are allusions to stories included in the *Kantapurāṇam,* which represents the amalgam of autochthonous indigenous traditions of Murukaṉ with the Sanskritic traditions, which portray the puranic personality of Murukaṉ. An attempt is made to blend the Dravidian Murukaṉ with the Aryan Skanda/Subramaṇyā through myths. Features of the deity deriving from the non-Tamil traditions i.e Sanskritic/Aryan, which do not figure in the early Tamil texts, relate to the birth of the God and his iconographic features (i.e. six faces and twelve arms); and victory over the *asurā* Cūrapaṉmaṉ is based on the puranic story of Subrahmaṇyā defeating Surapadmā[20]. The *Paripāṭal* and *Tirumurukāṟṟuppaṭ ai* do not narrate the legends/myths of Murukaṉ in full. Allusions to such legends are interspersed within the texts. It has been hypothesised that the poet resorted to these legends to portray the "superiority of Murukan over all others...by attributing to him qualities found in the *purāṇic* stories which the poets thought would be a source of inspiration to the readers too". Further, the poet may have used the legends to 'express his spiritual experience.[21] Murukaṉ is depicted with six faces and twleve arms in the second canto (Tiruccīralaivāy). Such desriptions can also be gleaned in the *Paripāṭal* and *Cilappatikaram*. Birth of Murukaṉ, the six-faced God to the six presiding deities of the Constellation Pleiades is mentioned in the *Paripāṭal*[22]. This fact of Murukaṉ's birth can be noticed in the *Tirumurukāṟṟuppaṭai,* which alludes to the puranic story briefly. It is stated that this God, who has six forms, was born to six women in the lake which had *tarppai* grass on the summit of the Himalayas and was carried by one of them. These six women were the wives of six sages[23]. Passing references to the stories of Murukaṉ's birth are made in the *Tirumurukāṟṟuppaṭai* and *Paripāṭal* while the later *Kantapurāṇam* describes the birth of Skanda in great detail in the section *Urpattikāṇṭ am*[24]. Victory of Murukaṉ over Cūrapaṉmaṉ (*Cūr* in the early Tamil poems - who is considered frightful) is derived from the *purāṇic* story of Subramaṇya defeating Sūrapadmā. Sūrapadmā was not killed in the battle but when he transformed himself into a mango tree and was cut into two, the two parts were turned into a cock and peacock by Murukaṉ. While the cock was made the banner, the peacock was converted into the *vāhaṇa* (vehicle) of the God[25]. Allusions to this story are found in the *Tirumurukāṟṟuppaṭai* and *Paripāṭal*[26]. Two references in the *Tirumurukāṟṟuppaṭai* mention the God with the *vēl* (spear) who entered the sea and destroyed Cūrapaṉmaṉ, king of the *asurās*[27]. Another indicates the God with the red spear who subjugated the *avuṇar* (*asurar*) by chopping down the mango tree which had flowers and destroyed the *asurā cūr* who was half man and half horse[28]. This is compared by a scholar to the cutting down of the tutelary trees of enemy kings by the victorious kings[29].

Another *purāṇic* study alluded to is the story of the fight between Tārakaṉ and Subramaṇya. The *vēl* of Murukaṉ is said to have pierced the Kiravuñcam hill where an *asurā* hid his brother. Tārakaṉ fought with Murukaṉ and was annihilated. Murukaṉ is said to have split the hill and freed the warriors imprisoned in it. There is one reference to Murukaṉ splitting the hill in the *Tirumurukāṟṟuppaṭai*[30]. The legends of Murukaṉ's exploits of cutting down the mango tree, diving into sea to conquer *Cūr* by throwing the *vēl* and the splitting of the hill by the *vēl* are also referred to in the *Cilappatikāram*[31]. Thus from the above it is clear that the poet's descriptions of Murukaṉ represent the commingling of both the indigenous and the Sanskritic traditions.

The *Tirumurukāṟṟuppaṭai,* along with the *Paripāṭal,* is viewed as a work, which expresses the devotee's love and *bhakti* (devotion)[32]. Apart from describing the shrines and singing of Murukaṉ's glories, the poets talk of love and submission to the feet of God as the path to salvation. This salvation can be achieved if the devotees pursue the path of righteousness to reach the feet of Murukaṉ[33] and by the devotees praising and adoring him with hands folded on the head when they arrive at his feet[34] i.e. at the shrines.

While in the *Cilappatikāram* Murukaṉ is still conceived of within the earthly reality, the *Tirumurukāṟṟuppaṭai* appears to view Murukaṉ as a transcedental absolute.

Viṣṇu in the *Paripāṭal* is conceived that way. Murukaṉ is conveyed by the poet to be incomprehensible, incomparable and immeasureable.[35] Further, Murukaṉ is described to be one who grants blessings and boons to the devotees who seek his feet and worship him. One of his faces is said to be diffusing rays of light which put an end to darkness of the world[36]. His arm is described to cause rains[37]. Another face looks on the devotess who praise him graciously and lovingly grants them boons for which they pray[38] Another face keeps guard over the sacrifices performed by the *brāhmaṇās*[39]. Besides, Murukaṉ is mentioned as the lord who grants salvation to those who ask for it[40] and grants grace to those who are distressed.[41] We find that such ideas were not prevalent in the early forms of worship. The concept of a transcendental God and the merging of Murukaṉ with Skanda was a new feature in religion. The seed of *bhakti* (devotion) also seems to have been sown in this period. It is however only in the early medieval religious poetry viz., *Tēvāram* and *Tiviyaprapaṉṭam* that the idea of the devotee's total surrender to him and his mystical union with the God is developed. Despite this idea of an incomprehensible absolute, Murukaṉ was still conceived of as within the *akattiṇai* (love) traditions and within the confines of the real and poetic landscape. From the above it is clear that attempts were made at the universalisation of Murukaṉ-from a *tiṇai* deity into a deity of universal importance.

Koṟṟavai, the deity of the *pālai tiṇai,* is the third important deity who gets transformed into a puranic (Sanskritic) goddess namely Durga. In the case of Koṟṟavai it is interesting to note that the process of amalgamation of folk traditions and Sanskritic elements can be recognised more clearly through the descriptions in the *Cilappatikāram*. This text refers to three types of ritual dances.

The one relevant to Korravai is the *vēṭṭuvavari,* while the *āycciyarkuravai*: the dance of the cowherdesses and *kuṉrakuravai*: the dance of the *Kuṛava* girls (girls of the hills) are relevent for Māl and Murukaṉ. These three ritual dances/drama were enacted on certain occasions, the first two significantly ending with songs in praise of the Pāṇṭiya ruler. It is relevant to note that these dances were folk/tribal in nature but show evidence of Sanskritic influences. All the three dances were danced in times of crises within the communities i.e *eyiṇar, āycciyar* or the *kuṛavar.*

The various stages and action of the *vēṭṭuvari* is described in great detail in Canto XII of *Cilappatikāram* which consists of 74 lines of prose interspersed with songs. It begins with the priestess/oracle of the *eyiṇar* community announcing that the goddess is offended on account of the community not making any offerings to her. By dancing in the *maṉram* of the settlement of the *eyiṇar* encircled by a thorny fence she warns them that they will not be victorious if the goddess is not given her offerings. From the *eyiṇar* tribe a virgin girl was chosen to represent the Goddess. Her short hair was twined in a tuft and ornamented with a small silver snake and a crescent like semi-cirucular tooth from the boar which had destroyed all the plants in the fields. her necklace was made of the teeth of a strong tiger, She wore a girdle of cleaned tiger skin with spots and stripes, had a bow in her hand and rode a stage with antlers. The *eyiṟṟiyar* (women folk) who offered dolls, wild fowls of soft feathers, blue peacocks, balls and *kaḻaṅku* (beans) followed her carrying paints, boiled grains, sweets of sesamum seeds, rice with meat, flowers, incense and fragrant scents. When she was taken to the cult spot i.e. shrine of *Aṇaṅku* (deity) various instruments like the drum, trumpet and pipe were played simultaneously with the ringing of the bells during the procession to the shrine. Then the girl got possessed and in that state uttered the oracle pointing towards Kaṇṇaki.

Then the praise of the girl was sung. She was taken to be one who wore the moon in her hair, had an unwinking eye in her forehead, coral lips, a darkened throat (by poison?), had the serpent Vāsuki as her girdle, wore the hide of an elephant as an upper garment and the skin of a lion (or tiger) as a lower one; had a trident in her bangled hands; wore a *cilampu* on her left foot and her right foot had small bells. She, (Koṟṟavai) who was skilled in sword fighting who stood on the head of the double-bodied *Āvuṇaṉ* (*asurā* i.e. Mahisāśurā) was worshipped by many. She who was Kumari, Cavuri and Camari, the holder of the trident, was taken to be the younger sister of Viṣ ṇu and her colour was blue. Then she truly resembled Durga, the goddess Lakshmi and Saraswati whom Viṣṇu and Brahmā came to worship. She was Cālini, the virgin girl who was to be possessed by the Goddess and speak with the voice of the Goddess (*Aiay*). Praises of this virgin girl Cāliṇi (who assumed the form of the Goddess of victory) and the *eyiṉar* tribe into which she was born were sung. The 'goddess' joined the dance which had been started by others. Then the songs sung mention the success of the *eyiṉar* in cattle raids. This ritual was performed to propitiate the goddess so that the *eyiṉar* could get more cattle. As part of the victory celebration some offerings were made to the 'goddess'. It is possible that some cattle were killed at the ritual and the blood offered to her. Songs sung towards the end request the goddess to accept their offerings and bless them with more. Finally the *eyiṉar* ended the ritual by wishing the ruler (Pāṇṭiyaṉ as they perform it near Madurai) victories[42]. The folk elements in the *veṭṭuva vari* comprised the selection of the virgin girl to represent the goddess, the dance of the *eyiṉar*, singing of the songs praising the cattle raids of the *eyiṉar* and the offering (sacrifice?) to propitiate the goddess. The Sanskritic element is evident from the transformation of the goddess Koṟṟavai (deity of the *pālai tiṇai*) into the Sanskritic Durga or mahisasuramardini.

The source through which the *eyiṉar* got to know of Durga is not clear and the processes of the virgin goddess becoming Durga are not easy to trace. Yet, this goddess is totally transformed into the Sanskritic Durgā and made the sister of Māl (viṣṇu). A special attribute of Koṟṟavai, not found in the northern form of Durga was that she had a deer and not a lion as her vehicle and she is also a virgin goddess. The worship of a virgin girl possessed by the goddess is a typical folk form although here she is endowed with all attributes of Durga. In fact she is even addressed as Sanskari, Antari, Nīli, who wears in her head the serpent and the crescent moon, which are the attributes of Śiva in Puranic religion.

In this context, it is significant to note the discovery of a Pallava sculpture of

Durgā in the village of Periyavēṇmaṇi in the Madurantakam taluk of Chingelput district of Tamil Nadu. This particular sculpture of the goddess which measures about 3 1/2 feet by 2 1/2 feet dateable to 8th-9th centuries A.D has all the attributes of Durga with one exception. The goddess has a deer instead of a lion as a *vāhana* which is a unique feature. This sculpture fits in with the description of Koṟṟavai provided in the *Cilappatikāram* discussed above. On account of the presence of the deer this icon may be styled as the Mrigavāhiṇi Durga[43]. Durga with the deer as *vāhana* is represented in late Pallava sculptures and in some early Cōḻa sculptures i.e upto the 10th century A.D.

Thus under the increasing Sanskritic influences Koṟṟavai is transformed into Durga and made the sister of Viṣṇu. But the tribal moorings are seen in the sacrifices offered to her (probably animals like cattle were killed and blood offered). Essentially the *vēṭṭuvavari* seems to be a ritual folk dance associated with sacrifices performed for gaining success in cattle lifting and with prayers for victories in the future. In the *Tirumurukāṟruppaṭai* Koṟṟavai is denoted as the mother of Murukaṉ[44], thereby establishing her identiy with Parvati.

One of the two major Purāṇic deities Śiva as we have seen in an earlier section is not a *tinai* deity although he is mentioned in various ways in the anthologies and in the later texts. What is however of specific interest is that the *Cilappatikāram* explicitly mentions Murukaṉ as Ālamar Celvaṉ Putalvaṉ i.e. son of the one who sits under the banyan tree; in other words, Śiva, the god who resides in Mount Kailāsā[45]. Together Murukaṉ, Koṟṟavai and Ālamar Celvaṉ who were thus brought together into a single imagery are later incorporated in the Pallava shrines as the cult object in the form of Soma-skanda. This is an iconographic form with Śivā as the central deity which was evolved only in Tamiḻakam particularly by the Pallavas whose ideology was derived from the Purāṇās[46].

A unique feature of cultic development in Tamiḻakam in the later phase is the evolution of the Pattini Cult or the cult of the chaste wife.

This does not seem to be directly related either to the cult of Koṟṟavai or any form of Mother Goddess usually associated with folk cults in South India. It makes its appearance in the story of the *Cilappatikāram* and the establishment of the Pattini cult is attributed to the Cēra ruler Ceṅkuṭṭuvaṉ who built a temple for Kaṇṇaki (the heroine of the epic)[47]. However, this cult did not take root in Tamiḻakam except in the Cēra region. It seems to have migrated to Sri Lanka after the 7th-8th Centuries A.D and the story of Pattini also seems to have assumed several versions viz, the Buddhist and the Hindu in that island in medieval times[48]. There is however, no doubt that they are all derived from the *Cilappatikāram* version and at the same time incorporated local (i.e. Sri Lankan) elements as well as northern Sanskritic traditions. The worship of Pattini or the Pattini cult survives even today in Sri Lanka among the Tamils of the eastern region of the island[49]. In South India particularly the Cēra region (i.e. Kerala) the cult seems to have transformed into the cult of Bhagavati or Kāli; although the latter forms of the Mother Goddess had no relation whatsoever with the origin of the cult[50]. It has been suggested that the cult itself as described in the *Cilappatikāram* owes its origin to the pre-Cilappatikāram period in Tamiḻakam when the Buddhists and Jains had evolved a cult of the Pattini. It is further suggested that the worship of the Pattini was enacted through a ritual drama probably in Madurai which influenced the composition of the epics *Cilappatikāram* by Iḷaṅkō Atikaḷ and *Maṇimēkalai* by Cīttalai Cāttanār[51].

In the earlier section the identification of Māyōṉ/Māl with Viṣṇu/Kṛṣṇā has been discussed particularly with reference to Balarāma and Kṛṣṇa as Vṛṣṇi viras, to the influence of the *Kṛṣṇa carita,* and some of the attributes like discus given to Māl. It is the *Paripāṭal* of the later phase which makes Māl a universal deity and a transcendental absolute. In this work worship of Māl also shifted to a new locale i.e. temple. In the hymns of the *Paripāṭal* one comes across the temple environs and the worship of the *vigrahā,* a symbolic representation of the God[52]. The praise of temple/shrine or Māl at Tirumāliruṅkuṉṟam of Tirumāliruṇcōlai (12 miles north of Madurai) is sung[53]. Māl is looked upon by the poets of the *Paripāṭal* as a transcendental absolute who is the one[54] beyond comprehension[55], beyond description;[56]. beyond comparison;[57] and transcending time[58]. Further, he is described to be the first of all the beings,[59] the one who belongs to the four yugas[60] and the universe,[61] and hence omnipresent. As in the worship of Murukaṉ, the devotees' love for God and their desire to live at the feet of Mal is an important feature in the *Paripāṭal*[62].

The descriptions in the *Paripāṭal* would even suggest the predominance of purāṇic forms over other folk elements in the worship of Māl/Viṣṇu, as Viṣṇu is said to have assumed endless forms among which even the *virāṭa* or *visvarupā* form seems to be included[63].

At the same time the folk elements continued to prevail among the pastoralists as seen in the description of the *āycciyarkuravai* in the *Cilappatikāram* (Canto XVII).

Here, the *āycciyarkuravai* was performed by the cowherd girls of the cowherds settlement on the outskirts of Madurai. When Kōvalaṉ was killed in Madurai, some bad omens were noticed at the settlement of the cowherds. Milk did not curdle when it was churned for butter, the bull with the big hump shed tears from his eyes, the butter in the vessel did not melt and the cows shivered. On seeing this, i.e. ill omens foreboding disaster, Mātāri (the woman who looked after Kaṇṇaki) called her daughter to dance the *kuṛavai* which Māyavaṉ (Kṛṣṇa) and his elder brother had danced with Piṉṉai to ward off the impending evil. This was the enactment of kṛṣṇa's mythical dance with the *Gōpis*. Seven girls participated in this song and dance which ended with the *āycciyar's* prayer to Māyōṉ for the benefit of their cows and the victory of the Pāṇṭiya ruler[64]. According to F.Hardy there is elaborate treatment of the myths of Krsna connected with Vrajā (Vrindāvaṉ) which were adapted to the Tamil cutural milieu. In Hardy's view, this dance is a kind of religious folk dance in which are enacted the mythical bullfight and *kuṛavai* (a non, *Caṅkam* form). Though it represented a mythical event the dance was highly structured and formalised. The *kuravai* was not part of the traditional repertoire of the *mullai tiṇai*. So Hardy opines that the author of the epic would have had knowledge of the *kuravai* in folk culture and written about it under the influence of the *akam* conventions and mythical episodes[65]. Here again the mythical bullfight and *kuravai* were essentially folk elements while the myths of Kṛṣṇa in Vriṇdāvaṉ constituted the Sanskritic elements.

As during this phase (by 5th-6th centuries A.D) the temple had become an important centre of worship and even a centre of 'pilgrimage' (for eg. Tirumāliruñcōlai or Tirupparaṅkuṉṟam), it may be stated that the beginnings of formal religious systems can be traced to the later phase of early historical Tamiḻakam. The reference to temples are indeed numerous. For example, there were temples (*kōṭṭam, kōyil*) of deities like the six-faced God (Murukaṉ), the fair-complexioned God Balaramā (Vāliyōṉ), the dark-coloured God Neṭiyōṉ (Viṣṇu) and the God of the victorious umbrella and garland Maṉṉavaṉ (Intirā) in Pukār according to the *Cilappatikāram*[66]. Archaeology, however, is silent on this aspect. These temples also seemed to have been involved in the Intira *viḻa* celebrations as rituals seemed to have been held here during the *viḻa*[67]. Besides these temples the shrines of Viṣhṇu at Pukār (the deity was called Maṇivaṇṇaṉ[68]) and at Turutti[69] (the island of Srirangam) and Vēṅkaṭam[70] are mentioned in the course of the journey Kōvalaṉ and Kaṇṇaki undertake to Madurai. Another shrine mentioned in the *Cilappatikāram* is that of Viṣṇu at Āṭakamāṭam (Tiruvanantapuram)[71]. The *Paripātal* also refers to the shrine of Viṣṇu at Tirumāliruñcolai[72].

One gets to know of the non-brahmanical religions from the *Cilappatikāram* and *Maṇimēkalai*. These religions, i.e. Buddhism and Jainism, co-existed with the Brāhmanical religion. In fact these two works are primarily Jain and Buddhist works. The author of the *Cilappatikāram* was a prince who become a Jain monk and relinquished his right to the throne. In fact in the epilogue the author mentions the monastery at Kuṇavāyir Kōṭṭam where he stayed. The *Maṇimēkalai* exalts Buddhism and considers the Buddhist philosophy to be the best among the six systems of philosophy. Both these creeds may have been extended royal patronage. Further, since both the epics are set in the urban centres of these times, the urban centres are described elaborately. These urban centres were loci of wealthy traders and merchants. The *Cilappatikāram* describes the *paratar* (traders) of Pukār to be wealthy and of high lineage. It can be assumed that these religions found followers among the prosperous mercantile community. There seems to be a close association between the trading community and the heterodox religions especially Buddhism. In fact, Kōvalan, the hero of the epic *Cilappatikāram* was born into a family of *paratar.* His father was Mācaṭṭuvaṉ (great caravan leader). In the earlier period we had highlighted the donations of caves made to the monks of the heterodox sects. Such donations of caves/ monumental structures do not figure in the epics or didactic works or in the archaeological records of the later phase of the early historical period. In the *Maṇimēkalai* we are informed of Kōvalaṉ's father joining the Buddhist order. He joined the Intira Vihāra Pukar. Mātavi also joined the nunnery (*mātavor paḷḷi)* i.e. became a nun. Kannaki's father renounced worldly pleasures and became a follower of the Ājivika seet.[73]

Pukār, the Cōḷa port par excellence, was a city in which traders and merchants resided and which housed temples of different deities. The intira Vihāra at Pukār is mentioned by both the epics.[74] Further, the Buddhist association at Pukār is confirmed by the Māhābodhi (tree) on the outskirts of the city.[75] There are similar references to Jain monasteries (*paḷḷis*). Kōvalaṉ and Kannaki met the Jain nun Kāvuṇṭi Aṭikaḷ in her *palli*[76] which was in the grove of trees. They undertook the journey to Madurai with her.

Mention is made of (*Kantaṉpaḷḷi*) (the sacred hall of the Jains), at Uraiyur, the *Aṛavōr paḷḷi* (monastery of the Jains?) at Pukār and the Jain *silātalā* built by Jain householders for the *cāranar* in the suburbs of the city[77].

The Cēra capital Vañci is also described to have a *caityā* constructed by a predecessor of Kōvalaṉ (who became a monk after distributing his wealth) and an Intirā Vihārā like the one at Pukār[78]. It has been postulated that the "references to the Intirā Vihārās suggest that Buddhist establishments came up in the outskirts of big urban centres and it became a common literary tradition to ascribe them to dirive authorship or to great kings like Asōkā by pilgrims and foreign travellers visiting Buddhist centres. In a few cases they may have been erected by merchant or trading organisations and later traditions provided them with great antiquiety"[79]. And in this context it may be pointed out that Intira vihārās existed at Pukār and Vañci, two important 'urban' centres of those times.

Kāñcipuram was an important centre of Buddhism and the *Maṇimēkalai* refers to the *caityā, stūpā* and *vihārā* located there.[80] Maṇimēkalai, the heroine of the epic *Maṇimēkalai,* is said to have travelled to Kañci to study the Buddhist philosophy from the saint Aṛavaṇa Aṭikaḷ. Due to the influence of Maṇimēkalai the Cōḷā king is said to have converted a prison house into a *vihāra* with a kitchen and a dining hall[81]. She is said to have been charitable i.e. miraculously produced food from her divine bowl (*amudacurabi*) and provided food and medicines to the needy[82].

It may be stated that royal patronage was extended to Buddhism by the Cōḷa ruler. No hostility between the two creeds is reflected in the texts though in the *Maṇimēkalai* an attempt is made to place Buddhism over the others[83]. References to religious conflict and persecution are not found in the texts. That *brāhmaṇās* were well treated and given respect is fairly clear from the *Cilappatikāram.*

Archaeological evidence of this period is meagre as compared to the wealth of literary references. Some sort of a Buddhist structure assignable to an earlier date (4th century) has been noticed at Kañcipuram in the area adjacent to the Kamākshi Ammaṉ Temple. However, diggings at Pukār seem to be more illuminating. The monastic complex with an apsidal caityā excavated is dated to about 4th-5th centuries A.D. i.e. the period under discussion[84].

These heteredox sects may have gained importance on account of possible royal patronage and increased membership especially among the wealthy traders. Unlike in the Western Deccan where merchants made elaborate grants to the monasteries and huge rock-out *caityās* and *vihārās* were excavated (made) the Tamil region does not show any archaeological or monumental evidence of such monuments although literary descriptions are found in the epics. It has been pointed out that "the transitional phase of the 3rd-6th centuries A.D. was one of Jain and Buddhist ascendancy probably under the patronage of the Kalabhra rulers. This is indirectly confirmed for Jainism by the fact that the Drāviḍa Saṅgha of the Jains was established at Madurai by one Vajranandi in C.A.D. 470[85]. In this context, it is relevant to note that some of the minor didactic works like *Nālaṭiyār, Paḻamoḻi Nāṉūrū, Cirupañcamūlam* and *Ēlati.* were perhaps written by people of the 'heterodox' sects. The author of '*Ēlati*', Kaṇimētaviyār is definitely a Jainā. Moreover, since the texts lay emphasis on non-violence (*ahimsā*), vegetarianism, abstinence of the young, alms given to ascetics and the needy, public works of utility etc, their temper appears co correspond to the Jaina and Buddhistic principles and ethics.

One of the most significant differences between the early and later phases is the idea of renunciation which under the influence of Buddhism and Jainism in particular seems to have become an accepted norm. Not only were the monks and nuns of the Buddhist and Jain orders upholders of this norm, even the householders or *upasakās* and *śravakās* are seen to be renouncing the material world seeking salvation under the Buddhist and Jain ideologies[86]. This would indicate different levels of renuciation hardly known to the early anthologies and texts. In this context the Buddhist and Jain organisation into Saṅghas seem to have become quite common as evidenced by the epics and the archaeological evidence. This would represent another aspect of development of formal and organised religious system particularly in the congregational religions of Buddhism and Jainism which developed the sense of the *communitas* i.e the development of the community of believers.

As in the first phase of the early historical period there was an absence of a dominant religious ideology. The 'heterodox' religions seem to have gained ascendency and followers (even among the laity) especially in the urban centres. With the gradual influx of Purāṇic/Sanskritic notions and ideas, attempts at integration of theDravidian autocthonous traditions with the Puranic traditions is best represented by cults of Koṟṟavai (Durgā/Pārvati) and Murukaṉ (Skanda). It is only from 7th Century onwards with the land grant system that Puranic religion with the emphasis on *bhakti* became a new ideological force to reckon with. Correspondingly, a change can be seen in the genre of literature. The literature of the later period is definitely more religious and devotional in nature. The *Tēvāram* and *Tiviyaprapaṉtam* contain the experiences of the *bhaktas* (the *Nāyanmārs* and *Āḻvārs*). In this period, the temple also emerged as an important centre of worship. One can state without doubt that the seeds of all these developments were sown in the period of the epics and the eighteen minor works.

FOOTNOTES

1. Paraṅkuṉṟam is said to be to the west of Madurai-*Tirumurukaṟṟuppaṭai* 1.71.
2. Tiruvāiṉaṉkuṭi is identified with the modern Paḻani—A Kandiah, *Cult and Worship of Murukaṉ as reflected in the Paripāṭal and Tirumurukāṟṟuppaṭai,* Sri Lanka, 1984, pp. 22-23.
3. Tiruvērakam is popularly identified with Swāmimalai (four miles from Kumpakōṇam and 20 miles from Tañjavūr). It is also said to be a shrune of Subramaṇyā in the hill country of Malabar-Kandaiah, 1984, p. 23, *Journal of Tamil Studies* Vol.9, June 1976, p. 8.

4. Aḻakarmalai is 13 miles from Madurai- K.Zvelebil, 1976, p. 8
A.Kandiah, 1984, p. 24.
5. *Tolkāppiyam, Poruḷatikāram, Akattiṇai Iyal* 5.
6. *Paripāṭal* VIII.
7. *Tirumurukaṟṟuppaṭai* 11 218-20.
8. *Paripāṭal* VIII: 97-102; XVII: 1-4.
9. *Paripāṭal* XVII: 7, XIX: 14-15.
10. *Paripāṭal* VIII: 109; 22; XVII: 9-16; IX: 72-3.
11. *Tirumurukāṟṟuppaṭai* refers to the sound of the drums of the Gods, blowing of horns and conches and the beating of drums in the canto on Tiruciralaivāy (11. 119-21) and to celestial girls playing sweet music on the *yāl* in the canto on Tiruvāviṉaṉkuṭi (11. 140-43).
12. *Tirumurukaṟṟuppaṭai* 11.12-41.
13. Ibid 11. 47-56.
14. Ibid 11. 190-217.
15. Ibid 11. 227-44.
16. Ibid 11. 218-26.
17. *Cilappatikāram* XXIV.
18. *Tirumurukāṟṟuppaṭai* 11.94-96.
19. Ibid 11. 177-89.
20. A. Kandiah 1984, pp. 67-69
K.Zvelebil, *Tamil Traditions on Subrahmaṇyā Murugan,* Madra, 1991, p. 75.
21. A. Kandiah, 1984., p. 67.
22. *Paripāṭal* V:11; XIV:21 ; XXI: 67
Also *Cilappatikāram* XXIV : *Paṭṭumaṭai.*
23. *Tirumurukāṟṟuppaṭai* 11 253-55 *Paripāṭal*-V.
24. A. Kandiah 1984, p. 68.
25. Ibid, p. 68.
26. *Paripāṭal* XVIII: 1-4; V:1-4; XXI: 8,28; XIV 18; IX:70.
27. *Tirumurukāṟṟuppaṭai* 11. 45-46.
28. Ibid 11. 58-61.
29. A. Kandiah 1984, pp. 69-70.
30. *Tirumurukāṟṟuppaṭai* 1.266
A. Kandiah, 1984, p. 70.
31. *Cilappatikāram* XXIV : *Pāṭṭumaṭai.*
32. There is a legend about the author of the text Nakkīrar being saved in time of distress when he chanted the poem in honour of Murukaṉ. It runs like this "Nakkīrar was ordered by Śiva to make a pilgrimage to atone for his presumption after the dispute with Siva at the Tamil Literary academy in the city of Maturai. He was caught by a demon on his way while performing his daily *puja* on the bank of the river in the forest. He was later confined in a cave along with 999 other men in order to make a huge sacrifice. When the demon was preparing himself to consume all the 1000 prisoners in the sacrifice, the poet invoked the help of the god Murukaṉ to save him and chanted this poem in his honour. At the end of the chanting of the poem, the god Muṛukaṉ appeared and killed the demon. Thus Nakkīrar and the other were saved." Therefore A. Kandiah is of the view "that many Saivites believe even

at present that the chanting of the *Tirumurukaṟṟuppaṭai* still has the same saving power. This legend is undoubtedly a creation of later date to make the work a popular and inspiring one among the people." - Kandiah, 1984, pp. 54-55.

33. *Tirumurukāṟṟuppaṭai* 11.62-66.
    Paripāṭal VIII: 81-82.
34. *Tirumurukāṟṟuppaṭai* 11. 250-2.
35. Ibid 11. 278-81.
36. Ibid 11. 91-2.
37. Ibid 11. 115-6.
38. Ibid 11. 93-94.
39. Ibid 11. 94-96.
40. Ibid 1. 270.
41. Ibid 1. 271.
42. *Cilappatikāram* XII: 1-74 and songs after this. K. Sivathamby is of the view this ritual is similar with the modern Tirayāṭṭam - exorcistic ritual performed in kerala - *Drama in Ancient Tamil Society,* Madras, 1981, p. 288.
43. For the iconographic details of this see R.Champakalakshmi's and A.Swamy's "Pallava Antiquities in Periyaveṇmaṇi" (Rp.) *Journal of the Madras University,* Volume XL1, Nos 1 and 2, January - July 1969, p. 130;, pp. 132-35.
44. *Tirumurukāṟṟuppaṭai* 1. 258.
45. *Cilappatikāram* XXIV.
46. I am thankful to Dr. R.Champakalakshmi for this information.
47. *Cilappatikāram* XXVII and XXVIII.
48. Gananath Obeyesekere, *The Cult of the Goddess Pattini,* Chicago, 1984, p. 509. Also chapters 13, 14,15.
49. Ibid. Chapter 15.
50. Ibid., pp. 540-52.
51. Ibid., pp. 603-07.
52. F. Hardy, *Viraha bhakti,* New Delhi, 1983, p. 202.
53. *Paripātal XV*
    F. Hardy, 1983, p. 204.
54. *Paripāṭal* I:5; 43; XIII:37.
55. Ibid I: 29; III: 46-50.
56. Ibid I: 31; 49-54.
57. Ibid I, 49-54.
58. Ibid II: 16-19; III:61.
59. Ibid: I: 53.
60. Ibid: III: 80.
61. Ibid I: 37-48; III: 63-72; IV:25-35.
62. Ibid I: 65; II: 72-73; XV: 65.
63. R.Champakalakshmi, *Vaiṣṇavā Iconography in the Tamil country,* New Delhi, 1981, Chapter 3.

64. *Cilappatikāram* XVII. It contains a lot of musicological details. Also see F.Hardy, New Delhi, 1983, pp, 172-80.
65. F. Hardy, 1983, pp. 180-83. Mention is made of the *Valacaritai nāṭakankaḷ* i.e dramas depicting Kṛṣṇa's boyhood.

    Sivathamby opines that the *āycciyar kuṛavai* and bull baiting constitute living traditions even today but in modified forms. In this regard he mentions Vanamamalai's views on the *Kolāṭṭam* festival which is a relic of the *āycciyar kuravai*. In this festival, the songs are sung by brahmin girls and ritual is performed by the Brahmin girls whereby a miniature image of a cow is taken round the streets in processions. He also quotes A.K. Majumdar's views on the *kuravai,* "it is most likely.....that the *Kuṛavai* dance of South India became known in the north first as the *Hallisaka* and then as *Rāsa* and that the dance was adopted in the north along with the legends surrounding it." Further, Sivathamby states that Majumdar traces the Radha cult to Piṉṉai of theTamil Tradition-K.Sivathamby, 1981, pp. 291-92.
66. *Cilappatikāram* V:11.168-81.
67. Ibid.
68. Ibid X 1. 10.
69. Ibid XI: 11 35-52.
70. Ibid XI: 11 41-42.
71. Ibid XXVI: 11 62-64. Some identify it as the temple of Padmanābha Swamy at Trivandrum while Dikshitar identifies it with a Vaisṇava shrine found in the suburbs of karūr.
72. *Paripāṭal* XV.
73. *Cilappatikāram* XXVII: 11. 90-95; 98-100, 103-09; XXIX: 7.
    Maṇimēkalai, XVII: 11. 7-8.
74. *Cilappatikāram* X: 1.14; XXVII-1-92
    Maṇimēkalai XXVI: 1. 55.
75. *Cilappatikāram* X: 11. 11-12.
76. Ibid X: 1-36.
77. Ibid X: 11. 15-25; XI: 1.5; V:11.178-79.
78. *Maṇimēkalai* XXVIII : 11. 122-31; XXVIII: 11. 69-72; XXVI: 1.55.
    Cilappatikāram X: 11. 13-14; XXVII: 11.92-93.
79. R. Champakalakshmi, 1992, p. 29.
80. *Maṇimēkalai* XXVIII 11. 170-76; XXI : 11.161-74.
81. Ibid XIX, XX.
82. Ibid XVII.
83. Ibid XXVIII.
84. *IAR* 1962-63, pp. 163-65; 1964-65, p. 42;1965-66, p. 35.
85. R. Champakalakshmi, 1992, p. 8.
86. Kōvalaṉ's father renounced the material world.

CHAPTER - IV

EARLY TAMIL POLITY : FROM CHIEFDOM TOWARDS KINGDOM

Early historical Tamil society cannot be described as a state society, although evidence of different levels of political authority may be recognised among the *Vēntar,* Vēḷir and other chiefs. The *Caṅkam* poems use the terms *vēntar* and Mūventar interpreted as "crowned Kings" and "three crowned Kings" respectively, to refer to the three main ruling families/lineages namely Cēra, Cōḷa and Pāṇṭiya[1]. The nuclei of these three major chiefdoms, often described as kingdoms, arose in the three major fertile reverine belts which were said to be the main rice producing areas. Besides the *mūvētar,* there were petty chiefs who were known as *kuṛunilamaṉṉar,* which would literally mean lords of lesser tracts. (*kuṛu*= short)[2].

Conventional historians like Subrahmanian are emphatic about the presence of a states society in early historical times. Their theory of a state society is based on a number of assumptions like the presence of a regular and elaborate administrative machinery, standing army, and a full-fledged tax structure with officials to extract the taxes. Such 'facts' as we shall see later, are not substantiated by literature.

The early Tamil Kings/chieftains were known as *Kō, Kōmāṉ Maṉṉaṉ, Vēntan* etc. and their place of residence or palace was known as *kōyil.* In later times, the *kōyil* denoted the house of god or temple. Seneviratne has pointed out that in the hilly and pastoral regions there was a correlation between the eco-zone represented by the physiography economy and habitat and the epithets/titles and personal names taken by the leadership and the community. He indicates that the term *ko* could mean mountain and its parallel term is *malai.*Terms such as *kōmāṉ,* Malaiyamāṉ and Neṭu (māṉ) are interpreted by him to mean hill chieftain. The texts refer to chieftains such as Vēlāvi Kkōmāṉ , Paṭumāṉ, Malaiyamāṉ Tirumuṭikkāri. Another term used in the texts viz, *Nāṭan* could also indicate an association with a hilly region. Further, he goes on to show the pastoral affiliations from epithets of certain chieftains. Certain chieftains like Pēkaṉ, Eyiṉaṉ, Aṇṭiraṉ had epithets like Āy, Āvi, Āviyar, which indicate a pastoral association[3]. There were some like Erumai, a name which also suggests a link with pastoralism as it appears to have derived from *eru* which means bull.

Another term *perumakaṉ/perumāṉ* taken by certain chieftains is interpreted by

Seneviratne to mean "great descendant/scion/ son—eg. Perumakkaṉ Pēkaṉ[4]. Next to the *Mūvēntar* (vide Appendix 10) two of the more important chieftaincies of Tamiḻakam were those of Tiraiyars in the Pālār Valley (Toṇṭaināṭu) and the Atiyamāṉs of Takaṭūr (Dharmapuri) identified with the Satiyaputras of Aśokan edicts on the basis of the Jambai inscription[5]. The Āviyars (Paḻani hills-A chieftain Pēkaṉ is also said to have ruled over the Paḻani hills) the Āys (south Travancore region), the Porunar (Kodai hills), the Iruṅkōvēḷs of Kodumbalur (near Pudukottai), the Ōviyars (Chingleput region), the Malaiyamāṉs of Tirukkōvalur (South Arcot) and the Oris of Kolli hills (Koṅgunāṭu)[6]. These were some to the Vēḷir chieftaincies. In addition to these there were other vels such as Vēḷ of Aḻuntūr[7]. and Vēḷ of Aḻumpil[8]. (See diagram 1 and Appendix 11).

The term Vēḷir, which is the plural of 'vēḷ', is interpreted to derive from *vēḷvi* or 'sacrifice' and '*veḷ'* meaning bright desire (beloved of the people)[9]. Another derivation suggested is from *vēl* meaning earth (or mud) or land. The Vēḷir are referred to in the *Caṅkam* texts as ancient clans (Mutumākkaḷ) or ancient Vēḷir people (Toṉ Mutir Vēḷir)[10]. Further in the *Puṟanāṉūṟu* the chieftain Iruṅkōvēḷ (Vēḷir) is said to be the descendant of those who ruled over Tuvarai for 49 generations[11], after appearing from the sacrificial pot/pit of Vaṭapāl Muṉivaṉ-a northern sage. Nacciṉārkkiṉiyar one of the commentators of the *Tolkāppiyam* mentions that Agastya led a group of Kings, 18 clans of the Vēḷir and the Aruvāḷar from Dvaraka to the south. The Vēḷir belonged to the lineage fo Kṛṣ ṇa (Yadavas vṛṣṇis) of Dvaraka[12]. Accepting this tradition of linking the Vēḷir with the Yadavas, Raghava Iyengar states that the ancestors of Iruṅkōvēḷ may have migrated to Tamilnadu in the 10th century B.C[13]. These Vēḷir were located in fertile/coastal areas as well as hilly/pastoral tracts. There is a definite coincidence of the urn burial with the Vēḷir settlements of the fertile/coastal areas[14]. In this connection, Seneviratne interestingly noted that there were no Vēḷir settlements south of the Vaigai river in the extreme southern parts of the Tamil macro region (i.e. districts of Tirunelveli and Madurai) even though urn burials, cairn/stone circles occur profusely in these areas[15]. One of the reasons for this can be attributed to the establishment of the Pāṇṭiya power in this region, whereby the other minor chiefs could have been sidelined.

The Vēḷir located in the *marutam* could have been one of the earliest large scale agricultural communities of Tamiḻakam. Some of their territories were not only located in fertilse areas but also had access to or were rich in mineral deposits. Due to the presence of these factors the Vēḷir could have come into conflict with the *Mūvēntar* when the latter made attempts to extend territories under their away, and therefore, encroached upon lands of the Vēḷir. The number of *Vēḷs* mentioned varied from five to seven[16]. These *Vēḷs* were very munificent and poets frequently glorify the gifts given by them. Sudrashan Seniviratne likes the *perumaka* group of Sri Lanka (figuring in inscriptions) to the proto historic megalithic BRW context. In his opinion, some of them may have belonged to the Vēḷir clan[17].

Besides the Vēḷir a number of other chieftains are referred to in literature (vide

Appendix 12). Like the Vēḷir they held sway over agrarian or hilly/pastoral zones. They are not referred to as *Vēḷ* although they were quite similar to them except in terms of origin as the Vēḷir are described to be old and traced their ancestry to the Yadavas. Some of these chieftains were Ātaṇuṅkaṉ and Pulli of Vēṅkaṭa nāṭu, Paṇṇaṉ of Ciṟukuṭi, Kumaṇaṉ of Mutermalai, Puṭṭain coṟṟan of Kutiramalai etc[18]. Though some of these chieftains had scarce resources their munificence is praised by the poets. Most of the Vēḷir and non-Vēḷir seem to have distributed prestige items such as gold. horses, chariots etc apart from the basic necessity such as food.

The *Kiḻār* represented another category of chiefship. The *Kiḻār* was one who possessed rights in land. The *Kiḻār* could have emerged as heads of major households with the expansion of settlements and growth of private property. In several respects the *Kiḻār* may be compared to the gahapati of north India[19], Deccan and Andhra.[20] who were householders figuring prominently in Buddhist texts and as donors in early historical epigraphical records. The *Kiḻār* were heroes of some poems. In course of time some of the *Kiḻār* could have been important personages in the clan settlements (*ūrs*). Eight such *Kiḻār* are mentioned ruling over different *ūrs* (places) (vide Appendix 13).

The *mūvēntar* as powerful lineages tried to establish their hegemony by integrating various groups or sublineages under their control by the beginning of the Christian era. In a poem[21] the poet Kōvūr Kiḻār tries to reconcile the differences between two scions of the Cōḻa royal family Nalaṅ Kiḷḷi and Neṭuṅ kiḷḷi. These two could have belonged to two sub lineages of the Cōḻas and fought to assert the superiority of one over the other or in the process became integrated into a single polity. The Cēra case is also interesting. Tamil textual tradition refers to two ruling families among the Cēras-the Irumpoṟai and Ātaṉ. Is this indicative of the fact that there were two lineages of the Cēras which gained politicial supremacy? In the case of the Pāṇṭiyas they were known as *Pañcavar*[22] (meaning five) Were there five lineages initially among the Pāṇṭiyas out of which one powerful lineage integrated the others? In other words, all the three had the potential to become monarchies within a territory.

For the Gangetic Valley of north India it has been brought to light that the status of the ruler (*rājaṉ*) changed from *gopati* (indicates that the ruler was a tribal leader) in the early Vedic period to *bhūpati* (or lord of the earth) in the later Vedic period whereby he culd collect taxes and tribute from the people[23]. In fact R.S. Sharma also shows how the titles assumed by the ruler emphasize the ruler's lordship over all categories of people. The titles assumed are *nṛpa, nṛpati, nareśvara, naradhipa* and *manujadhipa.* These terms show how the change occurred from the protective aspect of the ruler to mean lordship or authority.

There are no similar titles assumed by the early Tamil rulers. As it was the duty of the rulers to protect the people, they were known as *kāvalar* (i.e. those who provide protection). However, the idea of territoriality is evident from the terms used to denote the territories of the *mūvēntar* viz. Cōḻa nāṭu, Pāṇṭiya nāṭu and Kuṭanāṭu (Cēra) (vide

Appendix 2). Moreover, the Cōḻa King is referred to as Kāviri nāṭaṉ which would indicate his association with the region of the Kāveri river. Performance of eleborate coronation rituals like *Rācacūya* by some kings would also strengthen the idea of territoriality as we shall see later in this section. The rulers would have got land through wars.

Besides the *mūvēntar* and other chieftains, there were other groups of people associated with different parts of the region, suggestive of territorial links.

The Koṅkar inhabiting Koṅkar nāṭu are described in literature to be possessing cows[24]. Initially they could have been pastoralists inhabiting the Coimbatore-Salem regions i.e. the *mullai* tracts. They could have come into conflict with the Cēra[25] when the Cēras made attempts to defeat the Koṅkar in order to get control of the land they inhabited and the cattle which they bred. Abundant Roman coins were found here. Did the Cēra's defeat the Koṅkar in order to participate in commercial activities? Another possible association is that of the Koṅkar with the Western Gangas, who established their dominance over Talakkad and the region around it from at least the 5th century A.D[26].

The identity of the Kōcar is puzzling. They are described in various ways: as warriors with spears, as honest, truthful people, as people speaking four languages and living in Tulu country rich with gold and also near Cēllur near the sea, and as cruel people[27]. On the basis of all the references Dorai Rangaswamy is of the view that the Kōcar represent a mercenary army[28] The Kōcar could have been warriors fighting for various chieftains. They allied with the Mauryas in their invasion of Mōkūr[29].

The frontier groups occupying the northern border of Tamiḻakam were the kaḻvar and vaṭukar. The vaṭukar are said to be living in the region beyond the Vēṅkaṭam hills and speaking a different language. The Vaṭukar seem to be hunters basically (probably like the vēṭṭuva as they had dogs) killing animals and drinking toddy and also carrying arms[30].

The *kaḻvar* chief Pulli ruled in the region of the Vēṅkaṭam hills which was well known for festivals. Pulli was also described to be munificent[31].

As highlighted earlier, the nuclei of the three chiefdoms lay in the river valleys with the capitals of the three being Karūr, Madurai and Uṛaiyūr all being strategically situated on the banks of rivers. They three chiefdoms had dual centres of power, inland and coastal, the latter being consciously developed by them as ports of trade. Muciṟi, Korkai and Kāveripaṭṭiṉam served as the second important centre for the Cēra, Pāṇṭ iya and Cōḻa respectively. The establishment of hegemony by a ruling lineage would have led the Pāṇṭiyas, Cēras and Cōḻas to issue coins with their respective royal symbols.

It is interesting to note that the *mūvēntar* stuck to the tribal traditions while at the same time they were influenced by Sanskritic elements or Vedic-Śāstraic forms of kingship.

Kingship meant possession of certain features, attributes such as the staff (*kōl*), drum (*muracu*), the tutelary teree (the *kaṭimaram* or *kāvalmaram*) and the umbrella[32]. All this, especially, the drum and tree are pronounced tribal features. The gory war sacrifice (*kalavēḷvi*) performed on the battlefield by rulers chieftains is clearly indicative of tribal leanings.

Further, the chieftain's involvement in cattle raids[33]. and *uṇṭāṭṭu, peruñ cōṟṟunilai*[34], in which they ate and dined with warriors also support the tribal basis of chiefship. Though marked social differences existed between the 'ruler' and 'ruled' because of the rulers' access to prestige goods and other resources it was offest by close contacts between the 'ruler' and the 'ruled', The *uṇṭāṭṭu* and *peruñcōṟṟunilai* could well have been occasions for bringing the rulers and the warriors in closer contact by sharing of wealth or food.

Receprocity through gift or patronage to poets, bards and kinsmen in return for eulogy, service in war etc. underlined the tribal kinship basis of socio-political organisation.

Some of the early rulers were known by various epithets which praised their qualities of leadership and bravery in war[35].

The influence of the Vedic/Śāstraic notions of kingship is visible from the following. Some ruling families claimed impressive lineage connections with epic heroes presumably to stress and validate their position[36]. A few rulers even boasted of supremacy over their northern counterparts[37]. More importantly, some of the rulers performed brahmanical sacrifices like the northern rulers.

The term generally used for the sacrifice is *vēḷvi*[38]. It could donote a brahmanical or a non-brahmnical sacrifice. Poems refer to some of the Cōḻa and Pāṇṭiya kings performing sacrifices brahmanical or non brahmanical. The war sacrifice or sacrifices performed on the battlefield constituted the non brahmanical sacrifice where the *antaṇar's* (*brāhmaṇas*) participation may not have been necessary. In the brahmanical sacrifices the *antaṇar* would have officiated as priests. It has been pointed out that only the *vēntar* performed sacrifices and not the Vēḷir[39].

The name of the Pāṇṭiyaṉ King Palayākacālai Mutukuṭumip Peruvaḻuti itself suggests that he built many sacrificial halls[40]. He is said to have performed *vēḷvi*[41] though we do not have details on the type of the sacrifice. Another pāṇṭiyaṉ king Talaiyalaṅkāṇattuc ceruvenṟa Neṭuñceḻiyaṉ is also mentioned as a performer of *vēḷvi*[42].

Cōḻa Kings Karikāla Cōḻa and Nallaṅkiḷḷi[43] also performed sacrifices. It is only in the case of the Cōḻa king Perunaṟ Kiḷḷi that we explicitly know that he performed the *Rācacūya* sacrifice as evident from the epithet to his name Iracācūyam vēṭṭa Perunaṟ kiḷḷi[44]. The *Rājasūya* was essentially a consecration ritual according to the Vedic texts. It was the most elaborate of the royal sacrifices encompassing many ceremonies spread over a considerable period of time. By performing the *Rājasūya* a chieftain is elevated to the status of a King. This meant that it could be performed by a powerful chieftain. It included ceremonies like the *ratna havimsi, abhisecaniya,* a cow raid, a game of dice and chariot race[45]. With the exception of the *ratanahavis* the other ceremonies like the cow raid, chariot race, game of dice could be the remnants of the tribal society[46]. Only the *ratnahavimsi* ceremony indicates the dissolution of the old tribal polity to a certain extent with the elevation of certain members of the tribe to a higher position over the others and the recruitment of non-Vedic people into the ranks of the Vedic community[47].

It has also been pointed out that major sacrificial rituals such as *rājasūya, aśvamedha and vājapeya* served as occasions for the consumption of wealth in numerous ceremonies stretching over many months accorpaniesd by lavish libations of milk and *ghī*, offerings of grain in various forms and the sacrifice of the choicest animals of the herd. There was elaborate gift giving between *kṣatriyas* and *brāhmaṇas*. In addition to this, gifts were brought by other chiefs as prestations to the *yajamāna* (the king). The chiefs also competed with each other while giving gifts as the value of the gifts reinforced their status and further entailed a return of a more valuable gift when they performed the *rājasūya*[48]. The lengthy ceremony of the *rājasūya* (spread over two years in later vedic texts) itself necessitated having a fixed place. Also the *ratnahavimsi* ceremony meant that the *ratnins* lived in permanent dwellings[49]. This indicated the emergence of the idea of territoriality-possession over the land. The necessity of extensive consecration rituals has been explained by Romila Thapar as follows: "initially the position of the *rājā* as a superior among other *rājās* was not so secure and required validation. If the *rājā* was selected to be the chief then he would not only have to prove himself but would also have to be invested with the requisite powers which would demarcate him from other *rājanyas*[50]". In effect the performance or the *rājasūya* turned a chieftain into a King.

Viewed in this light the performance of the *rācacūya* by Perunaṛ Kiḷḷi has some relevance. In order to establish himself as king vis-a-vis other chieftains, Kiḷḷi would have performed the *rācacūya*. Also in this period the notion of territoriality was emerging in Tamiḷakam with the three kings (*mūvēntar*) laying claims to territory and trying to acquire nuclear/strategic areas to control. So in effect the *rācacūya* was a validation ceremony conferring the status of a king.

Nicholas Dirks has stated that "these royal sacrifices when performed were the kingly arenas par excellence. It was through the sacrifice that the king became identified with the Gods through the sacrificer[51]". In this early period, the sacrifices performed in the presence of *brāhmaṇas* were few unlike in the early medieval period (of the Pallavas and Cōḷas) when sacrifices were performed to enhance status and thereby acquire legitimation for the King's rule by *brāhmaṇas*.[52] Legitimation of a chieftain's rule in early Tamiḷakam was mostly provided by bards/poets who composed eulogies i.e. *puṟam* or war poems in praise of a king glorifying his heroism and redistribution of gifts.

The Vedic rituals, as mentioned in the texts, consumed a lot of wealth. It entailed the availability of an economic surplus which could have been provided by the *grhapati/ gahapati* in the form of tribute to the *rājā*. Further, booty could have been brought by a successful raid or victory in battle in which the heroism of the *rājā* was reflected[53]. For the *rācacūya* in Tamilkam booty from raids or battle could have provided the wealth. Could the *kiḻāṉ* of Tamil region have provided a certain amount of wealth through tribute for the *rācacūya* of the Cōḻas like the *grhapati* of the North? This question is important because Perunaṟkiḷḷi, the Cōḻa who performed the *rācacūya*, could well have belonged to the later part of the first phase of the early historical period when the Tamil rulers were making attempts to legitimise their sovereignty through the performance of the Vedic sacrifices relating to the distribution of agricultural and other wealth. This would mean that they were also consciously trying to evolve an agrarian base. The traditions regarding Karikāla's attempts to improve irrigation and expand the cultivated area would also support such a view.

However, no gifts of land to *brāhmaṇās* at the culmination of the *vēḷvi* is mentioned in the *Caṅkam* texts.

The three *Vēntar* /rulers also came into conflict with the Vēḷir on account of the latter possessing fertile areas in *marutam* and coastal exchange centres in *neytal* and rich mineral deposits or forest resources, in the *kuṟiñci/mullai;* in other words, a good material base. The *mūvēntar* tried to destabilise the Vēḷir by gaining control over the areas held by them and thereby undermining their material as well as political base. It was necessary to subordinate the Vēḷir as they posed a great threat to the *mūvēntar.* Sudarshan Seneviratne has vividly explaned this process of subordination and later integration of the Vēḷir with the *mūvēntar*[54]. The *mūvēntar* did so by directly acquiring territory which they annexed after subjugating the Vēḷir; by marrying into the families of the Vēḷir and by making the Vēḷir serve under the *mūvēntar.* Other territories of the non-Vēḷir chieftains were also invaded (if not annexed as stated by Seneviratne[55]) for loot and plunder and also hegemonic control.

Conventional scholars like N. Subrahmanian and Arokiaswami[56] would make us believe that there was a regular and an elaborate administrative machinery in the territories of the *mūvēntar.* They, particularly Subrahmanian, devote a number of chapters to discuss the government at the capital, municipal and village government, law and justice, revenue and finance. Contrary to this view, the sources do not indicate the existence of such an elaborate sophisticated administrative apparatus. There are no references to a highly developed bureaucracy as Subrahmanian has delineated. What we hear of is *cuṟṟam*[57] which means relatives or people surrounding the king and they may have not been royal advisors or ministers as Subrahmanian takes them to be[58]. The *Maturaikkāñci* refers to *Kāviti* who could have been a counsellor[59]. There are references to institutions such as *nāḷavai maṉṟam, avai and avaikkaḷam* but these were basically tribal councils[60].

Evidence from the texts goes against the presence of a standing army. The texts refer to some personages designated as *ēnati* such as Ēṇāti Tirukiḷḷi, Ēṇāti Tirukaṇṇaṉ and Enati Tirukuṭṭuvaṉ[61] who were heroes of poems. Certain scholars have considered *Ēṇāti* as a corrupt form of *senapati*[62]. In view of the limited information on the subject it is not clear as to whether the *ēṇāti* was an honour conferred or (as it is prefixed to the name of a person) in recognition of his service or as an important personage of the army (probably *senapati* or commander).

Further, contrary to the conventional view a regular tax structure was absent[63]. There are scanty references to taxes paid to the ruler thereby implying that the ruler's right to tax had not yet been fully established. It has been pointed out that the rulers lacked the coercive power to directly impose and collect taxes from the people of the riverine zones[64]. Bearing in mind the strong tribal affiliations of the *mūvēntar* they could not have been in a position to tax the people. A regular administrative apparatus with officials to extract the revenue was absent despite what Subrahmanian would let us believe[65]. In the tribal set up of those times, tribute or voluntary contributions may have been given to the kings. Among the most interesting instances of suc tributes flowing into the royal court is that provided by Megasthenes who mentions that the country in the extreme south is ruled by a Pāṇṭiya queen (daughter of Herakles). Her territory consists of 365 villages each of which brings its products as tributes to the State treasury on an appointed day[66]. Such practices of paying tribute seemed to have continued till later times as attested by the late text *Cilappatikāram*. The text (in canto XVII) mentions that the cowherdesses took turns to supply ghee to the royal palace of the Pāṇṭiyās. Further, it provides another interesting description of the tributes brought by the hillfolk to the court of the Cēra ruler at Vañci. We are told that they brought as presents various items of flora and fauna such as "white tusks of elephants, loads of *akil,* whisks of deer hair, pots of honey, chips of sandalwood, lumps of red *sindura,* loads of *anjana* and beautiful *aritara,* cardamom stalks pepper stalks, *kuvainuru* (arrowroot flower), luxuriant *kavalai,* ripe coconuts, delicious mangoes, garlands of green leaves (*paccilai*), jackfruits, garlic, sugarcane, flowery creepers, rich bunches of areca nuts from luxuriant palms, bunches of the big variety of sweet plantains, āḻi cubs, lion cubs, tiger cubs, varutai deer that roam the hill sides, fawns of the timid deer, fawns of the musk deer, harmless little mongooses, peacocks with beautiful feathers, navi kittens (civet cats), wild hens and parrots with their honeyed words[67]."

It is only in the later texts such as *Kuṟaḷ* that one finds references to ministers army etc. Although the ruling ineages lacked the coerline power to tax and collect revenue, they made attempts to control certain areas with resources or certain aspects of production and trade. The Pāṇṭiya king controlled the pearl fisheries of the Gulf of Mannar as evident from the *Periplus,* the *Arthaśāstra* as well as the *Caṅkam* texts. It is possible that the rulers may have realised the advantages of the lucrative trade in pearls and hence took steps to make it a royal monopoly. Judging by the coins issued by the Pāṇṭiyās,[68] Cōḻas and Cēras, it may be inferred that they participated in the commercial activities. The Cōḻas, in particular, levied duties on goods i.e. *ulkuporuḷ* and appointed people or officers to supervise the control of such goods[69]. Besides it is possible that they maintained warehouses in which the dues, tributes, goods etc. were stored[70]. Also, the ruling families' interest in trading activities may have been responsible for the dual capitals which arose in the three kingdoms one in the interior and a port town on the coast[71]. Further, the objects imported from the West like gold, horses, wine etc were ideo-technic or socio-technic in nature and were accumulated by chieftains as prestige goods, which figured in the redistributive as prestige goods, which figured in the redistributive network. Finally it may be pointed out that there were wars among the *Mūvēntar* through which they could gain access to and control the other's resources[72].

From the above survey it is clear that physiography influenced the nature of political organisation. As discussed in the section on historical geography the movement of the Vēḷir was associated with the spread of the megalithic culture, particularly BRW and Iron, and this may be said to have led to the emergence of different types of chiefships in the various zones depending on where the Vēḷir settled. Hence, the hill chiefs and pastoral chiefs seem closer to tribal polity while the *marutam* chiefs were more advanced politically and had the potential to develop towards a territorial kingship or state. It is only the three ruling families of *marutam* who performed brahmanical sacrifices.

A certain degree of socio-economic diversity characterised the *marutam* and *neytal tiṇais* . The dual centres of power which arose in these tiṇais housed heterogenous populations like the King's officials. craftsmen, *brāhmaṇās,* traders, members of the non-brahmanical sects of Buddhists and Jains etc. The ramification of trading activities brought about further diversification noticeable in the presence of individual traders/ merchants (Indian and foreign i.e. *yavaṇās*), groups of them (*cāttu*), king's officers or customs agents and warehouse guards in the dual centres.

The ruling families interest in trade can be gauged from the Cōḷa attempts to levy duties on goods which could have served as althernate source of revenue. It has already been pointed out that the *mūvēntar* lacked the coercive power to tax the farmers and siphon off the excess for other requirements i.e. a 'surplus'. The ruling families had no sustainable resource base even though the Cōḻas in particular made some attempts at agricultural expansion by deforestation and introduction of cultivation and provided irrigation facilities by damming the river Kāveri. If traditions are to be believed the damming of the river is attributed to Karikāla Cōḻaṉ. Though the *mūvētar* had the potential to evolve into a State they never could do so. The reasons for this could be attributed not only to the sudden arrest of urban growth due to the withdrawal or decline of the western trade around the 3rd century A.D. but also due to lack of coercive power and institutional mechanism to draw out the surplus from the farmers of the *marutam.*

On the basis of what is mentioned above it is clear that the political organisation of the Cēra, Cōḻa and Pāṇṭiya was in a process of transition from non-state to a state situation i.e. from a tribal to a territorial organisation. While certain trends indicate the processes towards state formation, the continuity of the tribal features is also attested.Thus these early *mūvēntar* societies seem to correspond to Claessen and Skalnik's concept of an 'inchoate state[73]' or Webb's transitional state[74]'.

To give a more precise assessment of Tamil polity in the early historical period, it may be said that it was in the process of developing into a territorial monarchy but did not reach its maturity due to the lack of institutional means of establishing a stable resource base. the process was one of 'primary state formation' and not 'secondary state formation[75]' which was arrested due to a crisis of material resource base. A comparison with the Deccan under the Sātavāhanās would illustrate this point. The Deccan under the Sātavāhanās represents the case of secondary state formation and this has been shown to be the result of the region's internal political process under Mauryan influence. The region had reached a certain degree of political development under the Mauryas and hence could imbibe or adapt Mauryan forms under the Sātavāhanās who continued to use the earlier Mauryan structures of administration. The Sātavāhanās adopted both the Vedic/brahmanical ideology for legitimation of their sovereignty and sponsored Buddhist ideology and monuments for promoting trade[76]. The influence of the Mauryan State is minimal as far as Tamiḻakam is concerned. None of the official designations of the Mauryan State such as *rajukas, yuktās, mahāmātrās* are known in Tamiḻakam evidently because the local/regional chiefs had not been incorporated in any administrative structure that was evolved under the Mauryas. In Tamiḻakam, the *janapada* type of polity persisted at various levels of the *Vēntar,* Vēḷir and other chiefs. The concept of a large empire with vast territory is not known in Tamiḻakam but the Cēra, Cōḷa and Pāṇṭiya were associated with specifice region within Tamiḻakam which thenceforward became traditionally and historically the Cēṛa, Cōḷa and Pāṇṭiya nāṭus.

This does not mean that contact between north India and early Tamiḻakam at the political, apart from econimic and cultural levels has to be ruled out. M.G.S. Narayanan points to contacts between the Mauryas and the 'kingdoms' of the extreme south[77]. However, that the nature of this contact was different from the Mauryan contact with the Deccan was not examined by him. He merely points out the references to *Mōriyar* in the poems of Māmūlanār in *Akanāṉūru* on the basis of which he stated that the Nandas and Mauryas were the first to introduce chariots and roads[78] into Tamiḻakam. Further, he suggests that the passages of *Akanāṉūru* alluding to the Mauryas should be placed side by side with references in the *Arthaśāstra* to the trade routes and the value of mines and pearl fisheries[79].

Here, it may be added that one of the Aśokan edicts mentions the Cēra, Cōḷa, Pāṇṭiya and the Satiyaputras of the extreme south[80]. While the Cēra, Cōḷa and Pāṇṭiya were the *Mūvēntar* of the early Tamil texts, the Satiyaputras were identified as the Atiyamāṇs of the *Caṅkam* texts on the basis of a Tamil Brahmi inscription found at Jambai in south Arcot district. Of the four mentioned in the edict, the Atiyamāṇs did not rise above the level of a chieftain, lesser in political importance than the other three ruling lineages.

There is evidence to establish that the Cēra, Satiyaputra and Pāṇṭiya had indirect, cultural or economic ties with the Mauryas or with the north. For the Cōḷa, we have no specific evidence to show such a relationship.

As far as the Cēras are concerned, M.G.S. Narayanan has traced the relationship between the Cēras and the Mauryas. Titles such as Vāṇavarampaṉ and Imayavarampaṉ which the Cēra kings took convey the same meaning as the title of Aśoka Devanāmapiya i.e. Beloved of the Gods[81]. It has been suggested that the Cēras may have taken this title as a mark of respect and also a symbol of differentiating themselves (from other chieftains) such as those who had the backing of the Mauryan state. Cēra rulers possibly patronised the Jains as is evident from a Tamil Brahmi inscription from Pukaḷūr which records a Jaina endowment and which mentions three generations of Cēra rulers[82]. In this context, it may be added that Ilaṅkō Aṭikal, the author of the *Cilappatikāram,* embraced Jainism and stayed at Kuṇavāyiṟ Kōṭṭam[83]. after his renunciation. Sudarshan Seneviratne further points out that interaction between the Cēras and Mauryas was "probably a natural sequel to the economic ties that linked Kerala exchange centres to the north from pre-Mauryan times." The large number of punch marked coins found from Eyyal and Kottayam belong to a pre-Mauryan phase[84].

We have already indicated the importance of the Jambai inscription in aiding the identification of Satiyaputras. In this connection, Seneviratne points out the acceptance of the term Satiyaputra by the Atiyamāṉs, use of the Brahmi script (in the inscription) and also the patronage which was granted to the Jain priests (as places like Villupuram, Ellananur and Tirunarkulam situated near Jambai have ancient Jain temples) are indicative of the acculturation process.[85]

The association/ relation between the Pāṇṭiyās and the north is apparent from references in the *Arthaśāstra* to cotton fabrics and pearls of the Pāṇṭiya country[86]; the discovery of Northern Black polished ware (NBP) sherds[87]; the dense location of the Tamil Brahmi inscriptions in the modern districts of Madurai, Ramanathapuram and Tirunelveli (or present day Tamilnadu, which were a part of the Pāṇṭiya country)[88] and recovery of issues of early Pāṇṭiya punch marked coins which carry apart from the fish symbol, many other symbols categorised as pre-Mauryan and Mauryan ones which are found in the northern punch marked coins[89].

The ideology of war, heroism and generosity dominated Tamil polity, which led to the development of a redistribution system based on kinship ties and patronage to bards and poets i.e. a system of redistribution wherein the rulers and chieftains gave away gifts[90]. The poets, bards, singing and dancing groups (*pulavar, pāṇar* etc.) went mostly in search of patrons who liberally showered them with gifts. There were others like the *Iravalar* and *paricilar* who also visited courts of Kings/chieftains for gifts.

Gift giving was a two way process—a return gift had to be made for a gift received[9]. In a gift exchange the giver is usually regarded as superior to the receiver[92]. Gift exchange, according to Gregory, established personal qualitative relationships between the subjects transacting[93].

In the region under study the ruler/chieftains gave gifts and the bards, poets and others who got gifts did not returns gifts as such, what they did instead was they sung glories of the King/chieftain and legitimised their rule. Thereby a personal relationship between the patron and client i.e. between ruler and poet was established. Both the giver of the gift and the receiver were in a state of reciprocal dependence. In a way the giver of the gift i.e. ruler or chieftain was superior to the receiver.

Giving of gifts indicated development within the kin centred redistributive relations[94]. Not only were kinsmen but others were also entitled to gifts. Apart from the sharing of resources/food at the *uṇṭāṭṭu* and *peruñcōṟṟunilai* there was a perceptible change in gifts given by rulers/ chieftains of Tamiḻakam. Initially gifts were in the form of horses, chariots, elephants gold, gems and food. Evidence of grants of land is meagre. However, the *patikams* (colophons) of the *Patiṟṟuppattu* mention gifts or land/ settlements to poets[95] some of whom were *brāhmaṇās*. In some instances, the warriors who were given land as reward insisted only on *marutam* and not a small settlement where gram was grown (possibly *mullai?*[96]). It has been remarked that "food is usually the primary instrument of intra-clan gift giving. Distribution of food within a clan and its shared consumption is not simply concerned with biological nourishment, it serves as an important symbol of clan solidarity and identity[97]". Feasts such as *uṇṭāṭṭu, cirucōṟṟuviḻa* and *peruñcōṟṟunilai* could be taken as symbols of clan solidarity and identity.

Early Tamil rulers, Vēḷir and non-Vēḷir chieftains were great distributors of wealth. The leader of a societal unit played a crucial role in the distribution of materials according to anthropological studies. The early Tamil ruler was at the top of a social pyramid where there was a flow of goods towards him (possibly through plunder, tribute, levies on articles of trade) and from him the goods flowed downwards to the bards and kinsmen. In other words, the ruler was at the head of a redistributive netweok[98].

Such efforts at redistribution of wealth by rulers of Tamiḻakam were eulogised by poets. Certain *tuṟais* of the *Tolkāppiyam* also extoll the act of gift giving[99].

About the Cōḻa ruler Karikāla the poet says:

"He ceases not to do kind deeds; And spends his income giving gifts to others free"[100]

Another chieftain spoken of in praise was the Toṇṭai chieftain[101]. In fact the munificence and generosity of Vēḷir chieftains like Pāri, Kāri, Ōri etc was extolled by poets more than that of the *mūvēntar*[102]. Since some of the chieftains (Vēḷir and non-Vēḷir) ruled over hilly or pastoral regions, their subsistence base may have been limited. This did not deter them from giving gifts. They resorted to plunder raids in order to get resources or gain control over them for redistribution purposes. For instance, *Puṟanāṉūṟu* 180 highlights the fact of a *Kiḻāṉ* of Īruntūr in a *vaṉpulam* region depleted of all resource summoning his blacksmith to make a new *vēll* (lance) to be used in a raid to satisfy a hungry bard.

Rivalry between the *vēntar* and the Vēḷir/ non-Vēḷir could have resulted in strife between the two[103]. Some of the Vēḷir territories lay in fertile and raw material producing areas. While a few of these raids could have been plunder oriented, some could have aimed at acquiring control over resources. Further, it has been pointed out that "the poetic flower symbolism associated with the different kinds of raids such as *veṭci* (cattle raid), *karantai* (cattle recovery), *vañji* (a chieftain's raid), *kāñji* (defence against a chieftain's raid), *tumpai* (preparations for resisting the enemies) shows exactly how institutionalised and common was a plunder raid[104]".

Objects such as gems and gold were precious and were redistributed by important people like rulers and chiefs presumably for creating or symbolising a superior position.

In the region under study the gifts were not elaborate or monumental[10] and were restricted to gold. gems, horses, chariots, good etc. No monumental architecture was sponsored by the chiefly or ruling families or elite groups as in the Deccan and Andhra region. Yet, the patronage extended to the Buddhist and Jain sects in the form of rock beds, caverns made suitable for the retreat of the monks by all elite groups, traders, craftsmen etc. would show that gifts served as the main instrument/mechanism of legitimation depending upon resources.

No particular religious ideology was central to the legitimation process. This may be substantiated by the fact that *vēḷvi* which was a generic term for any offering or sacrifice was of different kinds and included the *kalavēḷvi* or the war sacrifice apart from the Vedic sacrifice. Both were performed by the ruling familes. Similarly, the acts of gifts to the poets and bards including *brāhmaṇās* are more conspicuously mentioned in the literary texts, while the gifts made to the Buddhists and Jains are known only from the epigraphic records, thus indicating that the texts provide only a partial picture as they contain very few references to poets of the Buddhist and Jain persuasion.

The building of shrines is not specifically associated with the ruling families, with the exception of the references in the epics to temples. Given the fact that *tiṇai* deities were central to the worship of the people of the different zones and universalisation of any one particular deity or any particular form of worship was absent, it may be inferred that no single religion was central to the process of legitimation of authority and patronage.

As for war ideology, the *puṟam* genre of literature i.e. the texts *puṟanāṉūṟu* and *Patiṟṟuppattu* idealise war, heroism and chivalry. Early Tamil poems are pervaded with martial aspects and their purpose is to glorify war. The thematic context of the poetry (*tuṟais*) as delineated by the *Tolkāppiyam* also extolls heroism/ death on the battlefield[106]. The *mūtilmullai*[107] songs describe the women folk of the *maṟavars* to be as brave as their husbands as is evident from the following poem:

"Her purpose is frightening, her spirit cruel.
That she comes from an ancient house is fitting, surely In the battle the day before yesterday,
Her father attacked an elephant and died
there on the field
In the battle yesterday,
Her husband faced a row of troops and fell
And today
She hears the battle drum
And, eager beyond reason, gives him
A spear in his hand
Wraps a white garment around him,
Smears his dry tuft with oil,
And, having nothing but her one son,
"Go!" she says sending him to battle"[108]

Uvakkai Kaluḻcci tuṟai[109] songs praise the warriors' wives and mothers rejoicing at the sight of their husbands and sons wounded or dead. For instance,

"The son of the old woman or whose soft dry arms flesh hangs and veins are raised and
Stomach is like a full lotus leaf has failed in battle and fled"
At that enraged, she said
"If he has been routed in the thick of battle I will cut off these breasts from which he sucked",
And sword in hand, she turned over fallen corpses groping her way on the red field.
Then she saw her fallen son, lying, cut in pieces,
And she rejoiced more than the day she bore him"[110]

The *Kuṭinilaiuraittal tuṟai, Ēṟāṇmullai tuṟai* and *vallāṇmjllai tuṟai* songs praise the tradition and lineage of the warrior chiefs. In the *Patiṟṟuppattu* the *centuṟaippātāṇ-pāṭṭu* and *Vañcittuṟaippātāṇ* glorify the warriors' strength[111].

Emphasis on war and heroism can be gleaned from references to the bloody sacrifices (*kalavēḷvi*) and dances (*Kuṟavai, tunaṅkai*) performed on the battlefield. It is also referred to in other poems but it is described in detail in *Puṟanāṉūṟu* 372[112]. Pāṇṭiyaṉ king Neṭuñceḻiyaṉ is credited with having performed the *Kalavēḷvi* as well as other *vēḷvi's*[113].

According to Hart gruesome objects of the battlefield are identified of discussed in association with productive processes in peaceful pursuts like agriculture and its allied operations. The war sacrifice is invariably compared with the processes of harvesting. Basically agreeing with Nacciṉārkkiṉiyar the medieval commentator of the *Tolkāppiyam*, Hart explains this as a parallel in terms of post harvest operations on the threshing floor[114]. In contrast to this Sivathamby does not equate the war sacrifice (ritual in his view) with agricultural activities as he considers it as a martial one essentially connectedwith the battlefield[115] which seems more plausible.

Dances of Kings in the battlefield along with the warriors probably as part of the war sacrifice or victory celebrations also prove the heroic aspect of those times[116]. Another gruesome dance of the battlefield vividly portrayed in the texts is the *tunaṅkai* of the peymakaḷir or dance of the female goblins. These female goblins/demonesses are described to be dancing amid the corpses of elephants and men in the battle field and sucking the blood from these dead bodies[117]. Besides the war dances, warriors also rejoiced during *uṇṭāṭṭu*[118].

In this age death in the battlefield with injuries on the chest was considered the hallmark of bravery. *Puranāṇūru* 93 mentions that warriors who died a natural death were cut with swords so that they looked/seemed like soldiers who died in battle and could enter paradise. In another poem a king is addressed by the poet in the following words "your body full of sword scars, you have good fame but are ugly to look at. They (your enemies) because when they see you they turn their backs (and flee) are good to look at, their unmarred bodies untouched by affliction, but they are ugly to hear of[119]". It was shameful for a warrior to run away from the enemy or to have a wound on his back, so much so that when Ceramāṉ Peruñcēralātaṉ was wounded by a spear on his back he faced north and starved himself to death (*vaṭakkiruttal*[120]).

Weapons were to be frequently used in battle The poetess Auvvaiyār sang this song when she saw an enemy King

> "These spears kept in large guarded place are adorned with peacock feathers
> and with garlands.
> Their strong, thick shafts
> are handsome,
> anointed with ghee
> But those spears
> have tips and joints broken
> from spearingenemies
> They are in the blacksmith's hut
> those sharp-tipped spears
> of our great king
> who surrounds himself
> with the destitute,
> who gives if there is food enough
> and shares if there is not"[121].

Practices of plunder raids to facilitate the distribution, predatory marches of chieftains, destruction of agricultural settlements and crops were eulogised in the poems. *Puṛanāṉūṛu* 15 describes the destruction of enemy land wherein donkey yoked to ploughs ploughed the roads, chariots were driven in the fields and sources of water were ruined by driving elephants into them. Poems praise the Cōḷa ruler Perunaṛ kiḷḷi burning his enemy's *marutam* tracts which were full of sugarcane and Pantiyan Naṉmāṛaṉ's buring of enemy crops[122].

Heroic aspect is not only evident from the poems which eulogize war and valour but can be also gleaned from the megalithic burials and hero stones. Hero stones were erected for warriors who fell in battle or while lifting or recovering cattle. They seem to have been venerated as there are references to worship of such hero stones in the poems. The megalithic burials have also revealed a predominance of weapons of war such as sword, dagger, trident, lance made of iroṇ which reflect the heroic nature and militaristic tradition of those times. Perhaps the burials with numerous weapons represent those of warriors. Kailasapathy indicates that the chieftains of Tamiḻakam had epithets which signified their prowess in weapons of war. Such epithets included *palavēl* (of many lances) and *vāyvāḷ* (sword that never goes awry[123]).

In short one could sum up by stating that "the ethos of war dominated and moulded contemporary sociopolicical ideals and institutions[124]", but a gradual change and complexity even in the ideological forms and its instruments (such as land gifts etc) may also be perceived.

FOOTNOTES

1. *Puṛanāṉūṛu* 110:11; 375:2.
2. G.L. Hart 1976, p. 51.
3. Seneviratne, 1985, pp. 213-16.
4. Ibid, pp. 217-18.
5. Reported by the State Department of Archaeology Tamil Nadu.
6. R. Champakalakshmi, 1975-76, p. 116.
7. *Akanāṉūṛu* 24:4; 196:11.
8. Vēḷ of Aḻumpil is referred to as Manalviral vēḷ-*maduraikkāñci* 11.344-45.
9. R. Champakalakshmi 1975-76, p. 119.
   Raghave Iyengar in his *Vēḷir Varalāṛu* suggests that Vēḷir could be form *vēḷvi*, p. 16.
10. *Akaṉāṉūṛu* 372: 3-4
    Puṛanaṉūṛu 289.5
    Vēḷir of Kuṉṛūr are called ancient Vēḷir people *Kuṛuntokai* 164;3.
11. Verse 201. tuvarai is identified with Dvaraka by Nacciṉārkkiṉiyar or Dvarasamudra by N. Subrahmanian—*Pre Pallavan Tamil Index*, p. 445.
12. R. Champakalakshmi, 1975-76, p. 120.
13. See *Vēḷir Varalāṛu,* pp. 26-27.
14. An excellent analysis of the Vēḷir settlements has been done by Sudarshan Seneviratne on the lines suggested by R. Champakalakshmi-see Sudarshan Seneviratne 1989, pp. 16-17.

15. Seneviratne, 1985, p. 322.
16. The five Vēḷir (Tiṭṭaṉ, Eḻiṉi, Erumai, Iruṅkōvēḷ and Porunaṉ formed an alliance with Cōḻa and Cēra and fought against Neṭuñceḻiyaṉ at Talaiyālankānam- *Akaṉāṉūṟu* 36: 13-22, Iruṅkōvēḷ fought against Karikāla - *Paṭṭinappālai* 1. 282 Neṭuñceḻiyan also overran the Vēḷir territory of Aḻumpil - *Maṭuraikkāñci* 11.344-45.
17. Seneviratne, 1985, pp. 375-77.
18. Ātanuṅkaṉ : *Puṟanāṉūṟu*; 175, 389
    Pulli : *Akanāṉūṟu* 175, 389
    Paṉṉaṉ : *Puṟanāṉūṟu* 70; 73; 181; 388
    Kumaṇaṉ : *Puṟanāṉūṟu* 158-65
    Piṭṭaṅ Koṟṟaṉ : *Puṟanāṉūṟu* 168-72.
19. Romila Thapar, From Lineage to State, 1984, p. 105, p. 109.
20. H.P.Ray, *Monastery and Guild : Commerce Under the Sātavāhanās,* Delhi, 1986, pp. 197-198.
21. *Puṟanāṉūṟu* 45.
22. *Puṟanāṉūṟu* 58.
    Subrahmaniam 1980, p. 43. He is of the view that since the Paṇṭiyaṉ land comprised of all the five *tiṇais* the rulers were called *Pañcavar* or the rulers of the five lands..
23. R.S. Sharms "From, Gopati to Bhūpati (A review of the changing position of the king)", in *Studies in History,* Vol.II, no.2, 1980, pp. 1-10.
24. *Patiṟṟuppattu* 77.
25. *Patiṟṟuppattu* 22 mentions the Cēra ruler Palyāṉaiccelkeḻu Kuṭṭuvaṉ defeating the Koṅkar. The Koṅkar could have also been warriors who fought with spears. Āy Aṇṭiraṉ is said to have driven these Koṅkar to the sea coast on the west. Also M.A. Dorai Rangaswamy, *the Surnames of the Caṅkam Age: Literary and Tribal,* Madras, 1947, pp. 124-27.
26. M. Arokiaswami in *"The Kongu country: being the history of the modern districts of Coimbatore and Salem from the earliest times to the coming of the British,* Madras, 1956 argues that the Gangas from Talakkād settled in Kongu-Chapters V, VI, VII.
27. *Akanāṉūṟu* 15; 90; 113; 205
    Kuṟuntokai 15
    Maṭuraikkāñci 11. 508-10: 11. 773-74.
28. Dorai Ranagaswamy 1947, pp. 47-48, p. 133.
29. *Akanāṉūṟu* 251.
30. *Akanāṉūṟu* 107: 11-12, 295: 11-17, 381
    Naṟṟiṇai: 212:5-6.
31. *Akanāṉūṟu* 83: 8-11; 209: 8-11; 393: 17-20.
32. G.L.Hart 1975, pp. 15-18.
33. For Cattle raids see MGS Narayanan's "Cattle raiders of the Sangam Age", *Indian History Congress, Proceedings,* 1977, pp. 102-109.
34. In the *Tolkāppiyam uṇṭāṭṭu* was a feature under *veṭci turai*. In this the warriors rejoiced before and after stealing cattle. They were fed toddy and food by chieftains. Poems of the *Puṟanāṉūṟu* dealing with *uṇṭāṭṭu* are 257, 258, 262, 269, 297 *peruñcōṟṟunilai* (grand rice feast) was an aspect of *vañci tuṟai* of the *Tolkappiyam*. The King/chieftain fed lot of rice to the warriors when they were in the war camp- *Puṟanāṉūṟu* 292. In fact one of the Cēra kings was known as Peruñcōṟṟu Utiyañ Cēral Ātaṉ as he said to have fed the armies of 100 and five (interpreted as the Kuravas and Pantavas and the Andhras.) Were *peruñcōṟṟunilai*

and *uṇṭāṭṭu* given to warriors who were members of the claṅ/kin to which the kings/chiefains belonged?

35. Names such as Cōḻa Uruva paltēr Ilañcētceṉṉi (Cōḻa Ilaṉceētceṉṉi; the possessor of numerous chariots): Cōḻa karikālan Peruvāḷattāṉ (Karikalā Cōḻa the one who brought about great prosperity); Cōḻa Kuḷamuṟṟatt-tuñciya kiḷḷivalavaṉ (Cōḻa Kiḷḷivaḷavaṉ who died a glorious death on the battlefield of Kuḷamuṟṟam) and Pāntiyaṉ Karuṅkkai-oḷ-vāl Perrumpeyar Vaḻuti (Perumpeyar Vaḻuti, the stronghanded one with a glittering sword.)
R. Sumathi, 1984, p. 170: 6ff
36. The Cōḻas considered themselves to be descendants of legendary Cempiyaṉ (Cipi) *Puṟanāṉūru* 37:39. Also Hart 1975, p. 62. The Pāṇṭiyās claimed descent from heroes of the *Mahabhārata* according to Clarence Maloney
-R. Sumathi, 1984, p. 17: 8/ff.
In the later period i.e early medieval period the Pallavas and Cōḻas also did so in their attempts to achieve *Kṣatriya* status-Kesavan Veluthat 1982, pp. 147-57.
37. We are told of Āriyappaṭai Kaṭanta Neṭuñceḻiyaṉ (Neṭuñceḻiyaṉ who won victory against the Northerners) or of Imayavarampaṉ Cēralātaṉ (Cēralātaṉ who had the Himalayas as his boundary). Again, we are informed that the northerners became helpless on hearing the attack of Karikāla Cēḻa on their country -*Paṭṭinappālai* 1. 276 or that the Kings of the north (passed) many a sleepless night on hearing the invasion of Coḻa Nalaṅkiḷḷi *Puṟanāṉūṟu* 31; R. Sumathi 1984, p. 171, 9ff.
38. Etymological meaning is sacrifice *DED* 4561, p. 384. *Tamil Lexicon* also furnishes the above meaning for *vēḷvi*, p. 3842.
39. R. Champakalakshmi 1975-76, p. 120.
40. Mukuṭumi Peravaḻuṭi (as he is mentioned in the colophon) is the hero of poems 6, 9, 12, 15, 64 of the *Puṟanāṉūṟu*.
41. *Puṟanāṉūṟu* 15.
42. *Puṟanāṉūṟu* 26.
43. *Puṟanāṉūṟu* 224; *Puṟanāṉūṟu* 400.
44. This name is mentioned in the colophons. He is the hero of poems 16, 125, 367, 377 of the *Puṟanāṉūṟu*.
45. For details and significance of the ceremonies see R.S. Sharma *Aspects of Political Ideas and Institutions in Ancient India,* Delhi, 1991, 3rd rev. ed.
Romila Thapar *From Lineage to state,* New Delhi. 1984.
C. Dreikmeier, *Kingship and community in early India,* 1962.
J.C.Heesterman, *The Ancient Indian Royal Consecration* 1957.
R. Subramanyam, *The Tundi Copper Plate Grant of Vishnkundin King Vikramendravarma,* Hyderabad, 1962, vide Appendix II, pp. 38-40.
Also the authors of the various books point out the changes occuring in the consecration ritual due to the changing concepts of kingship from early Vedic times.
46. R.S.Sharma, 1991, p. 163.
47. Ibid, p. 169.
48. Romila Thapar, 1984, pp. 64-65.
49. R.S. Sharma, 1991, p. 359.
50. Romila Thapar, 1984, p. 64.
51. "Political Authority and change in South Indian History", *Indian Economic Social History Review,* Vol. XIII, No. 2, 1976, pp. 133-144.
52. For the various rites and sacrifices performed by Pallavas, Cōḻa's for legitimization of their

rule in the presence of *brāhmaṇās* see Kesavan Veluthat "the status of the Monarch: A note on the rituals pertaining to kingship and their significance in the Tamil country (600-1200) *Indian History Congress,* Proceedings of the 43rd Session, Kurukshetra, 1982, pp. 147-57.

53. Romila Thapar 1984, p. 65.
54. For details of the processes of subjugation, see Seneviratne, 1989, pp. 28-30.
55. Seneviratne 1984, pp. 357-60.
56. See chapters IV, V, VI, VII and VIII of N. Subramaniam's *Śaṅgam Polity,* Arokiaswami *The Classical Age of the Tamils,* Madras, 1972, pp. 49-65.
57. *Perumpāṇarruppaṭai* 1.447;
    Puṟanāṉūṟu 2: 19.
58. Subrahmanyam 1966, p. 375.
59. *Kāviti* is also interpreted as guild chief see chapter III Section A.
60. Sivathamby, 1986, P. 169. There are references to the kings agents in the *Paṭṭinappālai* who collected dues on goods coming into the port. (11. 120-24; 11.131-36) though the office is not designated by a specific term.
61. *Puṟanāṉūṟu* 167; 174; 394.
62. Subrahmanian 1980, p. 93
    R. Gurukkal 1989 (b), p. 22.
63. Poems hardly mention payment of land tax by people to their king. Term used is *paṭuvatu* (*Puṟanāṉūṟu* 17:6 that which is due to the King) A poem of the *Puṟanāṉūṟu* (184) gives us a picture of the attiude of the early Tamils towards taxes.
    If ripe paddy is harvested and made into food for an elephant,
    than even an field smaller than a *ma* gives enough for many days
    But if the elephant enters it alone, even a field of 100 *ceṟus* is useless,
    the paddy will be trampled unbeaten
    If a wise king taxes, aware of what is right,
    this land can give a crore and flourish still.
    But if a small man is king, and is greedy to take,
    with no thought of kindness;
    surrounded by men who do not know what is right,
    who are loud in their praises,
    then like the elephant that entered the field,
    he will not eat, and the world will perish.
    Hart (Tr.) 1979, p. 178.
64. R. Champakalakshmi 1986, p. 6.
65. See chapter VIII of *Sangam Polity.*
66. As quoted by Subrahmanyan, 1980, p. 222.
67. *Cilappatikāram* XXV: 11. 37-54
    V.R.R.Dikshitar (Tr.) 1978, p. 332.
68. R. Sumathy, 1984, p. 162.
69. *Paṭṭinappālai* 11. 120-36.
70. Ibid.
71. Maloney 1976, p. 19
    R.Champakalakshmi 1986, pp. 4-5.
72. *Akanāṉūṟu* 36; 125; 246; 253 and 345
    Puṟanāṉūṟu 7-9; 23; 25; 31-32; 33; 35-36
    Kuṟuntokai 393; Also R. Sumathy 1984, p. 163.

73. Claessen and Skalnik in *The Early State,* The Hague, 1978 have categorised early states as 'inchoate', 'typical' and 'transitional' in terms of their degree of progress towards a full blown, mature state. According to them, an 'inchoate early state' is one in which:-kinship, family and community ties still dominate relations in the political field.
-full time administrative specialists are rare.
-taxation systems are only primitive
and adhoc taxes are frequent.
-social differences are offset by
reciprocity and close contacts between
the ruler and the ruled.
74. Webb used the term 'conditional state to describe: "highly developed, sometimes durable chiefdoms, which at least superficially appear to be transitional to the state (although in fact, the transformation may never take place)....Although they may be almost exactly like small states in all ways except that they lack a reliable source of force which may be applied in a crisis, this very deficit means that the obedience of the separate segments of society to the leadership is conditional".
"The Flag follows Trade"- An essay on the necessary interaction of military and commercial factors in state formation". in Sabloff and Lamberg Karlovsky (ed.) *Ancient Civilization and Trade,* Albuquerque, 1975.
75. In the view of S. Seneviratne the expansion of the Mauryas into the Deccan was an attempt to exploit the resources and thereby acquire additional income to supplement the agrarian base of the Mauryas. They expanded into areas like Andhra which were agriculturally fertile and Karnataka and Kalinga which were rich in mineral deposits. According to Seneviratne the external impetus provided by the Mauryas together with the internal changes in Kalinga and Andhra resulted in the evolution of transitional type of early states through a process of secondarystate formation wherein Mauryan institutions continued in these States. "Kalinga and Andhra: The process of Secondary State Formation in early India" *Indian Historical Review* Vol.III, Nos 1-2, July 1980-January 1981, pp. 54-69.
76. R. Champakalakshmi, 1986, p. 11.
H.P. Ray *Monastery and Guild: Commerce under the Sātavāhanās* New Delhi, 1986, chapter 5.
77. M.G.S Narayanan presents a chronological scheme for the relations between the Mauryan empire and the Dravidians. He postulated that in the first place "commercial and cultural relations and probably political relations existed between the growing empire of Magadha and Tamilakam in the pre-Mauryan period of the Nandas. Secondly, that it turned into violent conflict and military confrontation during the early Mauryan period of Chandra Gupta and Bindusara as testified by the Maurya-Kosar invasion. Thirdly, it was again transformed into friendly political cultural cooperation as claimed by Ashoka. "The Ceras must have had a common boundary with the Mauryas and the rulers are said to have assumed titles such as Vanavarampan and Imayavarampan signifying "Beloved of the Gods". Ashoka is known as *Devanamapiya Piyadassi* (Beloved of the Gods) from his edicts. Further, Ashoka states his friendly relations with the Dravidian peoples in Rock Edict II. The imitation of Mauryan titles would suggest a cordial relationship between the Mauryas and Dravidan kingdoms in the times of Ashoka—'The Mauryan problems in Sangam works' in *Re Interpretations in South Indian History* , Trivandrum, 1977, pp. 83-98.
78. Poem 251 mentions the Kocar-vampa Mōriyar invasion of Mōkūr in the context of a love poem. Again in poem 281, like in the above, reference is made to the chariots of the

Mōriyar cutting across mountainous paths by which some sort of paths (roads?) are created. In addition to these references the *Caṅkam* poets also knew about the Nandas and their capital city Pataliputra. In another poem (*Akanāṉūṟu*265) Māmūlaṉār mentions that the Nandas hid their wealth under the waters of the river Ganga at Pātaliputra. Another poet Mocikiranār gives the location of Pataliputra on the banks of the river Cōṇai (Son) in *Kuṟuntokai* 75.

79. M.G.S. Narayanan, 1977, pp. 86-87.
80. Rock Edict II-Romila Thapar, *Asoka and the Decline of the Mauryas,* Delhi, 1973, (2nd ed.), p. 251.
    The Jambai inscription dated to 2nd Century B.C. reads "*Satiya puto atiyan neṭumāṉ an ce itta pali.*"
81. Titles have shown to depict two meanings on the basis of the splitting up of words. For example
    Vāṉam + Varampaṉ = Vāṉavarampaṉ = The one with the sky as boundary
    Vāṉāvar + ampaṉ - Vāṉavarampaṉ = The beloved of the Gods (residents of the sky)
    Imayam + Varampaṉ = Imayavarampaṉ = The one with the Himalayas as boundary
    Imayavar + Ampaṉ = Imayavarampaṉ = The beloved of the Gods (Residents of the Himalayas)
    MGS Narayanan 1977, p. 94.
82. Mahadevan 1966 (Inscription no. 57)
    Senaviratne 1985, pp. 340-41.
83. *Patikam* - of the *Cilappatikāram* mentions this fact.
84. Senaviratne, 1985, p. 341.
85. Ibid, p. 340.
86. *Arthaśāstra* refers to cotton fabrics from Madura and to Pandyakavataka - a pearl from the Pandya country - (Tr) R.P. Kangle, 1965, II, XI, 2 ; 114-15.
87. One sherd has been reported from Korkai and a number of them from Alagankulam vide-R.Nagaswamy "Excavations at Korkai District Tirunelveli" in *Damilica* II, December, 1970, p. 50 (There is a dissenting opinion. Some feel that it is not a NBP Sherd) For sherds at Alagāṅkulam see N.Kasinathan, Alagāṅkulam: *A preliminary Report,* State Department of Archaeology, Madras.
88. See I. Mahadevan 1966.
89. Seneviratne: 1985, pp. 353-44.
90. According to Polanyi "redistribution is centralization of goods or right over goods and their subsequent reallocation"—"The Economy as Instituted process" in K. Polanyi et.al. *Trade and Markets in the Early Empires*. Glencoe, 1959, p. 243.
    Also see Hindess and Hirst, 1979, pp. 45-59.
91. Marcel Mauss, *The Gift:Forms and functions of exchange in Archaic Societies* (Tr.) Ian Cunnison, London, 1970, p. 5.
92. C.A. Gregory *Gifts and Commodities,* London. 1982, p. 47.
93. Ibid, p. 41.
94. R.Gurukkal, 1989 (a), p. 169.
95. *II-patikam* mentions that Kummaṭṭūr Kaṇṇaṉār got 500 *Ur* in Umparkāṭu.
    VII : patikam mentions that Celvakraṭumikō Vāṭiyātaṉ stood on a hill and gave Kapilar land till the eyes could see. Perumkuṉrūr Kilār was given the (settlements) fields apart from either things.

96. See *Puṟanāṉūṟu* 297 for references of land to warriors-See M.G.S. Narayanan's "The Warrior Settlements of the Sangam Age", *Indian History Congress,* Proceedings 1982, pp. 102-09.
97. Gregory 1982, p. 52.
98. Marshall Sahlins *Tribesmen,* 1968, p. 87; 95. Also Sumathi, 1984, p. 153.
99. These are
Iyanmoḻi vāḻttu—poetising the context of praising the bounty of a chief.
Pāṇaṟruppaṭai—poetising the context of a bard directing another to a chief by praising his generosity.
Viṟaliāṟruppaṭai—poetising the context of a *viṟali* persuading another to a chief by singing his bounty.
pulavarairruppaṭai—poetising the context of a pulavar (scholarly bard) persuading another to a chief by singing in praise of his munificence.
Paricilturai—poetising the context of bard praising a chieftain's bounty to get a specific gift.
R.Gurukkal, 1993, p. 6.
100. *Porunaṟruppaṭai* 11. 173-74; J.V. Chelliah (Tr) 1962, p. 71.
101. "Approach the bounteous King whose counsellors are wise,
And who gives to those who beg from him,
And those who state their wants,
Rich gifts as each desires And he does his duty to supplicants"
Perumpāṇāṟruppaṭai 11. 443-447; J.V.Chelliah (Tr) 1962, p. 13.
102. The *Ciṟupāṇāṟruppaṭai* praises the 7 *Vaḷḷals* (chieftains).
103. Several such conflicts are mentioned in *Akanāṇūṟu* 36; 125; 246; 253; 345; *Kuṟuntokai* 393; *Puṟanāṇūru* 23; 25; 31-32; 33; 7-9; 35-36; 39; 40; 65-66, 203 and so on.
To state an example
The Pāṇṭiya rulers annexed the area of Travancore from the Āy Chieftain - *Akanāṇūṟu* 36, *Puṟanāṇūṟu* 24.
104. R.Gurukkal, 1989 (a), p. 171.
105. For a comparison see R.Thapar "Dāna and Dakṣsina as Forms of Exchange" in *Ancient Indian Social History,* New Delhi, 1978, pp. 105-21.
Vijay Nath: Dana: *Gift System in Ancient India* (600 B.C. C.A.D.300) *A Socio Economic Perspective,* New Delhi, 1989. In this the author focusses on developments in the practice of *dana* and *daksina* at different points of time vis-a-vis changes in material, conditions.
106. Known from *Puṟanāṇūṟu* 26 and *Tolkāppiyam, Poruḷatikāram* 60, 67, 79 etc.
For a hermeneutical analysis see R.Gurukkal "Towards the Voice of Dissent: The Trajectory of Ideological Transformation in Early India".
Puṟanāṇūṟu 312 explicitly states that it is the duty of the mother to give birth and bring up the son, the duty of the father to train him in warfare and educate him, duty of the *koḷḷan* to make proper spears and duty of the son to kill elephants and come back victorious.
107. Poems of this *tuṟai* from the *Puṟanāṇūṟu* are 288, 306, 308, 312.
108. *Puṟanāṇūṟu* 279; Hart (Tr.) *Poets of the Tamil Anthologies* 1979, p. 200.
109. *Puṟanāṇūṟu* 277, 295.
110. *Puṟanāṇūṟu* 278; Hart (Tr.) 1975, p. 38.
111. R. Gurukkal, 1989, pp. 173-74.
112. "The whole reasons I came to you,

beating loudly my tightly bound drum (Kiṇai)
was to take your necklace
shining as if it were moonlight
you have celebrated the war sacrifice
making the field of carnage resplendent
while arrow drops rained down
and shining swords were lighting up your
camp as you gained victory!
Kuvilam wood was fuel
for an oven made of severed heads
Lined intestines were cooked and boiled up
stirred with vanni sticks stuck in skulls.
by a barren sacrificial priestess
who scooped and stirred,
cooking on ball of food
that animals avoided
and that the male cook offered
saying
"May the fresh waler
poured from a little spout
for the quests
at the marriage festivel."

113. *Maturaikkāñci* and *Puṛanāṉūru* 26
114. Hart 1975, pp, 34-35
115. Siva thamby 1981, p. 187
116. Such dances are referred to as *Kuravas* and *tūṇaṅkai Purṇanūru* 22 *Patiṛṛuppaṭṭu* 45, 57, 77 *Akanāmīru* 142 mentions the *tuaṅkai performed by* chieftain *Niṁili and his* solders after defeating *Atikaṉ*.
117. *Maturakāñci* 1.26
Other dances of the pēymakaḷir are mentioned in *Puṛanāṉ*ūṛu 356; 359, 376, *Patiṛru-paṭṭu* 36, 67, ciṛupānāṛṛupaṭai 17, 196-200, *Paṭṭinappālai* i 260.
118. *Puṛanāṉūṛu* 257, 258, 262, 269, 297
119. *Puṛanāṉūṛu* 167, Hart (Tr) 1975; p 39
120. *Puṛanāṉūṛu* 65
121. *Puṛanāṉūṛu* 95; Hart (Tr) 1925; to 39
122. *Puṛanāṉūṛu* 16; 57
123. As quote by Senaviratne, 1985, p. 122
124. R. Gurukkal, 1981, p. 75

DIAGRAM-1

AUTHORITY STRUCTURE

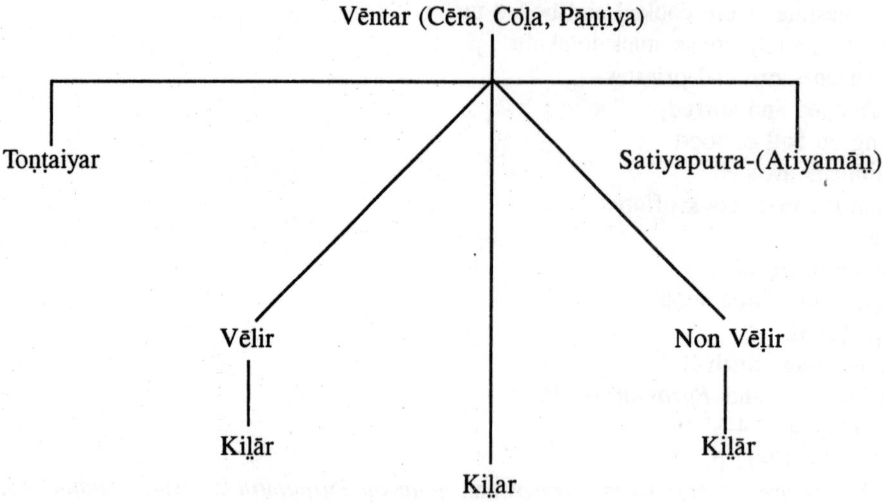

CHAPTER - V

RESUME

Historians in the past have often considered the emergence of early historical Tamil society and polity as a beneficial result of 'Aryanisation' particularly that of brahmanic/ sanskritic elements. This is also sometimes linked with early migrations from north to south, which are known from traditional accounts. While it is undeniable that northern influences assisted in the process of the transformation of a southern regional soci-cultural tradition with dominant Dravidian folk forms, the degree of the northern influences and the nature of synthesis that evolved from the meeting of the two different traditions are matters of continuing debate.

In this thesis, the main endeavour has been to show that while the debate cannot be laid at rest due to the nature of the major sources (Tamil texts) available for the period under study and the difficulties in interpreting them it is important to view these sources not as a single corpus but as located at relatively varying chronological points within a broad time span of about 600 to 900 years before the rise of the Palava-Pāṇṭiya ruling familes, which marks a definite change if not disjunction in societal organisation and polity. Such a relative chronology for different groups of texts (as shown in the present thesis) has been adopted here not only on the basis of the language, literary style and concepts used in them but also on their contents, ideas and processual differences reflected in the different groups of texts and their later collections, classification and the medieval commentarial efforts which interpreted them.

As for the process of "Aryanisation" it would be more correct to view it as northern influences coming with the brahmanical, Buddhist and Jain traditions and not entirely and solely with the brahmanical one. Migrations of people and cultural traits in the protohistoric context into peninsular India and Tamiḻakam in particular are to be seen in their proper perspectives i.e. not only as harbingers of new cultures and as acculturising agencies but also as adapting to a different cultural environment or as being, in turn, modified, influenced or shaped by the regional culture to evolve a new synthesis. It is this new synthesis of northern and southern cultural traditions (or Aryan and Dravidian, connoting cultures and not races) that emerged in pre 7th century Tamiḻakam to become more mature and culturally significant in the early medieval Indian context.

Agastya who is said to be the harbinger of "Aryan" civilization with the south, is associated with one such migration when he is believed to have led a group of three 'kings', 18 clans of the Vēḻir and the *Aruvāḷar* (from Dvaraka?) to the South. He is also believed to have deforested the land and made the land habitable and cultivable[1]. However, the legends and traditions that developed around Agastya show that the was a "sage" associated with both the Northern and Southern cultures and with the Sanskrit and Tamil languages and hence greatly revered in southern traditions. The Agastya tradition indicates that a synchronic process of acculturation in the proto historic period resulted in the development of a synthesis in early historical times.

In the course of such migrations. groups of people including the *brāhmaṇās* could have moved to the south and got assimilated in course of time. Nilakanta Sastri states that "the name of the section of south Indian Brahmins Brihaccarana is itself indicative of the great migration or movement towards the south[2]?" Migrations to south India from magadha are referred to in Jain traditions. For instance, a Jain migration under Bhadrabahu, the last of the Srutakevalins is recorded in medieval Jain texts. Due to a famine in the north, Chandragupts, the Mauryan emperor, is believed to have abdicated his throne and migrated to the south with Bhadrabahu the Jain saint and his disciples. They are said to have settled down at Sravanabelgola in Karnataka. According to Jain tradition some of them moved further south into Tamiḻaksm[3].

This thesis has tried to look at the development of early historical Tamil society in two broad phases i.e. from a tribal to a farming society, from uneven socio-econimic milieux in different ecozones to a dominant agrarian society in the major ecozones or areas of attraction (*marutam*) with potentialities for expanding into other eco-zones in varying degress of intensity. The ideology and technology for this development came from a merging of two different traditions *viz* the northern and southern. The major thrust of this study has been to analyse th nature of society of early Tamiḻakam. It has been maintained throughout the study that ecology and the physical environment influenced the emergence of various kinds of subsistence patterns, social and political institutions and religious beliefs. In the light of this, it has been argued that the social organization of the early Tamils cannot be explained in terms of a monolithic structure.

In the introductory chapter the dependence on a wide variety of sources for a stydy of this nature was indicated. Despite the limitations in understanding the hidden and symbolic meaning of the *Caṅkam* classics and the problems in using archaeological data an attempt was made to understand the nature of society of early historical Tamiḻakam in two broad phases.

The study commenced with an understanding of the region and its geography, ecology and settlement pattern. It was highlighted that the geographicalecological variations influenced the development potentialities of the region which in turn determined the distribution and nature of settlements. The early Tamil conception of ecology (or division into *tiṇais*) as referred to in the texts was also examined. A study of the *tiṇais* revealed unevenstages of development with the *marutam* and *neytal* emerging as the major zones of attraction. Textual as well as archaeological evidence indicate dense settlements particularly around the riverine areas in the proto historic and early historic periods. The nature of settlements which arose were also conditioned by the ecological factors. In contra distinction to the small settlements of the *kuṛiñci* and *mullai* the settlements of the *marutam* and *neytal* were bigger in size and accompanied by socio-economic diversification. Further, it was stated that the basic elements of civilization which emerged in the protohistoric period (megalithic), like sedentarization and establishment of settlements, paddy cultivation and irrigation, further intensified in specific ecozones like *marutam* and *neytal* with greater emphasis on agriculture and irrigation, craft specialization, emergence of exchange centres and expansion of the exhange newwork in the early historic period. In other words by the early historic period greater sedentarization and increased agricultural production resulted in the emergence of major and minor chiefdoms, diversification of economic activities through craft specialization (albeit rudimentary) and trade and social differentiation in certain areas.

The major thrust of this study has been to point out changes in society over a long chronological time span of nine centuries i.e. from 3rd century B.C. - 6th century A.D. It has already been stated that uneven levels of development of the *tiṇais* on accourd of ecological constraints accounted for the presence of varied forms of organizations in the *tiṇais*. It was pointed out that at the level of the *kuṛiñci* and *mullai tiṇais* the 'tribal' basis of social norms and organization persisted while the *marutam* and neytal emerged as the regions characterized by socio-economic diversification.

Society in the first phase of the early historical period was essentially based on kinship which determined the production process and possibly regulated marriage ties. This was based on an analysis of the inhabitants of the various *tiṇais*. Such a Kin based society did not preclude craft specialisation at least in the fields of metal working, pottery etc though at a rudimentary level. Most of these a craftsmen were noticeable in the *marutam/neytal* regions. These regions also saw the rise of a mercantile community. emergence of markets and utilisation of money presumably by the merchant groups and emerging 'state' system (*mūvēntar*). Market places were areas where purchase and sale of luxury or exotic items along with necessary ones took place. However, the general populace living in the *tiṇais* were not dependent on the goods sold at the market places and exchanges within the *tiṇais* were based on barter and were not profit oriented. The ramification of trading activities resulted in the rise of 'urban' enclaves in *marutam* and *neytal* and the arrival and participation of foreign merchants (*yavaṇās*) in trading activities. Most of the urban enclaves were located at the mouths of rivers or on the coasts with rich hinterlands. The luxury goods entered the interior parts through redistribution (to bards and minstrels). Otherwise, it was mainly the urban/ruling elite who would have associated themselves with such luxury goods or 'ideo-technic' or 'socio-technic' objects.

These objects did not perocolate down to the lower groups of society. Thus. there were different levels of exchange at different points :

(a) long distance trade for prestige goods/luxury items.

(b) markets in urban centres which emerged due to maritime trade

(c) consumption points in the interior which were the seats of major chiefdoms

(d) inter *tiṇai* symbiotic exhcnage

(e) local level barter.

Such activities intensified in the *marutam* and *neytal* region which show a distinct tendency towards a more diverse and complex economy and hence social differentiation.

Instrumental to the rise of such a society and economy was the presence of a definite surplus. This 'surplus' produced in the riverine tracts facilitated the rise of the *mūvēntar,* although institutional forms for the regular appropriation of surplus could not develop. Realizing the advantages of a good subsistence base the colas in particular made efforts to increase the cultivated area by deforestation and providing irrigation facilities. Social differentiation and a nascent *varṇa* ideology is attested in the texts. It must be born in mind that all these developments are confined to the *marutam* and *neytal*. In contrast, the *kuṛiñci* and *mullai* were tracts of relative isolation (though they supolied the articles for export in the contemporary commercial cirucuit) characterized by simpler forms of socio-political organizations.

The striking transformation which took place in early Tamiḻakam was the emergence of a farming society characterized by incipient urbanism. Gordon Childe was the first to formulate the concept of the urban revolution and he provided a list of ten determinative critera to distinguish an urban society[4]. R. McAdams has argued that the urban revolution has to be understood in terms of changes in the underlying social organization that precipitated the technological changes outlined by Childe. He emphasizes the emergence of certain central factors ('core trends') which are characteristic of all civilized societies. These he enumerates as social stratification, urbanization, political differentiantion (or the emergence of the Sate) militarization and craft specialization[5] all of which are noticeable in early Tamilakam.

The Tamil country had potential for the growth of urbanism accompanied by social complexity and social differentiation. Increasing settlements particularly around the river valleys coupled with the establishment of agriculture and generation of surplus could have led to the onset of differentiation. Trade contacts could have also played an important role resulting in the accumulation of prestige certain prestige goods in the hands of the ruling elite. Further, certain groups like merchants could have been benefitted by indulging in trading activities. Their opulence is reflected in the fact that certain merchants even made donations to the non-brahmanical sects. The urban enclaves which developed in the *marutam* and *neytal* housed heterogenous populations and it was here that differentiation and *varṇa* were most pronounced.

In the sphere of religion the absence of a single dominant ideology and priestly class was highlighted. Instead, the worship of the deities specific to an ecological niche was characterised by folk forms of worship and the influence of the northern/ brahmanical/Puranic influence was in its nascent stages.

Thus we notice that new elements crept into the tribal/ kinship basis of organisation in some areas even during the early phase of the early historical period thereby paving the way for the emergence of a peasant society marked by incipient urbanism. To give a specific lable to early historical Tamil society in its first phase would be rather difficult as it does not correspond in every detail to the kind of concepts and models evolved through anthropological and ethnographical studies. For we have noticed that there were uneven forms and levels of development in different ecozones, some of which still remained in the tribal stages. However, to characterize them as tribal also would be inappropriate because of the presence of elements of change in different degrees in certain ecozones. One of the concepts which seems to apply to this phase would be the concept of a 'rank society' put forth by Morton Fried ableit to a limited extent. Rank societies are understood by Fried to be usually agricultural, characterised by high demographic density: employment of all individuals in labour tasks typical of their age and sex with the holder of a rank also compelled to work as he is expected to be more generous in his distributions; built on the framework of kinship; economic integration is brought about by redistribution, in which there is characteristic flow of goods into and out from a finite centre, persons were rich for what they redistributed and not for what they accumulated; villages were the characteristic mode of settlement; they tend to exist as largely independent autonomous social systems although some have points at which they are articulated with a larger and usually co-operative network; and werfare is serious and endemic in these rank societies[6].

In early historic Tamiḻakam it was pointed out that there was greater sedentarization accompanied by demographic expansion. Agriculture was carried on in certain pockets (mainly *marutam* while shifting cultivation was practised in the *kuṛiñci* and *mullai*). The holder of a rank in the early Tamil society would have been the chief/ ruler (either one of the *mūvēntar*, Vēḷir or non-Vēḷir chieftains / *kiḻārs*). Role of the chief as a great distributor is eulogised in the poems. Kinship was the basis of the production process and both man and woman participated in the production activities. The eco-zones or *tiṇais* are spoken of as *ulakams* worlds in themselves. In other words they were mostly self-sufficent units among which a symbiotic exchange (of basic essential commodities-mainly food products) was established. Warfare is idealized and eulogised in the early poems. The martial bias of the grave equipment of the megalithic burials also provides corroborative evidence. As a corollary, in such a society it is obvious that warriors and chiefly elites would have occupied a position of pre-eminence. Despite the general correspondence of Tamil society in this phase to rank society, there are certain important points of difference between Fried's rank society and early Tamil society. For instance Fried's rank societies are found on small islands and in remote areas. In Tamiḻakam society was not confined to such small areas. Further, war which although endemic was irregular in Fried's societies is a major insturment/mechanism for resource appropriation in Tamil society. Again inter village ceremonies or feasts which are "regular" and "which require a considerable period of elaborate preparation and play a significant role in regulating the general economy" in Fried's societies, are not the same as *uṇṭāṭṭu* and *peruñcōṟṟunilai* of Tamil society, for in the latter it is the rulers' initiative which brings about the sharing of food among his warriors and kinsmen and there is no inter village feast. As for the Tamil *viḻās* or festivals they are more in the nature of celebration of victories, religious rituals or ceremonies associated with the events in the ruler's personal life or his socio political status.

In the second phase, the transformation of Tamil society is much more clearly and conspicuously attested by the epics and the eighteen minor works. This phase is marked by agrarian expansion, growth of the urban settlements and marked social differentiation between the high born and the low born. Influence of *varṇa* is suggested by ritual pollution and the restriction on the low born from learning the *Vedas*. The didactic works lay stress on high birth and denounce the low born. In the religious sphere to there is a clear transformation. Folk elements of worship get adapted or merged with the Sanskritic elements resulting in the transformation of certain deities like Murukaṉ, Koṟṟavai and Māl under the Puranic/ Sanskritic influence, while certain folk practices continue in conjunction with the northern elements. More importantly an institutional form is given to religion and the temple emerges as the focal point of worship. The gods are envisaged as transcendental absolutes and *brāhmaṇās* began to function as temple priests. The nonbrahmanical religions seemed to have gained ascendancy and found followers in the urban areas. Presumably under their influence the whole corpus of didactic literature was composed.

By the end of the sixth century with the war ideology losing ground and with the expansion of agriculture (through the concept of the gift of land), society was moving towards a full fledged systemic agrarian organization characterized by social stratification. To integrate such diverse elements an ideology was necessary and this was provided by the *brāhmaṇās* through their *varṇa* framework. The *nāṭu* which in the earlier period did not necessarily connote an agrarian region came to be a peasant agrarian unit. Further the crystallization of the 'States' (like that of Pallavas or Cōḻas) and the rise of the ideology of *Bhakti* in the early medieval period helped in the integration of various ethnic groups / communities.

In the course of this work the experience of the Tamil country has also been contrasted with other regions of India namely western Deccan and north India (wherever necessary) in order to show the varied patterns of development between the regions.

This study has demonstrated the influence of ecology on the development of socio economic, political, religious life and their inter-dependence in early Tamiḻakam.

In the thesis the main endeavour has been to view society as non-static and point out the changes occurring in it and thereby make an integrated study.

FOOTNOTES

1. R. Champakalakshmi, 1975-76, p. 120. see Nilakanta Sastri's *A History of South India* 2nd ed, Madras 1958, pp. 65-76.

   G.S. Ghurye; *Indian Acculturation: Agastya and Skanda,* Bombay 1977, pp. 57-77.

   Agastya is not only glorified in Tamil traditions. The cult of Agastya is popular even in South east Asia.
2. Nilakanta Sastri, 1958, pp. 75-76.
3. R. Champakalakshmi, *Jainism in South India,* unpublished M.Litt. thesis, University of Madras, 1958, Chapter III.
4. "The Urban Revolution" in G.Possehl (ed.) *Ancient Cities of the Indus,* New Delhi, 1979, pp. 12-18.
5. *The Evolution of Urban Society,* Chicago, 1966, pp. 9-17.
6. *The Evolution of Political Society,* New York, 1967, pp. 109-84.

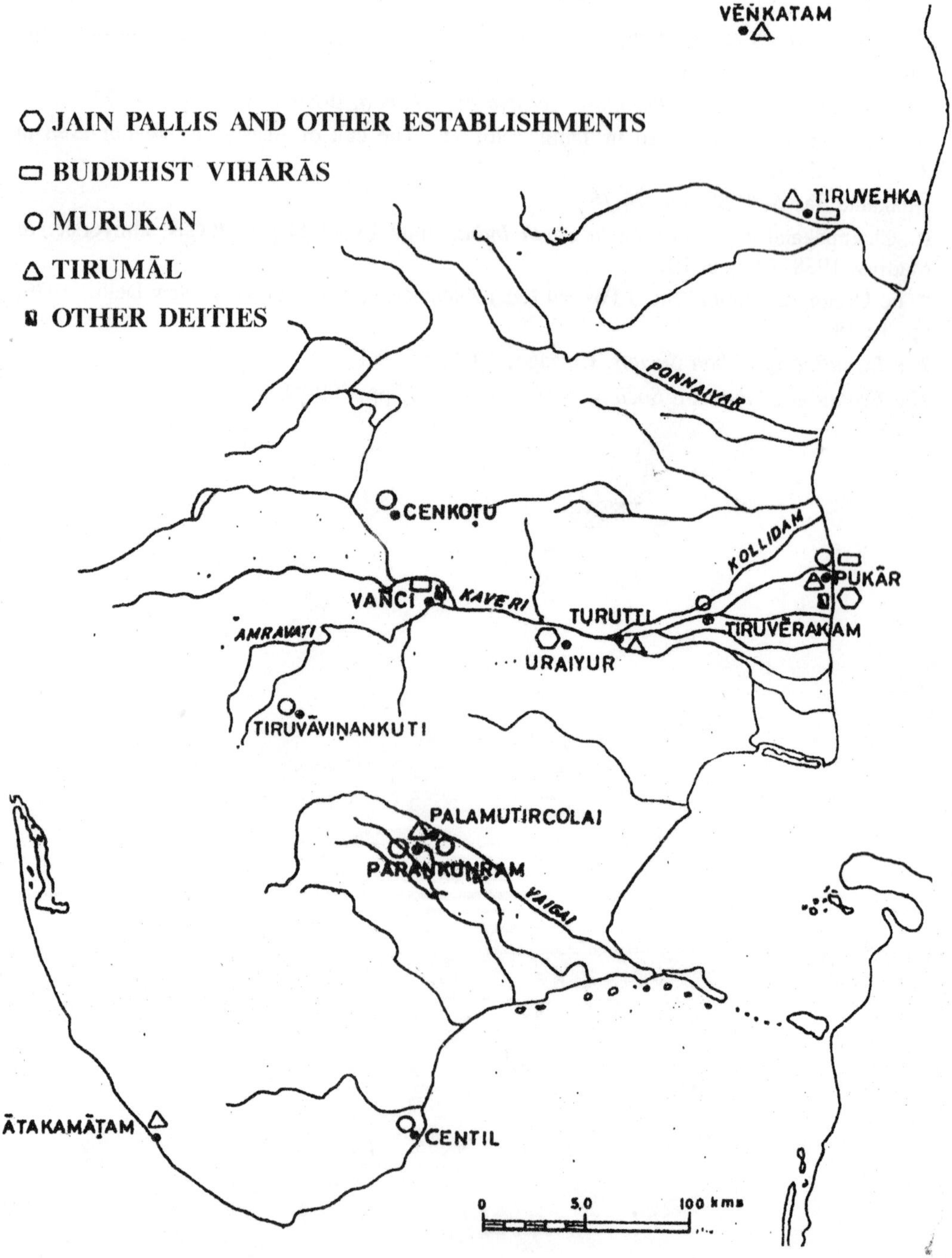

Map - I : Religious Centres of Early Historic Tamiḻakam

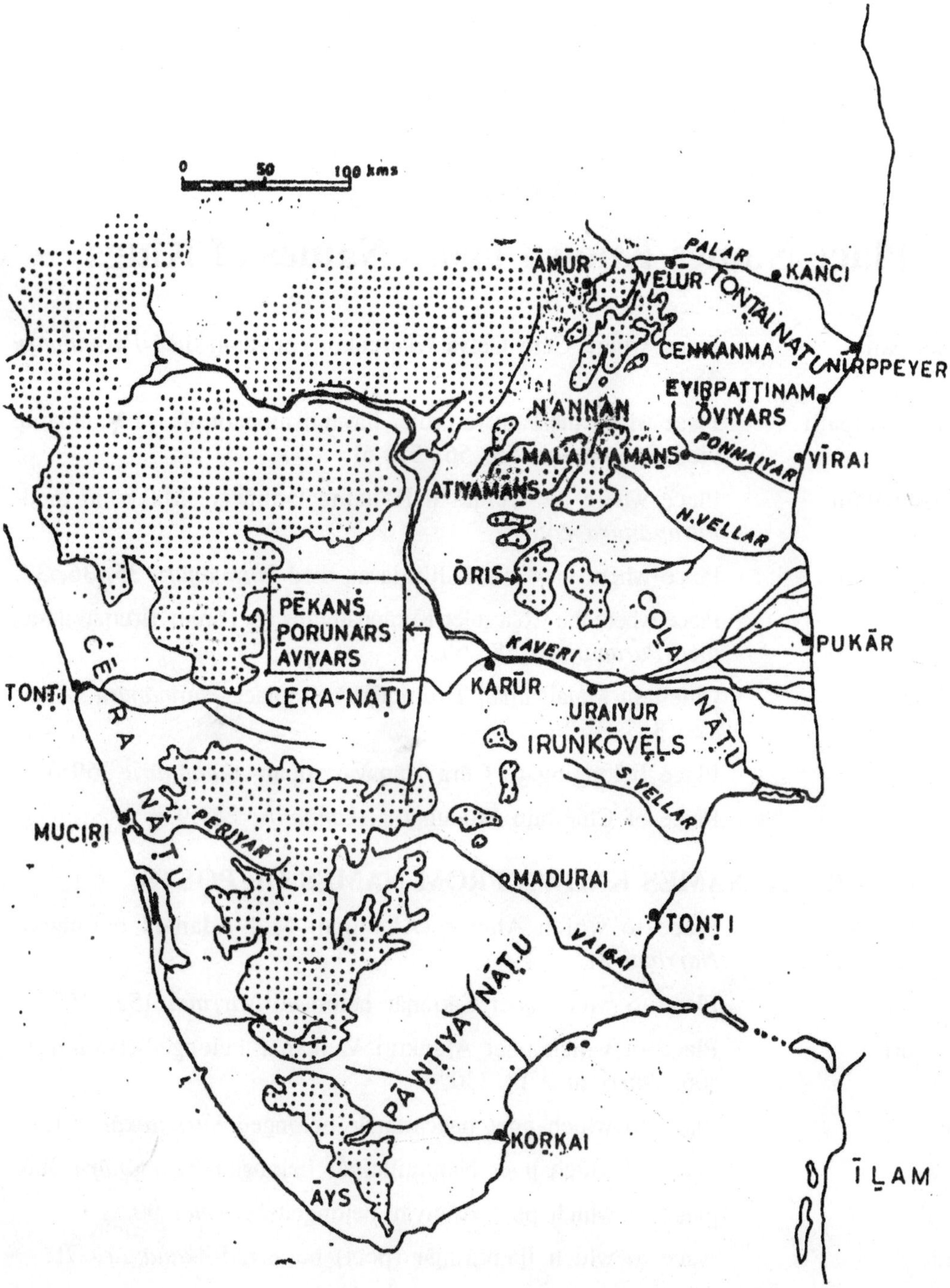

Map - II : Early Tamilakam : Political Configurations

APPENDIX-1

Place Names Known From Names of Kings

Cikkaṟpaiḻi	Place where Cēra Celva Kkatuṅkō Vāḻiyātaṉ died-*Puranāṉūṟu* 387.
Ilavantikaippaḷḷi	Place where the Paṇṭiyaṉ ruler Ilavantikaippalittuñciya Nanmāṟaṉ died *Purāṉāṉūṟu* 55, 56, 57, 61.
Kōṭṭampalam	Place where the Cēramān Kōṭṭampalattuñciya Mākkōtai died-*Puranāṉūṟu* 245.
Kulamuṟṟam	Place where the Cola Kiḷḷivaḷavaṉ died-*Puranāṉūṟu* 35, 36, 37.
Kurāppaḷḷi	Place where the Cōḻa ruler Kurāppaḷḷittuñciya Perum Tirumāvaḷavaṉ died-*Puranāṉūṟu* 58, 60.
Muḷḷur	Chieftain Malaiyamāṉ Tirumuṭikkāri's place-*Puranāṉūṟu* 123:5; 126:8.
Veḷiyam	Place belonging to Cēra Vāṉavarampaṉ-*Akanāṉūṟu* 359:6.
Vēmpi	Place of Chieftain Mūcuṇṭai, *Akanāṉūṟu* 249:9.

PLACE NAMES KNOWN FROM NAMES OF POETS

Akampaṉ Māl	Place to which Ātanār (Akampaṉ Mal Adanār) belonged-*Naṟṟiṇai* 81.
Ālampēri	Place to which poet Cāttaṉār belonged-*Naṟṟiṇai* 152, 255.
Ālaṅkuṭi	Place ot which poet Ālaṅkuṭi Vaṅkaṉār belonged-*Akanāṉūṟu* 106, *Naṟṟiṇai* 230, 330.
Aḻici	Place to which poet naccāttaṉār belonged-*Kuṟuntokai* 271.
Aḷḷur	place to which poet Naṉmullaiyār belonged-*Puranāṉūṟu* 306.
Añcil	place to which poet Añciyār belonged-*Naṟṟiṇai* 90.
Anti	place to which Iḷaṅkīraṉār (poet) belonged-*Akanāṉūṟu* 71.
Arimaṇavāyil Uṟattūr	*Akanāṉūṟu* 266.

Āṭuturai	poet Mācāttaṉār belonged to this place—*Puranāṉūṟu* 227.
Ciṟaikkuṭi	place to which Āndaiyār belonged—*Kuṟuntokai* 56, 57, 62, 132.
Erukkāṭṭūr	place to which poet tāyaṅ kaṇṇaṉār belonged—*Puranāṉūṟu* 397, colophon.
Erumaiveli	place to which Erumai veḷiyaṉār belonged—*Puranāṉūṟu* 273; 303.
Iruntaiyūr	place to which poet Koṟṟaṉ pulavaṉ belonged—*Kuṟuṅtokai* 335.
Iṭaiyāṟu	*Akananuru* 141
Kanccipēṭṭu	place to which poets Koṟṟan (*Kuṟuntokai* 213) and Naṉṉakaiyār
(Kacci or Kañci)	belonged (*Kuṟuntokai* 30, 180, 192) was a suburb of Kancipuram.
Kallāṭam	place to which poet Kallāṭaṉār belonged—*Kuṟuntokai 260, 269.*
Kaḷḷikkuṭi	place to which Pūtam Pullaṉār belonged—*Naṟṟiṇai* 333.
Kaḷḷiḷ	place to whi:h poet Attiraiyaṉār belonged.
Kāppiaṟu	place to which poet Kāppiyaṉār belonged—*Patiṟṟuppattu*: IV.
Kaṭaiyam	place to which Kaṭaiyāṭṭār father of Veṇṇakaṉār belonged.
Kaṭampaṉūr	place to which poet Cāṇtiliyaṉ belonged (*Kuṟuntokai* 307).
Kaṭum Toṭaikka	A place to which poet Kaṭumṭotaikkāvaṉār belonged *Akanāṉūṟu* 109.
Kaṭiyalūr	place to which poet Uruttiraṉ kaṇṇaṉār belonged-*Kuṟuntokai* 352.
Kōṭṭīyūr	place to which poet Nallantaiyār belonged—*Naṟṟiṇai* 211.
Kumaṭṭūr	place to which poet Kaṇṇaṉār belonged—*Patiṟṟuppattu*:II.
Kumili Ñalal	place to which poet Nappācalaiyār belonged.
Māṅkuṭi	place to which poet Marutaṉ belonged—*Puranāṉūṟu* 72 *Maturaikkāñci* colophon.
Miḷai	place to which Mīḷaipperum-patumaṉār belonged—*Naṟṟiṇai* 109.
Miḷai	place of poet Vēḷ Tittaṉ—*Kuṟuntokai* 284.
Mukaiyalūr	place to which poet Ciṟu Karuntumpiyār belonged—*Puranāṉūṟu* 181.
Mukkal	place to which Mukkal Acān Nalveḷḷiyār belonged—*Naṟṟiṇai* 272.
Muppēr	place to which Muppēr Nākaṉār belonged—*naṟṟiṇai* 314.
Murañciyūr	place to which poet Muṭinākarāyar belonged—*Puranāṉuru* 2.

Nallūr	*Naṟṟiṇai* 282. place to which poet Ciṟu Mētaviyār belonged.
Naṟavu	*Patiṟṟupattu* 60:12.
Okkūr	place to which poetess Macāttiyār belonged.
Olaiyūr	*Akanāṉūṟu* 25 *Puranāṉūṟu* 71, 242.
Otuṅkāṭu	*Akanāṉūṟu* 91:12.
Paṭumaram	place to which Moci Kiraṉār belonged.
Peruṅguḷam	*Naṟṟiṇai* 340:3.
Peruṅkōḻi	place to which poetess Nakkaṇaiyar daughter of Perunkōḻi nāyakaṉ belonged—*Puranāṉūṟu* 83, 84, 85.
Peruntalai	place to which poet Peruntalai Cattanār belonged—*Puranāṉūṟu* 151, 164, 165.
Peruvāyinmuḷḷi	place to which the author of the text *Acārakōvai* Peruvāyiṉ Muḷḷiyār belonged.
Poruntil	place to which poet Iḷaṅkīraṉār belonged—*Puranāṉūṟu* 53.
Potukkayam	place to which kūranṭai belonged—*kuṟanloka* 337.
Pullāṟṟūr	place to which poet Eyiṟṟiyaṉār belonged—*Puranāṉūṟu* 213.
Taṅkāl	place to which poets Poṟkollaṉār (*Puranāṉūṟu* 326 and Veṇṇākaṉār belonged *Naṟṟinai* 313)
Urōṭakam	place to which Kantarattaṉār belonged—*Kuṟuntokai* 155; *Naṟṟiṇi* 306.
Uvarkkaṇṇūr	place to which Pullaṅkīraṉār belonged—*Akanāṉūṟu* 146.
Veḷiyam	place belonging to Cēra Vāṉavarampaṉ *Akanāṉūṟu* 359:6.
Veḷḷaikkuṭi	place to which poet Nākaṉār belonged—*Puranāṉūṟu* 35.
Veḷḷiyam	*Naṟṟiṇai* 101.
Vempaṟṟūr	place to which poet Vempaṟṟūr Kumaraṉār belonged—*Puranāṉūṟu* 317.
Vempi	place of Chieftain Mūcuṇṭai—*Akanāṉūṟu* 249:9.
Veṇṇi	place where Cola Karikāla fought his battle against Cēra Peruñ Cēral Ātaṉ-*Puranāṉūru* 66:6. Poetess Vennikuyattiyār belonged to this place.
Viḷaṅkil	place of Kaṭalaṉ- *Akanāṉūṟu* 52:4; 81:13.
Viriyūr	place to which poet Nakkaṉār belonged—*Puranāṉūṟu* 332.
Viṟṟūṟṟu	place to which poets Mūteyiṇaṉār and Vaṇṇakaṉ Tattaṉ belonged—*Kuṟuntokai* 372: *Naṟṟiṇai* 298.
Viyalūr	a coastal town—*Akanāṉūṟu* 97:13.

PLACE NAMES KNOWN FROM NAMES OF KIḶĀRS WHO WERE CHIEFS/IMPORTANT MEN

Ampar

Cirukuṭi

Karumpaṉūr

Koṇkāṇaṇ

Malli

Nalai

Poṟaiyāṟṟu

Vallār

PLACE NAMES KNOWN FROM NAMES OF KIḶĀRS WHO WERE POETS

Aiyūr

Ālattūr

Aricil

Ārkkaṭu

Āvur

Cellūr

Iṭaikuṉṟūr

Kampur

Kāri

Karuvūr

Kayattūr

Kāṭṭūr

Kiḷḷimangalam

Kōṭiyūr

Kōvūr

Kuṅṟur

Kuṟuṅkōḻiyūr

Kuṭalūr

Māṅkuṭi

Maṟṟūr

Maruṅkūr

Maṭalūr
Miḷai
Nallavūr
Nīṭūr
Nocci Niyamam
Perunkunrūr
Potumpil
Turaiyūr
Ukaikkuṭi
Umaṭṭūr
Vellūr

PLACE NAMES (EARLY HISTORICAL) KNOWN FROM CANKAM LITERATURE, FOREIGN ACCOUNTS AND ARCHAEOLOGICAL RECORDS

*Alagarai	
Aḻantūr	identified with modern Tiruvaluntur near Mayavaram.
*Aḷḷur	
Aḻumbil	
Āmūr	
Āṭuturai	
Bacare	identified with Porkad/Varkkalai
Ceṇkaṇmā	Cengam, N.Arcot
Eyirpaṭṭiṇam	(Soptama?) (Marakanam?)
*Karaikkadu	
Kaḻār	
Kāveripaṭṭiṇam (Pukār)	
*Kodumanal	Kodumanam of the *Patiṟṟuppattu*
*Koṟkai	
Kutantaivāyil	
Kutavāyil	
Kuṉṟūr	
Kuṭalūr	
*Madurai	Capital of Pāṇṭiyās

Māṅkatu	
*Maruṅkūrpaṭṭiṇam	identified with Alagankulam
Māvilaṅkai	
Miḻalai	
Muciṛi	identified with modern Cranganore
Mūtaveḷḷilai	
Naura/Nitra	identified with Cannanore/Mangalore
*Nattamedu	
Nelcynda	identified to be near Kottayam
Neṭuntēru	
Nīrppeyaṛṛu	identified with modern Vasavasamudram
Pāmallur	
Pērur	
Piṭavur	
Pōr	
*Tirukkāmpuliyur	
Toṇṭi	identified with modern Ponnani
Umparkāṭu	
*Uṛaiyur	capital of Cōḻas
*Vañci (Karur)	capital of Cēras
Vayalūr	
*Vīrai	Vīrai of the *Caṅkam* texts identified with Arikamedu

* Denotes sites which have been excavated.

APPENDIX-2

LIST OF NĀṬUS

Cōḻanāṭu	The Cōḻa country (*Puṟanāṉūṟu* 67:8; 382:3)
Cōṉāṭu	Nāṭu to which the *brahman* Kauṇiyaṉ Viṇṇantāyaṉ belonged (*Puṟanāṉūṟu* 166)
Kāṭṭu nāṭu	Jungle tracts (*Naṟṟiṇai* 59:6)
Koṅkar nāṭu	Primarily pastoral land was a part of the Cēra country for sometime ruled by the Iḷam Kōcar-(*Patiṟṟuppattu* 22:15; 77:10-11) (Subrahmanian, 1966, p. 322)
Kuṭanāṭu	Western part of Tamilakam-Cēra Country (*Puṟanāṉūṟu* 177:12) (*Patiṟṟuppattu*)
Miḻaikūṟṟam	Chieftain Evvi ceded this to Neṭuñceḻiyaṉ (*Puṟanāṉūṟu* 24:19) (becomes an agrarian unit in early medieval times)
Mukkavaranāṭu	in Toṇṭaimaṇṭalam to which poet Āmūr Mallaṉ belonged (*Puṟanāṉūṟu* 80 colophon.)
Muttuṟṟu kuṟṟam	*kuṟṟam* in *marutam* land ruled by a vēḷir. The vēḷir ceded this to Pāṇṭiyaṉ Neṭuñceḻiyaṉ (*Puṟanāṉūṟu* 24:22) (becomes an agrarian unit in early medieval times)
Nīr Nāṭu	Land of the waters-Cōḻa country (*Kaḷavaḻi Naṟpatu* 3:3, 8:4; 17:4; 19:3 and so on)
Ōyma nāṭu	ruled by chieftain Nalliyakōṭaṉ (*Ciṟupāṇāṟṟuppaṭai* colophon)
Pāṇṭināṭu	The Pāṇṭiya country (*Cilappattikāram* XXX:148; *Maṇimēkalai* XIV: 55)
Parampunāṭu	ruled by Chieftain Pāri (*Akanāṉūṟu* 303:10; *Puṟanāṉūṟu* 108:4; 109:1; 110:2-3; 113:7)
Pūḻi nāṭu	part of Cēra land
Puṉal nāṭu	The fertile Cōḻa country on account of the river Kāveri (*Kaḷavaḻi Nāṟpatu* 1:4; 2:4; 9:3; 14:3 and so on)
Pūṅkunṟa nāṭu	Land of beautiful hills, probably a part of Ramnad district near Mahipalampatti (*Nālaṭiyār* 128, 212; Subrahmanian, 1966, p. 588)

Puṉṉāṭu	A division in Cēra nāṭu (*Akanāṉūṟu* 396:2; Subrahmanian, 1966, p. 586)
Teṉṉātu	Cēra land (Subrahmanian, 1966, p. 456)
Tulunāṭu	The Tulu country South Kanara area Land of the Kooar (*Akanāṉūṟu* 15:5)
Vēnāṭu	Ruled by the Āys (Veḷir) R. Champakalakshmi, 1975-76, p. 121
Vēṅkaṭa Nāṭu	The hilly region around Vēṅkaṭam hill (Puṟanānūrn 381 : 22).
Yāṟṟunāṭu	Island (*Paripaṭal* IV:67)

APPENDIX-3

LIST OF KIḺĀRS WHO WERE POETS

Aiyūr Mulaṅ Kiḻār	: *Puṟanāṉūṟu* 21
Ālattūr Kiḻār	: *Puṟanāṉūṟu* 34; 36; 69; 225
Aricil Kiḻār	: *Puṟanāṉūṟu* 146; 230; 281; 285
Ārkkaṭṭu Kiḻār Makaṉār	: *Akanāṉūṟu* 64
Āvūr Kiḻār	: *Puṟanāṉūṟu* 322
Āvur Mulaṅ Kiḻār	: *Puṟanāṉūṟu* 38; 40; 166; 177
Iṭaikuṉṟūr Kiḻār	: *Puṟanāṉūṟu* 76-79
Kampūr Kiḻār	: *Naṟṟiṇai* 294
Kāri Kiḻār	: *Kuṟuntokai*
Karuvūr Kiḻār	: *Kuṟuntokai* 170
Kāṭṭūr Kiḻār	: *Akanāṉūṟu* 85
Kayattūr Kiḻār	: *Kuṟuntokai* 354
Kiḻḻimaṅgalam Kiḻār Makaṉār Cērako vaṉār	: *Naṟṟiṇi* 365
Kiḻḻimaṅgalam Kiḻār	: Kuṟuntokai 76, 110,152, 181
Koṭiyūr Kiḻār makaṉār neytaltattaṉār	: *Akanāṉūṟu* 243
Kōvūr Kiḻār	: *Puṟanāṉūṟu* 31-33, 41, 44-47
Kuṉṟūr Kiḻār makaṉār	: *Puṟanāṉūṟu* 338
Kuṟun Kōḻiyūr Kiḻār	: *Puṟanāṉūṟu* 17, 20, 22
Kuṭalūr Kiḻār	: *Puṟanāṉūṟu* 229
Māṅkuṭi Kiḻār	: *Puṟanāṉūṟu*24, 26, 313, 335
Māṟṟūr Kiḻār makaṉār koṟṟaṉ koṟṟaṉār	: *Akanāṉūru* 54
Māṭalur Kiḻar	: *Kuṟuntokai* 150
Miḻai Kiḻāṉ Nalvēṭṭaṉār	: *Naṟṟiṇai* 210, 349
Nallāvūr Kiḻār	: *Naṟṟiṇai* 154

Nīṭur Kiḻavōṉ	: *Akanāṉūṟu* 266
Neitarcāittuitta Āvūr Kiḻār	: *Akanāṉūṟu* 112
Nocci Niyaman Kiḻār	: *Puṟanāṉūṟu* 293
Perunkunrur Kiḻār	: *Puṟanāṉūṟu* 147; 210; 211; 266
Potumpil Kiḻār Makaṉ veṇkaṇṇi	: *Naṟṟiṇai* 375
Potumpil Kiḻār makaṉār	: *Naṟṟiṇai* 387
Sellūr Kiḻār makaṉār	: *Akanāṉūru* 250
Perum Putaṁ koṟṟaṉār	
Tuṟaiyūr Ōṭai Kiḻār	: *Puṟanāṉūṟu* 136
Ukāikruṭi Kiḻār	: Kuruntokan 63
Umaṭṭūr Kiḻār makaṉār paraṅ koṟṟaṉār	: *Akanāṉūṟu* 69
Vaṭamōtaṅ Kiḻār	: *Puṟanāṉūṟu* 260
Veḷḷūr Kiḻār Makaṉar veṇputiyār	: *Kuṟuntokai* 219

APPENDIX-4

LIST OF POETS BELONGING TO THE ARTISAN/CRAFTSMEN COMMUNITY

Kaccippēṭṭu Iḷam Taccaṉār	: native or resident of Kaccippēṭṭu. We do not know if taccaṉār was a proper name or indicated the profession of carpentry (*Naṟṟiṇai* 266)
Kaccippēṭupperum Taccaṉār	: probably a 'carpenter' and resident of Kaccippēṭu (*Naṟṟiṇai* 144; 213)
Maduraipperuṅkoḷḷaṉ	: probably a 'blacksmith' of Madurai (*Kuṟuntokai* 141).
Maduraippoṉceykollaṉ veṇṇ-Kamar	: 'goldsmith' from Madurai (*Akananaṉūṟu* 363).
Taṅkāl poṟkollaṉār	: Goldsmith belonging to Taṅkāl (*Akanāṉūṟu* 355)
Taṅkāl poṭkollaṉār	: Goldsmith (*Puṟanāṉūṟu* 326)
Taṅkāl poṟkollaṉ veṇṇākaṉār	: goldsmith belonging to Taṅkāl (*Naṟṟiṇai* 313)
Vaṭama Vaṇṇakkaṉ pamōtaraṉār	: lapidary from North India (*Kuṟuntokai* 85; *Puṟanāṉūṟu* 172)
Vaṭama vaṇṇakkaṉ peruñcāttaṉū	: lapidary from the north (*Puṟanāṉūṟu* 125)
Vaṭama Vaṇṇakkaṉ pēri *Cāttaṉ (ār)*	: lapidary from the North (*Akanāṉūṟu* 38; 214; 268; 305) *Kuṟuntokai* 81, 159, *Naṟṟiṇai* 299, 323; 378; *Puṟanāṉūṟu* 198)
Veṇṇikkuyaṯṯiyār	: A woman potter (*Puṟanāṉūṟu* 66)
Viṟṟuṟṟuvaṇṇakkaṉ Tattaṉār	: perhaps a 'lapidary' belonging to Viṟṟuṟṟu (*Naṟṟiṇai* 298)

APPENDIX-5

LIST OF POETS BELONGING TO THE MERCANTILE COMMUNITY

Kāviripumaṭṭiṉattu Poṉvaṇikaṉār Makaṉār Napputaṉār (the gold trader Kaviripumpaṭṭiṉam)	:	(*Mullaipaattu*)
Madurai Aṛuvai Vāṇikaṉ Ilavettanar (Iḷavēṭṭaṉār, the trader in cloth' from Madurai)	:	(*Akanāṉūṛu* 302; *Kuṛuntokai* 185; *Naṛṛiṇai* 344; *Puṛananuru* 329)
Madurai Kūla vāṇikaṉ Cittalai Cāttaṉār (Cittalai Cāttaṉār, the trader in grains from Madurai)	:	(*Akanāṉuṛu* 3066; 320; *Kuṛuntokai* 154; *Puṛanāṉūṛu* 59)
Madurai Ōlaikkataiyattār Nalvellaiyar (nalveḷḷaiyār) 'the owner of a palmleaf mart jewellery shop' from Madurai	:	(*Naṛṛiṇai* 250)
Uṛaiyūr Iḷampoṉ Vāṇikaṉār (trader in gold from Uṛaiyur)	:	*Puṛanāṉūṛu* 264)

APPENDIX-6

LIST OF POETS FROM THE BRĀHMAṆA COMMUNITY

Erukkattur Tayaṅkaṇṇan̤ār	*Puṛanān̤ūṛu* 397
Kapilar	*Akanān̤ūṛu* 2, 12, 18, 42, 82, 118 etc.
	Kuṛuntokai 13, 18, 25, 38, 42, etc.
	Naṛṛiṇai 1, 13, 32, 59, 65, 77, 217etc.
	Puṛanān̤ūṛu 8, 14, 105-111, 113-24 etc.
	Kuṛiñcippāṭṭu
Kaṭiyalūr Uruttiraṅkaṇṇan̤ār	*Kuṛuntokai* 352 *Akanān̤ūṛu* 167
Māmūlan̤ār	*Akanān̤ūṛu* 1, 15, 31, 55, 61, 65, 91, 97, 101, 115, 127, 187, 197, 201, etc.
Maturai Kaṇakkāyanār	*Puṛanān̤ūṛu* 56, 189
Makan̤ār Nakkīran̤ār	
Pālai Kautaman̤ār	*Patiṛṛuppaṭṭu* III
Peruṅkaucikan̤ār	*Naṛṛiṇai* 44, 49
Tāmppal Kaṇṇan̤ār	*Puṛan.ān̤ūṛu* 43

APPENDIX-7

LIST OF POETS HAVING GOTRA NAMES

Atreya Gotra	Kaḷḷil Āttiraiyaṉar (author of *Kuṟuntokai* 293)
Gautama Gotra	Āmūr Kautamaṉ Sātevaṉār (author of *Akanāṉūṟu* 159; *Paripāṭal* 19:51)
	Pālai Kautamaṉār (author of *Patiṟṟuppattu* III)
Kausika Gotra	Iraniyamuttattupperuṅkuṉṟūrūrpperum kaucikaṉār
	Peruṅkaucikaṉār (author of *Naṟṟiṇai* 44, 139)
	Madurai Ilankanni Kaucikanar (author of *Puṟanāṉūṟu* 309)
Kauntinya Gotra	Maduraikavuṇiyaṉ Puttattaṉār (author of *Akanāṉūṟu* 74)
Vatula Gotra	Kotimankalattuvatuli-Narsentuvanar (author of *Akanāṉūṟu* 179; 232)

APPENDIX-8

LIST OF WOMEN POETESSES

Añci attai makaḷ nākaiyār	*Akanāṇūṛu* 352
Añcil añciyār	*Naṛṛiṇai* 90
Ātimanti	*Kuṛuntokai* 31
Auvvaiyār	*Akanāṇūṛu* 11, 273, 303
	Kuṛuntokai 15, 23, 28, 29 etc
	Puṛanāṇūṛu 87-104, 140, 187 etc.
Kākkaippāṭiṇiyār	*Patiṛṛuppattu* 51-60,
Naccеḷḷaiyār	*Puṛanāṇūṛu* 278
	Kuṛuntokai 210
Kumiḷiñaḷalār	*Akanāṇūṛu* 160
Nappacalaiyār	
Kuṛamakaḷ Kuṛieyiṇi	*Naṛṛiṇai* 357
Maṛōkkattu Nappacalaiyār	*Puṛanāṇūṛu* 39, 126, 280,
	Naṛṛiṇai 304.
Maṛpittiyār	*Puṛanāṇūṛu* 251, 252
Nakkaṇṇaiyār	*Akanāṇūṛu* 252
	Puṛanāṇūṛu 83, 84, 85
	Naṛṛiṇai 87
Naṇṇakaiyār	*Kuṛuntokai* 180, 192
Neṭumpalliyattai	*Kuṛuntokai* 178, 203
Okkūr Mācāttiyār	*Kuṛuntokai* 126, 186, 220
	Akanāṇūṛu 324, 384
	Puṛanāṇūṛu 279, etc.
Pārimakaḷir	*Puṛanāṇūṛu* 112

Puṅkaṇuttiraiyār	*Kuṟuntokai* 48, 171
Pēymakaḷ Iḷaveyiṇi	*Puṟanāṉūṟu* 11
Tāyaṅkaṇṇiyāṟ	*Puṟanāṉūṟu* 250
Varumulaiyāritti	*Kuṟuntokai* 176
Veṇmaṇipputi	*Kuṟuntokai* 299
Vennikkuyattiyar	*Puṟanāṉūṟu* 66
Veṇputiyār	*Kuṟuntokai* 97, 174, 219

APPENDIX-9

LIST OF POETS BELONGING TO NON-BRAHMANICAL SECTS

Pakkuṭukkai Naṉkaṇiyār	*Puṟanāṉūṟu* 194
Ulōccaṉār	perhaps a Jain
Munṟuṟai Maṉṉavaṉ	Jain
Kaṇiyaṉ Puṅkuṉṟaṉ	Jain

APPENDIX-10

LIST OF MŪVĒNTAR

CĒRA

Cēramāṉ Antuvañcēral Irumpoṟai: *Puṟanāṉūṟu* 13
Cēramāṉ Kaṭaloṭṭiya Velkeḻukuṭṭuvaṉ: *Puṟanāṉūṟu* 369
Cēramāṉ Katunkō Vāḻiyātaṉ: *Puṟanāṉūṟu* 8
Cēramāṉ Kaṇaikkāl Irumpoṟai: *Puṟanāṉūṟu* 74
Cēramāṉ Karuvūreṟiya Oḷvātkōpperuncēra Irumpoṟai: *Puṟanāṉūṟu* 5
Cēramāṉ Kuṭṭuvan Kōtai: *Puṟanāṉūṟu* 54
Cēramāṉ Kuṭakkō Cēral Irumpoṟai: *Puṟanāṉūṟu* 210, 211
Cēramāṉ Kuṭakkō Neṭuncēralataṉ: *Puṟanāṉūṟu* 62, 63, 368
Cēramāṉ Kōkkōtai Marpaṉ: *Puṟanāṉūṟu* 48, 49
Cēramāṉ Kōṭṭampalattuttuñciya Mākkōtai: *Puṟanāṉūṟu* 245
Cēramāṉ Cikkarpaḷḷittuñciya Celvakkaṭuṅkō Vaḻiyataṉ: *Puṟanāṉūṟu* 387
Cēramāṉ Celvakkaṭuṅkō Vāḻiyataṉ: *Puṟanāṉūṟu* 14 *Patiṟṟupattu* VII
Cēramāṉ Takaṭūr Erinta Peruñcēral Irumpoṟai- *Puṟanāṉūṟu* 50; *Patiṟṟupattu* VIII
Cēramāṉ Pamūḻureṟinta Neytalaṅkaṉal Iḷañcētceṉṉi: *Puṟanāṉūṟu* 203
Cēramāṉ Pālai patiya Peruṅkaṭuṅkō *Puṟanāṉūṟu* 11
Cēramāṉ Peruñcēralātaṉ: *Puṟanāṉūṟu* 65
Cēramāṉ Peruncōṟṟu Utiyañcēralātaṉ: *Puṟanāṉūṟu* 2
Cēramāṉ Mantarañcēral Irumpoṟai: *Puṟanāṉūṟu* 125
Cēramāṉ Māri Veṇkō: *Puṟanāṉūṟu* 367
Cēramāṉ Yaṉaikkatcēy Māntarañcēral Irumpoṟai: *Puṟanāṉūṟu* 22
Cēramāṉ Yāṉaikkatcēy Māntarañcēral Irumpoṟai: *Puṟanāṉūṟu* 20
Cēramāṉ Vañcaṉ: *Puṟanāṉūṟu* 398
Cēramāṉ Māntarañcēral Irumporai: *Puṟanāṉūṟu* 53
Imayavarampaṉ Netuñceralātaṉ: *Patiṟṟuppattu* II
Imayavarampaṉ Tampi Palyāṉaicel Keḻu Kuṭṭuvaṉ: *Patiṟṟuppattu* III

Kaḷaṅkāykkaṇṇi Nārmuṭi Cēral: *Patiṟṟuppattu* IV

Kaṭalpirakku Ōṭṭiya Ceṅkuṭṭuvaṉ: *Patiṟṟuppattu* V

Atukkōtpāṭṭuc Cēralātaṉ: *Patiṟṟuppattu* VI

Kutakkō Iḷañcēral Irumpoṟai: *Patiṟṟuppattu* IX

CŌLA

Cōḻāṉ Irācacūyam Vēṭṭa Perunaṟkiḷḷ - *Puṟanāṉūṟu* 16, 125, 367, 377

Cōḻāṉ Ilavantikaippaḷḷittuñciya Nalaṅkiḷḷi Cētceṉṉi: *Puṟanāṉūṟu* 61

Cōḻāṉ Uruvappal Tēr Iḷañcētceṉṉi: *Puṟanāṉūṟu* 4, 266

Cōḻāṉ Karikāṟ Peruvaḷattāṉ: *Puṟanāṉūṟu* 7, 66

Cōḻāṉ Kurāppaḷḷittuñciya Kiḷḷivaḷavaṉ: *Puṟanāṉūṟu* 373

Cōḻāṉ Kurāppaḷḷittuñciya Peruntirumāvaḷavaṉ: *Puṟanāṉūṟu* 58, 60, 197

Cōḻāṉ Kuḷamuṟṟattuttuñciya Kiḷḷivaḷavaṉ: *Puṟanāṉūṟu* 34-42, 46, 69, 70 etc.

Cōḻāṉ Ceṅkaṇāṉ: *Puṟanāṉūṟu* 74

Cōḻāṉ Ceruppāḻi eṟinta Iḷañcētceṉṉi: *Puṟanāṉūṟu* 370, 378

Cōḻāṉ Nalaṅkiḷḷi: *Puṟanāṉūṟu* 27-33; 44, 45, 68 etc.

Cōḻāṉ Nalaṅkiḷḷi: Tampi Māvaḷattaṉ: *Puṟanāṉūṟu* 43

Cōḻāṉ Nalaṅkiḷḷi: *Puṟanāṉūṟu* 44, 45

Cōḻāṉ Neytalaṅkāṉal Ilañcētceṉṉi: *Puṟanāṉūṟu* 10

Cōḻāṉ Pōrvaikkōpperunarkiḷi: *Puṟanāṉūṟu* 80-85

Cōḻāṉ Muṭittalaikkōpperunarkiḷḷi: *Puṟanāṉūṟu* 13

Cōḻāṉ Veṟ Paltaṭakkaip Peruviṟṟkiḷḷi: *Puṟanāṉūṟu* 62, 63, 368

Kōpperuñcōḻaṉ: *Puṟanāṉūṟu* 67, 212, 213, 219, 222, 223

PĀṆṬIYA

Pāṇṭiyaṉ Arivuṭainampi: *Puṟanāṉūṟu* 184

Pāṇṭiyaṉ Ilavantikaippaḷḷittuñciya Nanmaṟan: *Puṟanāṉūṟu* 55-57, 196, 198

Pāṇṭiyaṉ Karuṅkai Oḷvātperumpeyar Vaḻuti: *Puṟanāṉūṟu* 3

Pāṇṭiyaṉ Kānappērtanta Ikkirapperuvaḻuti: *Puṟanāṉēūṟu* 367

Pāṇṭiyan Kūtrkarattuttunciya Nammaraṉ, Purammam 51, 62

Pāṇṭiyaṉ Cittiramāṭattuttuñciya Naṉmāṟaṉ: *Puṟanāṉūṟu* 59

Pāṇṭiyaṉ Talaiyālaṅkanattuc ceru veṉṟa Neṭuñceḻiyaṉ: *Puṟanāṉūṟu* 23-26, 76-79

Pāṇṭiyaṉ Palyākacālai Mutukuṭumi Peruvaḻuti: *Puṟanāṉūṟu* 6, 9, 12, 15

Nampi Neṭuñceḻiyaṉ: *Puṟanāṉūṟu* 239

Kāṇappēraeyil Kaṭanta Ukkiraperuvaḻuti: *Puṟanāṉūṟu* 21

APPENDIX-11

LIST OF VĒḶIR

Ancient vēḷir people	*Kuruntokai* 164:3
Āy	*Puranāṉūṟu* 127-36, 240-241,
Āy Aṇṭiraṉ	*Puranāṉūṟu* 129, 374, 375
(Lord of Aykuṭi in Potiyil hills)	
Eḻiṉi	*Puranāṉūṟu* 158, 230, 392
Evvi	*Puranāṉūṟu* 24, 202, 233
(Milalai Kurram)	
Eyiṉaṉ	*Puranāṉūṟu* 351
Iruṅkovēḷ	*Puranāṉūṟu* 201, 202
(Kotumbalur)	
Malaiyamāṉ Tirumuṭikari	*Puranāṉūṟu* 121-24, 126
(Kovalur)	
Mānalvira Vēḷ (Alumpil Vel)	*Maduraikkāñci* 11. 344-45
Nannan (konkana)	*Malaipatukaṭām*
Naṉṉaṉ (i) (Parampu)	*Akanāṉūṟu* 356
Naṉṉaṉ (Venman) (ii) (Pāḻi)	*Akanāṉūṟu* 15, 97, 142, 349 etc.
Naṉṉaṉ	*Akanāṉūṟu* 396
Neṭuvēḷ Āvi	*Akanāṉūṟu* 1, 61
(Potiyil hills)	
Ōymāṉ Nalliyakōṭaṉ	*Puranāṉūṟu* 176
Pēkaṉ	*Puranāṉūṟu* 158 *Ciṟupāṉāṟruppaṭai*
Valvil Ōri (Kolli hills)	*Puranāṉūṟu* 152, 153, 158, 204
Vēḷ Pāri (Parampunāṭu)	*Puranāṉūṟu* 105-09, 11, 236
Vēḷ of Aḻuntūr	*Akanāṉūṟu* 24:4

APPENDIX-12

LIST OF CHIEFTAINS (NON *VĒḶIR*)

Akutai	*Akanāṉūṟu* 208
	Puṟanāṉūṟu 233, 347
Āmūr Mallaṉ	*Puṟanāṉūṟu* 80
Aṉṉi Miñili	*Akanāṉūṟu* 196; 262
Āntai	*Puṟanāṉūṟu* 71
Antuvaṉ cāttaṉ	*Puṟanāṉūṟu* 71
Ātaṉ Aḻici	*Puṟanāṉūṟu* 71
Ātanuṅkaṉ	*Puṟanāṉūṟu* 175; 389
Atti	*Akanāṉūṟu* 44
Ēnāti Tirukkiḷḷi	*Puṟanāṉūṟu* 167
Ēṟaikkoṉ (Kutiramalai)	*Puṟanāṉūṟu* 157
Ēṟṟai	*Akanāṉūṟu* 44
Erumai (Kutanatu or Erumaiyūr)	*Puṟanāṉūṟu* 36, 155, 253
Iḷaṅ kanṭirakkō	*Puṟanāṉūṟu* 151
Iḷaṅ kumaṇaṉ	*Puṟanāṉūṟu* 165
Iḷaveḷimāṉ	*Puṟanāṉūṟu* 207, 237
Iḷaviccikkō	*Puṟanāṉūṟu* 151
Kaḻuvuḷ (Kamur)	*Akanāṉūṟu* 135; 365
Kaṅkaṉ	*Akanāṉūṟu* 44
Kanṭirakkōperunaḷḷ (Totti hills)	*Puṟanāṉūṟu* 148, 149, 150
Kaṭiya Neṭuvēttuvaṉ	*Puṟanāṉūṟu* 205
Katti	*Akanāṉūṟu* 44, 226
Matti (Kalar)	*Akanāūṟu* 6, 211
Mucunṭai (Vempi)	*Akanāṉūṟu* 249
Mūvaṉ	*Puṟanāṉūṟu* 209

Nāñcil Vaḷḷuvaṉ	*Puṟanāṉūṟu* 137-40
Ñimili	*Akanāṉūṟu* 142; 148
Ōymāṉ Nalliyātan	*Puṟanāṉūṟu* 376
Ōymāṉ Villiyātan	*Puṟanāṉūṟu* 379
Paṇṇaṉ	*Puṟanāṉūṟu* 70; 173
Piṭṭaṅkoṟṟan (Kutiramalai)	*Puṟanāṉūṟu* 168-72
Pulli (Vēṅkaṭam hills)	*Akanāṉūṟu* 61, 83
Ṭittaṉ	*Akanāṉūṟu* 6; 122
	Puṟanāṉūṟu 80, 352
Talumpan (Unūr)	*Puṟanāṉūṟu* 348
Veḷimāṉ	*Puṟanāṉūṟu* 162, 237, 238
Viccikkōṉ	*Puṟanāṉūṟu* 200

APPENDIX-13

LIST OF KIḺĀR

Ampar Kiḻān Aruvantai	: *Puṟanāṉūṟu* 385
Cirukuṭi Kiḻān Paṇṇaṉ	: *Puṟanāṉūṟu* 173, 388
Karumpaṉūr Kiḻāṉ	: *Puṟanāṉūṟu* 381, 384
Koṇkaṇaṅ Kiḻān	: *Puṟanāṉūṟu* 154-56
Malli Kiḻān Kāriyati	: *Puṟanāṉūṟu* 177
Nālai Kiḻavaṉ Nākaṉ	: *Puṟanāṉūṟu* 179
Poṟyaṟṟu Kiḻāṉ	: *Puṟanāṉūṟu* 391
Vallār Kiḻāṉ Paṇṇaṉ	: *Puṟanāṉūṟu* 187

BIBLIOGRAPHY

PRIMARY SOURCES : TAMIL

Eṭṭutokai

Aiṅkuṟunūṟu (1980) U. V. Swaminatha Aiyer (ed. with Tamil commentary) U.V. Swaminatha Aiyer Publication, Madras, (6th ed.)

Akanāṉūṟu (1951-54) Vēṅkaṭacāmi Nāṭṭar and Venkatacalam Pillai (ed. with Tamil commentary), South India Saiva Siddhanta Publishing Society, Tirunelveli, Vol. I, 3rd ed., Vol. II-3rd ed., Vol. III, 2nd ed.

Kalittokai (1958) Rajamanikkanar (with Tamil commentary), Valluvar pannai, Madras.

Kuṟuntokai (1978) P.V. Comacuntaraṉār (ed. wtih commentary) South India Saiva Siddhanta Publishing Society, Tirunelveli (4th ed.)

Naṟṟiṇai (1976) A. Narayancāmi Aiyer (ed. with commentary) and P.V. Comacuntaranar (supplementary commentary), South India Saiva Siddhanta Publishing Society

Paripāṭal (1956) P.V.Comacuntaraṉār (ed. with Tamil commentary), South India Saiva Siddhanta Publishing Society, Tirunelveli, (4th ed.)

Patiṟṟuppattu (1955) Auvai Duraicāmi Pillai (ed. wtih Tamil commentary), South India Saiva Siddhanta Publishing Society, Tirunelveli (2nd ed.)

Puṟanāṉūṟu (1956) Auvai Duraicāmi Pillai (ed. with commentary) South India Saiva Siddhanta Publishing Society, Tirunelveli, Vol. I (3rd ed.), Vol. II (2nd ed.).

Ibid (1963) U.V. Swaminatha Aiyer (ed. with commentary), Tamil University, Tancavur (6th ed.)

Pattuppāṭṭu

Pattuppāṭṭu (1961) 1986	U.V. Swaminatha Aiyer (ed. with commentary), Tamil University, Tancavur (Rp.)
Ciṟupāṇāṟṟuppaṭai 1972	P.V. Comacuntaraṉār (ed. with Tamil commentary), South India Saiva Siddhanta Publishing Society, Tinnevelly (Rp.)
Kuṟiñcippāṭṭu (1972)	P.V. Comacuntaranar (ed. with Tamil commentary), South India Saiva Siddhanta Publishing Society, Tinnevelly (Rp.).
Maturaikkāñci (1971)	P.V. Comacuntaranar (ed. with Tamil commentary), South India Saiva Siddhanta Publishing Society, Tinnevelly (Rp.)
Malaipaṭukaṭām (1970)	P.V. Comacuntaranar (ed. with Tamil commentary), South India Saiva Siddhanta Publishing Society, Tinnevelly (Rp.)
Mullaippāṭṭu (1970)	P.V. Comacuntaraṉār (ed. with Tamil commentary), South India Saiva Siddhanta Publishing Society, Tinnevelly (Rp.)
Neṭunojvāṭai (1967)	P.V. Comacuntaraṉār (ed. with Tamil commentary), South India Saiva Siddhanta Publishing Society, Tinnevelly (Rp.)
Paṭṭinappālai (1972)	P.V. Comacuntaraṉār (ed. with Tamil commentary), South India Saiva Siddhanta Publishing Society, Tinnevelly (Rp.)
Perumpāṇāṟṟuppaṭai (1967)	P.V. Comacuntaraṉār (ed. with Tamil commentary), South India Saiva Siddhanta Publishing Society, tinnevelly (Rp.)
Porunarāṟṟuppaṭai (1970)	P.V. Comacuntaraṉār (ed. with Tamil commentary), South India Saiva Siddhanta Publishing Society, Tinnevelly (Rp.)
Tirumurukāṟṟuppaṭai (1971)	P.V. Comacuntaraṉār (ed. with Tamil commentary), South India Saiva Siddhanta Publishing Society, Tinnevelly (Rp.)
Pattuppāṭṭu (1961)	V.M. Gopalakrishnamachariar (with commentary), Madras.

Epics

Cilappatikāram (1992)	Vēṅcatacāmi Nāṭṭar (ed. with commentary), South India Saiva Siddhanta works Publishing Society, Tinnevelly Tinnevelly. (Rp.)

Maṇimēkalai (1992) — Vencatacami Nāṭṭar (ed with commentary), South India Saiva Siddhanta Works Publishing Society, Tinnevelly (Rp.)

Patinüeṇkiḻkaṇakku

Patiṉeṇkiḻkaṇakku (1981) — New Century Book House, Madras (2nd ed.)

Ācārakkōvai (1976) — Aḻakar Aṭikal (commentary) South India Saiva Siddhanta Works Publishing Society, Tinnevelly (6th ed.)

Ibid (1992) — P.C. Punnaivananata Mutaliyar (commentary), South India Saiva Siddhanta Works Publishing Society, Tinnevelly (Rp.)

Aintiṇai Eḻupatu (1931) *Kaimilai* — Anantharama Iyer (commentary), South India Saiva Siddhanta Works Publishing Society, Tinnevelly.

Ēlāti (1975) — T.S. Balacundaram Pillai (with commentary), South India Saiva Siddhanta Works Publishing Society, Tinnevelly (6th ed.)

Iṉṉā Nāṟpatu (1973) — Vencatacāmi Nāṭṭar (with commentary), South India Saiva Siddhanta Works Publishing Society, Tinnevelly (10th ed.)

Mutumoḻikkāñci (1976) — Aḻakar Aṭikal (with commentary), South India Saiva Siddhanta Works Publishing Society, Madras, (Rp.)

Nāṉmaṇikkaṭikai (1980) — T.C. Balacundaram Pillai (with commentary), South India Saiva Siddhanta Works Publishing Society. Tinnevelly, (Rp.)

TOLKĀPPIYAM

Tolkāppiyam Porulatikāram (1983) Nacciṉārkkiṉiyar commentary, South India Saiva Siddhanta Works Publishing Society, Tinnevelly (Rp.)

Tolkāppiyam Porulatikāram (1951) Perāciriyar commentary, South India Saiva Siddhanta Works Publishing Society, Tinnevelly, Tinnevelly, First ed.

SECONDARY SOURCES AND TRANSLATIONS

Adams, R.M.C. (1956) — *The Evolution of Urban Society* Chicago.

Ibid (1979) — "The Natural History of Urbanism" in G. Possehl (ed.) *Ancient Cities of the Indus*, Vikas, New Delhi, pp. 18-26.

Adhya, G.L. (1966) *Early Indian Economics: Studies in the Economic life of northern-western India* (200 B.C.-300 A.D), Asia Publishing House, New Delhi.

Allchin, B. and Allchin, R. *The Birth of Indian* (1968) *Civilization,* Hammondsworth.

Ibid (1983) *This Rise of Civilization in India and Pakistan,* Select book Service, New Delhi.

Allchin, B. (1966) *The Stone Tipped Arrow, London.*

Arasu, M.R. (1974) "Naṭukallum Ilakkiyamum" in R. Nagaswamy (Ed.) *Seminar on Hero Stones,* Madras, p. 19-20

Arokiaswami, M. (1956) *The Kongu country being the history of the modern districts of Coimbatore and Salem from the earliest times to the coming of the Brithsh,* University of Madras, Madras.

Ibid (1972) *The classical Age of the Tamils,* University of Madras, Madras.

Arunachalam, M. "Puṛanāṇūṛu and a Rethinking on Ganapathi worship in Tamil Nadu" R. Nagaswamy (ed.) *South Indian Studies II*, Society for Archaeological Historical and Epigraphical research, Madras, 1979, pp. 31-46.

Arunachalam, P. (1968) "Vetci: or the first stage of war during the Sangam period", *Proceedings of the Second International Conference Seminar of Tamil Studies,* Madras, pp. 207-212.

Arunachalam, P. (ed.) (1986-88) *Śaṅga Ilakkiya Poruṭ Kaḷañjiyam,* 3 Vols. (Tamil University, Thanjavur)

Balambal, V. "Home life of the Ancient Tamils" in S.V. Subramanian, K.D. Thirunavukkarasu (ed.) *Historical Heritage of the Tamils,* International Institute of Tamil Studies, Madras, 1983, pp. 315-24.

Balakrishnan Nayar, T. (1977) The Problem of Dravidian Origins-A Linguistic, Anthropological and Archaeological Approach, Madras University, Madras.

Balasubramanian. C. (1976) *The status of women in Tamil Nadu during the Sangam Age,* University of Madras, Madras.

Balasubramaniam, K.M. (1987) *Pantai Tamiḻ Camutāyam Vaḷarcci: Oru Markciyapparvai,* Tamilap Puttakalayam.

Banerjee, N.R. (1965) *The Iron Age in India,* Delhi.

Begley, Vimala (1983) "Arikamedu Reconsidered" American Journal of Archaeology 87, pp. 461-81

Begley, Vimala "From Iron Age to Early Historical in South Indian Archaeology" Jerome Jacobson (ed.) *American Perspectives of South Asian Archaeology.*

Binford, L.R. "Archaeology as Anthropology" in L. Binford (ed.) *An Archaeological Perspective,* Seminar Press, New York, pp. 20-32.

Bonte, P. (1982) "Non-stratified social formations among Pastoral Nomads" in Friedman J. and Rowlands M.J. (ed.) *The Evolution of Social Systems,* Duckworth, pp. 173-200.

Bose, D. (1978) "Utilisation of Social and Cultural Anthropology in Historical Research:The case of the Impact of the Agriculture on some South Indian Societies in D. Chattopadhyaya (ed.) *History and Society,* Calcutta, pp. 25-45.

Bowra, C.M (1966) *Heroic Poetry,* London.

Burrow, T. & Emeneau, M.B. (1961) *A Dravidian Etymological Dictionary,* Oxford Clarendon Press.

Chakravarti, A. (1974) *Jaina Literature in Tamil,* with an Introduction, Footnotes, appendix and index, Bharatiya Jnanapitha Publications, New Delhi, Ist rev. ed.

Chakrabarti, D. (1976) "Beginning of Iron in India", *Antiquity,* Vol. L.

Chakravarti, UMA (1987) *The Social Dimensions of early Buddhism,* Oxford University Press, Delhi.

Champakalakshmi, R.& Swamy, A. (1969) "Pallava Antiquities in Periya Veṇmaṇi *Journal of the Madras University,* Vol. XLI, nos. 1 and 2, January-July, 1969, pp. 129-137 (Rp.)

Champakalakshmi, R. (1981) *Vaiṣṇava Iconography in the Tamil country,* Orient longman, New Delhi.

Champakalakshmi, R. (1982) 'Urban Process in Tamil Nadu'—occasional papers Urban History Association of India,.

Champakalakshmi, R. (1986) "Urbanisation in south India:the role of ideology and polity" in *Indian History Congress,* proceedings of the 47th Session, section I, Srinagar.

Champakalakshmi, R. (1989) (a) "Ideology and the State in South India"—Mamidipudi Venkatarangaiah Memorial Lecture, *Andhra Pradesh History Congress*, Proceedings of the thirteenth Session, Srisailam, 1989, pp. 278-307.

Champakalakshmi, R. (1989) (b) "The study of Settlement Patterns in the Cōḷa Period.: Some perspectives" *Man and Environment*, pp. 91-102.

Champakalakshmi, R. (1992) "Buddhism in Tamilakam:Patterns of Patronage" Paper presented at *International Seminar Buddhism* in Tamil Nadu, Madras, 25th-31st May.

Childe, V.G. (1951) *Social Evolution*, Watts & Co., London.

Childe, V.G. (1979) "The Urban Revolution" in G. Possehl (Ed.) *Ancient Cities of the Indus*, Vikas, New Delhi, pp. 12-18.

Chelliah J.V. (Tr.) (1962) *Pattupāṭṭu: Ten Tamil Idyls*, South India Saiva Siddhanta Works Publishing Society, Tinnevelly.

Claessen and Skalnik (1978) *The Early State*, Mouten, The Hague.

Clothey, Fred, W. (1978) *The many faces of Murukaṉ : the history and meaning of a South Indian God*, Mouton Publishers, The Hague.

Danielou, A. (Tr.) (1965) *Shilappadikāram* (*The Ankle Bracelet*) George Allen and Unwin, London.

Daryll Forde, C (1971) *Habitat, Economy and Society*, London (Reprint)

Deo, S.B. (1981) "Some aspects of Megalithic Technology", M.S. Nagaraja Rao (ed.) Madhu: *Recent Researches in Indıan Archaeology and Art History, Shri M.N. Deshpande, Festschrift*, Agam Kala Prakashan, Delhi, pp. 33-35.

Deo, S.B. (1983) "The megaliths : their culture, ecology, economy and technology". Paper presented at an international Conference on *Recent advances in Indian archaeology*, Deccan College Post graduate & Research Institute, Pune, December, pp. 1-19.

Dikshitar, V.R.R. (1936) *Studies in Tamil literature and history, University of Madras*, Madras.

Dikshitar, V.R.R. (Tr.) (1949) *Tirukkuṟal* of Tiruvaḷḷuvar Adyar Library, Madras.

Dirks, N.B (1976) "Political authority and structural change in early South India". *Indian Economic and Social History Review*, Vol. XIII, no. 2, pp. 125-57.

Dorai Rangaswamy, M.A. (1968) *The Surnames of the Caṅkam Age:Literary and Tribal,* University of Madras, Madras.

Dsekmeier, Charles (1962) Kingship and Commnity nearly India, Stanford, University Press, California and Oxford University Press, Bombay.

Dubianski, Alexander, M. (1979) "An analysis of the Mullai-Pālai Fragment of Anicient Tamil Poetry", *Journal of Tamil Studies,* Vol. 15, pp. 88-103.

Earle, T.K. and Brumfiel, E.M. *Specialisation, Exchange (ed.)* (1987) *and complex societies,* Cambridge University Press, Cambridge.

Ekambaranathan, A. (1981) *Iconographic Concepts and Forms of Śiva in the Tamil Country (as revealed by literature and epigraphs upto 9th Century A.D.) unpublished Ph. D thesis, Department of Ancient History and Archaeology, University of Madras, Madras.*

Ekholm, Kajsa (1982) "External Exchange and the transformation of Central African Social systems" in Friedman, J. and Rowlands M.J. (ed.) *The Evolution of Social Systems* Duckworth

Eliade, Mircea (1958) *Patterns in comparative Religion* (Tr. Rosemary sheed)

Encyclopaedia of Tamil Literature 1990, Vol. one Introductory Articles, Published by Institute of Asian Studies, Madras,

Finnegan, Ruth (1982) *The Penguin Book of Oral Poetry*

Friedman, J. & Rowlands M.J. (1982) "Notes towards an epigenetic model of the evolution of civilisation" in Friedman J. and Rowlands M.J. (ed.) *The Evolution of Social Systems,* Duckworth, pp. 201-78.

Fried, M. (1967) *The Evolution of Political Society;* Random House, New York.

Friedberg, Claudine "The development of traditional agricultural practices in Western Timor:from the ritual control of consumer goods production to the political control of prestige goods." in Friedman J. and Rowlands M.J. (ed.) *The Evolution of Sicial Systems,* Duckworth, 1982, pp. 137-171.

Gandhimathi, R. (1986) *Historical Gleanings from Paripādal,* unpublished M.Phil Dissertation, University of Madras.

Ghurye, G.S. (1972) *Two Brahmanical Institutions. Gōtra and Charana,* Popular Prakashan, Bombay.

Ghurye, G.S. (1977) *Indian Acculturation Agastya and Skanda,* Popular Prakashan, Bombay.

Girija, C. (1976) "Elimalai in Sangam polity", *Indian History Congress,* Proceedings of the thirty seventh session, Calicut, 1976, pp. 56-91.

Godelier, M. (1977) "Salt Money and the circulation of commodities among the Baruya of New Guinea" - *Perspectives of Marxist Anthropology,* Cambridge University Press, pp. 127-51.

Godelier, M. (1977) *Perspectives in Marxist Anthropology,* Cambridge University Press, Cambridge.

Godelier, M. (1982) "Economy and religion: an evolutionary optical illusion" in Friedman J. and Rowlands M.J. (ed.) *The Evolution of Sicial Systems* Proceedings of a meeting of the Research Seminar in Archaeology and related subjects held at the Institute of Archaeology, London University, Duckworth.

Godelier, M. (1982) "Politics as 'infrastructure' :an anthropologist's thoughts on the example of classical Greece and the notions of relations of production and economic determination" in Friedman, J.and Rowlands M.J. (ed.) *The Evolution of Social Systems* Proceedings of a meeting of the Research Seminar in Archaeology and related subjects held at the Institute of Archaeology, London University, Duckworth, 1982.

Gloria Sundaramathy, L. (1975) "The Women poets of Caṅkam Age", *Journal of Tamil Studies,* Vol. 8, pp. 62-79

Gregory, C.A. (1982) *Gifts and Commodities,* Academic Press, London

Goody, Jack (1982) "Population and polity in the voltaic region" in Friedman J and Rowlands M.J. (ed.) *The Evolution of Social Systems,* Duckworth, pp. 535-46.

Gupta, P.L. (1965) "A bibilography of the hoards of punch marked coins of Ancient India" *Journal of the Numismatic Society of Ancient India,* Vol. XVII, pp. 15-19.

Gururaja Rao, B.K. (1970) "Development of Technology during the Iron Age in South India (c. 1000 B.C. to the beginning of the historical times) *Indian Journal of History of Science,* Vol. 5, No.2, pp. 253-271 (Reprint)

Gururaja Rao, B.K. (1971) "Megalithic Culture in Tiruchirapalli District' in *Prof. K.A.N. Sastri Felicitation Volume,* Madras, pp. 202-05.

Gururaja Rao, B.K. (1972) *The Megalithic Culture in South India,* Mysore.

Gurukkal, R. (1981) "Aspects of Early Iron Age economy:problems of Agrarian Expansion in Tamilakam", *Indian History Congress,* Proceedings, pp. 7-82.

Gurukkal, R. (1989) (a) "Forms of Production and Forces of change in Ancient Tamil Society" *Studies in History,* 5, 2 ns, pp. 159-75

Gurukkal, R. (1989) (b) "Political process and social formation in early Tamilakam" Paper presented at the seminar on *The State in Precolonial South India* held at Jawahar Lal Nehru University.

Gurukkal, R. (1993) "Towards the voice of Dissent, The Trajectory of Ideological Transformation in Early India."

Harm de Blij (1971) *Geography: Regions and Concepts,* USA.

Handoo, Jawaharalal (1976) "Levi Strauss and Cilappatikāram Myth and Method" in *Journal of Tamil Studies,* Vol. 10, pp. 13-22.

Hanumanthan, K.R. (1977) "Was there untouchability in early tamil Society" *Indian History Congress,* Proceedings of the thirty eighth session, Utkal University (Bhubaneshwar), pp. 90-91.

Hardy, Friedhelm (1983) "*Viraha-Bhakti:The early history of Krishna Devotion in South India",* Oxford:University Press.

Hart III, George L. (1974) "Some aspects of kinship in ancient Tamil Literature" Thomas R. Trautamnn (ed.) *Kinship and history in South Asia,* Ann Arbor

Hart, George, L. (1975) *The poems of ancient Tamil : their mulieu and their Sanskrit counterparts,* University of California Press, Berkeley.

Hart, III George L. (1976) (a) "Ancient Tamil Literature:its scholarly past and future", B.Stein (ed.) *Essays on South India,* New Delhi, pp. 41-64.

Hart, III George L. (1976) (b) *Relation between Tamil and classical Sanskrit literature,* Wiesbaden

Hart George L. (1979) *Poets of the Tamil Anthologies—Ancient poems of Love and War*, Princeton University Press, Princeton.

Hart, George L. (1987) "Women and the sacred in Ancient Tamil Nad" George W. Spencer (ed.) *Temples: Kings and peasants: Perceptions of South India's past,* New Era Publications, Madras, pp. 1-28

Heesterman, J.C. (1957) *The Ancient Indian Royal Consecration.*

Hindess, Barry and Hirst, Paul Q. (1979) *Pre Capitalist Modes of Production,* Routledge and Kegan Paul, London, (Rp.)

Hikosaka, SHU (1988) "The Age of Cilappatikāram and Maṇimēkalai" *Journal of the Institute of Asian Studies,* Vol. V, No.2, March, pp. 91-114 (Institute of Asian Studies, Madras).

Ilakkuvanar (1963) *Tolkāppiyam* (in English) with critical Studies, madurai.

Jaiswal, S. (1977) "Studies in the Social Structure of Early Tamils' in R.S. Sharma and V.N. Jha (ed.) *Indian Society: Historical Probings,* (Reprint), pp. 124-55.

Jaiswal, Suvira (1991) "Varna Ideology and Social Change" *Social Scientist,* Vol. 19, Nos. 3-4, pp. 41-48.

Jesudasan, C & Jesudasan, H. *A history of Tamil Literature,* Calcutta.

John, K.J. (1975) "Early Man in Wynad" *Journal of Kerala Studies,* Vol. II, pp. 125-31.

John Samuel, G. (1978) *Studies in Tamil Poetry,* Mani Pathippakam, Madras.

John Samuel, G. (1979) *Collected Papers on Tamil Literature,* Mani Pathippakam, Madras.

Jotimuthu, P. (Tr.) (1984) *Ainkurunuru* (with commentary) Christian Literature Society, Madras.

Kailasapathy, K. (1968) "Tamil heroic Poetry :A comparative Study", *Proceedings of the Second International Conference of Tamil Studies,* Vol.II, Madras, January, pp. 152-57

Kailasapathy, K. (1986) *On Art and Literature,* New Century Book House, Madras

Kanakasabhai, V. (1956) *The Tamils Eighteen Hundred years ago,* Madras (2nd edition)

Kandaswamy K.N. (1981) "The Age of Tolkāppiyam". *Journal of Tamil Studies,* Vol. 20, pp. 37-71.

Kandaswamy, S.P. (1984) "The Kongu and Roman coins" Journal of the *Numismatic Society of India,* Vol. XLVI, pp. 39-44.

Karve, Irawati (1968) *Hindu Society an inter pretation* 2nd. ed. Poona, 1968.

Kasinathan, N. (1988) "The Date of Tamil Brahmi Inscriptions", paper presented in the Seminar on Tamil Brahmi Scripts.

Kasinathan, N. (1992) *Alagankulam:A preliminary Report,* State Department of Archaeology, Madras.

Kennedy Richard, S. (1976) "The King in South India as Chieftain and Emperor". *Indian Historical Review,* Vol.III, July, pp. 1-15.

Kersenboom Story, S.C. (1981) "Viṟali: (possible sources of the Devadasi tradition in the Tamil Bardic period)", *Journal of Tamil Studies,* Vol. 19, pp. 19-41.

Krishnaswami Aiyangar, S. (1918) *The beginnings of South Indian History,* Modern Printing Works, Madras.

Krishnaswami Aiyangar, S. (1923) *Some contributions of south India to Indian Culture,* University of Calcutta, 1923.

Krishnaswami Aiyangar, S. (1929) *Beginnings of South Indian History,* Madras.

Krishnaswami, V.D. (1949-50) "Megalithic Types of South India" *Ancient India,* No.5-6, pp. 35-45.

Kuppuram, G. (1983) "Tribes of Tamil Nadu" S.V. Subramanian, K.D. Thirunavukkarasu (ed.) *Historical Heritage of the Tamils,* International Institute of Tamil Studies, Madras, pp. 75-89.

Kuppuswamy, T.V. (1978) "The Brahmanas and Brahmanism in Sangham literature" *Bulletin of the Institute of Traditional Cultures,* Madras, pp. 131-64 (Reprint).

Kuppuswamy, T.V. (1978) "Matrix of the Social structure of the early Tamils" *Indian History Congress,* 39th Session.

Kuppuswamy, T.V. (1984) *Sangam Chieftains and their times,* Tanjore.

Leshnik, Lawrence, S. (1974) *South Indian 'Megalithic' Burials : the Pandukal Complex,* Franz Steiner Verlag Gmbh, Wiesbaden, 1974.

Leshnik, L.S. (1975) "Nomads and Burials in the early history of South India", in Leshnik and Sontheimer (ed.) *Pastoralists and Nomads in South Asia,* Weisbaden.

Mahadevan, I. (1966) 1968 "Corpus of the Tamil Brahmi Inscriptions" R. Nagaswamy (ed.) *Seminar on Inscriptions,* Madras, pp. 57-73

Mahadevan, I. (1968) "Tamil Brahmi Inscriptions of the Sangam Age", *Proceedings of the Second International conference, Seminar of Tamil Studies,* Vol.I. Damilica II, pp. 60-64.

Mahadevan, I. (1970) *Tamil Brahmi Inscriptions,* Madras, 1970.

Mahadevan, I. (1974) "The Shorter U in Tamil Brahmi Script" Paper read at the *Fourth All India Conference of the Dravidian Linguistic Association,* Madras, June.

Mahalingam, T.V. (1974) The Naga Cult in India, *Bulletin of the Institute of Traditional Cultures,* Madras, pp. 11-18 (Rp.)

Mahalingam, T.V. (1966) "Inscribed potsherds from Alagarai and Uraiyur" in R. Nagaswamy (ed.) *Seminar on Inscriptions,* Madras., pp. 42-43.

Mahalingam T.V. (1970) *Excavations in the Lower Kaveri Valley,* Madras 1970.

Mahalingam T.V. (1974) *Early South Indian Palaeography* Rp. Madras

Maloney, Clarence (1969) "The Paratavar:2000 years of Culture Dynamics of a Tamil Caste", *Man in India,* Vol. 49, 3, September 1969, pp. 224-240.

Maloney, Clarence (1970) "The beginnings of civilization in South India" *Journal of Asian Studies,* Vol. XXIX, no. 3, pp. 603-616.

Maloney, Clarence (1976) "Archaeology in South India-Accomplishments and Prospects" in B.Stein (ed.) *Essays on South India,* Vikas, New Delhi, pp. 1-40.

Mangalam, S.J. (1982) "Roman Coins from Kerala" in A.V. Narasimha Murthy (ed.) *Studies in South Indian Coins,* Vol.II, New Era Publications, Madras, 1992, pp. 61-66.

Manickavasagom, M.E. "Administrative system of the anicient Tamils" in S.V. Subramaniam. K.D. Thirunavukkarasu (ed.) *Historical heritage of the Tamil, International Institute of Tamil Studies,* Madras.

Manickam, V.T. 1966 (1968) "Harlots in Ancient Tamil literature", *Proceedings of the First International Conference Seminar of Tamil Studies* Kuala Lam put, pp. 338-45.

Margbandhu, C. (1983) "Ancient sea ports of South India their trade relationship with the Western world during the First century B.C. to Second Century A.D." in B.N. Mukherjee, D.R.Das, S.S. Biaswas et al. *Sri Dinesa-candrika Studies in Indology, Shri D.C. Sircar Festschrift,* Sundeep Prakashan, Delhi, pp. 185-202.

Marr, J.R. (1968) "The lost decades of patiṟṟuppattu" Proceedings of the Second International Conference Seminar of Tamil Studies, Madras.

Marr, J.K. (1985) *The Eight Anthologies* : a study in early Tamil Literature, Madras.

Mauss, Marcel (1970) *The Gift : Forms and Functions of Exchange in Archaic Societies* (Tr.) Ian Cunnison, Cohen and West, London.

Meenakshisundaram, T.P. (1965) *A history of Tamil literature,* Annamalai Universtiy.

Muller, J. (1987) "Salt, Chert and Shell : Mississipian Exchange and Economy" in E.M. Brumfiel and T.K. Earḷe (Ed.) *Specialisation, Exchange and Complex Societies,* Cambridge, Universtiy Press, London.

Murphy, William, P. (1978) "Oral Literature", Annual Review of Anthropology, Vol. 7, pp. 113-36.

Murugesa Mudaliar, N. (1971) "Polity in Tirukkuṛal" in Tirukkural Lectures,1959-1960—1968-69, Part-I, English, *Thirumathi Sornammal Endowment Lectures,* University of Madras, pp. 499- 623.

Muthuswamy, E.S. (1987) "State Formation in An cient Tamil Nadu", *Journal of Tamil Studies* Vol. 31, pp. 95-102.

Nagaraju, S. & Gururaja Rao, B.K. "Chronology of Iron Age in South India" D.P. Agarwal & Dilip Charkabarti (ed.) *Essays in Indian Protohistory.* B.R.Publishing Corporation, Delhi, 1979, pp. 329-329.

Nagaswamy, R. (1973) *Yāvarum Kēḷir,* Vacakar Vattam, Madras.

Nagaswamy, R. (1973) *Kaveripattinam—A guide* Tamil Nadu State Department of Archaeology, Madras.

Nagaswamy, R. (ed.) (1974) *Seminar of Hero Stones,* State Department of Archaeology, Government of Tamil Nadu, Madras.

Nagaswamy, R.& Majeed, A. (1978) *Vasavasamudram,* Tamil Nadu State Department of Archaeology, Madras.

Nagaswamy, R. (1981) "An outstanding epigraphical discovery in Tamil Nadu", *Proceedings of the Fifth International conference Seminar of Tamil Studies,* Madurai, Section 2, pp. 67-72.

Nagaswamy, R. (1991) "Alagankulam: An Indo Roman Trading Port" *Indian Archaeological Heritage, K.V. Soundara Rajan, Festschrift,* Vol. I, Agam Kala Prakashan, Delhi, 1991, pp. 247-255.

Nandakumar, Prema (Tr.) (1989) *Maṇimēkalai,* Tamil University, Thanjavur

Nandakumar, Prema (1992) "Inspirer of the sacred Narrative in Tamil literature", paper Presented at International Seminat: *Buddhism in Tamil Nadu,* Madras 25th-31st May.

Narayanan, M.G.S. (1975) "The Vedic Puraṇic-Sastraic Element in Tamil Sangam society and culture: (a study of Purananuru-First section), *Indian History Congress,* Proceedings of the thirty Sixth Session, Aligarh, pp. 76-91.

Narayanan, M.G.S. (1977) (a) *Re Interpretations in South Indian History,* Trivandrum, 1977.

Narayanan, M.G.S. (1977) (b) "Cattle reiders of the Sangam Age" *Indian History Congress,* Proceedings of the Thirty Eighth Session, Utkal Universtiy (Bhubaneshwar), pp. 70-82.

Narayanan, M.G.S. (1982) "The Warrior Settlements of the Sangam Age", *Indian History Congress,* Proceedings of the 43rd Session, Kurukshetra, pp. 102-09.

Narayanan, M.G.S. (1987) "A critique of the history of South India and a proposal for a new conceptual frame" *South Indian History Congress,* 7th Session, 9-14th of January, 1987, Madras University.

Narayanan, M.G.S. (1989) "The cult of war as class ideology in the Sangam Age in South India", *Indian History Congress*-Proceedings of the 49th session, Karnatak University, Dharwad, 1988, pp. 109-113.

Narayanan, M.G.S. (1990) "Social History From the Text Book of Poetics in the Sangam Age" (A study of Tolkappiyam-Section

IV-Porulatikaram)" *Indian History Congress,* Proceedings of the 51st Session, Calcutta, December.

Natarajan, B. (1971) "Economic ideas of Thiruvalluvar" in *Thirumathi Sornammal Endowment lectures on Tirukkural,* 1959-60 to 1968-69, Part-I-English, University of Madras, pp. 55-106.

Nath, Vijay (1987) *Dānā : Gift System in ancient India* (c. 600 B.C-c. A.D. 300) *A Socio-economic perspective,* Munshiram Manoharlal Publishers Pvt. Ltd., Delhi.

Nilakanta Sastri, K.A. (1939) *Foreign Notices of South India,* Madras.

Nilakanta Sastri, K.A. (1958) *A History of South India: from Pre historic Times to the fall of Vijayanagar,* Oxford University press, Oxford (2nd edition)

Nilakanta Sastri, K.A. (1972) *Sangam Literature: its cults and cultures,* Swati Publications, Madras.

Nilakanta Sastri, K.A. (1987) "Sanskrit Elements in Early Tamil Literature" in K.M. Shrimali (ed.) *Essays In Indian Art, Religion and Society: Indian history Congress,* Golden Jubilee Year publication, series Vol. One, Munshiram Manoharlal, New Delhi, pp. 45-58.

Pandian, A. Bhaskar (1974) "Ilakkiyattil Naṭukal" in R. Nagaswamy (ed.) *Seminar on Hero Stones,* State Department of Archaeology, Tamil Nadu, 1974, pp. 72-74.

Pannerselvam, R. (1966) "An important brahmi Tamil inscription a reconstruction of the genealogy of the cera kings", *Proceedings of the First International Conference of Tamil Studies,* Volume I, Kuala Lumpur, April, 1966.

Paramasivam, K. (1983) "Religion and Kingship in Caṅkam literature in S.V. Subramanian, R. Vijayalakshmi (Ed.) *Philosophical Heritage of the Tamils,* Interantional Institute of Tamil Studies, Madras, 1983, pp. 141-50.

Paranivitana, S. (1970) *Inscriptions of Ceylon.*

Parpola, A (1973) *Arguments for an Aryan Origin of the South Indian Megaliths,* Tamil Nadu State department of Archaeology, Madras.

Pearson, Michael Parker (1984) "Social Change, ideology and archaeological record" Mathew Spriggs (ed.) *Marxist Perspectives in Archaeology* (new Directions in Archaeology) Cambridge University Press, pp. 59-71.

Pillay, K.K. (1969) *A Social History of the Tamils,* Pt. 1, University of Madras, Madras.

Pillay, K.K. (1979) "Naṟṟiṇai in its Historical setting" in Studies in Indian History (with special reference to Tamil Nade), Madras, pp. 121-84.

Pillay, K.K. (1979) "Rise and growth of the caste system in Tamil Nadu", *Studies in the History of India with special reference to Tamil Nadu,* Madras, pp. 292-416.

Pope, G.U. (Tr.) (1958) *Nālaṭiyār,* South India Saiva Siddhanta Works Publishing Society Ltd. Tinnevelly, 1958.

Purnalingam Pillai, M.S.(1985) *Tamil Literature,* Tamil University, Thanjavur, (Revised and enlarged)

Raghava Varier, M.R. (1988) "Marine Technology in ancient Tamilakam" *Indian History Congress,*

Proceedings of the 49th Session Karnatak University, Dharwad, 1988 (1989), pp. 114-21.

Rajamanickam, M. (1966) "Aspects of social life of the Tamils in the Sangam Age" *Proceedings of the First International Conference Seminar of Tamil Studies,* Kuala Lampur, Vol. 1, pp. 332-37.

Rajan, K. (1991) "A chronological note on the punchmarked coins of Tamil Nadu" A.V. Narasimhamurthy (ed.) *Studies in South Indian coins* Vol.I, New Era Publications, Madras 1991, pp. 17-22.

Rajan, K. (1990) "New light on the Megalithic culture of the Kongu Region", Tamil Nadu, *Man and Environment*, Vol. XV, January-June, pp. 93-102.

Rajalakshmi, C. (1975) "Women in the Age of the Caṅkam", *Journal of Tamil Studies,* Vol. 8, pp. 88-92.

Raju, S. (1983) "The Chieftains of the Sangam Age" in S.V. Subramanian, K.D. Thirunavukkarasu (ed.) *Historical Heritage of the Tamils,* International Institute of Tamil Studies, Madras, pp. 253-265.

Ramachandran, B. (1958) Study of weight standards of silver punch marked coins of Mambalam and coins of Mambalam and Bodinayakkanur hoards. *Transactions of the Archaeological Society of South India,* 1957-58, Madras.

Ramachandran, C.E. (1971) "Sangam Literature as a source" S.C. Malik (ed.) *Indian Civilization. The First Phase/problems of a source book* (Based on the Proceedings of a Seminar), Indian Institute of Advanced Study, Simla, 1971, pp. 165-70.

Ibid (1974) *Ahananuru in its Historical setting,* University of Madras, Madras.

Ramachandran, K.S. (1962) "Some Aspects of the Economy of the Indian Megalith Builders", *Indian Historical quarterly,* Vol. XXXVIII 1, 1962, pp. 102-09.

Ibid (1980) *Archaeology of South India Tamil Nadu,* Sandeep Prakashan, New Delhi, 1980.

Raman, K.V. & Shanmugam, p. "Terracotta coin moulds (1991) from Kanchipuram," A.V. Narasimhamurthy (ed.) *Studies in South Indian coins* Vol. I, New Era Publications, Madras, 1991, pp. 23-29.

Raman, K.V. (1968) "Some Ancient crafts and Technology in Tamil Nad as revealed in Excavations" *Proceedings of the Second International Conference Seminar of Tamil Studies,* Madras Vol.II, January, pp. 394-401.

Ibid (1975) Brahmi Inscriptions of Tamil Nad: A historical Assessment" in Z.A. Desai and A.M. Shastri (Ed.) *Studies in Indian Epigraphy,* Mysore, pp. 104-118.

Ibid (1976) "Archaeology of the Sangam Age" *Indian History congress* Proceedings, Calicut, pp. 50-56.

Ibid (1978) "Tamil Nadu and Kerala: Archaeological Investigations in the Recent past in B.K. Gururaja Rao (ed.) *A Decade of Archaeological Studies in South India,* Dharwar, pp. 1-10.

Ramanujan, A.K. (Tr.) (1967) *The Interior Landscape: Love Poems from a classical Tamil anthology,* Indiana University Press, Bloomington, 1967.

Ibid (1985) *Poems of Love and War: from the Eight Anthologies and the Ten long poems of classical Tamil,* Oxford University press, Delhi.

Ray, Himanshu Prabha (1986) *Monastery and Guild : Commerce under the Sātavāhanās,* Oxford University Press. Delhi.

Renfrew, Colin (1982) "Space, time and polity" in Friedman J. and Rowlands M. J. (ed.) *The Evolution of Social Systems,* Duckworth, 1982, pp. 89-114.

Sadasivan, D. (1968) *"Māmūlaṉār—A Sangam Poet",* Madras University Journal-Humanities," Vol. XL, No. 1.

Sahlins, Marshall (1972) *Stone Age Economics London.*

Sanjeevi, N. (1973) *Śaṅga Illakkiya Āraicci Aṭṭavaṇaikal* (research Tables on Sangam Literature) Published by the University of Madras.

Santhakumar, R. (1985) (*Roman coins in Tamil Nadu*) unpublished M.Phil. Dissertation,. University of Madras.

Sarangapani, R. (1984) *A critical study of Paripāṭal*. Publications Divisions, Madurai Kamaraj University, Madurai.

Sarma, I.K. (1992) "Archaeological Evidences Pertaining to Buddhism in Tamil Nadu", Paper presented at International Seminar; *Buddhism in Tamil Nadu,* Madras 25th-31st May.

Saroja, G.V. (1992) "History of Buddhism in Tamil Nadu", paper presented at International Seminar:*Buddhism in Tamil Nadu,* Madras, 25th-31st May.

Schoff, W.H.Tr (1912) *Periplus of the Erythrean Sea,* New York.

Shanmugham
Shan mugham, R. (1962) *The Social Life of the Tamils* unpublished M. Phil. Thesis, Madras University.

Selvanayagam, S. (1968) "The Regional Concept in geography and the classification of land in the Ancient Tamil Country" "*Proceedings of the Second International conference Seminar of Tamil Studies*" Madras, Vol. II, pp. 218-25.

Seneviratne, Sudarshan (1980-81) "Kalinga and Andhra. The process of Secondary State formation in early India Indian Historical Review" Vol. VII, Vol. 1-2, pp. 54-69.

Ibid (1985) *Social Base of Early buddhism: South East India and Sri Lanka 3rd Century B.C.-3rd Century A.D.* unpublished Ph.D. dissertation, Jawaharlal Nehru University, New Delhi.

Ibid (1989) "Pre-tate is State Societies : Transformations in the Political Ecology of South India with special reference to TamilNadu" paper presented at a *Seminar on the state in Pre-colonial* South India", Jawaharlal Nehru University, New Delhi.

Sharma, R.S. (1972) *Indian History Congress,* proceedings, 33rd Session, Muzaffarpur.

Ibid (1980) "From Gopati to Bhūpati "(a review of the changing position of the king)", *Studies in History,* Vol. II, No. 2, pp. 1-10.

Sharma, R.S. (1987) *Urban Decay in India* (c. 300-c. 1000), New Delhi.

Ibid (1991) *Aspects of Political Ideas and Institutions in Ancient India* (3rd rev. ed.) Delhi.

Shrimali, K.M. (1988) "Religion, Ideology and Society, *Indian History Congress* Proceedings, Dharwad.

Shulman, David (1982) "Poets and patrons in Tamil Literature and Literary legend" in Barbara Stoller Miller (Ed.) *The Powers of Art : Patronage in Indian Culture*, Oxford University Press, Delhi, p. 89-119.

Singaravelu, S. (1966) *Social life of the Tamils, The Classical period,* Department of Indian studies, University of Malaya, Kuala lampur.

Singh, R.L. (1971) *India : A Regional Geography,* National Geographical Society of India, Varanasi.

Siromoney, Gift & Jebarajan Emmanuel "A new Tamil Brahmi Inscription from Vikramangalam Madurai" Madras Christian College, Department of Statistics, *Scientific Report,* No. 37.

Sivaraja Pillai (1984) *Chronology of the early Tamils,* New Delhi (Repring)

Sivathamby, K. (1966) "An Analysis of the Anthropological significance of the Economic Activities and conduct code ascribed to Mullai tinai", *Proceedings of the First International Conference Seminar of Tamil Studies,* Kuala Lampur, pp. 320-31.

Ibid (1974) "Early South Indian Society and Economy; the Tinai Cancept" *Social Scientist,* Vol. 29, pp. 20-37.

Ibid (1981) *Drama in Ancient Tamil Society,* New Century Book House, Madras.

Ibid (1986) *Literary History in Tamil (a historiographical analysis)*, Tamil University, Thanjavur.

Smith, C. (1982) "Conditions of change in social stratification" in Friedman, J. and Rawlands M. J. (ed.) *The Evolutions of Social Systems,* Duckworth.

Soundararajan, K.V. (1967) "Determinant Factors in the Early History of Tamil

Nad" (Part I) *Journal of Indian History,* pp. 647-71.

Ibid (1968) Determinant Factors in the early History of Tamil Nadu" (Part-II) *Journal of Indian History,* pp. 39-64.

Ibid (1969) "Megaliths and black and red ware" A.K. Narain (ed.) *Seminar Papers on the problems of Megaliths in India,* memoirs of the Department of Ancient Indian History, Culture and Archaeology, No.3, Department of Ancient Indian History, culture and Archaeology, Faculty of Arts. Banaras Hindu University, Varanasi, pp. 69-89.

Spate O.H.K. & Learmouth (1972) *India and Pakistan, A General and Regional Geography,* London (Reprint with corrections).

Srinivasan, K.R. & Banerjee, N.R. (1953) "Survey of South Indian megaliths' in *Ancient India,* No. 9, 1953, pp. 103-115.

Srinivasan, K.R. (1946) "The Megalithic Burials and Urn fields of South India in the light of Tamil Literature and Tradition", *Ancient India,* No. 2, July, pp. 9-16.

Ibid (1958-59) The Megalithic monuments of South India-Literature and tradition" *Archaeological society of South India Transactions,* pp. 1-14.

Srinivas Iyengar, P.T. (1983) *History of the Tamils : from the earliest times to 1000* A.D. Asian Educational Services, New Delhi, (Reprint)

Srinivasan, T.M. (1970) "A brief account of the ancient irrigation engineering systems prevalent in South India" from *Indian Journal of History of Science,* Vol. 5, No. 2, pp. 315-25 (Reprint).

Srinivasan, T.M. 1970 (1971) "Water Lifting Devices in Ancient India: their origin and mechanisms (from the earliest times to c. A.D. 1000) from the *Indian Journal of History of Science,* Vol. 5, No. 2 (Reprint), pp. 379-89.

Srivastava, Balram (1964) "Economic significance of Roman coins found in India", *Journal of the Numismatic Society of India,* Vol. XXVI, Part II, pp. 222-27.

Stein, Burton (1980) *Peasant State, and Society in Medieval South India,* Oxford University Press, Delhi.

Subramanian, A — "Terracotta Art in Ancient Tamil Nad" (Rp.) from *Annals of Oriental Research,* Silver Jubille Volume, pp. 139-44.

Subramaniam, A.V. (Tr.) (1980) *The Ten Decades (patiṟṟuppttu: A Sangam poetical work),* Tamil Nadu Government's Translation of Classics Series : 5, Tamil Nadu Text Book Society, Madras.

Subramanian, A.V. (Tr.) (1989) *Naṟṟiṇai* (An Anthology of Amour) Department of Tamil Development-Culture, Govt. of Tamil Nadu, Madras.

Subrahmanian, N. (1963) "The Colophons of the Padiṟṟuppattu" *Uournal of the Madras University* (Section 'A' Humanities), Vol. XXXIV, No. 2, January, pp. 115-30, Reprint.

Ibid (1963) "Perum Choṟṟu Udiyaṉ Chēral Ādaṉ" *Journal of Indian History,* Vol. XLI Pt. II, August, Serial No. 122, pp. 465-474, Reprint.

Ibid (1966) *Pre-Pallavan Tamil Index* (Index of historical material in Pre Pallavan Tamil Literature), University of Madras Madras.

Ibid (1980) Śaṅgam Polity : *The Administration and Social Life of the Sangam Tamils,* Ennes Publications, Madurai, (Rev. ed.)

Subrahmanyam, R. (1962) *The Tundi copper Plate Grant of Visnukundin King Vikramendra Varma,* Hyderabad.

Sumathi, R. (1983) "*The Proto-history of Northern Tamiland : assessment of the potentiaities and processes of change*" —M.Phil Seminar Paper No.3 Centre for Historical Studies, Jawaharlal Nehru University, New Delhi.

Sumathi, R. (1984) "Trade and its impact on the early Tamils-The Cola experience"- unpublished M.Phil dissertation, Centre for Historical Studies, JNU, New Delhi.

Sundara, A. (1979) "Typology of megaliths in South India" in D.P. Agrawal, Dilip K. Chakrabarti (ed.) *Essays in Indian Protohistory,* B.R. Publishing Corporation, Delhi, pp. 331-40.

Sundaram, J. (1968) "Some Features of the Brahmi inscriptions of the Tamil Country", in R.Nagaswamy (ed.) *Seminar on Inscriptions: Speeches & Papers,* Books (India) Pvt. Ltd. Madras, pp. 74-77.

Suresh. S. (1992) "Recent" Antiquarian finds from Karur (Tamil Nadu) and their historical significance" Paper presented at *Indian History Congress,* Proceedings of the 52nd Session, New Delhi.

Tamil Lexicon (1982) University of Madras, 6 volumes and supplement

Thaninayagam, Xavier, S. (1953) *Nature in Ancient Tamil Poetry : Concept and Interpretation,* Tamil Literature Society, Tuticorin.

Ibid (1968) "The period of ethical literature in Tamil: third century the seventh century A.D." in J.C. Heesterman, G.M, Schokkker and V.I. Subramoniam (ed.) *Pratidānam : Indian,* Iranian and Indo-European Studies, Mouton, the Hagne, Paris, pp. 601-14.

Thaninayagam, X.S. (1970) *Tamil culture and civilisation Readings : The Classical Period,* Asia Publishing House, Bombay, pp. 1-54.

Ibid (1971) "Aspects of Tamil Humanism" in *Thirumathi Sarnammal Endowments lectures on Tirukkural,* 1959-60 by 1968-69, Part 1-English, University of Madras, pp. 1-54.

Thapar, (1969) "The impact of Trade c100 BC-300 A.D. in India" in Kunwar Muhammad Ashraf Memorial Volume, New Delhi, pp. 30-38.

Thapar R. (1978) *Ancient Indian Social History : Some Re-Interpretations.*

Ibid (1984) *From Lineage to state,* Oxford university prer, New Delhi, 1984.

Ibid (1987) *Megasthenes : Text and Context, The Mauryas Revisited* (S.G. Deuskar lectures on Indian History), Centre for Studies in Social Science, Calcutta, pp. 32-60.

Thurston, Edgar (1987) *Castes and Tribes of Southern India* (Rp.) Asian Educational Hense, New Delhi.

Trautmann, Thomas.R (1987) "The Study of Dravidian kinshlip" G.W. Spensr (ed. *Temples, kings and peasants : Perceptions of South India's Past,* New Era Publications, Madras, pp. 29-5.

Terray, E. (1972) *Marxism and Primitive Societies,* New York.

Usha, I. (1985) *Trade and mercantile community during the Sangam*

Period, unpublished M.Phil. Dissertation, University of Madras, 1985.

Vaidyanathan, K.S. (1968) "Ancient Geographical Divisions of Tamil Nadu" handbook (Kaiyedu) II *International Conference Seminar of Tamil Studies,* Madras : International Association for Tamil Studies.

Vaiyapuri Pillai, S. (1956) *History of Tamil language and Literature* (beginning to 1000 A.D.), New Century Book House, Madras.

Vanamamalai, N. (1974) "Naṭukarkalum Nampikkaikalum", in R. Nagaswamy (ed.) *Seminar on Herostones,* State Department of Archaeology, Tamil Nadu, pp. 45-54.

Vansina, Jan (1965) *Oral Tradition : A study in Historical Methodology* (H.M. Wright. Routledge & Kegan Paul London.

Varadaraja Iyer (Tr.) (1948) *Tolkappiam-Porulatikaram,* Vol. I, part I, Annamalai University, Annamalai Nagar.

Varadarajan, M. (1969) *The Treatment of Nature in Sangam Literature* (Ancient "Tamil Literature). South India Saiva Siddhanta Works Publishing Society, Tinnevelly. 2nd ed.

Vasudevan Sreelatha (1991) "Iconographic concepts and forms of Koṟṟavai (Durga) in Sangam literature" "Nanditha Krishna (ed.) *Shakti in art and religion,* C.P. Ramaswami Aiyar Institute of Indologicla Research, Madras, 1991, pp. 36-40.

Veluthat. Kesanvan (1982) "The status of the Monarch: A note on the rituals pertaining to Kingship and their significance in the Tamil country (600-1200 A.D.)", *Indian History Congress,* Proceedings of the 43rd Session, Kurukshetra, pp. 147-57.

Venkataswami, Mayilai Seeni "Ilakkiyatil Naṭukal", in (1974) R. Nagaswamy (ed.) *Seminar on Hero stones,* State Department of Archaeology, Tamil Nadu, pp. 38-44.

Venkatasubramanian, T.K. "Social Roots of Tamilian Religions", paper presented at *Indian History Congress.*

Ibid (1980) "The pattern of Economy of the Early Tamils" in *Indian History Congress,* Proceedings, pp. 169-76.

Ibid (1982) "Growth of Urban Centres in Early Tamilakam", *Indian History Congress,* Proceedings, 1982, pp. 134-46.

Ibid (1983) "The pattern of political structure in the Sangam age" S.V. Subramaniam, K.D. Thirunavukkarasu (ed.) *Historical Heritage of the Tamils,* International Institute of Tamil Studies, Madras, pp. 75-89.

Vittiyanantan, S. *Tamiḻar Cālpu (Canka Kalam),* Pari Puttakappannai, Madras.

Warmington. E.H. (1974) *The Commerce between the Roman Empire and India,* London, 2nd ed. (Rev. and enlarged).

Wheeler, R.E.M. (1646) "Arikamedu : An Indo-Roman Trading Station on the East coast of India", *Ancient India,* No. 2, pp. 17-124.

Ibid (1951) "Roman contact with India, Pakistan and Afghnistan" in Grimes (Ed.) *Essays presented to O.G.S. Craw ford,* London, pp. 345-81.

Ibid (1954) *Rome beyond the Imperial Frontiers,* London.

Zeuner, F.E. and Alichin B. "The Microlithic sites of Tinnevelly District, Madras State", *Ancient India,* No. 12, pp. 4-20.

Zvelebil Kamil (1963) "Tamil Poetry 2000 years ago" *Tamil Culture,* Vol. X.

Ibid (1968) *Introducing Tamil Literature.*

Ibid (1973) *The smile of Muruganฺ on Tamil Literature of South India,* Leiden.

Ibid (1975-77) "A Guide to Murukaṉ", *Journal of Tamil Studies,* Vol. 9, pp. 1-22; Vol.10, pp. 40-55; Vol. 11, pp. 82-105.

Ibid (1986) *Literary conventions in Akam poetry,* Institute of Asian studies, Madras.

Ibid (1987) *Tiru Murugaṉ,* Indian Institute of Tamil Studies, Madras.

Ibid (1991) *Tamil Traditions on Subrahmaṇya, Murukaṉ, Institute of Asian Studies.*

INDEX

B

D

I

J

L

M

O

P

T

◇◇◇